THE *ULTIMATE*
WEB DEVELOPER'S
SOURCEBOOK

Ben Sawyer

CORIOLIS GROUP BOOKS

Publisher	*Keith Weiskamp*
Project Editor	*Toni Zuccarini*
Copy Editor	*Chris Kelly*
Proofreader	*Shelly Crossen*
Cover Art	*Gary Smith*
Cover Design	*Tony Stock*
Interior Design	*Michelle Stroup*
Layout Production	*Kim Eoff*
Indexer	*Elizabeth Friedel*

The Coriolis Group, Inc.
7339 E. Acoma Drive, Suite 7
Scottsdale, AZ 85260
Phone: (602) 483-0192
Fax: (602) 483-0193
Web address: http://www.coriolis.com

ISBN 1-57610-000-6: $49.99

Printed in the United States of America

10 9 8 7 6 5 4 3 2 1

*This book is for my mother, who taught me the power of networking
long before Dr. Tim Berners-Lee did.*

Contents

Chapter 2 A History of the Internet and the World Wide Web 27

Chapter 3 The Web Today 45

Chapter 4 Tomorrow's Web 57

Chapter 5   An Overview of Web Design   67

Chapter 6   Web Sites: Planning, Techniques, and Examples   89

Chapter 7   The Details of Designing for the Web   109

Chapter 8   Web Site Benchmarks: Specific Examples   145

Chapter 9   Design Implementation Benchmarks: Specific Examples   183

Chapter 10   Web Content Types: An Overview   207

Chapter 11   Web Graphics: Tips, Tricks, and Software   221

Chapter 12   Web Music and Sound   281

Chapter 13   Web Animation: From Pageflips to Digital Video   313

Chapter 14   Multimedia Content Solutions   347

Operating System   381
Hardware   381
Connection   382
The Major Server Options   382
ISP and Online Service Personal Home Pages   382
Local ISP Hosting   383
Web Outsourcing   384
Ready-To-Run Server   386
Custom-Developed Servers   388
The Connection Primer   389
56 K Frame Relay and ISDN   389
T1/Fractional T1   389
T3/Fractional T3   389
Domain Names and IP Addresses   390
No Half-Steps   392

Chapter 16   Web Server Details   395

Remember, Try Before You Buy   396
Windows NT-Based Servers   396
Windows NT Varieties   396
The NT Workstation/Server Controversy   397
Software   398
Hardware   401
Unix-Based Servers   402
Software   403
Hardware   404
Macintosh Servers   407
Software   407
Hardware   408
Server Software Stuff   409
Commerce Tools   409
Search Engines   412
Security and Firewalls   416
Messaging and Chat   421
Web Sites   425
Books   426

Chapter 20   Java and ActiveX Resources   475

Chapter 21   Macromedia's Shockwave Resources   499

Chapter 22   Overview of the Web Business   507

Chapter 23   Jobs and Hiring in the Web Industry   523

Chapter 24   Web Market Analysis: Forecasting and Surveys   541

Special Thanks

First I would like to thank Keith Weiskamp, publisher of The Coriolis Group, for his support. None of what has taken place in the last 18 months would have happened without Keith. Of course, other thanks to the rest of the people at Coriolis: Jeff Duntemann, Carol Duntemann, Dave Friedel, Tony Potts, Tony Stock, Donna Ford, Kim Eoff, and the entire production staff. You won't find a more dedicated group in publishing.

I'd also like to thank the many developers, vendors, and other professionals I talked to over the course of this book. The amount of dedication and passion in the developer community over the Web is so incredibly infectious it's amazing.

Finally, I've got to thank the people who, aside from me, are most responsible for this text. First, my copyeditor Chris Kelly and my proofreader and fact checker extraordinare Shelly Crossen. Then there is Toni Zuccarini, my project editor at Coriolis, who deserves more praise than I can give. While I have to find a substitute gift for her (she doesn't eat lobster), I can't find any substitute praise other than that Toni has been one of the best people I've ever worked with. Some people dread calls from their editor—I always look forward to hearing from Toni. As I move on to a new project and new editor with Coriolis, I will look forward to coming back and working with her again.

Ben Sawyer
October 1996
Portland, Maine

Introduction

When Keith Weiskamp and I first discussed the computer book market over a year ago, we both centered on the same idea, "Most computer books don't address the needs of professional developers." The books are either simplistic rehashes of manuals or they're not really focused on the needs of professional developers. Thus we cooked up the idea of a "Developer's Sourcebook," the first of which was *The Ultimate Game Developer's Sourcebook*. The idea was to try and corral the information and ideas professional developers need on a day-in, day-out basis into one book. After *The Ultimate Game Developer's Sourcebook*, the most logical sequel was a similar book for Web developers. And so *The Ultimate Web Developer's Sourcebook* was born.

The Web has transformed the entire computer industry. Whether it is an Internet site or a corporate intranet, the Web has become the center of the computer revolution. The speed at which this happened and continues to happen is so unreal that just blinking leaves even the most experienced of developers scrambling to catch up. So in creating this book I've tried to help you catch up. It has always been my experience that good developers don't have trouble figuring out something new once they've got good information, but they do have trouble finding that information in the first place. This book solves the first 20 percent of the battle of learning something new.

There are so many tools, so many ideas, and so much possibility that the challenge was to construct a book that touched on as much Web development as any one text can. As I write the last pages, I sincerely think this book comes as close to that goal as I hoped it would when I started out.

What This Book Is About

This book is meant to complement your knowledge and the existing pool of knowledge out there about Web development. In each section I try to share my own ideas that I've collected, as well as present a large package of information that can truly bring you up to speed on a number of key development topics. In this way, the book acknowledges one of the most fundamental

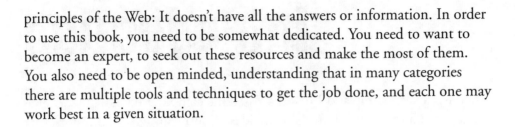

principles of the Web: It doesn't have all the answers or information. In order to use this book, you need to be somewhat dedicated. You need to want to become an expert, to seek out these resources and make the most of them. You also need to be open minded, understanding that in many categories there are multiple tools and techniques to get the job done, and each one may work best in a given situation.

There's No Single Path

One axiom I believe strongly is that there is no one way to approach the field of Web development. The field itself isn't old enough to have developed a set solution. Sure, you can (and I have) identify some right and wrong ways to accomplish certain tasks, but finding "one right way" isn't easily accomplished. So, in the end, there are a lot of different ways to attack developing and producing a Web product. Any book that presents a "my way or the highway" premise would be misleading at best.

My approach is to present many different options and let you figure out which one is best for your situation. I'm not your ultimate evaluator, you are. As an author, I can't know whether you have a budget of $1 million or $1,000. Therefore, this book assumes that you will fit the information in it to your specific needs.

So What's Specifically Inside?

There is a lot of information contained in this book, but the stuff I think stands out is the following.

Contacts, Contacts, Contacts

One thing I find myself needing to do frequently is talk directly on the phone with vendors. While product literature and company Web sites are good first-round sources, I still find myself with specific questions that I need to have answered over the phone or via email. Therefore, wherever possible I've included the full contact information for every major company mentioned.

Books to Read

My shelves are filled with books about Web development. There are many excellent books out there and good developers should read as many as possible. I've tried to list as many good books on the topics described here as I could find. All are complete with author, publisher, and ISBN information to make ordering them from your favorite bookstore easy.

Sites to Visit

What would a book about Web development be without a bevy of Web sites to visit. In almost all of the Web site listings I've tried to add a quick summary of why I chose to list it. In most cases I've opted not to list every site, but stick to those I felt were either awesome indexes to other sites on that topic or were unique resources. A week spent surfing the sites listed in this book may be one of the best weeks you spend as a Web developer.

Product Development and Market Analysis

One thing professional developers always seem to be lacking is at least a basic understanding of markets. Far too many products are designed in the computer industry without the developer giving much thought to the most basic of product development questions: "Who is ready to use or buy my product or service?" This book spends a number of pages discussing these ideas.

The Focus on Professional Products

One thing that puzzles me about other development books (not all books, and not just Web books) is that they usually don't spend nearly as much time talking about the professional products and solutions that exist. I think this is because they're trying to avoid telling their readers to spend more money. Now if you're trying to be a professional developer and you're trying to save money, fine—I've included information about tons of free or shareware products and services, too.

However, if you're trying to be a professional developer without ever spending a dime on a key product like Photoshop or Fusion, well then I wonder how you call yourself a pro. The fact is, there are a ton of products and services you need to consider that will cost you some money. I've listed many of those here, some costing thousands of dollars. I didn't attempt to limit myself to anything, because depending on what you're trying to do, that sort of investment may be required. As the saying goes—you've got to spend money to make money.

An Attempt to Cover Things That Aren't Covered

In the end, this book tries to cover all the stuff other books don't spend as much time on. As I explained to my friend one day—this book is the "spackle" of Web development books. Then I explained in frustration, "And the Web is moving so fast I've probably still not covered it all." I've come close though, and as my friend said, "You've got to have something to write about next year."

CHAPTER 1

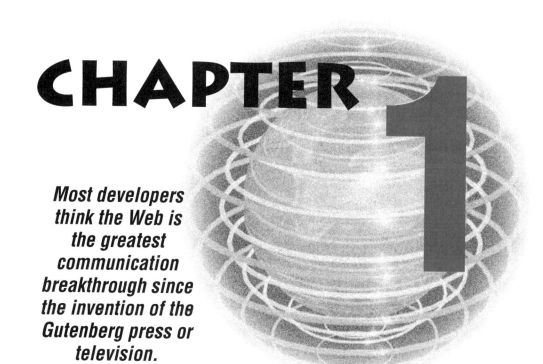

Most developers think the Web is the greatest communication breakthrough since the invention of the Gutenberg press or television.

A Web Developer's FAQ

What Is Web Development?

Web development involves the art of creating content and developing systems to make this content readily available on the World Wide Web or company intranets. Most Web developers spend the majority of their time creating interactive Web sites using a number of technologies, tools, and techniques: Web server software, Web page editors, CGI scripting languages, database software, and so on. In the past, Web development involved working with a simple markup language called *HTML* to create neatly "hyperlinked" documents that people could read with any simple Web browser software. The content featured in these documents consisted of mostly technical and academic information with a sprinkling of graphics. Today, however, Web content has exploded into all sorts of areas, ranging from annual reports and promotional material for companies to online magazines and news features, not to mention movies, games, corporate databases, government documents, and even the latest gossip about TV stars.

Web development involves a melding of content, technical software production, multimedia and design skills, marketing smarts, and overall publishing acumen. Oh yeah, Web development can also be exceedingly fun, frustrating, fulfilling, and fruitful, but not necessarily in that order.

What Are You Developing For?

This is one of the main questions most developers have when they first get introduced to the field of Web development. If you were planning to develop software for Macs or Windows-based PCs, you'd know right off what machines your users would have, the kinds of interfaces they'd expect, and for the most part what they liked and didn't like. The Web, though, is another story—think of it as a giant melting-pot operating system that any computer system can connect to. The content and software you develop will need to be compatible with not only the universe of Web browsers and other communications software in use today, but the galaxies that will be available in the near future. This means that you have to keep track of the standards for technologies like HTML, VRML, CGI languages like Perl, and other languages that Web browsers support (like Java, JavaScript, and Visual Basic Script).

What's Up with Web Browsers?

If you're reading this book, you probably know that a browser is a piece of software that displays Web pages. For now, most people use a standalone browser like Netscape Navigator as their main portal to the Web. However, this is likely to change in the near future.

Many companies are starting to incorporate Web browser capabilities and features into other types of software. One example of a unique approach to accessing the Web is PointCast. This software turns your PC into a dynamic news center where daily headlines and important information about the stock market, leading technology companies, and so on stream across your screen for you to select from at any time. In fact, PointCast also works in the background as a screen saver. Software like PointCast is especially important for Web developers because it introduces a new way of delivering Web content: instead of having the user go to the source, the source comes to the user!

In the future, browser technology will be embedded directly into the operating systems of our computers. Individual applications will then access Web content and interact with it in their own distinct way. Already, companies like Microsoft are introducing technologies like Sweeper that promise to reinvent the Web browser wheel and link the Windows operating system directly to the Web. The notion that a Web browser is a standalone application will go the way of the dinosaur (like the mainframe computer), and the Web and its components will evolve into the operating system of the future. So let's take a broader view here and define a browser as a piece of software technology that can be used by many types of software applications to enable major interaction between the user, the software, and Web sites containing dynamic, interactive content.

What Are the Leading Browsers?

As recently as 1994, a number of Web browser products were fighting it out to see who would be the leading contender. When Mosaic came along, it dominated the scene. Then came Netscape Navigator, shown in Figure 1.1, which now controls more than 70 percent of the market. Browsers like Mosaic and America Online's built-in browser are starting to disappear altogether.

Figure 1.1 Netscape Navigator—the current browser leader.

Netscape Navigator isn't the only browser in use, though. Let's look at a few of the other browsers and Netscape derivatives that are still major players:

- **Microsoft's Internet Explorer/Spyglass Mosaic**—Internet Explorer, shown in Figure 1.2, is based on Spyglass's Mosaic engine and represents Microsoft's effort to develop a browser as powerful as Netscape Navigator. While Microsoft is racing ahead in that area, Spyglass works the so-called *intranet* crowd by licensing its browser engine to large corporations looking to integrate the Internet into their corporate computing facilities. For the time being, Spyglass and Microsoft—although they are separate companies—are working together on this browser technology.

- **HotJava**—HotJava is the name of the browser Sun put together as an early showcase for the Java programming language. Don't confuse this browser with the Java language itself! In fact, now that Netscape Navigator is Java capable, the future of HotJava browser isn't clear. It's often talked about in conjunction with Sun's Java and Web efforts, though, so be aware of it.

- **Lynx**—Lynx, a text-only browser is still used by a small share of Web browsers who have very old equipment. Of all the text-only browsers out there, Lynx is perhaps the most popular.

Figure 1.2   Microsoft Internet Explorer—the up-and-coming challenger to Netscape.

- **Netscape Navigator Gold/Netscape Atlas**—Netscape is continuously creating new derivatives related to its core Navigator product. Navigator Gold includes Web editing functionality, and Atlas, which was a short-lived Netscape pre-beta browser that added voicemail and other communication facilities, to Netscape Navigator. This got renamed and repositioned as Netscape Navigator 3.0. Sometimes Netscape will beta-release a product under a different product name. We'll take a closer look at various Netscape derivatives later in this book.

So What Platforms Can Access the Web?

One of the best features of the Web is that it can be accessed by anything that can read and display HTML files. Because the Web's underlying networking protocols are extremely simple, it is easy for many different computer systems (and even high-end videogame consoles) to be Web accessories. In addition, much of the non-HTML content now on the Web (image files, video, animation, and so on) also can be accessed by different types of computer hardware because the content formats are open to the public. MIDI files, AU sound files, and GIF and JPEG image files are just some of Web-based materials that nearly every hardware platform can easily work with.

But not *everything* on the Web is universally accessible. There are content types that cannot be easily processed by some machines depending on which browser they run, how fast their connection is, and what additional software they have to handle special content. For example, if you are surfing the Web looking for multimedia action and you don't have the RealAudio player, your computer won't be able to play back RealAudio files.

So although many computers can access the Web in one way or another, the extent to which a specific hardware/software combination can access the entire World Wide Web is based on a variety of factors. This notion is very important, because many people believe that the Web is like a utopian universe where all machines and software are created entirely equal. Because all platforms are, in fact, not equal, Web developers need a careful understanding of what the term *access* means. I will explore this issue throughout this book.

By the Way—Who Invented the Internet and the Web?

Good (and curious) developers always know a little history of the medium they're developing for. That's one of the reasons I've included Chapter 2, which presents a brief history of the Internet and the World Wide Web.

The original idea for the Internet came from the RAND Corporation and the U.S. government's work to create a new national communications network that would survive a nuclear attack. From those original ideas, the federal government built something it called ARPANET, which set the standards for much of the current Internet technology. The Government shut down ARPANET in the late 1980s, but only after a significant number of other networks and infrastructure—developed independently by different organizations all around the world—had been built into what came to be the Internet.

The World Wide Web was invented by Tim Berners-Lee (shown in Figure 1.3), a software designer at the European Laboratory for Particle Physics (CERN). He wanted to create an easy-to-use system to retrieve and wade through data on the Internet. Once he created the basic ideas and software, many people quickly jumped on the bandwagon and began to expand the Web from there.

Figure 1.3   The creator of the Web, Tim Berners-Lee.

One of those people was Marc Andreessen, a student at the University of Illinois. Working at the school's National Center for Supercomputing Applications laboratory, Marc and his staff developed the first major browser for the Internet, which they called *NCSA Mosaic*. With the advent of Mosaic, use of the Web exploded—and in the aftermath emerged a slew of developers (Netscape, Spyglass, UUnet, PSInet, and many others) to construct the Internet and World Wide Web of today and tomorrow.

What Is a Web Server?

When little kids ask where babies come from, I like to tell them they come from Web servers. After all, it seems like everything else does these days. (Of course, given the slow access speeds I've gotten lately, I could just as easily say Web pages come via the stork.)

No matter what you say about Web servers—repeatable or not—they are certainly the driving force behind the Web. A Web server, like any other type of server, is a computer system that stores information, processes request for that information, and then spits out the answer to the requesting computer (called a *client*).

But what makes a Web server different from a standard network server? And as a Web developer, what do you really need to know about servers? Well, besides the many choices you have in software and systems (and you thought buying a house was easy!), the key thing to understand about your Web server is that there are many concerns you need to have about it than you probably have right now.

Like what, you ask? There are security issues (money lying on a sidewalk in New York City is better protected than some servers are) and special server software issues (for example, do you have RealAudio's server product? How about ichat?). There are also issues about connectivity (did you really think your clients were the problem?) and throughput, both of which can really affect what you want to deliver to the user. As with a human mother and her children, the quality of the Web pages your server is capable of producing is directly correlated to its own capacities. This book is going to spend a lot of time talking about server options and resources and how they affect the end result of your Web development process.

What Are Plug-Ins?

It seems plug-ins are everywhere in software these days. Photoshop has them, PageMaker has them, Studio 3D has them, and now so do two of the most popular browsers—Netscape Navigator and Microsoft Internet Explorer (the problem is, their plug-in schemes are incompatible!). The idea of plug-ins is simple: Programmers create a system by which other programmers can create integrated programs that run as seamless features in the mother application. Plug-in technology thus creates a living application that can continuously extend itself with new features.

For the Web, plug-ins take the form of programs that run directly inside of and with your browser. For example, Adobe makes a plug-in (called Amber) that allows you to view Adobe Acrobat files without leaving Netscape Navigator. Amber was created by rewriting the Acrobat program to act as a "sub-program" within Netscape, as shown in Figure 1.4, thanks to a special programming interface Netscape created for just this purpose. The ability of programmers to integrate their applications into browsers in this way represents a major advancement for the Web.

The problem with plug-ins is they're like my Lego bricks when I was a kid—all over the place! There are so many plug-ins (for video, audio, graphics, programming, multimedia, CAD drawings, and much, much more) that not everyone has them all. It's one big mess. Also, like regular software, plug-ins have to be ported to and recompiled for every new platform.

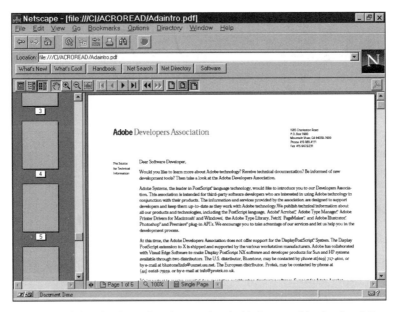

Figure 1.4 The Adobe Amber plug-in running in Netscape Navigator 2.0.

The key for Web developers is being in a position to sort through the various plug-ins and updates, as well as keeping abreast of the underlying technology (to develop content for many plug-ins, you will need a host of other programs). In this book I will spend a lot of time talking about plug-ins and plug-in resources. Because they dynamically and exponentially expand the types of sites and Web products you can develop, you should carefully consider using plug-ins.

How Do I Program for the Web?

You pick one of a million programming languages available and start coding. Some people seem to think you can only program for the Web in Java or JavaScript, but in fact there are dozens of specific ways to program for the Web.

The trick is learning on a situational basis what type of programming to do, which language is best to use, and what language-specific tools and techniques exist to help you do that. The answers are not simple. Because I have devoted a lot of time, research, and energy to exploring these questions, though, I'll try to answer them briefly here.

Essentially there are two ways to program for the Web. One is to use a Web-based language, like Java, JavaScript, Director, or Visual Basic Script. The other process is to use a programming language (such as C/C++, Delphi, or Pascal) to create a platform-specific solution that interacts with Web applications, content, protocols, servers, and so on. For example, plug-ins are C/C++ applications written to work in an integrated manner with a browser and Web-based content. The details of these two major types of programming you can do for the Web, however, are so numerous that I'm not even going to start dissecting them here.

What Tools Support Programming Web Applications?

How do you think people create software for the Web in the first place? They use tons of programming libraries and software development tools. There are TCP/IP libraries (TCP/IP is the underlying network protocol of the Web), Java compilers, visual form designers, libraries full of example code, and more.

Where there's smoke, there's fire—and where there's a programming language, there's a cottage industry of tools and libraries to help you program with it. If Tim Allen's character in "Home Improvement" were a programmer he'd be a happy man, because there are more tools to use in programming than there are in Norm Abrams' workshop. In addition, the rise of the Web has brought forth a slew of new tools and libraries to help programmers create fast and well-executed Web applications.

The Web may seem simple to the end user—point here, click there—but the work and programming that goes into producing this simplicity is significant. And where significant programming skill is needed, there are lots of programming tools.

I'll cover all of them in this book, from Java tools and libraries to C++ tools to OCXs. If there's a programming tool out there that I think is relevant to the Web, I'm going to talk about it and show you where to learn even more.

What Is Java?

What, you mean you haven't heard about Java? Where have you been? Unfortunately, though, the same hype that leads me to believe every living person has heard about Java has also resulted in misinformation about this highly versatile Web development tool. This book is going to help you put a lot of things into context, especially Java.

The Java programming language is based on the principles put forth in C++, but it is designed specifically for secure two-way, realtime interaction over networks—in particular, the Internet. It's also designed to be capable of running on any platform that supports the Java runtime (called the Java Virtual Machine). Thus, unlike with C++, there is absolutely no need to port or recompile your Java code for other machine types. Write it once, compile it once, and run it on many: It is this functionality that is giving Java its widespread fame and use.

Java was invented by Sun Microsystems, the workstation maker who supplies many of the servers that run the Internet. They originally were creating the language to work for major interactive television (ITV) systems and other hardware devices. But when it became clear that the market for ITV was a lot further in the future than Sun imagined, and the Internet started growing in popularity, Sun shifted the project's focus. After what certainly must have been countless cups of coffee in the early morning hours, Java was born!

It's a good thing for Sun that you can't spill Internet Java, because the programming language is probably hotter than the real java that got McDonald's sued. Just as I began writing this book it was announced that Microsoft, Apple, SCO, and other operating system companies would work to embed the Java Virtual Machine directly into their operating systems. Talk about a hot announcement!

Once upon a time, Web developers were pretty much stuck with HTML and special plug-in products. But now we have Java, which allows us to create almost anything our hearts desire and integrate it into our Web pages. No longer are Web sites merely vehicles for distributing cool-looking text and downloadable programs—the Web is now alive, and the blood for this organism is Java.

The dilemma with Java, though, is that although it is so powerful, it's also not for everyone. Java can be slow, it can be tough to work with, it's not accessible by every platform or browser, and there are (despite reports to the contrary) other solutions to consider. No one in his or her right mind would say Java isn't any good, but too few people have really tried to put it in context versus everything else that's available. In this book, I will put it all into perspective.

What Is JavaScript?

Perhaps the most powerful addition to the new Netscape Navigator is JavaScript. Because of its simplicity and its availability to millions of Netscape users, JavaScript is rapidly becoming the language most Web page authors are using to add more interactivity to their pages.

Originally, JavaScript was named LiveScript by Netscape, whose initial goal was to create a simple scripting language that would allow Netscape users to customize their browser and create more interactive Web pages. Soon after Netscape started the project, though, Sun Microsystems announced its Java programming language. Interest in Java grew so quickly that Netscape decided to work closely with Sun and turn LiveScript into JavaScript.

JavaScript is *not* Java. The two languages share a similar syntax, but they are used to handle different types of tasks. JavaScript is designed for light Web duties, where a heftier language like Java really isn't needed. With JavaScript you can process simple user actions (events), control how forms are processed, and add much more flexibility in the way HTML documents are displayed.

Soon after Netscape announced that its new browser would provide a scripting language adapted from Java, many people (developers and browser users alike) wondered if this approach would best serve the needs of Netscape users. As it turns out, Java is based on a powerful object-oriented system that makes it well suited for conversion into a scripting language.

What Is Visual Basic Script?

Visual Basic Script (VBScript) is an Internet-based scripting language that Microsoft derived from its Visual Basic language technology to serve as both an adjunct and a competitor to Netscape and Sun's JavaScript. Microsoft intends to offer VB Script to other browser companies—even Netscape—for use, hoping to establish it as a standard rather than a language inextricably linked to Microsoft's own browser. This significant step may result in more widespread use for VBScript than normal Microsoft practice would have made possible.

I will go into more depth later about VBScript and its similarities and differences relative to JavaScript. For now, look at it as a technology similar to JavaScript, not a product similar to Java.

What Is ActiveX?

ActiveX is a new Microsoft technology that is intended to provide the capability for "applets" (much like Java does) but also work like Netscape's plug-ins. Unlike Java, however, ActiveX programs are written in C/C++ or some other language, and thus you don't have Java's cross-platform compatibility unless you rewrite the control for another platform.

As with a lot of the subjects I'm previewing here, I will go into more depth about ActiveX later.

What Is Shockwave?

Shockwave is the preeminent multimedia plug-in technology on the Web. It's basically a Web-based playback engine for applications created using Macromedia's Director, which is the top-selling multimedia authoring package available for both Macintosh and Windows. The Shockwave plug-in is shown in Figure 1.5.

The key to Director's success has been Macromedia's creation of playback engines that help Director applications run on Windows, Macintosh, SGI, Sun, 3DO, and other platforms. As a result, it takes relatively little effort for

Figure 1.5 The Shockwave plug-in in action.

Director developers to write one program that runs on multiple platforms. So when the Web came along with its basically static text and graphic capabilities, the folks at Macromedia figured, why don't we make a way to distribute Director programs over the Web? Shockwave was the result.

Shockwave works by adding capabilities to Director to compress Director files, making them small enough to be suitable for the Web. Some additional Web-centered features have been added as extensions to Lingo (Director's programming language).

Director is a very powerful product, and Shockwave only makes it even more powerful and versatile. In addition, word has it Macromedia is working on a data-streaming technology that will make Shockwave applications load even faster, giving them a more immediate impact. In this book I devote an entire chapter to Shockwave: what it does, resources for Director and the Internet, and much more.

What Kinds of Web Sites and Applications Can You Create?

The great thing about the Web is that we, as developers, can create all kinds of neat sites. The Web is truly a digital blank slate for us to write on. A site devoted to chocolate chip cookies, a corporate information site, or a game—any wild creation is possible. Or is it? The Web has taken such a major turn toward more and more advanced development techniques that in order to create the Web site of your dreams, it's important to understand the *extent* to which you can create the kind of application or site you want. Your possibilities are directly proportional to your Web development capabilities.

It's one thing to say "I want to make a site all about 'Hogan's Heroes'!" but another thing to actually do it. There are legal issues (especially if you want to use video clips), the need for informational research, and an amazing assortment of other key obstacles. I will explore *all* of those issues in this book and try to attach to them the contacts, the tools, the techniques, and the tutorials you need to assemble the most brilliant Web site your mind can create.

How Do I Create Graphics for the Web?

The technical process of creating graphics for the Web is an art form in and of itself. There are, of course, two major still-graphic formats to which most Web developers are accustomed: GIF and JPEG. But if you think that graphics for the Web stop there, you're still caught in the first wave of the Web. Even for GIF and JPEG, there are derivative forms like Interlaced GIF and Progressive JPEG, not to mention a host of image reduction and processing techniques to improve the graphics you might already be generating.

Naturally, I'll cover those here—but wait, there's more! Graphical representation on the Web has expanded considerably; there's now digital video to consider, vector graphics (via plug-ins from Corel and Autodesk), Java-produced graphics, Adobe Acrobat, and much more.

Thus, when I talk about how to create graphics for the Web, you will need to focus on the two Ps: products and process. There are many products that can produce or display graphics on the Web. You will need to be familiar not only with the products, but with the actual design rules and practiced processes that create the best Web graphics.

What Options Are Available for Using Sound on the Web?

Sound is actually one of the cooler parts of the Web. There are many different options available, and each has its own strengths and weaknesses.

When we talk about sound, though, I'm not just talking about products like RealAudio (see Figure 1.6), perhaps the most famous of the streaming audio technologies available. There are standalone file types (like WAVs and AUs), QuickTime files, and MIDI files, to name a few of the other music data types I'll be discussing. Recently one company brought out a wonderful plug-in that streams MIDI files in Netscape.

What makes sound so exciting to develop on the Web is that even digital audio is easily compressed and sent out over the Internet in realtime, even on low-bandwidth settings. This accessibility has provoked a lot of development. I'll be wading through all of the resulting software options in an attempt to clear up which different applications are uniquely suited to each format.

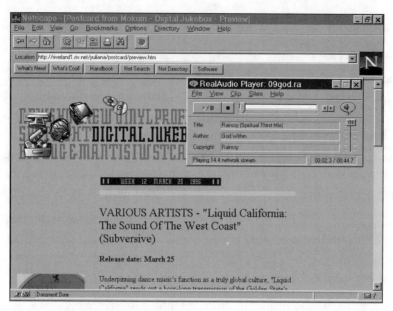

Figure 1.6 The RealAudio plug-in in action.

What Server Options Are There?

Well, I personally prefer a four-door with a sunroof on my servers, but I'm picky that way. But the truth is that when it comes to servers, there are more options than at your local GM dealer.

Servers are often the most mysterious part of Web development, if only because most Web developers don't deal with them on a daily basis (we leave that for an obscure bunch of wizards known as "Webmasters"). These developers, though, won't get away with avoiding this responsibility much longer.

The capabilities of the Web-based product you offer to people are directly related in many ways to the options, configuration, and performance of the server it runs on. Therefore, as Web development gets more complex, much more is going to be required of Web servers. Too many books (and other items I've seen) give people no real reason to be concerned with Web servers, because they fail to build on the relationship the server, browser, and client computers must have in order to offer up a good Web product. This book won't make that mistake.

Right now there are at least five major server product manufacturers: SGI, Sun, Digital, Intel-based, and Apple. In addition there are special server products (like RealAudio server and VDOLive) and other programs you can install and configure to offer additional server capabilities with your products. More are coming every day.

Can I Make Money Being a Web Developer?

Yes. How much is the real question. Some Web developers can make a small mint, whereas others—well, let's just say they shouldn't have quit their day jobs. Just because you can develop for the Web won't make you an in-demand, high-wage worker, nor does it mean that anything you develop will make millions of dollars.

The Web is simply a platform that delivers ideas, products, and services to others. Not all of these ideas, products, or services are worth other people's money. You may develop the world's coolest Web site, with a million technological wonders, but if someone else has already done this (or if it's a site titled "The Wonderful World of Pond Scum!"), it might not make you rich. There is much more to making money on the Web or as a Web developer than knowledge of the technical side of the Web.

This isn't to say you can't make money. People with awesome development skills are certainly in demand (I'll cover position and salary ranges later on), and good sites are beginning to see revenue stream in. Just understand that the Web is a business, and there are as many factors that combine to determine if you make money as there are in any other business.

How Hot Is Web Development?

Some folks would say it's too hot. In fact, the World Wide Web has been perhaps the number-one technology-related story of 1995 and 1996. Web development is probably the main focus of half the major players in the computer industry. Huge companies such as Microsoft are now rearranging their whole corporate structure to strengthen their ability to create products and development tools for the Web. We're talking about not just a new product line, but a change in the entire software development industry.

So, in short, it's pretty darn hot.

But how hot will it remain? Some say that the Web is still too far away from its promise, and thus Web development is really just a big, overblown black hole. Companies soon will back away from the Web, these skeptics tell us, and not spend the millions they're spending now.

This is "horse hockey," as Col. Sherman T. Potter used to say. Sure, the Web may be in an overhyped state for now, but that's not going to stop Web development. No one in their right mind can look at the Web and honestly say that in ten years it won't be the dominant force for software, computers, communications, and more. The "information superhighway" concept we've heard about for so many years finally has a tangible reality, and it's the Internet and the World Wide Web.

But if the Web is still more promise than reality, that means lots of work for Web developers. Development, after all, is the process of moving from promise to reality. To fuel the reality so many people want and need from the Web, it's going to take a lot of development, and that's why Web development is so hot. What has to happen to achieve that reality is what this book is all about.

What Does It Take to Be a Web Developer?

It takes a lot more than just Navigator Gold, let me tell you. In fact, let me make something clear here—this book is *not* about making Web pages. It's not even about creating Web sites. It's about major Web development and creating Web *products*.

When I talk about being a Web developer, I'm talking about all the facets that go into being a major Web developer: server knowledge, graphics knowledge, an understanding of sound and music, writing skills, marketing information, and much more.

Being a Web developer is not about firing up your favorite HTML editor and adding some tags. It's about having the background and ability to create interesting products (either for or on the Web) that people want or need to use. Go to the top sites around the Web and ask yourself what it took to make these sites so good. (Hint: It took a lot of work.) Then ask yourself what skills you would need to a develop a site like that. Clearly, a lot of different skills are required. If you want to specialize, that's fine. If you do, however, you will have to supplement your specialized abilities with those of other people, or limit yourself to designing products that can be done with just the skills you have.

As Web development has moved further along and gotten more complex, the skills to be a top-notch Web developer have increased as well. This book will help you develop those skills.

What Programming Experience Do I Need?

A good Web developer needs at least some programming experience. Why? Because the Web, despite some people's objections, is moving away from the original desktop publishing metaphor toward one that is more like regular software development—and that means programming.

This doesn't mean you need to run out and learn C++ today, but perhaps learning the principles of JavaScript or VBScript is a good idea. It's hard for a developer to learn one programming language, let alone every language in the world, but by understanding some of the basics you will gain insight that will help you deal with the programmers who might work with you on a particular project.

This book includes extensive resources to help you learn many types of Web-oriented programming. The resources are structured for beginners and professionals alike, so you can use them to expand your knowledge base regardless of your current level of programming ability.

Should I Develop for Netscape or Microsoft or...?

I just talked about there being a handful of World Wide Web browsers available, so the inevitable question comes up: Which one should I develop for? Certainly the easy answer is Netscape, since it's the browser that currently controls more than 70 percent of the market. Microsoft's Internet Explorer is catching up fast, however, and in the wake of deals like the one Microsoft recently signed with America Online (AOL), Internet Explorer is poised to become even more of a force.

So deciding on a browser to develop your Web products around isn't as clear-cut as it seems. You could develop for one browser only, develop the same site twice and offer specialized versions for each browser, or go for a common-denominator approach. My choice would be to develop in one of the ways that supports both—depending on the project, I would decide if that meant a common-denominator approach or two tracks of specialized sites.

Don't decide which browsers to support based on your own personal preferences. That would be a big mistake. Remember, you won't be able to control which browser your customers have—especially if the days of free browsers go away, an entirely possible prospect. Instead of deciding to stay focused on a particular browser based on the end result you need, let the site's design needs and/or the consumers you want to attract drive the decision. That also means keeping an eye on the "browser wars" to see which way the market is going.

Whatever browser(s) you choose to develop around, back up your preference with good reasoning and planning.

What Are the Changes in Access Speeds Going to Mean?

To put it simply, the faster access speeds that will be available to massive populations of Web users over the next three to four years are going to drastically change the face of Web development. ISDN and cable modems are close enough to becoming standards in much of the Web community that it's a mistake not to begin learning the development skills that the higher speeds will require.

Higher access speeds mean sites can pump out more graphics, more video, more sound, and more programmed applets. They mean more major database-capable servers, a higher production standard with more advanced graphics, and additions such as VRML (instead of just more HTML). This is the next generation of Web development, and it will spawn the next wave of new growth for the Internet.

The development tools, resources, and skill needed for the next-generation Web sites and products made possible by higher access speeds are going to mean you need to do your homework like never before. Consider this book your tutor.

What Is the *Intra*net?

It's an excuse for corporations to finally upgrade all their antiquated PCs.

Seriously, it's an internal corporate network that mimics the structure of the Internet. You see, the same things that make the Internet (and the World Wide Web) an easy-to-use, far-flung, and fluid system are the same things that can help internal corporate networks be useful. Right now, however, most corporate networks do very little besides distribute software and occasionally manage database information (in the most advanced settings).

The Internet and its associated software, though, make it much easier to have videoconferences, distribute corporate information, use cooperative computing, send email, and a host of other really cool things. Most Internet software is based on open standards. A lot of this technology can hook up incompatible machines like Macs and PCs in such a way that they can share information more easily than ever before. These internal corporate networks work just like miniature Internets, hence the name intranet. Corporations are learning to apply these Internet advantages to their internal networks and there is currently a huge shift underway toward turning traditional corporate networks into intranets.

Technology and tool-wise, there really isn't much difference between working on a Web/intranet project versus a Web/internet project. The major differences are in the application of the tools. A corporation building an internal Web site for its employees needs an entirely different approach in design and implementation than does, say an Internet site for a snack food company. Security issues can also be quite different. The resources, though—the things you'll need to read, buy, use, and know about—aren't different.

What's the Best Way to Develop Your Web Site Creation Skills?

The best way is to get "on-the-job" training by building sites. Of course, this again requires more effort than just firing up a Web editor and playing around with HTML files. Experience certainly counts—you've ultimately got to play with this stuff and gain your own ideas to build your development skills to their fullest. But don't for a second believe that's all you do.

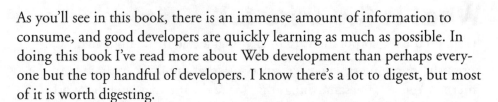

As you'll see in this book, there is an immense amount of information to consume, and good developers are quickly learning as much as possible. In doing this book I've read more about Web development than perhaps everyone but the top handful of developers. I know there's a lot to digest, but most of it is worth digesting.

In addition, though I do less than I should, I spend a lot of time surfing. One thing you can lose sight of when you're working on a Web project is that you need to spend time taking in other people's sites, too. I know it's dangerous to surf when you're under a deadline (you can wind up surfing right past it), but you've got to spend time experiencing what other people have created.

Also, spend some time looking at other types of computer-oriented development. Multimedia and game development skills and techniques have a lot of crossover potential. Multimedia designers, for example, know more about working with digital video than any Web designer could possibly hope to know right now. Game developers know more about 3D graphics. Spend time checking in with these camps, because they're also edging toward the Web—in fact, most of the corporate Internet sites for game companies are among the best around.

What Are Some of the Major Trends in Web Development?

Right now, the major trend is toward software-style construction of Web sites. The shift from HTML and text to full-service graphics and programmed applets is taking place faster than anyone could have imagined. Driving this change is the demand placed on the Web by consumers who enjoy all the Web has to offer, but still want more. In addition, with the advent of higher speeds, secure transaction technology, faster computers, and just better software, there are already trends toward heightened interactivity between users on a site (such as chat rooms and messaging). Online shopping is also growing quickly as people become more comfortable about purchasing items via the Internet. Oh, and did I mention Web-based games?

But all of these are short-term trends. Until recently, the ability to do things on or with the Web has been much more limited than I think people realized. The flip side, of course, is that as the Web gains the abilities that are within reach now, the flood of trends and possibilities will grow tremendously. So, for now, the real overriding trend is immense capability advancement.

What Design Experience Should I Have?

Design is very important to the Web, and there are many types of design I will be talking about in this book. For example, the Web is still primarily a two-dimensional, desktop publishing-like medium when it comes to design. This means that aesthetic skills similar to those held by top graphic designers are important. I'll provide a lot of good information about resources to help you learn more about this type of design.

However, don't make the common mistake of thinking that having good graphic design skills means you'll be a good Web designer. This is like saying someone is a good boat mechanic because he or she can fix cars. Sure, there are a lot of similarities, but they're still different beasts!

The Web is a much bigger medium than the traditional paper page that most graphic designers work with. As a result, other elements of design come into play—things like interface design, software design, and (perhaps most elusive) interactive design.

With the World Wide Web, your design skills can't just be deep; they have to be broad. This is never more evident than it is when you try to evaluate the design skills needed to create "killer" sites. Don't fret, though—not every Web product will require you to have every skill in the book.

What Does It Take to Be a Web Development House?

As the Web gets more complicated, teams of experts are forming into entire companies devoted to Web development. Some work to develop Web sites and products for themselves; a good example here is the AOL-backed iVillage or Paul Allen's Starwave. Other companies, like Magnet Interactive and Clement Mok, are primarily shops that develop sites for other companies (for example, Clement Mok did the Web site for Rocket Science games).

The reason Web development houses are forming is simple: A top site now takes several artists, programmers, writers, and producers working as a team. And as if that weren't reason enough, the development funds for top sites are already reaching into the millions of dollars, with many sites budgeted over

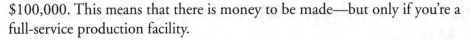

$100,000. This means that there is money to be made—but only if you're a full-service production facility.

So a Web development house needs a qualified team of production talent that covers all the bases of high-end Web development, but it also needs the key business and product development skills it takes to run a company well and deliver the quality of product that top clients will require. In order to form one, you'll need to hire on people, take on much larger projects, and carry an immense amount of responsibility that many lone-wolf Web developers haven't considered.

How Long Does It Take to Construct a Site?

Well, it depends—most software takes a year or more to develop, but most Web sites take a fraction of that time. A complex site can take a lot of time to build, however, and the thing we all know about a good Web site is that it's constantly being updated and improved. Web sites are like living creatures, and in that sense they're never truly finished.

In the interest of being more pragmatic and less philosophical, though, I would say that the average site takes around two or three months to devise and construct. As sites get more complex, I wouldn't be surprised to see the typical development time range from two months to eighteen months.

What Kind of Resources Do I Need?

Web development is a resource-intensive process. For today's cutting-edge sites, you need graphic tools galore, good sound tools, top-notch editing programs, perhaps several programming languages and tools—and that's just the tip of the iceberg.

Now you know why I wrote this book. The first step in determining the resources you need for development is knowing what really exists. What makes this especially hard for Web developers is that there are a lot of relevant resources you can use; I've tracked them down for you.

While I recuperate from all this work, you need to pore over the pages of this book and learn about the resources available. I haven't just listed the top two products—I've tried to list all the major players in each category. Once you've gotten an overview, then you can start using the follow-up information (including Web and snail-mail addresses) to find out even more about the product as you narrow down your decisions on exactly what resources to use.

So What Does This Book Offer?

You mean, after all this, you're still wondering? Well, I have a short answer and a long answer to this question.

This book offers context. That's the short answer.

Here's the longer one: I believe that Web development—like software development or any type of production, computer or otherwise—involves not a single idea, solution, tool, or process, but a dump truck full of things. Whether you're a novice Web developer or a pro, you need to look at Web development from a far larger viewpoint. You need to know not just about one thing or how to do one thing really well, but also what all the options are and how they relate to one another and your own ideas. That's context, and that is my goal in this book.

Toward that goal, I don't pretend to know everything. A doctor does not learn to help his or her patients by reading just one book or studying under just one teacher. Doctors learn from everyone and everything available, and they are constantly seeking new sources of information.

What makes this book special is that I try to present not only my thoughts and ideas, but everything else out there—from other books to Web sites to conferences to organizations—that can help you learn even more.

In other words, this sourcebook is both a reference guide and a trail map. I'll get you to one spot, then point out the many paths that take you even farther. After all, isn't that one of the greatest things about the Web—the links to ever more information and resources?

Okay....time to get to work!

CHAPTER 2

Before you get started with your own Web creations, it's important to know just how the Internet and World Wide Web began.

A History of the Internet and the World Wide Web

It surprises me how often people don't understand the history behind today's computer technology. Computers are so wedded to the future in our minds that we sometimes forget they have a past. But understanding the thirty-year history of what we now call the Internet and the World Wide Web can clue us in on better design ideas and give our development efforts more insight.

The Beginning

While the Internet and the World Wide Web, as we know them today, are only about eight years old, the original thinking behind a global computer network began in the early 1960s, as America prepared itself for a possible nuclear war with the Soviet Union.

One of the biggest concerns for Cold War strategists was how to maintain a semblance of military organization during a nuclear war. Atomic bombs can destroy tons of infrastructure in an instant, and just the magnetic pulse created by an explosion can destroy normal communications capabilities, especially radio signals. In addition, a central command and control center for phone lines and such could easily be targeted and taken out.

The RAND Corporation, one of the most advanced military think tanks, examined this problem intensely. The answer, designed by RAND employee Paul Baran, became known as the RAND proposal when it became public in 1964.

The RAND proposal was amazing in both its simplicity and its strategy. Essentially, Baran and his colleagues proposed that a new computer communications network be built from the ground up. It would be totally decentralized and designed to work even if parts of it didn't survive. In short, it would be built to fail.

All of the nodes on the network would be of equal stature, with each one able to send, receive, and forward messages. The messages themselves would be divided up into small components (called packets) that would all shoot out over the network separately and then be reassembled at their destination. There were no predetermined routes for these packets; they literally could bounce around until they got to the desired node. If any one node disappeared, the message would somehow find another route. In addition, the message would still be available even if the end node was destroyed, because the packets would still be in the system somewhere.

The ideas of a decentralized network and all nodes being equal have been the backbone of the Internet from its absolute beginning. You could even venture to say that these original two tenets are the "soul of the Internet."

From Paper to Practice: ARPANET

The RAND proposal quickly became more than an interesting theory. For several years after its 1964 debut, several major research universities built test networks and experimented with Baran's original ideas. The military took notice of this work and began funding a national network in 1969. Because the network was created under the auspices of the Advanced Research Projects Agency (ARPA), the builders called it the ARPANET.

ARPANET was a twofold project. First, it was a test of the very-decentralized-network principles originally outlined in the RAND proposal. Second, it was a way to link the nation's existing supercomputers together so scientists at various locations could work together and share computer time. The first nodes were established in 1969, but by 1972 ARPANET was already up to 37 nodes. From paper to practice, at every stage in its short life the Net was a smashing success.

If You Build It, They Will Come: Amazing Side Effects

An interesting aspect about computer history is how quickly workers found much cooler tasks for their computers than crunching numbers for the government, big corporations, and rocket scientists. In the 1960s, for example, a group of computer programmers invented a game called SpaceWar (the first computer game) while their coworkers thought they were just working late. Things were no different with ARPANET.

Instead of using the network to share computing time, it turned out that most of the people with ARPANET access were sending personal messages and news—in other words, email! As you might guess, many of the messages were decidedly not about military or research topics; in fact, one of the first electronic mailing lists kept subscribers updated about the latest science fiction books. And so, despite its humble beginnings and strict mission, the real strength of the eventual Internet broke through. Once its potential for instant communication became clear, nothing could pry the Net away from its new purpose—not even the U.S. military.

Almost every aspect of the World Wide Web we know today was invented as just such a side effect; its original purpose mutated into an entirely different use. Almost like a form of technological evolution, these mutated versions became the growth factors that created the phenomenal success of the Internet.

The Birth of Protocols

The original "language" of the first generation of ARPANET was called Network Control Protocol (NCP). NCP wasn't capable of handling lots of nodes, however, and so a more complex network protocol based on the same principles was needed. ARPA (now named the Defense Advanced Research Projects Agency, or DARPA) began working on a new protocol that eventually became Transmission Control Protocol/Internet Protocol (TCP/IP). In January 1983, ARPANET switched from NCP to TCP/IP, and the groundwork for today's Internet was complete.

More Nets Are Cast

As more and more organizations began understanding the power of a national (and even worldwide) computer network, other networks started sprouting up—all connected by or using the same basic technologies put forward by ARPANET.

As ARPANET began taking on a separate life, the U.S. military broke away to set up its own shop with MILNET. The computer science community followed suit with CSNET, and BITNET (the first three letters were an acronym for "Because It's Time") was created by the college community. Soon, all of these and other separate networks created gateways to let them interconnect as one big network—hence the word *Internet.*

Then the National Science Foundation (NSF), seeing the power of the developing Internet, joined in with NSFNET, which connected five big NSF supercomputing centers across the country. This and other high-speed networks—more commonly known as backbones—helped provide the capacity needed to support further growth of the Internet.

In 1989, with NSFNET and a dozen other networks operating together, the U.S. government closed down the network that started it all. ARPANET became a memory, and in its place was now the Internet: an amalgamation of far-flung networks and computers, all working on the original principles of decentralization, open systems, and equal opportunity that had been the foundation for the 1964 RAND proposal.

The Building of the World Wide Web

As more networks and nodes began populating the Internet, its growth demanded better organization and systems. In addition, as more and more people began using the Net from colleges and other locations, the demand for better email and communication systems brought forth a new round of features.

Users, programmers, and computer science departments created entities like USENET to post and distribute information across the Net. USENET, which is still quite active today, is a giant electronic bulletin board where hundreds of topics (broken into categories such as "rec.games.design" or "alt.sex") are discussed.

To improve its organization, a domain naming system was created. Nodes on the Internet were divided by country, and six fundamental Internet domains (with the extensions .com, .edu, .gov, .mil, .net, and .org) were established for naming sites. Nevertheless, the amount of data on the Internet and the number of computers attached to it were still growing enormously—and, despite the advent of USENET and other organized messaging entities, it was still a mess.

People responded with more solutions to the problem. Researchers at McGill University in Canada created Archie, a program that helped users to explore the Net and catalog information. Programmers at the University of Minnesota created an Internet database retrieval system called Gopher (in reference to both the "go-for" metaphor and the name of the school's sports teams, the Golden Gophers). A file transfer protocol (FTP) had already been in existence for a while, and FTP sites began organizing their information for easier downloading.

Despite all this refinement, there still was a need for more organization and user-friendliness before the Internet could reach its full potential. This need was answered when a little-known computer developer at a world-renowned physics research center created the World Wide Web.

Tim Berners-Lee: Father of the Web

Most people think of the Internet as an entirely American creation, yet perhaps its most important aspect—the World Wide Web—was born in Europe. The Web came to life at the European Laboratory for Particle Physics

(CERN) where Tim Berners-Lee, a software designer, was looking for a way to present and link together all the documents in various CERN databases. His idea was to create a "Web" of online documents that would be directly connected (or *hyperlinked*) to one another, as well as to other documents stored on the Internet.

CERN developed this idea privately, building on the core tenets that had made the Internet a success. The embryonic Web was decentralized, was simple to use, and focused on equality. By focusing on the data rather than any specific software or hardware, Berners-Lee created a file structure for Web documents that could be read by virtually any computer. All one needed was a program that could interpret the underlying language of Web documents (called Hypertext Markup Language, or HTML). Virtually any computer in 1990 could handle HTML.

Then Berners-Lee released his ideas, code, and file structure—for free—to the world.

Enter the Wonder Kids

People immediately began working to build up the Web and HTML. The watershed moment came in 1992, when students at the National Center for Supercomputing Applications (NCSA) at the University of Illinois—led by Marc Andreessen, who had been following Tim Berners-Lee's work closely—created Mosaic, the first major Web browser tool. Incorporating a graphical user interface (GUI) that displayed graphics and other information at the same time within the document, Mosaic gave people incredibly refined access to the Web.

The impact was almost as powerful as that of a nuclear bomb exploding in the middle of Times Square. Before anyone realized what had happened, a multibillion industry had been created. Mosaic propelled the Illinois NCSA center to the middle of the Web universe. People from around the world deluged the center with requests for technical support and information about Mosaic. People began putting up Web servers all over the place, and pretty soon the Web was growing at annual rates of more than 1000 percent. Andreessen and other members of the original programming team, who never got anything for their work on the original Mosaic browser, subsequently left to form other companies. Thus, the modern history of the World Wide Web began.

Browser Wars I

One of the original NCSA developers, Chris Wilson, left to work for Spry Inc. (makers of the infamous Internet in a Box product), where he created AIR Mosaic, a Windows browser. (Spry later was purchased for $100 million by CompuServe.) Andreessen moved to California, where after a brief programming stint he met up with James Clark, the founder of Silicon Graphics.

Clark had become an instant believer in the power of the Internet and the World Wide Web. His plan was to cash in on the success of the Web by building browser software so great that everyone would want his technology (as opposed to NCSA's or anyone else's). NCSA, however, had been working up licensing agreements with various interested partners to commercialize its browser—agreements that included a cross-licensing of features and code. In order to avoid an agreement like that (which would give any licensee his company's additions to the Mosaic technology), Clark decided to build the browser all over again.

That meant getting the original programmers. Clark and Andreessen wasted no time; they flew out to Illinois and recruited the majority of the team in a single weekend. Soon they incorporated under the name Mosaic Communications—later changing it to Netscape after NCSA complained that it had a copyright on the Mosaic name.

Netscape's major plan was to race ahead of the market by having its browser support more features and extended HTML tags. Up until then the HTML standards had been designed openly and approved by a community of Web developers. Netscape, however, decided to forge ahead on its own, and soon its browser was the only one to offer features like font sizing, centering of text, and tables.

People began to take notice, tailoring their Web pages to work with the extensions Netscape had added. This step created the exact cycle Clark was hoping for. People who didn't have Netscape soon wanted it so they could view the more "advanced" sites; meanwhile, as the number of people using Netscape expanded, more sites began customizing around it. Other browser developers either couldn't keep up or chose not to try.

Soon Netscape was the number one browser in the world; only a handful of others remain as alternatives to Netscape. Of these browsers, only one seems to have the potential to compete with Netscape.

Enter Microsoft

One of the companies that began to take notice of Netscape was Microsoft. Although it had been promoting its idea of "Information at Your Fingertips" for some time, Microsoft was caught by surprise when the Mosaic phenomenon exploded in front of it. While it once had been content to focus on new versions of Word, Excel, and Windows, Microsoft now saw that the Internet had grown to the point where Microsoft had to react.

Its first move (although this story is often disputed) was an offer to adopt Netscape's browser technology, but only if Microsoft was granted more than 20 percent of the company. When Netscape said no, Microsoft declared war. The software giant opened fire by working with the tiny Illinois startup that NCSA had granted the rights to the original Mosaic source code. (The venerable NCSA Mosaic itself had fallen by the wayside, unable to muster the resources to keep up with Netscape.) Interest in Spyglass Technologies skyrocketed when Microsoft announced it would develop a Web browser—called Internet Explorer—in conjunction with Spyglass.

Today Netscape still controls some 70 percent or more of the Web browser market, but Microsoft's Internet Explorer is catching up, with around 15 percent of the market at the time this book was written. However, with certain deals with America Online and CompuServe, Internet Explorer could reach 40 percent market share by the end of 1996.

The Online World Takes Off

By the 1990s the computer world had settled in with two basic machine types: Macintoshes and MS-DOS/Windows machines. Modem prices had dropped significantly, finally getting to the point where a 14.4 Kbps modem was in most people's reach. (Anyone who has tried to cruise the World Wide Web at a speed below 14.4 knows how critical this development was.) Not surprisingly, online networks like Prodigy, CompuServe, and a little-known upstart named America Online (AOL) began to grow rapidly. Subsequent price wars, coupled with the success of Windows 3.1 and even faster modem speeds, helped millions of users to flock online between 1992 and 1994.

Many of these newcomers to the world of modems and computer communications were joining online services that offered little in the way of Internet features. Once commercial companies and individual end users became aware of the online world, however, people inevitably began turning their eyes toward the Internet and the World Wide Web.

And so, while the online networks flourished—signing on as many as a million users every six months—many of their customers started jumping into the Internet, either through third-party Internet service providers (ISPs) or through the online services themselves when they started offering Web access. The Web hit its stride in 1994 when it really became commercialized and available outside universities and research labs—and once the press got hold of that news, well, all hell broke loose.

The Web as Global Superstar

In late 1993 and all through 1994, the mainstream press began taking notice of the online world, especially those odd things called the Internet and the World Wide Web. A new magazine called *Wired* (which billed itself as the *Rolling Stone* of the information age) enjoyed the most successful launch of any magazine in recent history.

Around the world—in school classrooms, corporate boardrooms, and people's bedrooms—millions of people began trying to understand what the World Wide Web was. The Web soon was featured almost daily on the business pages of the New York Times and Wall Street Journal. *Wired* jumped to monthly sales a year ahead of schedule, computer trade publications splashed their covers with Web information, and the major online services raced to expand access to the Web. Prodigy signed up 500,000 new members when its Web services debuted ahead of the other major networks. Meanwhile, AOL was growing so fast (and faster once its Internet services were available) that its infrastructure frequently could not keep up with the expanding subscriber base—some customers, in fact, began calling it America On-Hold.

Universal Resource Locators (URLs), the funny-reading **http://www.anywhere. com** addresses of Web sites, began creeping into ads and articles in mainstream newspapers and magazines, and even into television commercials. The number of domains on the Web rose from 20,000 in 1992 to 76,000 by the end of 1994.

As these developments began to sink in, people quickly saw that the entire world was going to redesign itself around the Internet and the World Wide Web. While some of the prognosticating got a little out of hand, the general idea that people everywhere would be connected to a global computer network through which they would work, communicate, shop, and more wasn't a farfetched notion anymore; it was becoming an absolute reality. Even so, the Web was still pretty simple compared to what was about to emerge.

Browser Wars II: Feature Race and API Explosion

Toward the end of 1995, Netscape introduced its long-awaited Navigator 2.0 browser software, which quickly set the stage for what will be a major advancement of the technology of the Web. In addition to a multitude of new features (such as plug-in technology and integrated reading of mail and news servers), Netscape Navigator 2.0 is able to interpret Java and JavaScript; as a result, the browser can download and run software that is directly integrated into the Web.

Netscape isn't the only company pushing new technology in its latest browser. The next version of Microsoft's Internet Explorer, Netscape Navigator's chief rival in the browser wars, is going to integrate Java and Visual Basic Script, Microsoft's own scripting language.

Microsoft and Netscape both are promoting so-called Application Programming Interfaces (APIs), which enable developers to create entire Web applications that work in conjunction with the browsers and/or Web server systems each company also offers. Both firms are also pushing the development of secure transaction technologies to encourage credit card purchases over the Internet.

Each company's goal is to establish its browser and server software as not just a standalone application (similar to your favorite word processor or spreadsheet program), but as the development platform for a new wave of Internet and Web applications. In essence, Netscape sees its browser technology becoming more of an operating system in its own right, while in Microsoft's view the browser will become more tightly woven into its existing operating system.

In both cases, though, it is clear that the days of a simple browser are gone. Today's Netscape Navigator and Internet Explorer will be replaced by an entire system of technology that enables a new round of software development to deliver on the promise of a true worldwide network and community.

Tomorrow's World Wide Web

Improved and expanded browsers are just part of the flood of new technology that's about to enter the World Wide Web. Once that technology has the kinks worked out, and more high-speed lines become commonly available, the Web's popularity will explode even further. The Web will also become far more of a realtime network, as embedded applets join with streamed content and data to make the idea of waiting for a Web site obsolete. When this transition takes place, the concept of the Web as a broadcast medium will be replaced by reality.

The immediate future of the Web will depend on the implementation of ideas for tools, products, and content that are already in place. As consumers, transfer speeds, and finished sites catch up to these plans, the World Wide Web will more than fulfill its current promise.

Where the World Wide Web will ultimately lead us, though, is hard to say. Even the Web's inventor, Tim Berners-Lee, says it has perhaps changed too much and too quickly from its humble beginnings at CERN. Berners-Lee and others openly worry that the principles of ease of use and open standards have been thrown aside in a commercial race for dominance of Web standards. Whether this is true remains to be seen, but there is a growing chorus of people calling for the Web to remain true to itself.

Yes, there is a plethora of proprietary or semi-open standards floating around the Net, but it's hard to see a total destruction of the founding principles of the World Wide Web. From the day the Web was conceived and through its many changes and additions, the core principles—equal opportunity, decentralization, and ease of use—have yet to be dislodged. Commerce may one day bring immense change to the Net, as some fear, but more often than not the fascination for historians has been (and will be) how much the Web and the Internet have changed the world, rather than how the world has changed the Internet.

Net and Web History Resources

The following books and Web sites contain even more useful information if you're interested in the history of the Internet and the World Wide Web.

Books

Eventually someone will write a great history of the Internet and the World Wide Web. Until then, I have found several books that are referred to as the best sources for Web background information and the fundamental history of the Internet.

Casting The Net: From Arpanet to Internet and Beyond by Peter H. Salus (published by Addison-Wesley, 1995; ISBN 0-201-87674-4)

An excellent book that covers all sorts of Internet history, including the people, the computer systems, and the events that made the Internet possible.

Whole Internet Users Guide & Catalog 2nd Edition by Ed Krol (published by O'Reilly & Associates, 1994; ISBN 1-565920-63-5)

This book has a lot more than history and background on the Internet—it's considered by many to be one of the best books ever about the Internet. It explains so much of what the Internet is and how it came to be that this book belongs in every Internet/Web enthusiast's collection.

Web Sites

Surprisingly, I couldn't find much *on* the World Wide Web about the history of the Internet and the Web. The few items I did find, however, were excellent resources for those of you looking for even more detail and enlightenment on this subject.

Hobbes' Internet Timeline
http://www.amdahl.com/internet/events/timeline.html

The Internet's History and Development: From Wartime Tool to the Fish-Cam by Scott Ruthfield
http://www.acm.org/crossroads/xrds2-1/inet-history.html

History and Development of the Internet from the *Magazine of Fantasy and Science Fiction*
http://caboose.com/altopics/internet/GUIDES_AND_HELP/HISTORY/

WWW Consortium History Page
http://www.w3.org/pub/WWW/WWW/

Net Thesis - History of the Net
http://www.ocean.ic.net/ftp/doc/nethist.html

From Arpanet to Usenet News: The Development of the International
Computer Network
`http://www.nac.gmu.edu/mon/Internet/HaubenFmArpanetToInternet.html`

A Brief Internet History Timeline

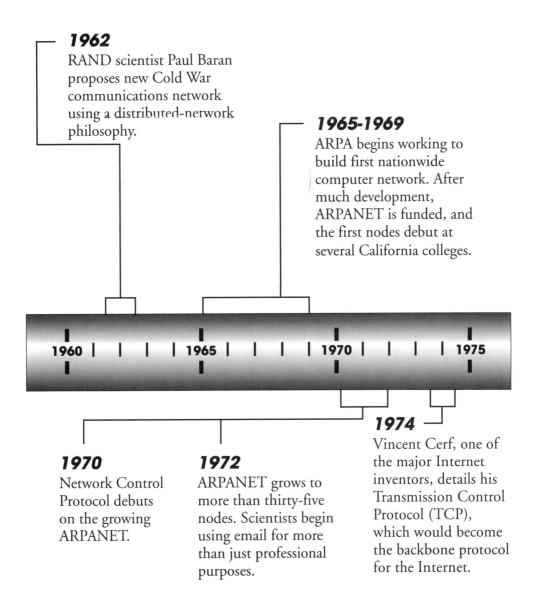

1962
RAND scientist Paul Baran
proposes new Cold War
communications network
using a distributed-network
philosophy.

1965-1969
ARPA begins working to
build first nationwide
computer network. After
much development,
ARPANET is funded, and
the first nodes debut at
several California colleges.

1960 | | | | 1965 | | | | 1970 | | | | 1975

1974
Vincent Cerf, one of
the major Internet
inventors, details his
Transmission Control
Protocol (TCP),
which would become
the backbone protocol
for the Internet.

1970
Network Control
Protocol debuts
on the growing
ARPANET.

1972
ARPANET grows to
more than thirty-five
nodes. Scientists begin
using email for more
than just professional
purposes.

1979-1981

BITNET, CSNET, and
USENET are launched. The
Internet begins to take shape.

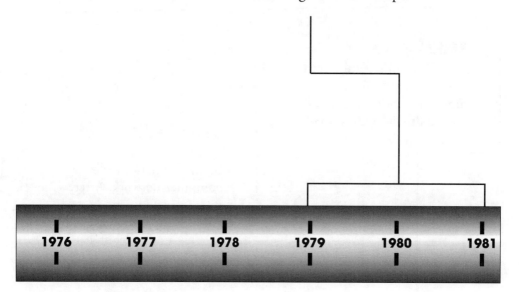

| 1976 | 1977 | 1978 | 1979 | 1980 | 1981 |

1983

TCP/IP becomes the protocol used on ARPANET. The greater Internet soon follows suit.

1984

Domain names are introduced, as well as moderated newsgroups on the USENET.

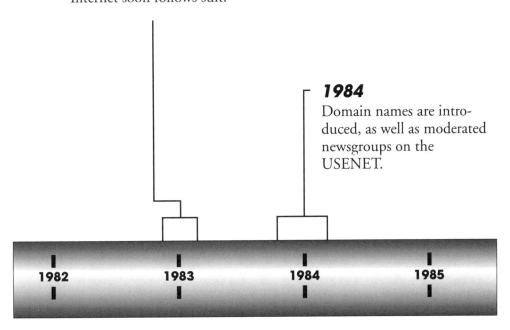

1989

The NSFNET backbone is upgraded to T1 (and two years later to T3), giving it even more capacity. Other companies begin to build and rapidly expand their own national backbones.

Internet Relay Chat (IRC) is developed.

Clifford Stoll catches an international spy ring on the Internet and writes a subsequent best-seller.

Online services begin to sign on large numbers of users. With online services growing further, the world continues to wake up to the coming age of global computer networks.

1986-1987

The National Science Foundation creates NSFNET, the major Internet backbone.

USENET completely reorganizes, in what becomes known as "The Great Change."

| 1986 | 1987 | 1988 | 1989 |

1988

Robert Morris writes a major virus on the Internet, causing many nodes to crash.

Public awareness of the power and reach of the Internet begins to grow.

1990

The government shuts down ARPANET.

A rash government crackdown on hackers and other computer users causes Mitch Kapor to form the Electronic Frontier Foundation (EFF) to act as a technological equivalent of the ACLU.

McGill University programmers debut Archie, an Internet search tool. The first commercial Internet service provider (ISP) begins operation.

1992

The World Wide Web and online services continue to expand. Mosaic makes its debut at the NCSA laboratory at the University of Illinois.

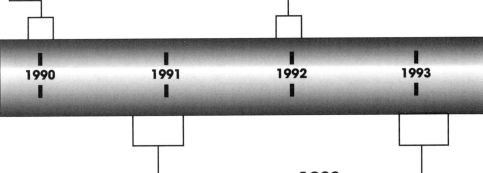

1991

With the commercialization of the Internet now a reality, major companies (such as UUNET and PSINET) begin working to make the Internet a major commercial network.

University of Minnesota programmers create Gopher.

Tim Berners-Lee invents the World Wide Web.

1993

The NSF creates the InterNic and other services to help manage the Internet, providing such services as assistant ISPs and managing and assigning domain names.

The World Wide Web begins to grow enormously.

Wired magazine begins publishing.

1994

The World Wide Web is every-where, and so is the hype associ-ated with it. As the Internet celebrates its twenty-fifth anniver-sary, the Web becomes the major foundation of the newly emerging global computer network.

James Clark and Mark Andreessen form Netscape Communications.

1996

Netscape Navigator 2.0 (and quickly after that 3.0, and perhaps even 4.0) and Internet Explorer 3.0 debut, offering an entire new suite of technologies (including Java and other programming options). Brows-ers are transformed from standalone applications to entire platforms upon which the next generation of Web applications will be built.

| 1994 | 1995 | 1996 |

1995

The Internet becomes a commercial success, with thousands of sites popping up monthly, URLs appearing in major corporate ad cam-paigns, and millions of people signing onto the World Wide Web. The entire consumer software industry realigns along Web development and implementation strategies. Companies begin building their own net-works based on Internet technology (called intranets). Online networks such as AOL and CompuServe have millions of users, and they now offer Web and other major Internet services.

Microsoft debuts its Windows 95 operating system (with built-in Internet access) and begins publishing a browser to rival the now-established Netscape Navigator.

It truly is a different Internet to many, as the NSF announces that registration of domain names will now cost $50 per year.

Sun finishes the majority of work on its Java language for the Internet.

CHAPTER

Don't jump the gun! There are some big issues today's developers need to be familiar with.

The Web Today

In the previous chapter, I briefly discussed the basics of the modern-day World Wide Web, but I glossed over most of the details. So much is going on, though, that I'm going to devote this chapter to current issues on the Web. Understanding them will help you make better sense of the huge amount of material I'll be covering later on in this book.

Sometimes I think the biggest problem with the Web today is that there is too much Web philosophy floating around. Everyone seems to have predictions and glorious visions of what the World Wide Web is or means. Personally, I think the majority of them are ridiculous because the people spouting them fail to tie them to anything that's actually practical, either right now or in the near future.

So I'm going to use this chapter to lay out today's key issues as they relate to the Web, the greater Internet, and Web development. Then, in the next chapter, I'll discuss how these issues will affect the Web of tomorrow. The rest of the book will build on and refer back to the key points explored in these chapters. All of the development, design, and resource information presented hereafter will be explained in terms of how each piece relates to the developmental issues shaping the Web of today and tomorrow. Ten of those issues are highlighted in this chapter.

The Progress of Browser Capabilities

The engines driving the actual progress of the Web are the two major browsers, Netscape's Navigator and Microsoft's Internet Explorer. While there are other advances, all of them must flow through one or both of these two competing Web access technologies. Java, for example, wouldn't have nearly the relevance it has now if Netscape had chosen to implement some other technology in its place.

So, when we examine the Web today, we have to look at it with one eye on Netscape and the other on Microsoft. Other players do matter—but only after we've done a reality check with these two companies.

Right now the competition between Netscape and Microsoft is brutally intense. Some of this competition has been applauded, simply because many people like the idea of someone sticking it to Microsoft—although an all-powerful Netscape is no better, is it? In any event, Microsoft is proving again that it does its best work when it's challenged. Already Microsoft has talked about being more aggressive in transporting certain technologies to the Macintosh (an area where the creator of Windows has lagged noticeably in recent years) because of the higher profile of Macs among Web developers and users. In addition, Microsoft has opened up more of its technology—for instance, Visual Basic Script is being openly submitted to the World Wide Web community as a scripting standard.

As a result of the competition between Microsoft and Netscape, each is proposing some technologies that are the same, but also some competing technologies that are incompatible (and guess who's in the middle when that happens?). So, despite some cooperation and overlap, we still have Netscape offering Unix derivatives while Microsoft instead offers its NT product and software. Similarly, Netscape promotes its plug-in technology and Java, at the same time as Microsoft is pushing ActiveX.

Netscape is devoted to establishing its products as the most open, most broad, and most advanced Web development and implementation system. It sees Navigator as not merely an application, but a complete platform upon which people build applications for the Web. Because of this view, the folks who run Netscape don't care if Navigator has to work with lots of Microsoft software (such as Windows or Word) around it, just as long as the Web and Internet go through them.

Microsoft, however, fears that if it fails to be a major force on the Internet it will jeopardize its operating system (especially Windows NT), development tools, and consumer software offerings. And it's not willing to cede these to anyone.

The resulting war has created an environment where two software titans, each dominating the market in its own way, are pushing different sets of technologies that overlap in some areas but conflict in others. Developers will have to understand when they can work with both sides, or when they must choose one or the other.

Sorting Out the Emerging Technologies

In some ways, the World Wide Web created an entirely clean slate for many software technologies. As a result, Web developers can't assume that the traditional major players in the software industry are going to be just as important on the Web. One case in point: Netscape, a billion-dollar company that didn't exist prior to the creation of the Web. Another case in point is Macromedia, whose move to the Shockwave system has solidified Director as a major authoring tool for many developers. Sales are now going through the roof for this company as a result of its Web technology.

While some people welcome this shakeup, it also creates havoc because developers need to reevaluate every tool, product, data type, and programming skill in terms of how applicable it is to the Web. This process isn't as easy as it should be. In fact, it is increasingly complicated by the phenomenon of every company giving away much of its technology for free in order to establish market share on the Internet. Discount market-share pricing is nothing new to the software business, but the Web has taken the practice to new heights.

This situation, though, creates a lot of uncertainty among developers. With products and technologies often costing nothing to adopt, it's much harder to gauge who's winning or losing. Perhaps, though, no one wins when things are free. For example, there are currently three major vector graphics plug-ins floating around (made by Corel, Autodesk, and Macromedia). If all are given away free and become equally established, then it's conceivable that you could mix and match all three on your site. But what if you find each has its own unique features and downsides? In this case (which is far more likely), the work to set up rules of use becomes a constant chore of evaluating all of the technologies for their strengths and weaknesses. You pay for this work, but none of it directly helps you build a new Web product.

As a result, one of the key issues facing developers today is knowing whether they are in an emerging software environment. If they are—whether they like it or not—they have a lot of work to do to evaluate a ton of new software, techniques, and technologies to keep pace with other developers in a quest to deliver the best Web products.

Building Dynamic Sites

When I talk about site building here, I'm after one thing: well-done, impressive sites. The days where a URL and some nice text could build up a good following are long gone. Today Web sites require major work just to stand out amid the thousands of sites and pages released daily. In 1995 and 1996, the Web has become an increasingly competitive environment. This is a business now, and the competition is cutthroat. In order to survive, a site has to be top notch and continually updated to retain users and build its viewing base.

Creating a dynamic site takes a significant amount of work. The content, for starters, has to be fresh and relevant. You have to utilize every edge and build a tight bond with users of your site. Some sites are quickly installing chat systems and other items to create more interactivity, which is seen as one way to create such a bond. Companies are even using email newsletters or direct mailings to build their communities. The interactive promotion of a site has become as important as the construction of the site itself.

Web developers are demanding the means to implement their ideas more widely and separate themselves from their competitors. Development tool companies and Internet technology companies are only happy to oblige. This relationship between developers and development companies is the reason why Web tools and technologies are multiplying so rapidly.

Now there are a dozen sites selling CDs over the Internet, a dozen or more selling videogames, and so on. Clearly, not all of these sites are going to survive. The ones that are more dynamic, more interesting, and better supported will win. These rules apply for any site now being built. And as access speeds increase, tools become more powerful, and more people come onto the Web, developers will have to respond with even more dynamic sites.

Determining Web Demographics

One of the raging debates going on among Web users and developers is about the demographics of the Web community. Not only are the results of the surveys taken thus far widely disputed, but a more fundamental argument exists about the processes used to gather and interpret the data in the first place.

This is a very important issue, because many of the Web revenue schemes that have been devised, especially those based on advertising revenue, depend greatly on the creation of a widely accepted and trusted auditing system. In addition, many planners still don't have an exact picture of who is "on" the Web, for how long, from where, and so on.

Of course, I'm not saying that there haven't been interesting studies—just that disputes exist about what they mean. Later in this book, in Chapter 24, I'll go into more depth on several published studies and numerous other examples of Web demographic information.

Web-wide studies aren't the only demographic issue that has come into play. More and more sites are working to build large databases of information about their customers on a user-by-user basis. Many of today's new server technologies help developers and site administrators specifically understand the demographics and Web surfing practices of the user base of their Web site.

The result is greater pressure to create a customizable Web-site solution—in other words, a site that tailors itself directly to the needs of each individual who browses it. In addition, developers need to be aware of the privacy and ethics issues related to Web demographics; never before has there been a system as encompassing as the Web for gathering information about people's profiles; with that has come entirely new sets of ethical dilemmas.

Databased Web Solutions— Building Sites in Realtime

The need for more dynamic sites and increased information about demographics has led to the newest wave of Web design and implementation, a wave that is already breaking at upper-echelon sites: realtime Web construction.

No longer are Web pages exquisitely planned single entities that are hard-coded by designers, one page at a time, with painstaking detail. Instead they are created on the fly—drawing content from large databases of information and spilling it into predefined templates (which may themselves be exquisitely designed), thereby creating customized or flexible displays of huge amounts of information in the blink of an eye (or at least a modem).

Combining this realtime construction capability with data about the current user might result in truly customized sites with Web browsing sessions tailored to the individual user. If, for example, I log on to ESPN SportsZone, the site might automatically know from past browsing sessions stored in a database to only display sports information about my favorite players, teams, and sports. I get ESPN's content but save a lot of time because it's displayed in a form that best suits my tastes. Microsoft's MSN (The Microsoft Network) already offers a customizable home page where you can create your own private menu of news, links, weather, and stock prices whenever you log on to **http://www.msn.com.**

Another example of realtime site creation is a databased publishing system. For example, a news organization like CNN might create a huge database of pictures of key people who pop up in the news from time to time, such as heads of state, corporations, and movie stars. Then as their writers create stories and log them onto their Web site, a database engine would automatically insert the pictures of these people into the page on the fly.

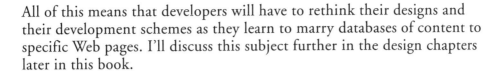

All of this means that developers will have to rethink their designs and their development schemes as they learn to marry databases of content to specific Web pages. I'll discuss this subject further in the design chapters later in this book.

Finding Emerging Revenue Streams

Another major issue is the development of real revenue streams from the Web. So far only a few companies have been generating revenue from their Web efforts, while the majority of commercially active sites haven't. On the Web, lots of sites are meant to be commercial entities, but they've yet to sell any ads or items, or generate any kind of income, let alone profit.

Some of this is due to logistics. Certain technologies—like secure credit card purchasing systems—are still in beta testing, and good database tools to support catalogs and other major development work are also just hitting their stride. When these technologies mature, though, more work nevertheless will be needed to develop the exact systems that can generate revenue on the Web.

Today, the majority of significant Web revenue falls into one of two camps: advertising and derived sales. In my book, advertising on the Web is defined as one source paying another source for the rights to space that promotes a product (which can be other Web sites) on the latter source's site. While I have reservations about advertising on the Web, it is the major revenue stream, other than derived sales, from which many developers plan to make money.

I use the term *derived sales* because not all sales from the Internet are actually completed there. A lot of sales, however, originate from the Internet and the World Wide Web. For example, my publisher (The Coriolis Group) maintains an online database of its books. A Web surfer browsing through the titles who sees a book he or she likes might pick up the phone to order instead of using the online system. Either way, the sale is still *derived* from the publisher's Web site. This is also how L.L. Bean uses its site: It doesn't accept orders over the Web, but uses a Web site rather than expensive catalog mailings to reach a wider consumer audience for its products at a much lower cost. As more purchasing occurs directly via the Web, I suspect that observers will split direct and derived sales into separate groups; for now, though, derived sales are the much larger category.

The challenge today is to find other revenue streams aside from the above two. The Web is a new medium, so you can be sure that new revenue ideas are going to emerge. For example, one developer might create a specialized piece of software needed to interact with a Web site, then sell this software directly to the user while the site itself remains "free." The revenue is derived from the direct software sale, but it is the need to use the software to visit the Web site that makes the sale happen. Other sites using various "E-cash" schemes might charge to serve up either Web pages or special content. Perhaps some sites will give out "cyber-coupons"—visit this site and earn $25 off your next flight to Florida (with the airline that gets the sale paying $10 a head for the booking).

In the end, some schemes will be fairly straightforward, but the nature of the World Wide Web and emerging technologies already point to some interesting and entirely new ideas for creating revenue from Web development or sites. Among the key issues will be who creates these ideas, and which ones become most effective. The next few years will yield boatloads of clues about these issues.

Developing Web Construction Processes

As software development continues to mature, developers have established some really good software construction skills. Microsoft has even published some excellent books (such as *Code Complete* and *Writing Solid Code*) that detail a very organized and systematic approach to creating good solid computer software.

The Web still has some distance to go in this effort, mostly because it's going through so much change, but also because it's still relatively young. This is no excuse, however, for not building a solid set of Web construction rules today. Already in my research I've come across a number of people, writings, and other resources that try to bring some Web-specific construction advice into focus.

Over the next few years, as some of the key Web technologies begin to fall into place, it will become increasingly important for major Web developers to create and maintain core construction principles and practices.

The Emergence of the Intranet

Over the next two to three years, the biggest Web development issue is probably not going to be related to the Internet. The Internet will still be significant, of course, but the effort to create internal intranets for corporations and organizations will bring a tremendous amount of development work to Web-savvy companies.

Much of corporate America has been particularly slow to catch up with recent technology breakthroughs. At one point it was spending billions of dollars, but lately—as Pentium PCs debuted, Windows 95 was launched, and the Internet became a reality—corporate buying has stagnated. Companies instead focused on utilizing the technology they already had in place.

All signs now suggest that a major wave of corporate computer re-engineering is going to take place. Much of this work will have to do with the development of intranets. The tools and capabilities of Web-based networks to create better information distribution and sharing among employees is light years ahead of anything that can be achieved by existing networking software (with all due respect to Lotus Notes).

And so the World Wide Web, with more direct benefits and a growing need for corporations to expand their productivity, has many companies justifying another round of massive computer technology investment.

Understanding the Infrastructure State

Many people—even Web developers—are very uneducated when it comes to the nuts-and-bolts infrastructure of the Web. In fact, it's easy to think of Web infrastructure as ending at the phone jack where you plug in your modem. However easy it may be to ignore the plumbing of the Web now, though, over the next several years a number of difficult structural issues will affect Web development.

First of all, there's an infrastructure shortage. If you wonder why things are slow on the Internet, stop blaming your slow modem; many times the real problem is the slow network and/or a slow server. The reason is related to the fundamental design of the Internet. TCP/IP protocol divides information into separate packets, which are then sent out with a destination address. Because nothing else is sent but that information, however, everything on the Internet is considered equal. The downside of this is that priority data—say, your realtime streamed video file—isn't going to be given any precedence over little Bobby in his bedroom, downloading Doom IV from **happy.puppy.com**.

The underlying problem is the wiring in the ground, which isn't yet up-to-date for the digital age. The majority of the world still uses traditional phone lines. And while ISDN is an amazing improvement, it's still not widespread

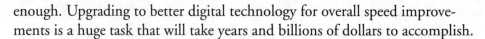

enough. Upgrading to better digital technology for overall speed improvements is a huge task that will take years and billions of dollars to accomplish.

As a developer, you need to pay attention to this issue today, because the moves to improve the infrastructure are being made now. The recent telecommunications deregulation act of 1995 is causing a drastic restructuring of the telecommunications and cable industries. All of the various components of these industries are looking at the Internet, too. Some companies will be more aggressive than others, and certain areas will be more competitive—which means that a lot of unevenness will be created.

Already you can see this phenomenon with ISDN, which is much cheaper in California than on the East Coast. In some areas cable modems might become more readily available, while in others wireless technology will be all the rage. As a developer planning today, you will need to examine how future infrastructure changes will impact your marketing, your development, and the rest of your business.

Applying and Fitting in with the Web

One issue many developers are learning about is the overall context of the Web. The World Wide Web and the Internet are very different beasts than what many people have been used to. The Web is *not* just like newspapers, radio, or television, and the Web is *not* just like multimedia or software development—it's a unique form of development.

Moreover, the Web is a changing entity. Many of the original pioneers in Web development now find themselves falling behind as the technology keeps changing. This ongoing revolution brings up some important questions about Web development and overall product design: How do you or your product ideas fit in with the Web? How does the World Wide Web really benefit you or your company? What does it mean to produce a Web site? Will it change the business you're in? What about the culture and practices of the Web community? Now that some of the initial hype of the World Wide Web has worn off, many companies and developers are reformulating what the Web means.

As a nice example, look at most magazine and newspaper Web sites, which are stale copies of their paper equivalents. As these publications are learning, they will have to do a lot more to survive on the Web. In addition, major newspapers that have enjoyed little or no competition in their hometown are finding

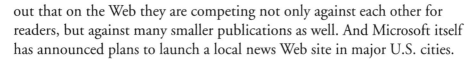

out that on the Web they are competing not only against each other for readers, but against many smaller publications as well. And Microsoft itself has announced plans to launch a local news Web site in major U.S. cities.

Newspapers and magazines are perfect examples of how the Web can force an organization or product to completely reinvent itself to ensure its survival. Most top developers hold this notion close to their hearts as they consult about or build new sites on the World Wide Web.

Pioneers, Stake Your Claim!

The Web is the new frontier. Its mere existence creates a whole new place to transfer existing businesses or develop entirely new ones. This is your chance to be one of the few who actually gets in on the ground floor. Every several years the computer industry has created new opportunities for pioneering developers. Never since the creation of the original personal computer industry, though, has there been an opportunity of such magnitude.

The biggest differences about this new opportunity, however, are that more people realize it exists and that the World Wide Web is far more complex in its implications than the original personal computer was. Thus, you have an opportunity to dream again—but also far more competition, learning, and developing to deal with.

Bill Gates likens the Internet to the old 49er Gold Rush, going on to say that some will get rich while others simply speculate and lose. I liken it more to the original pioneering settlements in America, where everyone staked a claim to build upon this Earth whatever they wanted. It wasn't all about panning for a big payday. Some folks simply wanted a home of their own, a family, and the means to enjoy life. Everyone, though, had to pioneer—to get in and work hard to produce what worked for them—and from that they built a much bigger community out of their individual efforts.

The Web is the same thing. Perhaps it's a little more competitive, but all in all it's about pioneering new opportunities and dynamic creations. There's always a lot of hype when this happens, whether it's the idea of a river flowing with gold in California or a handful of people turning an afternoon of HTML coding into a multimillion-dollar IPO. After all the hype is stripped away, there remains considerable room to believe that many new opportunities for lots of people have arrived. The opportunity is here, *and it's here today*—and that, perhaps, is the Web's most compelling issue.

CHAPTER 4

The time to begin preparing for tomorrow's Web is today.

Tomorrow's Web

I've talked about the history of the Web and the issues that face Web developers today, but what about the long-range future? Many people are promising that virtually every human problem will be solved by the Web, but we know that's not true. The Web does promise to change quite a bit, however—and, in turn, to change the world we know—so what we need to do is be somewhat realistic about what tomorrow will bring.

A Macroeconomic View Shows an Amazing Future

Most of the Web successes you and I will see will be entirely *micro*economic; we'll build sites and applications for private profit or as hired contractors. As we concentrate on the basic product we're developing, perhaps occasionally we will notice some industry-wide trends. When I get almost dumbfounded by the World Wide Web, though, is when I take a *macro*economic view of its impact. And so the first issue I want to discuss concerning the future of the Web is the shift in capital streams that will be caused by the Web's emergence.

Capital today is somewhat like energy—it can't be created or destroyed, but it can be transferred. Sure, I know this flies in the face of basic economic theory, but hang with me a second. I'm referring here to the large sums of capital (millions to billions of dollars) used to purchase or invest with. It's hard to create sums this vast out of thin air; instead, they have to be transferred from other parts of the economy. This is where the Web begins to rearrange things tremendously.

Macroeconomically speaking, the Web has two main effects: it immensely increases competition (especially in terms of pricing), and it drastically reduces distribution costs. Both of these result in huge shifts of capital.

The record industry provides a great example. A music CD currently costs about $2 to make, package, and ship. The record company then sells it to a distributor or retailer for about $6. The retailer then resells the CD to you and me for far more; the typical retail markup is 20 to 100 percent of cost. Now along comes the Web, where you can sample the album and view much larger selections. Because the costs associated with maintaining a database on the Web are minuscule compared to the cost of mailing millions of printed catalogs (which many record clubs and direct marketers do), the retailer's associated costs are reduced significantly. These savings can be passed on to

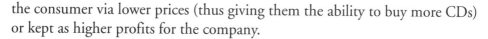

the consumer via lower prices (thus giving them the ability to buy more CDs) or kept as higher profits for the company.

But what if you could download music directly onto your own recordable CD or Digital Versatile Disc (DVD), a more advanced and larger capacity CD-ROM technology drive? It's entirely possible that this technology could be common within the next 5 to 10 years. Instead of dealing with Tower Records, or even Time Warner, you could buy the next U2 album directly from the band! And instead of the band members getting only a dollar per disc in royalties, they could sell it to you directly over the Internet for $5 (about one-half to one-third of today's store price) and still make five times as much money for themselves. Meanwhile, an entire industry making billions of dollars solely on its ability to *distribute* albums would vanish. But those billions of dollars won't disappear; they will go elsewhere. People would buy more albums, or maybe they would take more vacations or eat out more often. Maybe there would even be more bands making music, because even sales of 20,000 albums would net them $100,000.

And the changes won't stop there. What about the Internet Phone, a product that exists today? AT&T is worth $60 billion based on its long distance telephone service alone. What will happen when people begin using the Internet to communicate via voice with each other instead of using AT&T? Where will that $60 billion go? (Note that even if AT&T were to lose just 5 percent of its business, that's still about $3 billion!)

Now, I don't want to get too carried away, even though in my own mind I've concocted dozens of mind-boggling scenarios like the two mentioned above. There is no doubt that the Web will uniquely change many aspects of our economic lives, and the sociopolitical fallout of these changes will be substantial. The role Web developers get to play in this revolution is perhaps one of the most appealing aspects of our jobs. After all, actually creating the future beats dreaming about it any day.

How, Why, Where: Being Practical About the Future

I lose my temper with the Web faithful, though, when they stop their ideas about the Web at the previous paragraph. They lay out all of these fantastic future scenarios, and then they leave you hanging trying to sort out what is plausible rather than just wishful hyperbole. In addition, maybe I'm just self-centered, but I want someone to tell me where *I* fit into all this! Well, I don't want to be a hypocrite, so here is how I see how the future of the Web (at least for the next 5 to 15 years) and how these ideas relate to what this book is about—Web development.

Commerce Is King

The World Wide Web wasn't about commerce originally, but business is now the chief reason for the growth of the Web. The other reasons for which the Web exists (communication, artistic expression, research, and so on) will still exist, but most development efforts—yours, mine, and other people's—will be focused on business applications ranging from advertising to distribution, management, and transactions. Even entertainment-oriented sites such as The Spot, a sort of Web-based cross between MTV's "The Real World" and a traditional soap opera, are being created primarily for their advertising potential.

Via such technologies as microtransactions, digital cash accounts, and secure credit card processing, the Web of the future will become much more like a global market where bidders and sellers come together to transfer many types of products and services in realtime, 24 hours a day. Various Web applications will be developed to handle such commerce barriers as exchange rates, wire transfers, insurance contracts, and legal issues.

The cool thing about this development is that the Web has the potential to redefine business from the foundation up. It is plausible (and exciting) to expect that the top-echelon developers will be able to see the direct impact of their Web innovations on entire industries.

What This Means for Developers

For developers, this means their focus will be on technologies like secure transactions, catalog systems, and developing sites and applications which greatly increase commerce. Developers will also increasingly find themselves as consultants who can tell companies how Web-based commerce works.

Web commerce tends to focus on building narrow relationships with specific niche markets as opposed to building huge mass markets—the Web forces marketers to think about markets as large groups of distinct individuals, each with a specific need and desire. Web commerce is primarily an intense form of direct marketing, something many companies may not be familiar with. As a Web developer, your insights on how a company both attracts and enables consumers to purchase products through the Web will be a skill set companies will increasingly look for.

I'll Have My Agent Call Your Agent

Perhaps no technology brings more anticipation for the Web than the arrival of agents. Agents are programs that will automate your use of the Web, broadcasting your interests and interacting with sites to accomplish desired tasks—all without your presence.

For example, you might tell an agent program that you want to purchase a new refrigerator that meets a certain set of criteria. Then the agent would go to work on the Web, visiting stores and manufacturers that sell refrigerators. In each instance, it would interface with some specific system on the seller's computer to ascertain if there is a potential to do business. If there is, the agent program will report back the results, perhaps via email. Then all you would have to do is confirm the specific choice your agent made, and your refrigerator will be purchased.

The concept of agents may seem futuristic, but several companies (such as General Magic, AT&T, IBM, and Microsoft) already have some agent technology up and running.

What This Means for Developers

The advent of agents is quite significant, because it sustains the idea that Web sites in even the near future will need to handle actual as well as virtual browsers. A sign pointing to this sort of development already exists, as many developers add certain sections to their site to interact with the various "spiders" that roam the Web indexing pages.

In the future, as agents become more prevalent, Web developers will have to create sites that accommodate both real and "agent" browsers.

Not One Internet, but Many

We sometimes forget that the Internet in and of itself doesn't exist. Instead, it exists as a conglomeration of all sorts of different networks that follow a common set of standards and practices. What we consider the standards and practices of the World Wide Web, however, will in the future become a "common denominator" approach. This is because we can expect a lot of different infrastructures to be built over the next few years that, while being compatible with Internet standards, will look to extend their networks above and beyond them.

This is already evident in the success of online services like America Online and CompuServe. Both offer Internet access, but also have proprietary networks for their specific users. Other major providers, like PSInet and UUnet (now part of MFS Communications), are building systems that can prioritize certain data. For example, Mpath (the Internet gaming network) has a special deal to speed up its data through PSInet's section of the Internet.

Many suspected that the Internet would displace these types of networks, but instead it has strengthened them. By offering heightened security within their own network, or by containing additional content and customer service, or by using other mechanisms, these "extended Nets" are working to shore up the Internet's weaknesses.

What This Means for Developers

Developers will have to pay more attention to the various specialized networks and how they relate to their own ideas and developments. In addition to selecting providers that best suit their needs, developers will also have to note which consumers are using which networks.

The competition between these different networks will certainly result in the segmentation of Web users. For example, AOL might offer its users Internet access via cable modems very soon, but CompuServe may lag. While you're trying to service one large block of Web surfers clamoring for sites that take advantage of the bandwidth they've gained, you'll risk losing those who aren't caught up. The possibilities and limitations of each new way to access the Internet will require developers to think distinctly about the various routes people will use to access their specific site.

A Totally New Infrastructure

Tomorrow's Internet infrastructure will be incredibly diverse and speedy. Access speeds promise to be as much as 100 times faster than today's typical connection, and there are schemes emerging to broaden communications, and especially data network communications, with wireless, satellite, and cable systems.

Every time you double the speed of an online system, though, an entirely new look and feel are generated. Increasing processor speeds and advancing compression algorithms result in bandwidth that grows while the data needed to fit through it shrinks. In addition, the ideas behind certain wireless and satellite systems could bring parts of the world into Web-wired society far faster than many have predicted. One company, the Bill Gates and Craig McCaw (the founder of McCaw Cellular) backed Teledesic, is promising that a network of low-orbiting satellites providing data, voice, and video communications will be in operation by 2002. Many doubt that Teledesic will meet its self-imposed deadline, but remember that even 2010 is less than 15 years away.

What This Means for Developers

Developers will be required to keep pace with this infrastructure advancement. The speeds and power that will characterize the Internet 10 years from now will enable the creation of sites with tons of digital audio and video, 3D graphics, advanced applets, and more. The applications one can create with this type of power are far different than the majority of what is being created today.

Web Appliances

So far the World Wide Web is only accessible through personal computers and workstations, but many companies are racing to develop "Web appliances." These machines will be built specifically to access content from the Web. Right now, the first phase seems to be focusing on stripped-down PCs (such as Apple's Pippin device) or console systems (such as Sony's Playstation or Nintendo's Ultra 64). Beyond that, though, some companies are planning to create personal digital assistants (PDAs, like Apple's Newton) with Web access—and even to take the Web appliances a step further by building them into the infrastructure of offices and homes.

Some see the pursuit of Web appliances as foolish thinking; they argue that no one will want to work with a machine less capable than a state-of-the-art PC. This may be true, but most developers of Web appliances see a future where these devices are created to complement the PC in the household—indeed, they may be linked to that very PC. The PC would be the major computer, and the Web-surfing appliances around the house or office would be more like read-only accessors.

The basic point here is that not everyone in the future will access World Wide Web content via a full-fledged computer, because the Web has far too many applications in non-computer settings. For example, Boeing might set up a Web that disseminates continuously updated versions of all of its repair manuals. Someone reading this information would have no need for annotation or a keyboard, just a simple device that could navigate through the vast amount (probably millions of pages) of content. In this case, airline mechanics would perhaps use simple visual slates that would allow them to access the Web information.

What This Means for Developers

Developers will have to be much more vigilant about the types of devices that will be used to access Web content. Some won't be as capable as a Pentium PC or Sun workstation; instead, they could be simple PDAs or set-top boxes attached to a television monitor. Some will have keyboards, while others might use handwriting recognition.

What future hardware options might require of a site remains to be seen. The idea that the World Wide Web is a PC-only application is wrong, though, and eventually there will be a host of devices that open up the Web in unique and innovative ways. Developers should expect to work on sites created specifically to take advantage of whatever new Web access devices come along in the years ahead. For example, Excite, the search engine company, is creating a specialized version of their search engine site to work with the Web browser that Sega has for its Saturn video game console.

Where It All Leads: Digital Web Current

Ever think about electricity? It's an amazing invention. On a practical level, it's always on, all electrical devices use it with a standard interface, and it is available to virtually everyone. On a philosophical level, electricity in your living room is entertainment: your TV, stereo, and VCR are all electrical devices. In your kitchen, meanwhile, electricity is functional—it gives you the means to prepare and cook food.

As the Web matures, it will become just like electricity. There is every reason to believe that in the future the Web will become "plug and play," constantly on, and used by a number of devices that will connect to it. This universal application promises an incredible diversity of needed Web products, from a site to serve out recipes or order food from a terminal in the kitchen, to a games site accessed from the TV in the living room, to an entire array of business applications in the home office; the emergence of the Web as a digital current is upon us.

New Ethical Questions

Despite the relative newness of the World Wide Web, there are already entirely new ethical questions being raised about its uses. Some marketers have already used specific sites tailored for kids to find out what types of products the entire family uses (figuring the kids are far more willing to dispense the information).

As more technologies come into place—such as the agents mentioned above—the ethical dilemmas and people's awareness of them will increase. If developers and other members of the Web community can work steadfastly to deal with each problem as it arises, then users' long-term perceptions of the Web will remain overwhelmingly positive. If people begin to see marketers gathering information about them in unethical ways, or governments trying to control and introduce rigid regulation, or other threats of fraud or invasion of privacy, then the future of the Web could be severely hurt.

What This Means for Developers

As builders of the Web, developers are uniquely responsible for developing the ethical guidelines and enforcement mechanisms needed to ensure that the World Wide Web is used properly by all participants. At the same time, developers also need to ensure that other groups don't suppress the freedom of speech and other assets of Web culture that have made it special. It's a difficult task, to be sure. The speed at which the Web is growing and with which people are discovering both right and wrong ways to apply it to their lives doesn't make any of this easier.

Luckily, the Web promises so much to many different groups that—hopefully—there will be the proper types of pressure to guarantee fair, reasonable solutions to the concerns of Web surfers, developers, and the public in general.

Building Skills for Today and Tomorrow

When it comes to being practical about the future of the Net, I think it really boils down to identifying skills you can acquire today that will be just as useful in the future.

In a nutshell, this is how many companies are justifying the millions of dollars they're pouring into the Internet today. What they learn today, they reason, they can apply tomorrow when the use of the Internet becomes more widespread and improved technology allows them to bring in sizable revenue from their Web efforts.

So the reason we keep our eyes planted on the future is the same reason I spent time talking about the basic history of the Web. The value we gain from knowing where the Web is going is just as valuable as knowing where it's been—we gain a better understanding of what we should be doing today.

5

Good Web product design
requires a fundamental
understanding of basic
Web design principles.

An Overview of
Web Design

What Am I Designing?

All designing begins with a simple question: "What am I going to make?" Sometimes the answer is easy. In the short time I've been developing for the Web, though, I've found it difficult to say exactly what I'm going to make. Perhaps this is because of the wide-open possibilities of today's Web technology, or simply because many similar sites are likely to already be in existence for any idea a developer may have.

The best way to decide what you're going to make is to develop skills in all facets of Web product development. From brainstorming to planning, implementation, and simple do's and don'ts, there is a lot to be learned about how to develop for the Web. The developers with the best ideas tend to be the ones with the broadest understanding of the Web's purpose, capabilities, and existing offerings.

In this chapter I'll present some basic ideas of what it means to develop and design Web sites, and I'll touch on the key design aspects of the Web. The following chapters focus on specific ideas and resources for budding Web developers, but before you head there, it's best to think about some fundamental concepts.

Absolute Web Basics

The World Wide Web is really a very simple system, but developing for it requires that you understand the long and short of the Web. You need to broaden your concept of what Web development is, then break down common-denominator components of the Web.

The Long: Think of a Product, Not a Site

The first lesson in Web design is one that I can't stress enough. Today's developers *must* get away from the idea that Web development is just making a "site." A site is but one part of what you should consider the entire Web product.

For example, your Web product might be software that works in conjunction with a site to provide news and information on a "ticker tape" at the bottom of the screen. Every time users click on a scrolling headline, their browser is launched and your site serves up the complete text of the article. The site (which is merely a set of pages and content) is part of the product, not the product in and of itself.

Another example might be a specialty cookware store whose Web site takes online orders for merchandise. The real product includes the subsequent packaging and shipping of the materials, plus any other customer service that is provided (such as a follow-up email confirming shipment, or a downloadable recipe book tailored to the equipment purchased). Again, the Web site is but one part of the entire product being offered.

When you think in these larger terms, you may find yourself changing specific elements of the Web site as you flesh out other aspects of the entire product you're offering. Perhaps the most unique part of this book's approach to Web development is that I will take time to describe all of the factors—beyond just HTML and page design—that are going to fuel modern Web development. Moving from a site mindset to a product mindset is the first goal in this bigger-picture approach.

The Short: Begin by Breaking It Down

Having just expanded your view of what it means to develop for the Web, now I want to narrow it down. At its core, any World Wide Web product is made up of specific components. In trying to boil down these components into as small a list as possible, I came up with the following four essential building blocks.

Concepts

The first building block in designing any part of your Web product is a specific concept (or concepts): What essentially will this part do? What will it look like? What attributes will it take on? How does it fit into the reason this site exists? How does the user move to the next part of the site? All of these are conceptual items. You can't begin designing the other components of your product until you've created the concept they work to bring forth, so you should start here.

You may not realize it, but concepts are very physical items. Most concepts appear physically in such basic design items as treatments, brainstorming sessions, storyboards, and mock-ups. All good Web developers create concrete plans detailing the concepts of their sites before actually creating the sites.

Locations

From the outset the Internet has been a very geographical entity, and the World Wide Web is even more so. URLs alone give you actual addresses (many with country codes) that make you realize you're being connected to a specific place in the world from your personal location. But Internet locations aren't just the specific server site, they're also the specific server files you're linking to. Every server has some sort of specific location for each object that is part of the final site.

As I'll discuss a little later, the location component of Web design is perhaps its most amazing aspect. These locations—especially links to other sites and materials—are the reason it's called the Web in the first place. Additionally, locations remind us that our products are searching for and sending data to and from physical locations, and we need to account for that in our designs. Journalists may talk about "cyberspace" and such, but a good developer knows that the Web is as much about real estate as it is about some sort of virtual universe.

Areas

The visual relationships you create on a Web page (whether via frames, tables, or other layout characteristics) are composed of designed *areas* you create and present. Areas exist as a component because you create them. You decide if an object goes on the right, thus creating white space on the left; you decide to put a block of text here and a picture over there; and you decide the specific divisions frames create. All of these are examples of the creation of areas.

Objects

An *object* is any single item that exists on the Web. It can be a piece of text, a file, a picture, an applet, a 3D wireframe—whatever. We combine these objects into various pages and other files that are interpreted by a PC using browser technology, or downloaded for other applications to interpret. Remember, not all objects are visible; audio objects and CGI scripts are good examples of nonvisible objects.

The biggest part of Web development is the construction of objects. Not only do you have to spend time creating them in general, but many objects (such as graphics and audio files) require special optimization for the Web. Because there are so many instances of objects, I'll break them down further into specific categories:

- *Graphic*—There are several types of graphic objects, including static images, animations, and digital video. Before the advent of plug-ins, many developers became intimately familiar with the standard GIF and JPEG file formats and "server push-pull" technologies. Today, however, there are

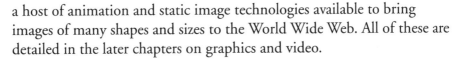

a host of animation and static image technologies available to bring images of many shapes and sizes to the World Wide Web. All of these are detailed in the later chapters on graphics and video.

- *Audio*—Audio objects break down into categories similar to those for graphics. "Static" audio objects (such as embedded WAV or AU files) are downloaded entirely and then played by the user. There are also a host of streaming audio technologies that can play digital audio or MIDI files in realtime over the Internet.

- *Text*—Text may not seem like an object, but it is. There is HTML text that is formatted for display in a browser, as well as the many files that exist as ASCII text, or even Microsoft Word documents (viewable via plug-in).

- *Programs*—As recently as 1995, the only program objects that resided on the Web were either downloadable EXE files or the occasional CGI script for processing forms. Today, though, an amazing amount of different programmed objects are available to Web developers, and Java, JavaScript, and Visual Basic Script have already begun filling up Web pages every-where. Aside from Web-specific languages, Web products and applets can also be created using such traditional computer languages as C/C++, Visual Basic, and Delphi/Pascal. In a later section of this book, I'll say more about the specific capabilities of each language as it relates to the Web and creating program objects for your Web products.

Putting It All Together: The Plan and the Pieces

Now that we've defined the bricks and mortar of the Web, let's think in terms of how those objects come together to build Web products. The best sites use all of these basic building blocks to their fullest potential and in innovative ways.

First, let's put the four fundamental elements in context. We start with *concepts*, because we must have a specific idea of what we're doing before we construct anything. Next we get to *locations,* which represent the physical placement of files and the infrastructure you create to serve up the files and objects you have on your site. Third we come to *areas,* the idea of which reminds us that objects aren't just listed in some sort of directory structure, but are arranged in visually appealing and orderly displays. (Essentially, when you think of this part of Web design, you're talking about the interface.) Finally, we get to objects—and in the end, what Web users are consuming are the objects you create for display and interaction.

Now let's associate each of these Web components with their role in your design efforts:

- *Concepts: Creative Design and Planning*—When you are trying to develop a site, it obviously starts as a creative design process. Creative design will certainly be evident in all aspects of your work, but most of all you will draw upon creative design principles to bring forth the fundamental reasons for inventing the site. When I refer to *concept design* in this book, I'm talking about working these creative ideas and plans out on paper and finally in a written plan.

- *Locations: Engineering and Structural Design*—When we work with locations (whether in terms of the server file system, links to other content and sites, or the overall hierarchical design of the location we're working on), we're dealing with engineering design issues: How do we lay out the object files logically? What server system do we use? Which sites do we link to? Do we use ISDN or leased lines?

- *Areas: Spatial, Aesthetic, and Interface Design*—After you've thought about the locations and structure of a site, you move on to areas, which, in Web development, basically translate into screen space. This term used to mean a Web page, but with the advent of frames, *screen space* is more appropriate, because frames can mean multiple pages in view all at once. In short, we're talking layout here, with a tinge of interface design as well.

- *Objects: Multimedia Design*—Developing the objects for your site is the most ambitious part of design. I refer to this task as *multimedia design* because there are so many types of objects (graphics, sound, text, programs, and so on). Each type of object requires different design skills, but the common label of "multimedia design" reminds us that in many cases these objects must interact with each other. Multimedia design therefore represents a combination of all these different medias into one complete presentation.

If nothing else, the exercise above shows that many types of design skills are needed for cutting-edge Web development. Beyond what I've briefly outlined, in fact, there are certainly other types of design that come into play. What's important, though, is to understand that Web products can be broken down into very specific components, and that focusing your design approach on these components is the best way to manage the overall construction of the product itself.

Web Thinking

The Web community is made up of developers and users, each basically searching for the same thing: useful (or entertaining), skillfully created Web products. In this section, I analyze a few key design issues from the viewpoints of developers and users.

Thinking Like a Web Developer

One of the keys to creating successful World Wide Web products is a good fundamental understanding of the Web's strengths. Specifically, you should be thinking about how the strengths of computers and the Web can bring added value to your particular product—*if* you tailor your product appropriately. With that in mind, let's examine what unique abilities the Web offers developers.

The Web Can Create Context

One of the biggest advantages of the World Wide Web is that your creation will exist among thousands of other sites and sources of information. The Web is a vast resource of ideas, artwork, sounds, text, news, programs, and more. Understanding how to create a context for your site amid this wealth of information is a great strength. In many ways, everything that exists on the Web that you can link to is content you can provide to your site's users via links. This additional content is how you can create a greater context to your own pages. The key way to do this is by creating "hyperlinks" to that content (in other words, to other locations) as it relates to your Web site. MSNBC (**http://www.msnbc.com**) news stories do this really well by offering lots of links to sites on the Web that are relevant to each story (see Figure 5.1).

The Context of Links

One of my favorite movies is *Miracle on 34th Street*, mainly because of a set of scenes that demonstrates a uniquely Web-like business strategy. At one point Mr. Claus, working at the Macy's department store in Manhattan, decides to tell people where in New York City they can get the best

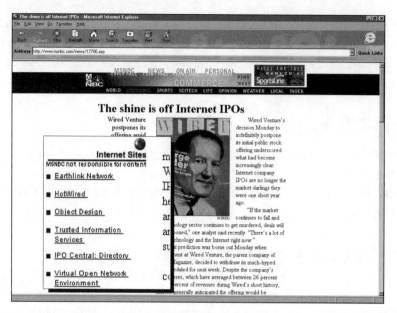

Figure 5.1 Some of the many links offered at MSNBC.

deal on whatever it is they're looking for—even if it's not Macy's. At first a manager immediately wants to fire Claus for doing so, because he thinks the bearded old man is driving away business. Mr. Macy overrules the manager, however, because he sees the bigger picture; in fact, he orders everyone in the store to do what Claus is doing. Macy foresaw that soon the first place customers would go shopping for anything would be Macy's, because they knew Macy's would tell them if there was a better place to look. Therefore, if the salesperson explained that Macy's really did have the best deal, the customer would have no reason to double-check elsewhere.

This tactic doesn't need movie magic to produce good results; the most successful World Wide Web sites work the same way. Indeed, links to sites with related content are the heart of the Web. When you develop a Web product, you must understand that you are not alone. There are bound to be other locations or objects that offer information or experiences similar to what your product offers.

There are three advantages to creating the context of your site through links. First, the more links you create, the more you become the hub to similar sites (making you the first stop on users' exploration of whatever topic or product you are offering). Second, you strengthen that entire portion of the Web, which in turn should increase the popularity of your specific site. Third, it forces you to check in on your fellow sites and the Web in general, thereby making you to stay ahead and giving you new ideas.

Lately, however, I've noticed that some sites are doing less of this context-based linking—perhaps because they fear the idea of people actually being led out of their site. Perhaps they need to watch *Miracle on 34th Street* a few more times.

Ways to Use Links to Create Context

- *Competitive Links—* Why not link your site to your competitors? If you've produced a killer Web product, why not back it up by giving your users the quick ability to see how inferior your competitors are? This approach combines context with quick and easy comparative advantages.

- *Supportive Links*—Are there sites that could support yours? For example, if you're building a site that describes a bed-and-breakfast resort, why not provide links to various nearby entities and stores so people can see why they should stay at your inn?

- *Navigational Links*—The Web is a big place, and you are but one stop; don't be a dead end. Why not offer offramps to places like Yahoo, or other indexes that can help like-minded surfers get around? They'll appreciate the help. For example, if your site is for a newspaper, why not link it to Yahoo's page listing other newspapers?

- *Relationship Links*—Relationship links are the best way to provide context, because they represent the virtual "fork in the road" that makes the Web so much fun. For instance, if you're building a site for a company in Maine, you might link it to the site for L.L. Bean, one of Maine's most famous companies. Other possible links might include the Portland Press Herald (Maine's largest newspaper) or the governor of Maine's home page.

- *Utility Links*—Many sites require certain technologies or knowledge in order to be used properly. Don't ever require them without offering links to places where those things can be acquired. If your site is Netscape enhanced, then offer a link to the Netscape home page.

The Web Can Repurpose Ideas, Content, and Products

Another definite strength of the World Wide Web is the ability to create new products with old or existing content, such as characters from a book being turned into characters on a Web-based game. Although there are incredibly bad examples of this ability littering the landscape of the Web—and few products with reused content will be as powerful as original products or sites—a product that draws upon the strengths of both the original product and the Web itself, while repackaging the content or using it for a new purpose, can be extremely satisfying.

Creating products with old or existing content from another medium, however, requires different tactics than other forms of Web product development. In a later chapter (Chapter 9) I'll present some interesting examples of how the Web can be an excellent outlet for existing content. For now, be aware that it's a strength, but only if you draw on the special features the Web can add, such as interactivity, links to other content, multimedia offerings, and the like.

The Web Is Made for Narrowcasting

No matter how many people go online, the World Wide Web will never be a "mass media" product. There are just too many different sites for any one of them (with the exception of perhaps some of the search engines or Netscape) to bring together a real cross-section of the world or even the country.

Good Web products find success in what marketers like to call *narrowcasting*, which is really just another term for niche marketing. Magazine and newsletter publishers have been doing it for years, so it's no wonder that they've been among the fastest to set up shop on the Web.

Narrowcasting is the idea of defining a very specific demographic or interest group, then creating a product specifically tailored to that group's needs. It works in only two instances, though: when the demographic or interest group is fairly large, or when you can reach its members very cheaply (thus making money off a small consumer pool). The ability of the World Wide Web to reach people on every continent at a minimal entry cost allows developers to reach pools of consumers that might have been too small to target before. And the Web's around-the-clock accessibility, interactive nature, and ability to handle a diverse amount of communication types and transactions makes it far better suited than other methods (such as newsletters, conventions, television, or radio) to deliver content to these narrow groups.

The Web Can Build Unique Communities

The key to a good niche Web product is the idea that you are fostering a community. For example, if you create a site dedicated to fly-fishing, you're really creating an outlet for the global fly-fishing community. This is one of the Web's most powerful traits. There may be more than a million fly-fishing enthusiasts in the world, but because they don't all live in the same town, they've never seen themselves as a single community. With the Web, they can be brought together like never before.

Creating a virtual online community is an effective way to market products to its members. Such a community, however, requires a Web site that not only is well designed, but also fosters interactivity between individuals. While online services like America Online have been accustomed to offering such things as interactive chat rooms, message boards, conferences, and celebrity guests, the technology to offer comparable services via Web sites is only now becoming possible. In addition, these types of interactions tend to require the presence of expert moderators and guests to generate lasting appeal.

Thinking Like a User

We're all Web users. Even if you spend most of your time developing products and sites, you've certainly spent some time surfing and using the Web. When you're a hard-core Web surfer, you begin to formulate basic opinions about what you consider the good, bad, and ugly parts of the World Wide Web.

Remember, the goals of a user are *not* necessarily the goals of the site producer. For instance, users don't want to pay for things. They also don't want to spend hours searching for and exploring a single site; they want sites to be ultra-speedy and always adding new content. While I'm sure producers want their sites to be that way, too, it's not always possible. Users, however, prefer results instead of excuses.

Users are a very fickle bunch, because there are so many sites begging to hold their attention—and they can jump through sites faster than a man with his hand on the TV remote control. So it's important to think about what users look for in well-designed sites—and what quickly turns them off.

Things Good Sites Do

What makes a Web site user friendly? What makes one a hit product? These aren't easy questions to answer, but putting on my user cap I came up with a list of things most Web surfers look for from their favorite sites.

- *Provide Excellent Navigation Tools*—Good sites provide a range of tools to make reaching all parts of the site an easy and quick process. The less effort users have to spend figuring out the structure of the site, the better.

- *Combine Intuitive Layout with Crisp, Clean Graphics*—The overall layout of screens and pages on a good site is easy to understand and consistent throughout the site. Graphics are clean, don't clash with the background or text, and are vital to the concept of the site (in other words, they're not just thrown in to jazz things up). Digitized photos are processed well, and don't look digitized.

- *Give Quick Access to Key Content*—Lots of sites exist to deliver primary pieces of content (for example, daily lead stories for a newspaper); this content should be easily accessible rather than "buried" several mouse clicks away. Remember, sites exist to *give* the user something, so don't put up too many barriers.

- *Make Repeat Visits Easy*—When users discover a site that makes it easy for them to come back often, they do. Sites like this send email newsletters to detail new material, use "cookies" to personalize their site, offer downloadable bookmark files for easy navigation, and update the site frequently with lots of new content.

- *Match Design with Infrastructure*—Good sites understand the limits of the World Wide Web and Internet infrastructure. Users want sites that work within their computer's capabilities, as well as within the capabilities of the server. Successful sites offer users text-only or lower-tech versions, frame-capable and frameless sites, pages tailored to specific browsers, and so on.

Things Bad Sites Do

Even beyond such obvious signs of amateurish development as large image maps or poor layout, there are a host of things that can ruin a site—most of which can be avoided if developers think about their product appropriately. The fact that even basic planning can prevent these mistakes is what drives users to believe that sites that do make them are not worth further investigation.

- *Give Any Form of Access to Incomplete Areas*—Whenever you show a zone that is "under construction," you're creating an aura of incompleteness. It's best either to wait or to build in complete but successive stages. Users hate the idea that a site is a *visible* work in progress.

- *Make Use of Unnecessary Technology*—Perhaps the worst Web design mistake is to employ objects such as chat rooms or Macromedia's Shockwave just because you can. There's a book full of reasons to use these two technologies, but if they're not integral to your overall product, why use them? Remember, you don't design sites to use technology—you turn technology into sites.

- *Spread Content Over a Million Different Pages*—Users want to get the most out of their time online. Not only does taking your Web site's content and dispersing it over a wide range of locations/pages work against this purpose, it can also c\reate navigational problems.

Sometimes, for organizational reasons, you will have to break up content. The trick then is to deliver the content in an organized but succinct way. For example, if your site for a daily newspaper is organized over eighty Web pages, why not also encapsulate all of it for easy downloading? (Better yet, encapsulate it in a downloadable Acrobat file for digestion via printed pages.)

Further Dimensions of Web Design

One area I haven't spent much time on yet is the role that Web economics plays in your design. Economics don't yet play as public a role in the design of Web sites as they will eventually, primarily because so much of the Web is still free. While most Web users pay a service provider for general Internet access, very few individual sites charge any viewing fees. Software for use on the Web is such a competitive market that many products are given away just to build market share.

Slowly, all this will change. No matter what changes, though, the economics of the Web must be a factor in your product design.

Start by developing a specific plan that details how you might derive revenue from your site (if that's what you intend to do.) Sometimes this can be as simple as saying, "We'll display paid advertising on the bottom fifth of the screen." Other plans might be more indirect. Kodak, for example, contends that it saves as much as $20 million on brochure and marketing material costs because of its product information site (see Figure 5.2). Whatever your ideas are, you should understand exactly what the economic goal of the site is.

The revenue strategy you pursue will definitely have an effect on your product's design. Sites that derive revenue from advertising, for example, will

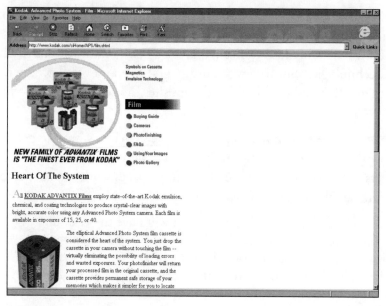

Figure 5.2 Kodak's money-saving information site.

need to provide a detailed analysis of their users—which means that you will have to design a process for gathering this information from the site. Sites that intend to make money via direct sales will need to incorporate good security and transaction systems. If you're creating a product that interacts with your Web site, do you intend to make money selling that product, selling subscriptions to the site itself, or a combination of the two?

Don't forget that the idea of subscribing to sites and paying for Web services is going to feel very foreign to most users. Many people, in fact, are attracted to the Web for its cheapness—asking this community to cough up cash for the privilege of browsing your site might not work, simply because most browsers don't expect to pay for things. Also, depending on your site, you might be susceptible to competition from some sixteen-year-old who builds a comparable site for free. You may be able to combat this vulnerability by offering special content that can't be matched without violating copyrights or that is simply too difficult to construct without a good supply of capital. In doing so, however, you've taken into account the economics of the Web—which is exactly my point.

An Alternative View of the Web: Store and Forward

With the abundant comparisons to broadcasting on the Web, as well as the popular metaphor of "Web publishing," I think that many people have forgotten that the World Wide Web is itself a computer network. Computer networks are not as much about broadcasting and publishing as they are about a concept called "store and forward."

My idea of the store-and-forward view is that Web servers actually forward information into the client computer to be used and manipulated later. The site then merely acts as a facilitator of the process of retrieving information from the Web.

I personally like this use of the Web. The fact is that Web surfing is an immense waste of time; what I seek from the Internet is information and software, not a constant online experience. Yet the majority of Web sites are made for online browsing. (You would think the site creators make money based on time spent browsing, but they don't.)

Although some sites and Web contents require you to be online browsing information and interacting with others, many products could be delivered as well (if not more effectively) by being downloaded to the local client—or at least by offering this option. For example, an online magazine that is completely accessible via a Web browsing session might also offer an Adobe Acrobat downloadable version. People could read this version offline at their leisure, then come back online to the site to offer comments, join chat sessions, or find links to additional content. When more secure Internet transaction systems come into play, one could even charge for the downloading of the magazine.

Another great example is PointCast (see Figure 5.3), a product that creates a profile of you and downloads news stories that you might want to read, all presented in a manner built perfectly for offline reading.

As I will discuss later, there are many compelling reasons and new technologies coming together to push more developers to make their Web products less broadcast-like and more downloadable. Some of the ability to do this in the future may be hindered by Web browsing appliances that won't have nearly as much capacity to facilitate offline content. As the PCs people use to browse

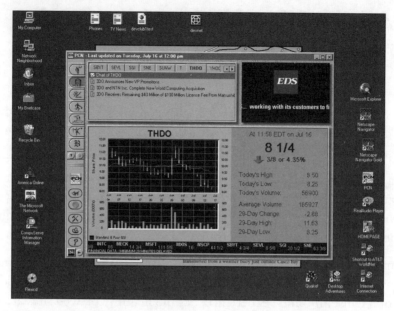

Figure 5.3 PointCast brings the news you want to your desktop.

the Web become more powerful, though, and as the need to optimize the time spent on the Web becomes more important, the practice of store-and-forward Web design and development will become more widely used.

The Fundamentals of Web Product Planning

There are a number of fundamentals you need to consider before you jump into creating your Web product. The following sections describe some of the most important—and overlooked areas.

Being Deliberate

The key to being a top-end developer of any sort—and not just for the Web—is what I call "being deliberate." This refers to undertaking development only after you've thought long and hard about what it is you want to create and *how you intend to create it*. Some would simply call this planning, but I don't look at it that way.

Planning comes after you've thought through most of the major questions and are trying to bring out the details you need to define in order to go forward with the project. "Being deliberate" comes earlier. In this stage, you want to develop the mindset that you're sure your idea is both good enough and original enough, and that you're capable enough to deliver on this idea.

This means you need to become determined enough to see the project through. Many Web products have died simply because people couldn't bring themselves to live up to the responsibility of finishing it, or because they rushed ahead and didn't do the things that could have ensured success. It also means knowing the Web and being able to understand early on the types of things that will (or won't) work.

So when I talk about how your product development needs to be a deliberate process, I'm referring to the need to guarantee that you've got a distinct, firm idea of what it is you'll end up with when you complete the product.

Research

The first task of good Web product planning is to be a diligent researcher. At the beginning of this chapter, I said that one of the problems with just jump-ing in and creating new Web products is that many people have probably beaten you to the punch. Despite its young age, the World Wide Web has seen a lot of ideas actually become implemented. This isn't to say your idea won't work, or all the good ones are taken—just that there are a lot of sites to check in on first. The good news is that even among similar ideas, there is plenty of room to break through on the Web.

Still, the first thing I do when considering a site idea is to see what else has been done along the same lines. Usually I find that while my idea isn't original by a long shot, my projected implementation of it would be light-years ahead of what most other sites have done. In addition, I often find that most of the sites that would potentially rival mine were not being created by entities that could sustain competition.

The other reason I begin by researching the Web is to build up lists of sites that I would want to offer links to from my site. Usually there are so many that I have to adjust the design of the site to add categories and organization to the different links.

Reverse Engineering: Start from the Desired End Result

One of the best ways to design Web sites is to start from the ending. Reverse engineering is at the heart of modern software (and Web) development. This is because there is more than one way to build software. Most developers tend to take the route most familiar to them—a route that used to work when the choices were less diverse. Today, though, a good developer has the skills and knowledge to define an end result, then select from a much wider range of products and processes with which to construct that product.

For example, you might be developing a virtual art museum. Do you first figure out what the tools will allow you to do, then define the design? Or do you imagine the ideal virtual museum, then evaluate what tools might exist to make that ideal a reality? I vote for the latter; the result is always a better design that pushes the envelope.

In addition, by starting from the desired end result, you guarantee a focus on exactly what your product is and what the user will experience. If you were to just start programming or creating a site, would you really understand where you were going to end up?

Get It Down on Paper: Planning and Writing

Perhaps the biggest unseen recent change in Web development is the amount of planning—and especially professional-level planning, in terms of major written plans, story boards, and mock-ups—that is being done. With so many options, much larger development budgets, and certainly higher stakes, today's leading Web product developers are taking the time to get their ideas just right.

Web Sites After Birth

Just because you've completed your site, doesn't mean that you're finished with it. Like any child, it needs to be taken care of after it is "born."

Creating Living Products: The Unique Edge of the Web

Unlike any previous medium, the World Wide Web is a living system. One thing Web product developers have to understand is that sites must constantly grow and change in order to create repeat viewership. Many sites now feature at least some sort of daily attraction. In addition, a growing number of sites include things like chat rooms and message boards to ensure lots of "lifelike" interactivity.

Watching Out for One-Upmanship

One thing to watch out for after the birth of your site is the one-upmanship that permeates the World Wide Web. For every good idea, there are plenty of folks who think they can do it better. Even worse, users on the Web can be quite a transient bunch. The moment someone else comes up with a better version of your concept, prepare for a flood of people to leave you for the next big thing.

A nice example here is WebCrawler. As one of the original Web "spiders," it was a good product. Yet it didn't take long for other developers to create Lycos and then AltaVista, both of which were much better search engines than WebCrawler. What happened? Users abandoned WebCrawler, of course. Even worse, C|Net has created search.com (see Figure 5.4): It acts as a "search engine to search search engines" and is essentially a one-stop shop for using all the major search engines, as well as specialized search engines. A perfect case of one-upmanship.

You can protect yourself by being ever vigilant. Keep surfing the Web for competitors, look to build unique technologies and ideas that are either difficult or illegal to clone, and constantly build these items into your site.

Reinventing Sites

At some point after your product has been completed, there comes a time when you need to completely overhaul your design and concept. The biggest problem along these lines right now is the breakneck speed at which Web technology is progressing. The time span between some site overhauls is frighteningly short.

At the same time, though, Web developers are becoming a little more cautious about jumping into new technology. An unwelcome byproduct of the speed with which new Web development products have debuted has been some very buggy programs.

This means that developers planning the design of the products must incorporate such concepts as the expected time between necessary overhauls. They also need to use tools and an infrastructure that will keep up with new technology, so that they don't have to start from scratch when the site has to be reinvented. MSN recently redesigned its entire start page, adding more hooks for its version 3.0 browser. The reinvention didn't change much of the basic content of this customizable start page, but the presentation got markedly better. (See Figures 5.5 and 5.6 for a quick look at the redesign.)

In the future, as the technology stabilizes, the need to overhaul sites as a result of breakthroughs will lessen to a more manageable pace. For the next few years, however, you should consider the potential need for complete reinvention of your Web product as early as the initial design.

Summary

Wow! We've covered a lot of ideas here. So many, in fact, that I think a brief recap of the key themes might help.

I talked first about widening your view of a World Wide Web product beyond just a specific site to encompass such ideas as integrated software and sites, or the surrounding services that support a site (for example, customer assistance). From there I explained how to think of Web products as the designed

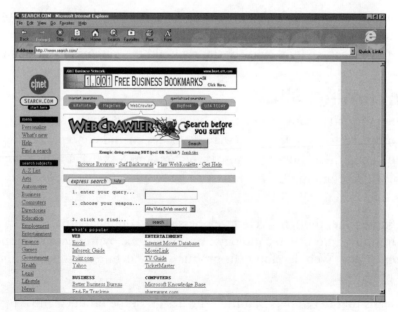

Figure 5.4 C I Net has created the ultimate search engine site.

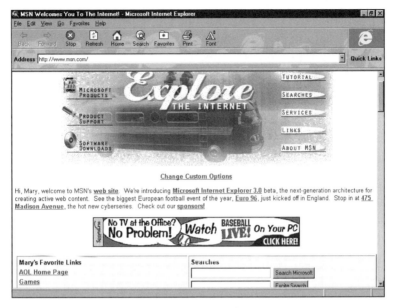

Figure 5.5 The Microsoft Network's original start page.

combination of concepts, locations, areas, and objects, with objects being the real content or meat of the Web, and the previous three being the process by which you present, deliver, and interact with that content and the user.

The next point I discussed was thinking about what the Web offers you as developer and user, including some specific ideas about how users might view

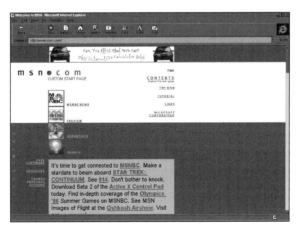

Figure 5.6 The redesigned start page.

sites. From the developer's viewpoint, I focused on what makes the Web special and how that might give us clues about overall design philosophy. As part of this discussion I examined "context" and especially how links and interaction with other Web sites and existing content can strengthen and contribute to your overall site. From the users' perspective, developers must understand what specifically turns them off and on about Web sites, and how we need to account for that in our products.

Then I explored the economics of the World Wide Web and how the "free" availability of most Web content has influenced product design. I also discussed the concept of "store and forward," which is an alternate view of the Web, instead of just following the dominant idea of it as a broadcasting-like or publishing-like medium.

Next I examined the key concepts behind planning for the Web. These included "being deliberative" (which means always approaching the planning process with a complete, cohesive, and feasible idea of what you want to make), intensive research, and planning on paper. I especially made the point of starting your design plans from the "desired end result"—that is, by figuring out the specifics of the site before working out how you will create them.

Finally, I explained that the design process for many Web products continues even after their debut, and that this necessary reinvention occurs at such a quick pace that you must prepare for it in the initial design stages.

Now the challenge is to apply these concepts and characteristics of Web design to specific ideas about how to construct pages, sites, and products. None of the principles I've discussed above will truly make sense to you until you see them applied. Over the next several chapters I will show you a number of ideas, resources, and especially sites that put these principles to use.

CHAPTER 6

Today's cutting-edge Web sites require thoughtful planning and written design documents.

Web Sites: Planning, Techniques, and Examples

What It Means to Plan a Web Site

Planning a Web site is a major effort these days. A typical site for a corporate client might take a million dollars to develop. When you consider all the art-work, programming, and sound design a cutting-edge site requires, a million dollars might actually seem like a pretty low figure. Some sites (like Pathfinder, GNN, and Sony's corporate site) probably cost millions more. With so much cash going into the development of top sites, perfect planning is essential.

The Basics of Web Site Planning

I created five key items to detail any site I'm developing, no matter how big or small it is.

1. An Overall Treatment of the Idea

A treatment is a brief explanation (usually one or two pages) of the basic ideas and planned implementation of a project. It should contain enough informa-tion to let anyone who might help you construct the site know what the end result of their efforts will be. It also might contain some data about estimated costs, target users, and time to complete. What it doesn't contain are hard details, which will be fleshed out from an approved treatment.

2. A General Storyboard of the Site

I use a three-step storyboarding process, which I'll summarize briefly here. The first thing I do is create a general storyboard that describes the key locations within the site and the basic structure of a possible layout. This board doesn't establish all of the links or the complete design of the pages. I merely give each page a name, show some simple branching (where the links will take users), and perhaps attach a few basic notes about what that area might look like. My goal is to explain how the overall site will divide up the content and what the further subdivisions of that content will be.

3. An In-Depth Storyboard

Once I have a general storyboard done, I begin creating a more detailed version. This is where the minute navigation and layout issues will be resolved. Every link is identified, and the basic contents of each page are listed. Depending on the breadth of the site, I may opt to leave out specific sketches of each page on the site, instead doing those as each page is actually created. Below I'll show you some ideas I've developed to create clean, impressive-looking site storyboards.

4. A Written Plan Explaining Each Specific Area

Accompanying any good storyboard is an overall written site plan. It's basically an elaborate and detailed treatment (including the major site components, as well as server systems and overall development approach) that may run ten to twenty pages or even longer. You might assume that such a plan is only necessary when you're developing a site for a client, but in fact it's a great tool for designing any site. Remember, putting your ideas on paper forces you to think very hard about your site before you really invest in it—paper now avoids mistakes and costs later. Later in this chapter I'll show you the basic outline of a site plan I've been working on.

5. Detailed Ledgers of All Objects Offered at the Site

The final aspect to a good paper plan is what I call a *content ledger*. Remember how I talked about sites being composed of objects? Well, every one of those objects needs to be created, named, placed in a server directory, and linked to a page, just for starters. You also will need to figure out such things as due dates, who is going to develop the objects, and how much each one is going to cost. If you manage the creation of each object well, you will have taken care of 80 percent of your content-creation headaches.

Key Ideas for Planning Consideration

Before I begin detailing the documentation of a plan, I think it makes sense to talk about some fundamental ideas related to site planning.

Concepts, Division, and Navigation

Planning out your site is mostly a process of translating your basic concepts into divisions of content, and then creating the navigation systems a visitor will use to access that content. Specifically detailed page layouts are still an issue, but those are essentially the final implementation of your plan. A lot of the specifics of your page-by-page design will come out when you actually construct the pages with an editor, rather than in your planning process. Even if the fine details are yet to be worked out, if you plan the links well and know the content you plan for each page, you'll more or less have a good idea of how the page will look.

Flattening Your Design

As you plan out the structure of your site, keep an eye on how hierarchical it is becoming. It's easy to find yourself designing Web sites that bury pages and content under so many layers of choices that users may give up and turn their attention elsewhere before they find what they want. At the same time, a very flat site might have so many links on one page that they confuse or overwhelm the user. Thus, you want to be careful about the process of flattening a design.

Step 1—Fundamental Site Navigation Analysis

One simple analysis I use sometimes is to set up a spreadsheet where I list the number of clicks it takes to move from one part of the planned site to another. Once that's done, I can begin to see where there might be navigation problems. In many cases, I only need to apply this idea to a part of the site. The example in Figure 6.1 demonstrates this technique. Aside from the link that goes from 2 to 7, the site follows a very basic hierarchical structure.

Table 6.1 maps how many clicks it would take to move from any one page in the site to another.

Since we're only working right now with the option to click forward with a link or use the default browser "back" button or menu option to move backward through the hierarchy, this table is actually a mirror image. Once you begin

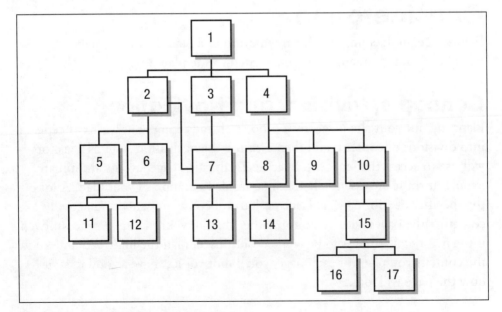

Figure 6.1 An example of a site plan.

introducing links that jump around (such as a "Go Home" button on every page), then you would start to construct a table that was less symmetrical.

Don't forget that when you introduce a new link to your site, it could radically change the results of this table. Allowing users to jump back to the home page of the site with a single click, for example, will make movement throughout the hierarchy much simpler and quicker.

I usually create this table once at the beginning of the site planning process, just to get an idea of where every page is relative to the others. Then I decide where to introduce links in order to cut down on the larger numbers of required clicks. Once those new links are implemented, my site's navigation options often are so complicated that doing a follow-up table would take too much work; I can probably isolate any problems more effectively through hands-on testing. When it's early and I'm trying to get a handle on a large number of potential problems, however, this table idea has helped.

Table 6.1   Counting the clicks.

To	From																	
	1	2	3	4	5	6	7	8	9	10	11	12	13	14	15	16	17	AVG
1	0	1	1	1	2	2	2	2	2	2	3	3	3	3	3	4	4	2.38
2	1	0	2	2	1	1	1	3	3	3	2	2	2	4	4	5	5	2.56
3	1	2	0	2	3	3	1	3	3	3	4	4	2	4	4	5	5	3.06
4	1	2	2	0	3	3	3	1	1	1	4	4	4	2	2	3	3	2.44
5	2	1	3	3	0	2	2	4	4	4	1	1	3	5	5	6	6	3.25
6	2	1	3	3	2	0	2	4	4	4	3	3	3	5	5	6	6	3.50
7	2	1	1	3	2	2	0	4	4	4	4	5	1	5	5	6	6	3.44
8	2	3	3	1	4	4	4	0	2	2	5	5	5	1	3	4	4	3.25
9	2	3	3	1	4	4	4	2	0	2	5	5	5	3	3	4	4	3.38
10	2	3	3	1	4	4	4	2	2	0	5	5	5	4	1	2	2	3.06
11	3	2	4	4	1	3	4	5	5	5	0	2	4	6	6	7	7	4.25
12	3	2	4	4	1	3	5	5	5	5	2	0	5	6	6	7	7	4.38
13	3	2	2	4	3	3	1	5	5	5	4	5	0	6	6	7	7	4.25
14	3	4	4	2	5	5	5	1	3	4	6	6	6	0	4	5	5	4.25
15	3	4	4	2	5	5	5	3	3	1	6	6	6	4	0	1	1	3.69
16	4	5	5	3	6	6	6	4	4	2	7	7	7	5	1	0	2	4.63
17	4	5	5	3	6	6	6	4	4	2	7	7	7	5	1	2	0	4.63
AVG	2.38	2.56	3.06	2.44	3.25	3.50	3.44	3.25	3.38	3.06	4.25	4.38	4.25	4.25	3.69	4.63	4.63	

Note: In cases where there are multiple routes to get to the same destination, I calculate the average number of clicks and use that figure.

Step 2—Ways to Flatten a Site's Structure

There are many ways to introduce a flatter structure to your Web site. Let's look at several key ideas, with an eye on the advantages and disadvantages of each.

- *Site Image Maps*—A site image map is really a visual index, usually located on the site's home page, to help people jump quickly to the content they want.

- *Index Pages*—Many sites are using indexes, especially as their content grows. Compared to a search engine, an index gives the developer excellent control over the information that is presented to the user. Additionally, many search engines might not return exactly the information needed as well as a handwritten index will.

- *Navigation Banners*—As popularized by Netscape's home page, a navigation banner is simply a small image map—usually displayed across the top of a page—that offers easy access to a range of areas in a site. The key thing to remember here is to keep a navigation banner constant across all parts of your site, so that users can become accustomed to it.

- *Search Engines*—A search engine can help the users of large sites quickly find their way to the specific content they're looking for. Microsoft has a very extensive site, for instance, and even though it's very well organized, it would be much harder for anyone to find individual items without a search engine. On the downside, search engines can also create ambiguous returns and don't always perform the way users or the site manager want them to.

Planning for Overall Consistency

One thing to keep in mind when planning out your site is the notion of consistency. Take the time to think about the overall look of the site from beginning to end, and make sure each page has a look that is consistent with and acts in a manner similar to the others.

A large portion of your Web site is really an interface. One of the biggest challenges of interface design is to make separate components act the same so that users don't get confused. When you plan your site, always be on the lookout for areas that should behave exactly like similar pages (for example, place navigation items in the same areas, and keep the graphical look consistent).

A key way to ensure consistency is to spend some time during your planning process defining "universals"—that is, aspects of your design that apply to the entire site. Universals might include the fonts you use in certain types of headings or graphics, the background color schemes, how links will be displayed, the size of banners, and so on.

A consistent style applied to all components will give your site a seamless, polished, and professional look. Good planning brings this about.

 Consistent styles are becoming a major need on many Web sites. One up-and-coming technology that will aid site consistency is Web style sheets, which I'll talk about later in this book. Style sheets will not instantly create consistency on a Web site, but they'll certainly make it easier to apply.

How Frames Affect Web Site Planning

A site that makes use of frames is an entirely different beast than a frameless site. Because frames dramatically change the layout, file structure, and navigation of your site, it takes some special attention during the planning process to really harness their power.

The main reason to use frames is to keep some content the same, while other content on the screen is changed. Although you could do this without frames, you'd need to design pages with certain elements repeated over and over, thereby wasting a lot of editing time. At the same time, when the user scrolled down the page, he or she would lose sight of those elements.

Frames solve this problem. Their most common applications have been to keep ad banners visible, to provide permanent titles, or to provide easy access to a table of contents. With frames, though, you move from a page-design planning system to a screen-design planning system. As a result, you need to change the way you plan your site.

When dealing with a frameless site, you can be sure that the current page loaded by the user contains all of the links and other interface elements he or she can select at that time. In contrast, framed sites mean more separate HTML files to handle, and you'll need to know which ones to load at which times to create the screen displays you want. In addition, my experience has been that frames work well when browsers are run at 800 × 600 resolution and much better at 1024 × 768. Of course, not everyone runs their browser at these resolutions, and I've yet to see complex framed sites set up to work at 640 × 480.

Still, depending on the purpose of the site, frames can be exceedingly useful. One site I'm planning has a lot of indexed material, and frames can help me guide people through several long lists of items. In other cases I can also provide a permanent banner that clearly displays where the user is, making it easier for him or her to move around.

The trick is being able to storyboard a framed site properly. It took me a while to get the hang of it, but later on I'll present a simple storyboarding system that helps with the planning of a frame site. It has allowed me to build the framed site I'm working on now more rapidly.

Planning Dilemmas

The planning process is where the majority of your design ideas will be put through the wringer. Now is the time to make the hard decisions about what your Web site is ultimately going to do. As you put your plan together, try to think through the various problems that might occur. Question everything!

Most of your time planning will be spent working out various dilemmas of what you can do versus what you want to do. You have to make tradeoffs, or figure out a way to avoid tradeoffs altogether. I use a simple figure, shown in Figure 6.2, to outline this idea.

For example, suppose your goal is to have a site that is extremely fast, as well as rich in graphics. The two notions for the most part are polar opposites; the more graphics you add, the slower your site is likely to be. Some developers would start planning compromises, trading fewer graphic elements for more speed. Not content to compromise, though, you decide to combine lots of graphics with speed by planning a T1 line connection (a hefty technological breakthrough).

The chart shown in Figure 6.2 represents the basic developer's dilemma, as well as the previous paragraph's. You want to end up at C, but in order to get there you need both A and B to be at their peak—and, unfortunately, the

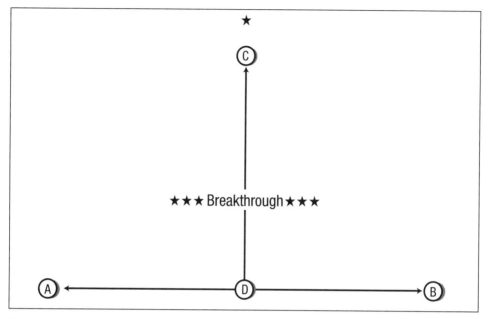

Figure 6.2 Working out potential site problems.

more you go for A the less you get of B, and vice versa. D represents the best possible compromise of both A and B. C, however, represents reaching that goal without any compromise, but instead through some sort of design or technological breakthrough.

As you work through your site plan, you will encounter numerous design dilemmas of this sort. Try to think in the terms I've describe above: If I go with this (A), what am I giving up (B), and to what degree? Is there a way to have (C)? If so, what's the breakthrough I need to make that available?

Creating Prototypes

One part of a good planning process is the creation of actual prototypes. As I constructed the basics of News-Junkie.Com (a site I'm currently working on), I often spent a day or two just working on prototypes of various screens and documents to see how they really looked. There is always a need to test out ideas before moving forward with the rest of a plan.

I frequently use prototypes to test frame layouts, sizes for graphic elements, navigation schemes, and text styles and color schemes. I've done very little so far with Java, JavaScript, and Visual Basic Script, so my prototyping experience with those languages is weak, but whatever your level of programming knowledge, prototyping is a definite necessity. Ideally you should constantly be working with these languages in order to build up technology libraries (code you can use over and over) as well as plain experience.

Especially if you're working alone, the key to prototyping is to not get bogged down in actually creating the site. Determine the several items you need to see in practice before writing your plan, and stick to doing simple tests of those items. Look for examples on other sites, too—you may find one and avoid having to mock up your own example as a result.

Documenting Your Plan

Once you've storyboarded your site to death, it's time to create an accompanying written plan to go with it. In instances when you are presenting a prospective site to clients or potential associates, a written plan is almost mandatory, but I can't stress enough that the writing of a site plan can help immensely even if you're working for yourself.

Basic Outline

In my mind, the biggest hurdle to writing a site plan is coming up with a basic outline. (The second biggest hurdle is writing a plan that really does help you during the construction phase.) Below is the basic outline I use:

- Site overview
- Site general storyboard
- Brief explanation of each area
- Detailed explanation of each area
- Summary of site content
- Content ledger
- Server information
- Detailed budget
- Construction calendar

- Marketing information
- Post-launch plan

Site Overview
Take the treatment you wrote earlier and adapt it as an opening section for your written document.

Site General Storyboard
Create a polished version of your general storyboards, showing the basic areas of the site in their intended layout.

Brief Explanation of Each Area
For each specific area in your plan, use a couple of paragraphs to describe what it offers the user and what content might be involved.

Detailed Explanation of Each Area
Following the brief description, provide a very detailed explanation of each area, including all of the content and the basic construction scheme (for example, do you need digitized or hand-drawn artwork? Streaming or down-loaded audio? Adobe Acrobat or just plain text?). You might include a basic sketch of the page/screen design as well. The more precise you can be, the better—skimping on the details here means more work later.

Summary of Site Content
The actual content objects you create for your site will take up the majority of your Web development resources, so devote a specific section of your written plan to describing the content.

Content Ledger
After you've summarized the content in paragraph form, create a spreadsheet of all the content items, including all of the basic aspects of its creation that you'll need to track.

Creating Content Ledgers
Web sites are chock full of content. From a multitude of text, graphics, and sound elements to programmed applets and CGI scripts, a killer Web site may call for an extraordinary amount of individual content

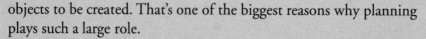

objects to be created. That's one of the biggest reasons why planning plays such a large role.

One specific planning tool that can help a lot is a *content ledger*, which basically is a spreadsheet detailing all of the objects you need to construct. Making a ledger forces you to be quite specific about everything you will need to create your Web site, and it also gives you an easy-to-manage system for tracking the various people you might need and which objects are done or not done.

There is no set template for a content ledger, but I'll share my personal version with you in Table 6.2. Feel free to modify it as you wish.

Server Information

Describe the server software, hardware, and connections your site will use. Don't forget to include details about additional server software (such as content servers like RealAudio, VDOLive, and back-end databases). You might also want to take some time to detail server security and maintenance programs.

Detailed Budget

Good sites have substantial budgets; don't dive into making your site without a good estimate of all costs. Decide how much you will be spending on

Table 6.2 Setting up a content ledger.

Name of Object	Front Page Image Map	Breakout Game
Object Type	GIF Graphic	Java Applet
Description	A graphical storyboard of the site with names of the pages for users to click for quick access	A simple game of Breakout written in Java—will reside on "Games Break Page"
Planned FileName	frontmap.gif	breakout.class
Server Directory	\frontpage\	\gamebreak\
Who Creates	John Smith Graphics	Developed in-house
Cost	$250	N/A
Due Date	July 30	Done
Associated Page(s)	frontpage.html	gamebreak.html
Special Directions	Should be only 16 colors, and resolution be 480×360	Resolution is 320×200

connections, servers, software, maintenance, graphics and sound construction, site programming, and promotion.

Construction Calendar

Once you've determined almost everything else about your site plan, take some time to put together a good construction calendar. This is important because with the pace of development, having a good calendar will be crucial for your actual implementation. Also, if you plan to attract other developers, or investors, to your site, a calendar is one of the first things many will ask to see.

Marketing Information

A good plan always includes basic marketing information. Who is the target audience? How many people are realistically expected to visit the site? What is their income level (and other characteristics)? Are there any competing sites, and if so, what are their threats or weaknesses in relation to your site (this is especially important if you're looking for investors)? How will you promote your site, especially if your audience requires you to do a lot of promotion off the Internet (for example, in newspapers or magazines)?

Post-Launch Plan

My design documents always conclude with several paragraphs about how the site will operate after it's launched. As I've already discussed, the Web is a living environment, and users expect sites to be updated frequently and to expand with new content. Some sites may involve such items as order processing, chat functions, and message boards. How many and what types of people are needed to maintain your site? If chat and messaging will take place, will there be special guests? How frequently? Is there an email newsletter? What types of updates will be needed and how often? These are the types of questions you need to answer in your post-launch section.

Web Design Documentation: Tips and Techniques

When planning the site I envisioned as News-Junkie.Com, I knew it was going to be large. I wanted to use frames to enable a number of navigational features, as well as to provide space for two permanent "ad banner" positions

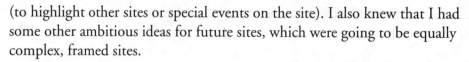

(to highlight other sites or special events on the site). I also knew that I had some other ambitious ideas for future sites, which were going to be equally complex, framed sites.

I realized that these complex ideas would require storyboards—not only to help me with the design, but to show to potential partners who might want to help develop the site. So I looked at several interesting sites and books, but I didn't find much about storyboarding sites. What I really wanted was a nice manual of style to copy, but apparently there wasn't one.

Since I couldn't find anything I liked, I decided to come up with something on my own (knowing that once I did, I would have a nice system to include in this book). Here's what I developed.

Example Site

For the purposes of this chapter, I thought it would be a good idea to share a site design from beginning to end, to emphasize some of the key points. In March 1996, I had an idea for a site I wanted to launch on my own. Although I was planning the idea for my own gratification (and perhaps some revenue), I realized that it would also be an excellent example site for this book (so if the site doesn't work, at least I got something out of it!).

The site I'm working on is called News-Junkie.Com. Its basic idea is to be a central resource for people looking for news on the Internet, as well as other periodicals (such as magazines) and more. My extensive site plan includes frames, many different locations, and a multitude of objects.

Pre-Storyboarding

The first thing I do is flesh out the specific "category" areas for the site. This is not so much a storyboard as a basic structure showing the main areas that will be used in a site on a title-by-title basis. I don't think about the detailed layout of the area, just the basic concept it will handle.

For this pre-storyboard I used one of those managerial chart programs (in my case, Microsoft PowerPoint). Figure 6.3 shows an example for my News-Junkie.Com site.

General Storyboarding

The first step in this phase was to create a general structure-oriented storyboard. I wanted a simple hierarchical structure that outlined all of the specific areas the site would have, so I developed the following scheme:

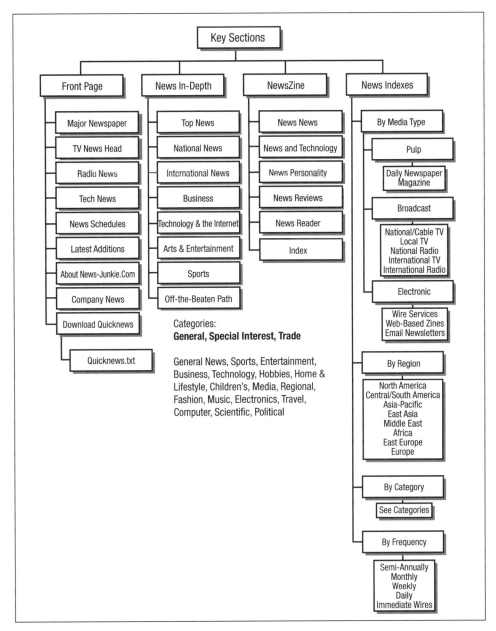

Figure 6.3 A look at the detailed layout of News-Junkie.Com.

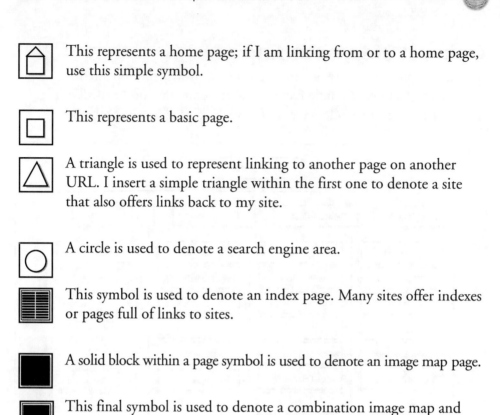

This represents a home page; if I am linking from or to a home page, use this simple symbol.

This represents a basic page.

A triangle is used to represent linking to another page on another URL. I insert a simple triangle within the first one to denote a site that also offers links back to my site.

A circle is used to denote a search engine area.

This symbol is used to denote an index page. Many sites offer indexes or pages full of links to sites.

A solid block within a page symbol is used to denote an image map page.

This final symbol is used to denote a combination image map and index.

Of course, there is room for more symbols. For example, I could see adding smaller symbols to indicate Java applets or Shockwave pages. You also could add other information, as I do in the working example that follows. As you'll see in Figure 6.4, there is a section where I multiply a part of the diagram by five with a "*5" note. I did this to denote that there would be five essentially identical links, so there was little need to diagram beyond that.

Working Example

I chose to diagram a specific part of News-Junkie.Com in Figure 6.4. This is an item called NewsZine, which features articles about news-themed sites and sounds on the World Wide Web.

NewsZine is a part of my site that branches off from the home page and offers six key sections:

- News about the news, with five or six articles offered from there.

- News about news technology.

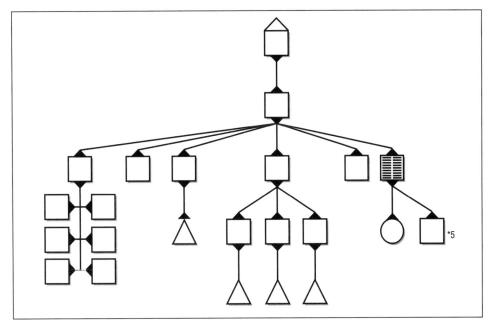

Figure 6.4 The storyboarding for my News-Junkie.Com site.

- A news personality profile.

- Reviews of news-oriented Web sites, with direct links to those sites.

- A column (called "News-Junkie Fix") that talks about being hooked on the news.

- A page that offers an index to the last five issues and a search engine for locating content among all back issues.

Storyboarding with Frames

It took a little bit of work to find a way to create a storyboard for my framed site. Framed sites are a detailed storyboarder's nightmare, because you are dealing with so many different documents. Even worse, as the user surfs through the site, not all of the frames change documents.

The solution I came up with used a simple numbering procedure to clearly denote what documents and frames would change from area to area as the user moved through the site.

First I start with a drawing package and sketch out the frame scheme(s) I plan to use, keeping them all standard. I make the drawing big enough so that when it is printed I can write in numbers or a simple note. Then I create a page full of duplicates of this blank frame design and print out enough pages to give me thirty or forty blank screens. A few minutes with a paper cutter after that, and I'm ready to go.

At this point I get a piece of poster board and a pencil, and I begin laying out the site. Each initial frame item is given a letter, followed by the number 1 as a subscript. On the side I note the title of the document and file name for that item. Each time a frame changes to a new document, I indicate the letter and use the next higher number (2, 3, 4, and so on) as a subscript, again indicating the document title and file name on the side.

The numbering system makes it really easy to see which frames are changing from link to link (see Figure 6.5). In addition, unless you make the frames

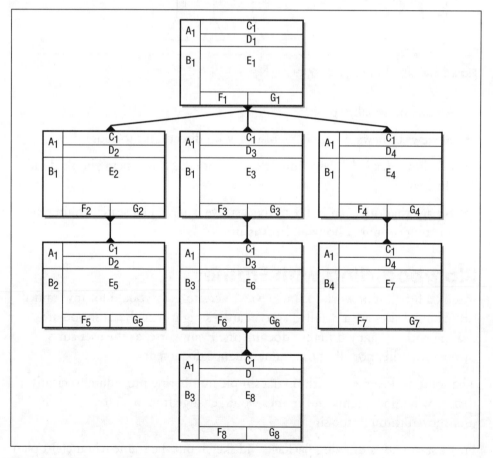

Figure 6.5 How to document a framed site.

really big, it's hard to pencil in the title and file names in the small spaces a framed site provides, so some kind of numbering is almost a necessity.

I Love It When a Plan Comes Together

Good plans work. That's primarily because good plans have a lot of thought and work put into them, and this effort pays off. Sometimes, though, the hard part is having the patience to put together a top-notch plan. When I was putting together the plan for News-Junkie.Com, I kept feeling like other people were getting the jump on me; I was sorely tempted to drop my plans and just crash ahead with building the site. I can't imagine what some of the more competitive site companies like iVillage must go through. At times, planning a Web site requires a real siege mentality.

When you charge into the implementation phase with a good, solid design plan, though, you feel like the wind is at your back. It's much easier to bring in assistance and to compare your site idea with what has already been implemented, because you have a complete idea of what you'll have when the site is finished and what it's going to take to get there.

CHAPTER 7

How can we become better Web developers? By focusing on our own details, as well as the influential work of others.

The Details of Designing for the Web

Page Design Is Not Just Page Layout

The layout aspect of building Web pages is certainly the most important part of this chapter, but don't let that overshadow other, less glamorous parts of the job. Page design also involves the use of forms, JavaScript, and even more mundane things (such as inserting comments for search engines to index your site more effectively).

However, the details of page design aren't always so visible; therefore, my main focus in this chapter will be the layout of your pages. I have some work to fall back on here, since more has been written about designing Web pages than about most other aspects of Web development. My intent here is to summarize much of that material, add some of my own thoughts, and then give you a barrage of suggestions for further reading. Because a lot of design principles are based on subjective opinions, it really helps to expose yourself to as many opinions as possible.

The Fundamental Rules of Web Page Design

Usually I hate simple "do's and don'ts" lists of rules—but not when it comes to Web page design. Despite the number of published design guides (both on the Web and on paper), many sites seem to make the same mistakes over and over again. And so I'll devote the first part of this book's Web design discussion to the lowest level of "Do this, and don't do this." While I find it hard to make rules I don't end up breaking myself, this list, hopefully, serves as some sort of foundation to build upon.

Use the <IMAGE ALT=> Tag to Define Your Images

A simple **ALT=** added to the **<IMAGE>** tag presents the user with text describing an image that has not been loaded (that is, fully displayed by the browser software). Whenever I see that a site isn't using these tags, I get angry. I do so much surfing that I regularly turn off image viewing or hit ESC to stop loading a page with time-consuming graphics. Sites that don't use **<ALT=>** tags give me the choice of either waiting for the graphics to load or simply ignoring the graphics (or the entire site) altogether. It only takes a second to add the **ALT=** extension to your <IMAGE> tag, so do it.

Make Sure Your Text and Background Color Always Create a Clear Contrast

Sometimes when you plan to use various backgrounds, you will change the text color to contrast with a "new" background. Be careful, though, that your fundamental background color and the new text color don't contrast. During loading of the new background, or if this background isn't loaded (if the user hits ESC, for example), the user will be trying to read your colored text against the original background—and having a heck of a time doing so if there's not enough contrast.

Also give some thought to users who might permanently set their own background color. Even though I think that as page design improves this will be less of an issue, it's certainly still worth consideration as you create your own color schemes.

Don't <BLINK> Unless You Have To

Blinking text was a simple addition to Netscape Navigator, but it got overused quickly. For the most part, in fact, it's a pain even when used sparingly. It can be useful for attracting attention to a warning message, but for anything else it's a clichéd gimmick that should be avoided. The emergence of animated GIF files should encourage you to create a more interesting and less annoying source of visual flair for your page.

Clearly Define Clickable Regions in an Image Map

Image maps are very useful items, but far too often users get confused by complex maps that do little to tell the user how to explore the site further. You don't have to go as far as creating a neon outline of each clickable element, but when you do place an image map on a page, look at it from a user's viewpoint, and make sure it's obvious which areas are links to additional content. In addition, can you tell where one clickable region pertaining to a topic ends and adjacent regions begin? (Few things annoy users more than thinking they've clicked on one item but getting another instead.)

Make Sure You Use a Title for Each Page

Many times developers forget to add in the <TITLE>...</TITLE> tag. In addition, sometimes that title isn't clear. Use the <TITLE>...</TITLE> tag and make it clear what the page is about.

Always Minimize the File Size of Your Images

High-quality graphic images are important, but so is speed, and small files load much more quickly. Fortunately, there are many things you can do—including reducing color depth, proper cropping, and translating files to the best-suited format (GIF or JPEG)—to shrink your file size without sacrificing quality. Not doing this resizing should be considered breaking the rules.

Reinforce the Interface with Graphics

Limited use of images that serve interface functions is a good idea. Make sure, though, that the graphics reinforce an interface that works with or without them. For example, a navigation bar with large icons to click on should be complemented by a section of text links. When planned right, images can make navigation much easier than text links, but remember that many users may not use graphics or may stop loading them for a particular page. By treating your graphics as a reinforcement of existing interface elements, you can be assured of no discontinuity for these users.

Don't Use Linked Content

While you can bring graphics and other content into your page from another site, the resulting speed and perhaps legal issues makes this a bad idea, except in the most unusual circumstances.

Fill Out Those Tags

Most of the tags used in HTML—and especially the various special tags offered up by Netscape and Microsoft—offer you a ton of different options. Many times you will use the defaults and not have to add in all the extensions. I find it good style, however, to code with all the options, even if the extra text simply shows I'm using the defaults. This makes it extremely easy to go back in by hand and make changes. In addition, there are lots of tags (such as the sizing for images) that speed up the display of your pages in browsers even

when set to the defaults (in this case, the actual size of the images). Use those extra tag options to their fullest extent!

Always Include Complete Contact Information for Site Visitors (and Don't Forget About Copyrights)

It's amazing how many sites I visit that don't tell me how to contact the company behind the site, the Webmaster, or anyone else. It drives me nuts—it's almost as if the company doesn't exist. Adding a physical location to your site helps to anchor it in the real world and can be key to how people perceive the site. Contact information should include the company's physical address, phone, fax, street, and mailing address, as well as email. Also, don't forget to have properly positioned copyright information on your page, clearly identifying your content as copyrighted. Don't hide copyrights or usage rules where someone has to be Sherlock Holmes to track it down. If you do, you'll only have yourself to blame for someone being confused about the rights.

Some companies have entire directories of world and local headquarters available at their sites, but at the least make sure you have the headquarters listed. This information should be available either directly on the home page or no more than one click away.

Don't Place "Under Construction" Signs on Your Site

Any part of your site that is still unfinished should remain either unseen or not be labeled as "under construction." Why promise people something they can't see? Build your site up in usable waves or wait until it's completely ready.

Clearly Define Links

Remember, many times people may arrive at a page on your site for the first time without going through other parts of your site. Unexplained links like "Back," "Forward," "Up," and "Down" can be quite confusing. Create links that are far more descriptive, such as "Next Page: Column Cont'd." or "Up to Technology Section."

Date Your Pages

Often visitors will return to your site just to see if there is any new or updated content. Other times it will be important for you to identify what needs to be updated or changed. Don't let dates be a guessing game in either case—at least place a date within comments in your HTML code, if not directly on the page display.

Spell Check Anyone?

Checking the spelling on Web pages isn't exactly the easiest thing to do, and the stray HTML brackets sometimes create misspellings or typos in documents. Be sure to search carefully for those spelling errors.

Pages Should Never Be Longer Than 2.5 Screens

For the most part, long pages don't work: They have been shown to disorient users (who lose track of past links), they take too long to load, and they generally don't work. Generally, the only time long Web pages are justified is when they are providing a document that is meant to be printed or saved by the user. In these cases you could offer a zipped version of the document for downloading and avoid displaying the Web page altogether.

Offer Access to Necessary Downloads

On the lead page of your site, offer all the necessary links to retrieve the plug-ins and best browsers for your site. Many of these items offer Web designers specialized button graphics to display to users on your page. Offering content without the automated means to access it is poor planning on your part. Clearly define optional and required items on your front page, so users can know what they need right from the start.

Use the <CENTER> Tag for Displaying Graphics

The use of a <CENTER>...</CENTER> tag almost always makes sense for images. Sometimes I like to place graphics flush left, but most of the time centering is best, since users' eyes tend to follow the middle of the page.

Centering works especially well when people like me run their browsers at
1025 × 768 or 1280 × 1024.

Avoid Long Horizontal Imagery

One of the most annoying parts of browsing the Web is being required to
scroll a page horizontally to view an image. Make sure you keep your imagery
within the borders of a window or frame at low resolution. Any image that is
breaking the horizontal margin should be resized. If you must offer such a
large image for technical reasons, consider placing a smaller version on the
page with text and offering a link to the full image.

Make Your Home Page Load Quickly

As noted above, a quick-loading home page doesn't mean that nice graphics
and other embellishments go out the window; but remember that most people
who access your home page will be doing so from another site. Long waits
while loading could encourage them to give up and head elsewhere, so it's
worth the effort to get them in quickly.

Make Your Home Page Sell the Site

The first thing most newcomers to your site will see is your home page—so it
goes without saying that the dominant job of your home page will be to pull
them further into the site. This means you need to design a home page that is
a competent salesperson for the entire site. Try to fit all the necessary information about the home page and the site in a low-resolution (or at least 800 ×
600) window size, and include information that tells the reader exactly what
the site has in store. And, as I've already pointed out, be sure to include
pointers to any plug-ins or software that users might want to have before
surfing your site.

Test Printing Your Pages

Don't assume that the computer screen is the only presentation of your site
that users will encounter. While almost everyone would agree that printing off
the Web has a long way to go, you can expect some of your users to print out
your site. As a result, you should check out what your site's pages look like
when printed. You may decide to change a few things to produce a better

printed product (such as adding page-numbers or title information, or making graphics black and white).

Keep Styles Consistent

Suppose your site has 150 distinct areas or pages in it. Why on earth would you not create a consistent style for all of them? Set headings and other style characteristics that work across the entirety of your site—there are few things worse than going from one page to another and feeling like you have changed sites completely.

Avoid Ambiguous Links

Links that say "Click Here" or "Here" (such as in "To go to the home page for Coriolis <u>click here</u>") can be extremely unintuitive. Make sure any link on your site tells users what the link does, as if it were the only thing on the page.

A few Web developers, including Michael Herrick of Matterform Media, like to have lots of little bullets or icons sprinkled throughout their pages to reinforce links and other components of their site. (I like this approach myself, as it makes it even easier for people to know what's going on.) Matterform offers what it calls "QBullets," which are small icons to append to your HTML links that explain the result of clicking on that link. As Matterform says "QBullets let you click with confidence." You can download QBullets at **http://www.matterform.com/mf/qbullets/aboutqbullets.html**.

Be Careful with That Color Scheme

Some style guides frown on changing the link color, but I don't. Just because you can change the color schemes of text, links, and followed links, however, doesn't mean you should. My general rules of thumb is to make sure you don't reverse the color scheme that Netscape Navigator defaults to (black text, blue links, purple followed links) and don't change schemes on your site from page to page. Finally, whatever scheme you use, make sure that users can clearly identify which links are followed and not followed. Some schemes don't—and if you're not sure, make sure you test them.

Clean Up Your HTML

Now that some good HTML editors finally exist, many people probably have cast aside their favorite text editor in favor of Microsoft's FrontPage,

Netscape's Navigator Gold, or Adobe's PageMill. All are very capable editors—but the underlying HTML may not be as clean-looking when you're done. Take some time to go back in with your text editor and clean up your code. Get things on the same lines, and add in some carriage returns.

Why? Well, a lot of times you'll find yourself going back to add in JavaScript or Visual Basic Script programs (or just generally to change things) without going through your editor. Clean HTML code makes this task much easier. You can also use this opportunity to remove "orphan" tags that are remnants of editing (and are common in Navigator Gold, for example). If you're just getting into the Web scene, form good habits now by keeping your code clean.

Ben's Subjective Web Page Design Tips

I consider the above principles to be more or less universally agreed upon (if not universally practiced). Now I'd like to offer some tips of my own. I consider these to be far more subjective, so don't flame me if you disagree—not all of these ideas will work for you or match your tastes. However, I would like to share my own feelings about page design.

Create a High Contrast between the Foreground and Background

If the background of your Web page distracts from the foreground, you're finished. In addition, if the background and foreground appear to sort of meld together (either in their color scheme or via pictures), then change it until you have a higher level of contrast. If you're trying to have some connection between the site and the background (say, musical notes or sheet music as a background for a site promoting something musical), by all means do it, but do everything you can to maintain a high contrast level.

Lighter Backgrounds Work Better Than Darker Ones

I've seen very few sites that work well with dark backgrounds. Of those, a pure black background with white text worked best. Softimage's site (see Figure 7.1), which uses a black background effectively, is another exception to the rule.

Figure 7.1 Softimage's Web page shows the exception to the no dark back-grounds rule.

Use Drop Shadows or Fades for a Smooth, Professional Look

One of the reasons I like very light backgrounds or very dark ones is that they lend themselves to graphics with very fine drop shadows or fades. These graphics either blend in with the page or pop up from it; either way, neither fights the page at all. Strong corners and borders tend to steal your attention and to separate elements in a far more rigid way than fades or shadowing. You also eliminate the "jaggies" that many transparent images acquire with this process. Figures 7.2 and 7.3 are some nice example pages that show off the use of drop shadows and fades.

Figure 7.2   These icons and photo from a page on the USA Today site (**http:// www.usatoday.com**) pop off the page from nice use of drop shadows.

Place Bars of Links at the Top and Bottom of a Page

If your page is even a couple of screens long, consider placing your navigation links at both the top and the bottom of the page. This makes it easier for people to get to the rest of your site's content.

Don't Be Afraid of Framed Sites— Just Be Careful

At first, framed sites were considered some sort of weird taboo. I'm not sure why; it probably had to do with some people overusing them, and several

Figure 7.3 The AT&T home page shown here (**http://www.worldnet.att.net**) makes good use of drop shadows and fades, and exemplifies the contrasts possible with a white background.

browsers not supporting their use. Today, though, people are getting more accustomed to navigating framed sites, and the two browsers used by the vast majority of Web users support them. While some may still decry frames, a nicely designed framed site offers some distinct advantages in interface design and overall design (such as being able to keep some content constantly on screen).

The trick is to be careful with them. Some framed sites offer entirely frameless versions, while others mix and match, using frames only when they provide a distinct advantage. The Web site for the electronic magazine Salon (**http://www.salon1999.com**) does this very well.

Anti-Alias All Your Graphics

There is no excuse for graphics that don't have smooth lines and soft corners. As noted earlier, it takes only a little more work to anti-alias (remove the "jaggies") from transparent graphics. Make sure you implement some form of anti-aliasing to reduce those jaggies!

Don't Change Font Sizes Within Links

One of my most annoying personal pet peeves are links that include one or more characters with a different font size. The result (until someone fixes it) is a link with an uneven underline—which, if you ask me, looks terrible. Drop caps are a tried-and-true graphic design technique, but they just don't work with links.

Break Up Your Text, and Consider Larger Font Sizes

Compared to normal writing, text for the Web means breaking up things more. Consider more paragraphs, shorter sentences, and larger typefaces. Why? Well, for simpler reading. Most in-depth text material on the Web can be shuttled to downloadable texts for printing.

Reading text from a computer monitor is an easy way to induce eye strain, so create both your layout and the underlying text with the intent to make the process more comfortable. To me, that means breaking sentences into small, digestible chunks, and using a larger typeface with more spacing between words. See Figures 7.4 and 7.5 for examples.

Don't Use Anything but Standard Separators

It took me some time to come around, but now I'm convinced that you shouldn't use anything but the standard <HR> tag for separators. A slew of different images have been developed to replace this tag, but substitute horizontal rules just don't work (they tend to steal your eye, rather than serve as a good transition into the next text paragraph). The <HR> extensions supported by Navigator and Internet Explorer offer plenty of options (I personally use a thicker rule than standard) to create variety from the default.

One other note is that with a white background, the <HR> tag doesn't look perfectly embedded (because the thin white line it uses to create this effect disappears on white backgrounds). The only compromises I've found to combat this are to use a single- or double-pixel black line, or to darken the white background slightly to create just enough contrast.

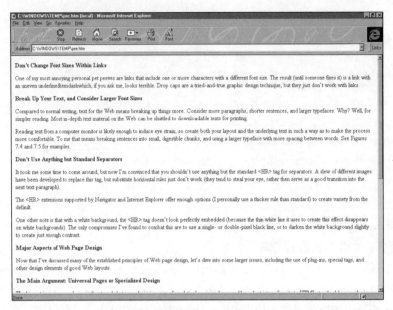

Figure 7.4 Lots of text can be difficult to read online, even at a normal point size.

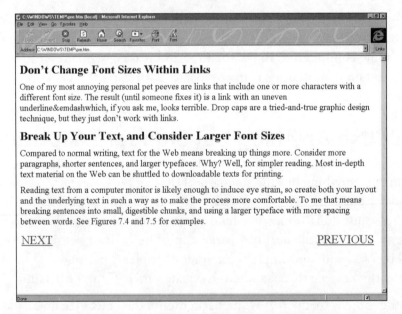

Figure 7.5 While much more could be done beyond this to break up text, large text in small doses can be an effective way to maximize online reading ability.

Major Aspects of Web Page Design

Now that I've discussed many of the established principles of Web page design, let's dive into some larger issues, including the use of plug-ins, special tags, and other design elements of good Web layouts.

The Main Argument: Universal Pages or Specialized Design

The biggest issue in page design is the struggle between designing pages for relatively universal access (through strict conformity to HTML standards) or employing new elements (like specialized tags, plug-ins, Java, or ActiveX) that can exclude segments of the Web-browsing public.

To decide where your Web product should stand, ask yourself the following questions each time you propose to design a more specialized page.

What Am I Trading Away as a Result?

Sometimes you don't really trade anything away. For example, using Microsoft's <MARQUEE> tag creates a "marquee" in Internet Explorer, but simply displays the text normally in other browsers. Using the Amber plug-in to display a Web 'zine you designed, however, will exclude all users who don't have Amber capabilities (and most users don't). Tradeoffs on the Web generally break down as those choices that exclude other users completely and those that simply cause items to appear in a degraded form on the "wrong" browsers. In many cases, the degraded tradeoffs aren't too bad, but every time you make an exclusion tradeoff you had better be able to answer the next essential question.

Is This Going to Make the Page Better Given the Tradeoff?

Every time you decide on an exclusion tradeoff, the justification has to be quite strong. For example, perhaps you want to use the Amber plug-in and base your site totally on the Adobe Acrobat technology. This may be essential to the needs of the site because of the flexibility Amber offers in displaying very technical pages. On the other hand, if the only reason you want to use Shockwave is so you can display rotating banners on all your headings, ask yourself if that is really essential to the site—so essential that you are willing to limit sharply how many users will be able to see it.

The most pragmatic approach would be to measure how much time users would spend gathering all the items to visit your sophisticated site. You could also look for various surveys or company reports that show you how many people have the various technologies you plan to require. Similarly, you could inquire about the hit ratio on various sites that require the same technologies or special tags as your intended product.

Can You Provide Alternative Paths to Your Content?

Sometimes you can offer multiple roads to the same material. While an Acrobat/Amber version of a newsletter or product brochure might be the best, why not also offer a scaled-down HTML version? That way every user can get the most out of your site. This is the same reasoning behind the many pages that offer both framed and frameless versions.

Thinking Vertical

A Web page has a vertical orientation to it that plays an important role in your page design work. Using things like columns of text created by tables, or text in one column and pictures in the other (again using tables for layout), can create a nice vertical look that complements the scrolling down of a page.

Other pages use a long background image, as shown in Figure 7.6, that creates a vertical orientation down a page. The major element of "thinking vertical" in page design and layout is to think beyond the borders of the window and about the page. Many designers storyboard their pages on 11 × 17 or longer paper so they can think in terms of the entire page's look.

On the flip side, think about how this vertical stress translates to the specific portion of the page the user might see at any point in scrolling through it. You might have a long, beautiful graphic on a page, but it could be a mess when someone is running the browser in a low resolution or in a smaller-sized window.

The Plug-In Situation

Plug-in technology has revolutionized Web page design options. Aided by the continued bandwidth push, plug-ins also are introducing such multimedia fare as video, interactive programs, and streaming sound to everyday Web use. Although I will explore these items extensively in other chapters, here I will discuss some aspects of how they influence page design.

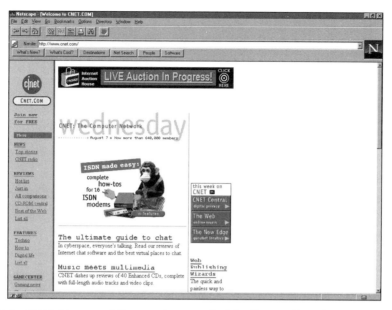

Figure 7.6 C I Net is one of the most recognizable sites on the Web, and its long yellow sidebar works perfectly with the vertical orientation of Web pages.

A wide range of plug-ins can be used in conjunction with Web page design. Some handle new graphics formats (such as Corel's CMX plug-in, which displays CorelDraw! graphics), while others simplify multimedia animation and interactivity (for example, Macromedia's Shockwave).

Many plug-ins, though, are of far more marginal use than you may think. Since for the most part you can create exciting, well-executed page designs without any plug-ins, be careful when adopting them into your designs. As with most software, only a select few are going to become generally accepted. Also, as programmers become more experienced with Java, you might find that they have created Java solutions to your design problems that are far more accessible (given the more universal reach of Java) than plug-in solutions.

Don't Mix and Match Plug-Ins

There are several different plug-ins for delivering sound, and several more for delivering multimedia content, video, or line art. Choose one plug-in to deliver sound for your site, one to deliver video, and so on. If your sound content is delivered via Progressive's RealAudio on one page and via Xing's StreamWorks on the next, you're multiplying the possible technical barriers for users—an approach that is guaranteed to cause you nightmares as well.

Offering Dual Plug-In Options, However, Is Fine

The point I just made doesn't mean that you can't support more than one plug-in that offers the same features. Many music sites on the Internet offer streaming audio in both StreamWorks and RealAudio; that way, the users of either one can hear everything the sites have to offer. This is perfectly acceptable, and you only shut out people who don't use either one.

Don't Use Plug-Ins When Content Can Be Delivered through Simpler Means

Always be aware of how to deliver your content through the simplest means that offer the most universal access. For example, you can create simple animations with animated GIF files instead of using Macromedia's Shockwave. If your audio is short enough, don't use a streaming audio plug-in when you can use WAV files (sure, it will take a little longer to download, but the format is far more universal). Plug-ins should be viewed as a way to deliver content that is beyond the technological capability of other means—not as general-purpose design aids.

Use the Plug-In Icons

Earlier I recommended offering the links to needed plug-ins on your home page. Most makers of plug-ins offer icons to use in your page layouts for precisely this purpose. Some, like Acrobat and RealAudio, have plug-ins to use as links to the content on your page, so when users click on the link, they know they're accessing material that requires a plug-in. Look for these icons on the home page of the plug-in's creator.

Screens Vs. Pages

In Chapter 6, I spent a little bit of time talking about how frames change the focus of Web site design from pages (which might scroll, giving you a larger canvas on which to present information) to single, static screen views. Sure, you can have scrolling elements to a frame—I use them all the time—but frames still cut down on the relative size of the element.

The biggest issue here is the resolution of the screen and how that affects the usability of a framed layout. I've seen several sites where the framed layout wasn't particularly good until the resolution reached 1024 × 768 pixels. Make sure you test your frames at every resolution (640 × 480, 800 × 600, 1024 × 768, and 1280 × 1024) and various window sizes. You'll be surprised by the results. I find it best to place a small note on framed sites—visible on the first page load—that informs users of the best resolution for viewing purposes (for example, "best viewed at 800 × 600").

 It's a smart idea to create a stable of frame designs that you can use as templates throughout your page-design career. Set aside time to do nothing but create frame layouts. Test them at different resolutions, keeping notes as to which resolutions work best with which layouts. You'll end up with a good understanding of frames in relation to screen space, as well as a lot of frame layouts you can readily call upon.

The Role of Graphics

I compare the role of graphics in Web page design to that of the special effects in *Star Wars*—they grab your attention, but there still has to be a good story to back them up.

Some designers are graphic and computer artists who fill their designs with gorgeous displays worthy of a top magazine layout without blinking an eye. Others are far more conservative, not in their design tastes but in their reluctance to sacrifice too much of a page's display speed in favor of superior design. In the middle are a select group of designers who manage to create artistic, fresh displays without sending the display speed into dog years. Above all, though, their graphics exist to serve the site, not the other way around.

A Note about Applets

Applets are almost like graphics; indeed, as with images, I think applets should be centered. Also, don't forget to provide proper instructions for the applet, if needed. Make sure that when the applet is at the top of the screen, instructions (or a link to the instructions) are viewable on screen.

Thinking About Sizes

As I explore Web development further, I find myself grappling more often with questions concerning resolution and size. The earliest implementations of HTML offered very little to help you control the pixel-by-pixel display of Web pages. Today, however, there are a slew of ways to engage in such micromanagement.

This wealth of options is complicated even more by frames and more powerful machines. As I write this, I can run Windows in graphic resolution modes ranging from 640×480 to 1280×1024 pixels. I usually prefer 1024×768; when I design a Web page optimized at that resolution, however, you can imagine what it looks like at 800×600, where a majority of browsers are running—and don't even ask about 640×480. And even someone running her browser on a 1024×768 display may be running it in a window that only fills half the screen (512×768).

What it all boils down to is that you can't take size for granted. If you want to be flexible, don't design sites that require rigid window sizing—this means that fancy frames and tables are problems. On the other hand, you can just be rigid and hope users comply and run their Windows at sizes that optimize your display—many sites have a simple message on their home page instructing optimal size to help with this process.

Using Tables for Polished Layout

At least until other display technologies come forward, many hard-core Web page designers make extensive use of tables to control the layout of their documents. When used to their fullest ability, tables can make a page look as if it came right out of Adobe PageMaker.

Tables give you more control over the alignment of items on the page. Want to have two columns of text running down the page? Just create a table with two columns, type away to your heart's content, and then simply turn off the gridlines so people can't see it's a table.

For an example of how tables can redefine the layout of your Web page, look at Figure 7.7.

Using Single-Pixel GIF Files to Control Layout

Another layout trick developers use is to combine the white space and margin abilities of Netscape with a single-pixel graphic (itself transparent). By loading in this graphic and increasing the white-space elements of the <IMAGE> tag (hspace and vspace), coupled with text flow support, developers can create more dynamic layouts. You can find an excellent tutorial on this process at the Web Wonk site located at **http://www.dsiegel.com/tips/index.html**.

Figure 7.7 Microsoft's home page packs a lot of information in a multicolumn format. A polished looking layout like this is only possible through tables.

Focus on Text

In the beginning—and still, to many purists—the World Wide Web was about the dissemination of information via text and not much else. As a voracious reader, I'm happy to see a medium that requires the amount of reading the Web does; its very existence has probably done more for reading skills than anything since the Gutenberg press or *Sesame Street*. While there are many reasons that the written word's grip on the Web will soften a little, text will always remain a top content item; so any focus on Web page design must include an exploration of text display.

First I should note that until technologies like Adobe's Bravo (which I'll discuss shortly) become major components of the Web, or until Microsoft or Netscape both incorporate more font flexibility (which will probably happen right after this book debuts), your choice of typefaces is pretty limited. Internet Explorer offers different fonts, but the vast majority of Web surfers use Netscape Navigator, which still doesn't. There are several ways to work around this problem, though.

Render Headings via Graphics, and Introduce Other Fonts to Break Things Up

One good idea is to create stylish headings with your favorite art package, using a different font and perhaps a few simple effects (such as 3D embossing or embedding). Keeping the color count and size on the low end should make these headings load quickly. Remember, your primary goal is just to add a different font to contrast with the Times Roman default offered up by browsers.

You could go even further by creating entire paragraphs as graphics to be loaded in. A 530 × 560 pixel image I constructed with a two-color depth (black and white) was only 37.1 K in size; larger images come in around 60 K. Such images shouldn't be a problem in terms of loading speed, depending on the other elements on your page.

One site that has used the text-as-graphics technique well is id Software's site—the makers of Doom (**http://www.idsoftware.com**). Since they may change their site, I've captured a screen shot from the current version to illustrate the idea (Figure 7.8). It took my 14.4 Kbps modem about twenty seconds to load this page, but the overall result was great.

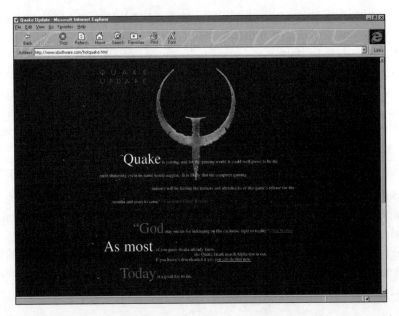

Figure 7.8 The Web page for Quake (by id software) shows the power and flexibility of rendering text as graphics.

Make Use of Various Type Sizes and Styles

With good use of <FONT SIZE=X> tags and the use of the <PRE> tag (which gives you a Courier font, plus boldface and italics), you can vary the overall text presentation just enough to present nice-looking pages. We all want access to dozens of fonts, but the best designers make good use of what they have, and this is all we have for now.

You can use additional fonts in Internet Explorer that will display as the default Times Roman font in Netscape. When you do this, though, consider working first to design a page that uses font size, the <PRE> tag, and graphics to create acceptable variety for Netscape users, then spice it up further for Internet Explorer. This route will help your design make the most of each program's font capabilities. A simple before and after example is shown in Figures 7.9 and 7.10.

Don't Forget About Forms

Forms are an aspect of Web page design I've seen little written about. With the advent of languages like Java, JavaScript, and VBScript, plus developers' growing mastery of CGI scripts and Perl, forms are becoming increasingly prevalent on the Web. For the most part, forms are pretty easy to design: The

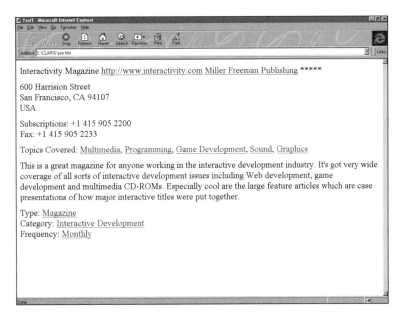

Figure 7.9   A page without a variety of fonts.

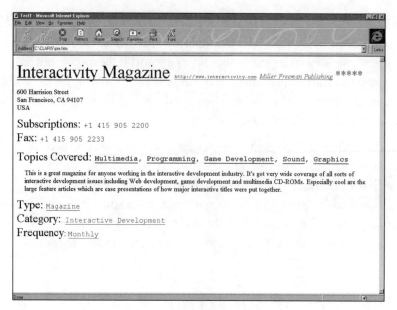

Figure 7.10   After varying font size and type.

designer just creates a vertical scrolling list of the components, followed by the obligatory "Submit" button at the end. There is, however, a lot more you can do to jazz up your forms—and as the need for more complex feedback systems comes into play, good form design will become a needed trait.

Use Tables to Create Justified Interfaces

When it comes to forms design, I almost always employ tables so I can create forms that have all the fields nicely aligned so they're easy to navigate. I can also combine radio buttons and text boxes into columns of checklists and group things together in an organized manner much more readily. Just look at Figure 7.11, which shows the advantage of using table formatting within a form.

Use a Forms Designer

Consider using a program created specifically for designing forms. Recently O'Reilly shipped PolyForm, a GUI-based forms designer that can help you create and organize dynamic form layouts so easily it's a crime.

Use JavaScript or VBScript to Control Input

One of the major reasons Netscape and Microsoft have implemented these two scripting languages is to give programmers a tool for entering form-based information. For example, if your form is intended to accept only capital

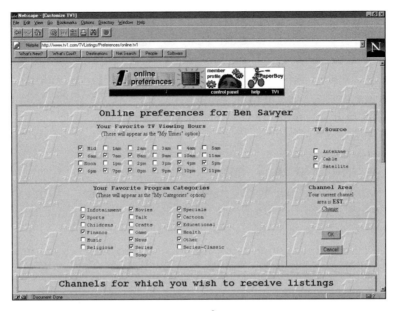

Figure 7.11 The page for customizing your personalized TV listings on TV1 (**http://www.tv1.com**) is very clean looking, thanks to lots of table formatting.

letters, you could use these scripting languages to automatically change all the forms fields to capital letters before submission to the server.

In short, you can create a more foolproof and intuitive input system for your forms by using a scripting language. Since forms are one of the more unintuitive parts of the Web for many users, the more you do to reduce their burden, the more complete, correct, and frequent your forms-based feedback will be.

Use Graphics to Reinforce the Data Input

If you have form-based items that *must* be filled in, or are especially important, consider using some icons or other graphic elements to explain or draw attention to the item. Again, the idea here is to give the user even more clarity in how to fill out the form.

Create Onscreen Fill-in Instructions

I like using a small font to include simple instructions about each field. The easier it is for the user to understand what information each field should contain, the better. Sometimes this might mean adding in a simple example of what you want.

Create Clear Descriptions of Form Elements

When you label your fields, take extra care to make sure the field names that you assign make sense. Sure, "Address" seems to be clear to anyone, but some users might think you mean their email address. Even "Home Address" might cause some people to type in their home page address. The rule of thumb I use here is to think as precisely as I can and design fields that rule out anything other than what I want.

Provide Links Upon Submission

The worst thing about poorly designed forms usually shows up after the user submits a page. Always provide links on the resulting page so that users can go somewhere after a correct submission. In addition, if you require them to fill out a form again because of an error or omission, provide the exact information explaining what needs to be filled out and how.

HTML: Netscape Navigator vs. Microsoft Internet Explorer

In the battle of the World Wide Web browsers, Netscape's Navigator is ahead of Microsoft's Internet Explorer for now, but the real victor won't be known for three or four years. Until there is either a clear winner, a combination of features, or a commonly supported display technology (such as Adobe's products), no discussion of Web page design would be complete without examining the differences between the Netscape and Microsoft browsers.

Should I Support One over the Other?

As I've said elsewhere, customizing your site for either Navigator or Internet Explorer is fine, as long as you understand and accept the implications of your decision. Deciding on a common-denominator approach is also fine, as is creating a site that offers separate tracks designed specifically for each browser (a rather ambitious choice).

There is no easy answer to this question right now. In the future, the two browsers may be so similar that the question goes away, or perhaps one will ultimately force the other into obscurity. Until then, you have to make a decision and stick to it. Just make sure you back it up with good reasons (and not personal vendettas against either company), and let your users and site designs be part of that reasoning process.

What Layout-Oriented Tags Does Each Offer That the Other Doesn't?

This is another tough question to answer, because at any moment each browser is scrambling to adopt its rival's unique features. At one point, different-colored backgrounds in tables were in Explorer but not in Navigator; however, one download later Netscape had them, too. For the moment, at least, the Microsoft browser still has some unique features, including type styles, marquees, and borderless frames.

The best thing to do as a developer is to download the latest copies of both programs regularly. While you might not adopt every new feature right away, the only way to stay on top of each browser's improvements is to check in on both. Later in this book, I provide a comprehensive HTML reference guide. It's the most up-to-date summary of each browser you'll find.

Check the following pages for the latest in the tag wars:

Introducing HTML 3.2
`http://www.w3.org/pub/WWW/MarkUp/Wilbur/`

This is the home of the latest WWW Consortium document on HTML, now up to version 3.2. Always check in here to see the latest HTML standard being pushed by this very influential Web organization.

Microsoft Internet Explorer Author's Guide and HTML Reference
`http://www.microsoft.com/workshop/author/newhtml/default.htm`

Microsoft updates and explains all the supported HTML and Microsoft extensions to HTML for its Internet Explorer program at this URL.

Creating Net Sites by Netscape
`http://www.netscape.com/assist/net_sites/index.html`

From here you can access the pages which detail Netscape's extensions to the most current HTML implementation.

What's the Breakdown on Which Platforms Are Supported?

The biggest difference here is that Netscape Navigator is available for several implementations of Unix (such as Sun and SGI workstations), while Internet Explorer supports only Windows 95/NT and Macintosh hardware. Since the majority of Web users do not have Unix-based machines, this may not seem to be a problem for you. If you stick with Netscape, however, you can create nicely tailored pages for users of those machines—with Internet Explorer, you can't.

What about ActiveX and Plug-In Technology and the Scripting Languages?

Right now, beyond various tag differences, the major layout and page design differences that will crop up have to do with the programming foundations of the two browsers. Because Netscape's plug-in architecture is different from that of Internet Explorer, things like Shockwave have to be slightly changed to work properly with each program. As a result, some types of plug-in controls may be available for one and not the other (at least until a port is created). In addition, while Microsoft says its product will offer Java and JavaScript support, there is no news on whether Netscape will use Visual Basic Script or support ActiveX.

So it's up to the developer of a site to work out the differences, and to make sure that the plug-ins you plan to use are available to the browser(s) you plan to support. Unless VBScript offers a distinct advantage (which at times it can), JavaScript seems to be the way to go for simple scripting items, since both browsers support it.

Is One Faster than the Other?

My experience has been that Internet Explorer usually is somewhat faster than Netscape. Given the rate of progress on new revisions, however, there is no telling what the answer to this question is today. If you are looking to speed issues to settle on a development choice, consider mocking up several sites and experimenting with each browser's latest version, comparing retrieval times and such. And remember, just because each one may perform similar functions doesn't mean that they perform those functions exactly the same way.

Nonphysical Aspects of Web Page Design

For the most part in this chapter, I have concentrated on the physical side of Web page design. Things like graphics, text, tables, and visual applets make up the bulk of design elements of a Web page. As I pointed out earlier, however, many elements in a Web page's design aren't physically present on the page.

Chief among these nonvisible elements is sound, even though a sound file might be physically represented by a link or icon graphic. Just add a simple MIDI file that works with Live Update's Crescendo plug-in to your page, reload it, and see how different it feels with the music. Or, for a nonsound example, add a JavaScript routine that updates the date and time on your page whenever the document is reloaded. Both of these items demonstrate how objects other than graphics or text can distinguish a specific page on your site.

The Future of Web Page Design

Ironically, for all of the progress in Web technology, the work on improving the overall design and presentation of Web pages has been slow to develop. One primary reason is the ever-present problem of bandwidth. Another is that many display-oriented improvements require other technologies to blossom first—plug-ins, type formats, and compression schemes, to name just a few. Yet another reason is the continued education of many Web page developers who aren't exactly schooled with good design skills.

Thankfully, bandwidth is improving, and several of the technologies needed to bring better display options to Web pages are falling into place. With this in mind, let's look over several items that will change Web page design in the next couple of years.

Amber and Bravo

Perhaps more than any other technology, Adobe's display technology—in the form of the Acrobat plug-in Amber and its new Bravo system—has the potential to revolutionize Web page design. I'll take some time to discuss the background of these items to help you understand the changes that are coming as a result.

For years, Adobe has been the king of page description languages (PDLs) and font technology. In fact, while it was originally designed for printers, Adobe saw PostScript as a completely universal display technology. The company later created Display PostScript, which first shipped as part of the NeXT computer system, then turned this technology into what is now known as Adobe Acrobat. With the advent of the Internet, the concept of a universal display language is becoming a major component of many developers' next-generation Web plans. Thus, there is no doubt that Adobe's technology is going to play a central role in that effort.

The major thrust by Adobe to bring a more robust device-independent display technology to the Internet is represented by Amber and Bravo. Amber is a plug-in control for Netscape (and soon Internet Explorer) that allows you to view Adobe Acrobat files (PDF files) directly within the browser.

Bravo is the further evolution of the Display PostScript–Acrobat–Amber legacy. Bravo is much more integrated with the Internet and features more compression tools to shorten load times (PDF files can be rather large). In addition, Bravo incorporates a new type technology (called OpenType) that finally creates a unified type model between Adobe's Type 1 fonts and Microsoft's competing TrueType. Bravo recognizes and works with both of these major typeface file formats.

Bravo has also been licensed by Sun to become the two-dimensional API and imaging system for the next implementation of Java. Java thus will work in an integrated manner with Bravo to bring far more complex type and two-dimensional graphics capabilities to the Web.

The goal of Bravo enthusiasts is to finally deliver World Wide Web pages that are as exquisitely designed as the state of the art in printed pages. As Bravo technology becomes increasingly available, there will be a rapid change in page design possibilities for the Web. Just imagine—unlimited font availability and easy positioning of graphic elements just like you find in your favorite page layout application. With Bravo, it will all be possible.

Web Style Sheets

Another big change headed for the Web is the movement toward style sheets. Specifically, the proposal known as Cascading Style Sheets (CSS), developed by the W3 consortium, looks like it will become the basis of a new way of creating Web pages.

Web style sheets work to define an overall template for HTML components. You still code your documents with tags like <H1>, <BODY>, and the like, but you use the style sheets to define the look of those HTML tags. For example, your style sheet might dictate that all <H1> tags are to be displayed with the Helvetica font in red. Now suppose you have a site with 500 pages—if you wanted to change the heading color to green instead of red, currently you would have to change every instance of the header code in every document. With style sheets, however, all you have to do is redefine the style sheet—one step, instead of hundreds!

Style sheets will be essential elements of Web design, especially for larger sites containing lots of pages. They'll also be welcomed by developers looking to create a quick way to change the look of a site during the development process. Want to check out a new color scheme or background? How about changing the navigational images at the bottom of every page? With style sheets it will be easier than ever for developers to test out new looks.

Dynamic Pages

Let's face it: From a design standpoint, 90 percent of Web pages suck. The World Wide Web may be a wide-open medium that almost anyone can participate in, but that doesn't mean everyone is suddenly blessed with awesome graphic design skills. Conversely, traditional graphic designers and artists have sometimes erred on the Web by not adjusting to its technological constraints or some of the Web's other idiosyncrasies.

Creating appealing pages is much harder than it looks. Major sites backed by sizable production budgets can employ professional artists to spice up their looks dramatically. Well-executed graphics can go a long way toward creating an appealing site, and sites with good budgets are able to leverage that money against lower-cost sites by spending it on killer artwork and professional designers.

Even without a big budget, though, some of the simplest rules I've listed in this chapter can lead you to a polished-looking page. Sure, you could settle for a functional page, with the most basic layout and little or no graphics. But if you take some time with your page design—just a little effort to vary the margins and fonts, create some attractive headers, sprinkle in some icon graphics, and/or add some crisp graphics with drop shadows and smooth lines—the difference can be dynamic!

Summary

In this chapter I've tried to identify all of the major points that go into designing a single Web page. I'll recap these points here so you can make sure that all of them sink in.

First, I outlined a series of standard do's and don'ts that form a basic foundation of page design style and practices. Then I explored several key aspects of page design, such as recognizing the medium as strongly vertical in layout,

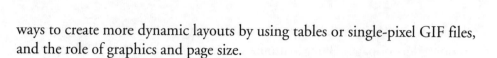

ways to create more dynamic layouts by using tables or single-pixel GIF files, and the role of graphics and page size.

I talked about the differences between the two leading browsers, Netscape Navigator and Microsoft Internet Explorer, citing the key differences as being the platforms each one supports and the programming options (for example, ActiveX vs. plug-ins, and VBScript vs. JavaScript). Instead of citing individual tag differences and advantages, which can change all too frequently with updates to each product, I gave you a few URLs to check for the most up-to-date information on browser tag developments.

I also didn't forget about forms, outlining several key design points that can create better-looking and more intuitive forms on Web pages.

I ended with a discussion of two major technologies that will dramatically change the process of designing Web pages: Adobe's move to a universal display language for the Web with Amber and the newer Bravo technology, and Web style sheets. Still under development, the latter technology will make it easy to define universal styles and make quick changes to those styles for all the pages on a given site.

Web Page Design Resources

Oh boy, get ready; there's a lot to cover here.

I've tried to list only resources that deal with layout and interface construction help. Resources for other elements that are key to page design, but are more directly concerned with the construction of the page objects rather than the page as a whole, can be found in the chapters specifically devoted to those objects.

Suggested Books

Some of these books cover design and style manuals not directly associated with the Web—but I have found several to be useful in helping construct general principles useful to any Web page designer. Others I have culled from other Web developers. Those which aren't Web specific are noted.

Creating Killer Web Sites: The Art of Third-Generation Site Design by David Siegel (Hayden Books, 1996, ISBN 1-56830-289-4)

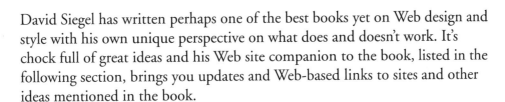

David Siegel has written perhaps one of the best books yet on Web design and style with his own unique perspective on what does and doesn't work. It's chock full of great ideas and his Web site companion to the book, listed in the following section, brings you updates and Web-based links to sites and other ideas mentioned in the book.

HTML Manual of Style by Larry Aronson (Ziff Davis Press, 1996, ISBN 1-56276-352-0)

This is the second version of this popular book. The HTML 3.0 Manual of Style is billed by its publisher as "The Strunk & White of the HTML programming language." The book includes 30 double-page spreads with code down one side and a picture of a Web page on the other, so you can see exactly how certain items are coded in HTML.

Clement Mok's Designing Business: Multiple Media, Multiple Disciplines (Adobe Press, 1996, ISBN 1-56830-282-7)

Clement Mok is one of the most well-known graphic and new media designers in the world. His work for Apple, Microsoft, and other major clients is legendary. His design studio, Studio Archetype, is one of the Web's leading design shops. In this book, which isn't a Web book per se, he shows you a ton of information that is very relevant to good Web design and style. A must-have book for the serious designer.

The HTML Sourcebook: A Complete Guide to HTML 3.0, 2nd Edition by Ian S. Graham (John Wiley & Sons, 1996, ISBN 0-471-14242-5)

This is one of the most popular Web books so far, because it's both an excellent HTML reference and a good guide to advance Web page development techniques, especially as they relate to HTML itself.

The Web Page Design Cookbook: All the Ingredients You Need to Create 5-Star Web Pages by William Horton, Lee Taylor, Arthur Ignacio, and Nancy L. Hoft (John Wiley & Sons, 1995, ISBN: 0-471-13039-7)

Inside this book you'll find hundreds of templates to help you create good, fast Web pages. It also includes tons of do's and don'ts about Web page design.

Note: This list may seem small because I've narrowed it to books that talked about either HTML style, or overall design and interface issues. There are a slew of other books listed in Chapter 11 about graphic design for the Web that will also be equally as useful. Rather than list them here, I chose to list those Web design books which were the most graphical in nature.

There are some other influential reading sources you might also consider to help you focus on the details of stellar page design. Though none of these books deal specifically at all with the Web, you nonetheless can garner some good ideas from them. Consider getting or browsing through at the local book store books on:

- *Interface Design*—There are several books on interface design available. Check with your favorite computer book publishers and look through their offerings. Lately there have been several new books published on this subject that are quite good.

- *Typographic Design*—As someone who studied graphic design as my minor in college, I appreciate and learn a lot from the finer points of type design. It's the foundation for lots of graphic design and hence, Web design. Fonts got off to a slow start on the Web, but they're heating up fast. There are several good books from Adobe Press and in your local megabookstore's graphic design section.

- *Business and Graphic Design Texts*—While I refuse to say that Web design is graphic design (it isn't), there certainly is a lot to learn from many graphic and business design books (I mentioned one already) and many of these books can be found in a good library. I especially like to go and read graphic design books that are from the precomputer age. There are also many coffee table books on graphic design that can be quite influential on your overall page design ideas.

Suggested Web Sites

Of course, the best Web style guides are on the World Wide Web itself. Also be sure to check in with your Internet provider if you're using a hosting service—some have specific style guides of their own that you will need to incorporate into your own personal guide. By no means is this the most exhaustive list of style guides and page design links; but what's here is what I included in my first major reading list when I started designing pages.

How to Create Killer Web Sites Companion Page
http://www.killersites.com

The companion site to the book of the same name, well designed itself, it's a site filled with interesting help and tips on Web style.

Top Ten Ways to Tell If You Have a Sucky Home Page
http://www.winternet.com/~jmg/Sucky.html
The "David Letterman meets Beavis and Butthead" of Web style guides.

Bob Alison's Tips for Web Spinners
http://gagme.wwa.com/~boba/masters1.html
A bevy of content with lots of links to other major Web design sites.

Sun's Interface Design Guide for the WWW
http://www.sun.com/sun-on-net/uidesign/
Sun has a lot of experience with both the Web and traditional GUI design. This large document spends a lot of time explaining good GUI design; especially as it relates to creating well-designed Web pages.

Art and the Zen of Web sites
http://www.tlc-systems.com/webtips.shtml
An awesome list of tips with a really cute introduction!

Style Guide for Online Hypertext by the World Wide Web Consortium
http://www.w3.org/pub/WWW/Provider/Style/Overview.html
A very good style guide to the Web written by Tim Berners-Lee himself.

The Ten Commandments of HTML
http://web.canlink.com/webdesign/ten.html
A simple list of ten major tips to good page design.

Webcraft Style Guide
http://www.atdesign.com/content/base/at/webcraft/05/index.html
A nice collection of information with page design details and style tips.

Web Style Manual by Patrick J. Lynch
http://info.med.yale.edu/caim/StyleManual_Top.HTML
One of the best style guides around, this is a must read with lots of information that can make you a better Web page designer after just one read.

CHAPTER 8

Despite thousands of junk pages, the Web is full of awesome sites you can and should learn from.

Web Site Benchmarks: Specific Examples

I'll say it even before I start: *Don't flame me on these picks.* There are dozens more "benchmark" Web sites than I could possibly list. If your site isn't here, I probably just haven't seen it yet. The ones I've selected are by no means alone in terms of quality (and may not even be the absolute best in their category); they're just the sites I happen to have learned from and been influenced by. Feel free to send me suggestions of others—I may update this book at some point, and even if I don't, I always love to see innovative new ideas, or old ideas that are executed really well.

The bottom line is this: Look at this chapter as a learning experience, not a beauty contest. If you really want to argue with somebody, go flame the computer magazines when they hand out their various Internet/Web design awards.

Benchmark Sites

Whenever I come across anything I think is done well and might be useful in my work—a piece of software or music, a movie, or a Web site—I try to make a mental note of it. If I'm really on the ball, I jot it down in my scrapbook of ideas. What do I do with these influences? I steal them, that's what. Call me a copycat, but design and development are (and always will be) incremental processes that require you to incorporate the ideas of others.

This doesn't mean you should copy a site verbatim—well, unless you like courts and lawyers. But if you come across a particularly nifty navigation scheme or color layout that clearly is not copyrightable, then by all means steal it. For example, when I saw early in my Web life how some sites used email newsletters to generate repeat visits, that idea went directly into my mental toolbox. And when I discovered that pages with white backgrounds and drop-shadowed graphics looked somehow better than most others, I stuffed that thought in, too.

In that spirit, let's cover a list of interesting sites that showcase Web design and development ideas you can use. Just as any good book, document, or product can be an important developer's resource, so, too, can any good Web site.

Retail Sites

A lot of action in the coming year will center around selling retail products on the World Wide Web. So far, sales via the Web have been held back by concerns about security measures for electronic transactions. By the end of 1997, though, there will be a considerable amount of new technology and software in place to make Web retailing easier and more secure. Many sites are already using a variety of secure means to implement Web sales. Let's look over several sites which are working hard to be at the top of Web retailing.

1-800-MUSIC NOW

MCI Communications
http://www.1800musicnow.com

MCI has been one of the most aggressive companies (especially among telephone companies) in recognizing the Internet's potential and redefining itself for the telecommunications revolution. One major component of this effort is its subsidiary 1-800-MUSIC NOW. Not only is the service itself—which lets you sample and purchase records over a simple phone line without an operator—a breakthrough, but MCI has a great Web site for it as well.

Like the sites for many record companies and retailers, MCI uses RealAudio throughout the 1-800-MUSIC NOW site to support its music offerings. What I especially like, though, is how MCI has worked to have the site generate sales. Every time I go into a record store, I really need help in selecting music—it's not that I don't know what I like, but I like so many different things that I sometimes need a little direction before I can make a decision. MCI's site features several different elements designed to help turn casual browsers into buying customers.

For example, one page allows the user to see what large-market radio stations are playing in their top-ten rotations; for each song or album title there is a link to hear and/or purchase the record. 1-800-MUSIC NOW also features different theme pages, like the love-songs page displayed in Figure 8.1. Essentially, these are a Web retailer's virtual equivalent to a real store's end-of-aisle displays. This site is a great benchmark for retailers (especially those with lots of items) because it does so much to suggest and sell specific items rather than just letting users sift through a simple A-Z index.

Throughout the site there are clean graphics, useful tables and cross links, and other examples of good fundamental design principles at work.

Figure 8.1 1-800-Music Now's page helps people who don't have any particular music in mind.

L.L. Bean

http://www.llbean.com

You don't have to live in Maine to understand the sort of cautious attention to quality and care of its customers that L.L. Bean exemplifies. L.L. Bean is considered one of the best-run mail-order companies in the world—in fact, other mail-order firms visit Bean to learn about the business practices that have made it so successful.

L.L. Bean's site (shown in Figure 8.2) shows how a company focused on customer service (which almost every retailer has to be) can translate that philosophy to the World Wide Web. For example, visitors to the site are told that L.L. Bean won't accept orders of any kind via the Web (offering mail, phone, or fax ordering options instead) until the company is 100 percent certain that its customers' credit card information will be protected. The reason for this stance is that Bean values its customers' trust, which could be severely damaged if the firm rushed ahead with a less-than-secure Web-based ordering system. As another service to its customers, the site also reminds visitors that the colors they see may vary greatly from monitor to monitor—a point that less customer-oriented retailers might overlook.

In addition, the L.L. Bean site offers a database guide to all the U.S. national parks, a great service that certainly attracts users who would be prime Bean customers. This is a perfect example of a retailer leveraging its expertise about not only its wares, but the world in which they are used, to create new business on the Web.

Some Ideas for Retail-Oriented Sites

- Create pages that act as end-of-aisle displays, using themes and stories to promote the products you offer.

- Translate your customer-service ethic to the Web by including information on returns and other store policies.

- Present additional content that will attract potential customers. For example, if your company sells cookware, build a recipe database and offer it as a free service on your Web site.

- Pay close attention to security issues and credit card use. The more comfortable users of your site are about the security of their transactions, the better off you'll be.

Figure 8.2 The cautious warnings uphold the L.L. Bean tradition of excellent customer service and trust.

- Explain to your customers the "tricks" of shopping via the Internet by providing information about such things as color variance and how transaction security works.

- Offer downloadable tools such as Adobe Acrobat order forms or catalogs for offline browsing. Consider even creating a custom program to do shopping offline (Shaw's supermarket, at **http://www.shopat.com/shaw's**, does this).

- If you're selling products that are featured at other Web sites (for example, Kodak cameras) offer links to those sites so customers can get the most information possible. Make it a point to search out "linkable" content.

Corporate Identity and Information Sites

Most corporate sites on the Internet tend to focus on the products the company makes, but a corporation is far more than a set of products and services. Corporate home pages try to explain the company itself—including its employees, executives, policies, logos, pension plans, and history—as well as offer information about how to interact with that company. This information can help people understand your company better, attract prospective employees, educate customers about your services, and serve as a handy reference for investors.

General Electric

`http://www.ge.com`

GE is one of the world's biggest companies, employing more than 100,000 people worldwide in dozens of divisions and countries. Its corporate site, while a little on the subdued side (as might be expected for such a long-established company), is nonetheless a benchmark in terms of disseminating very important corporate information. Its "Inside GE" page (shown in Figure 8.3) offers a good outline of the types of things you might offer visitors to any company site:

- *Get an overview of GE*—This section includes annual reports, links to GE divisions, and press releases, among other things.

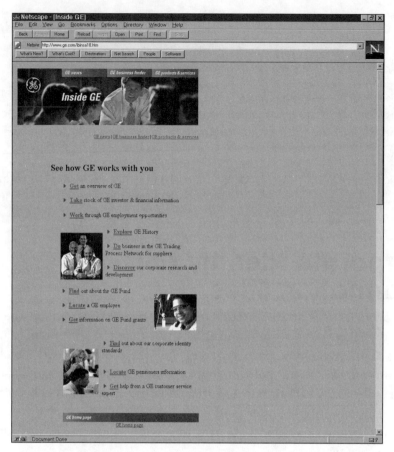

Figure 8.3 GE's home page has a multitude of information about GE and how it works with employees, customers, and vendors.

- *Take stock of GE investor & financial information*—GE has thousands of investors; distributing information to them via the Web may eventually save the company a sizable amount in investor-relations costs.

- *Work through GE employment opportunities*—Whether you employ thousands of people or just a few, one of the best things to do is post employment information.

- *Explore GE history*—Does your firm have a history? Presenting it can be a great way to trumpet past accomplishments and experience.

- *Do business in the GE Trading Process Network for suppliers*—Do you do business with other companies? If you purchase products, offer prospective suppliers information about how to pitch their services to you.

- *Discover our corporate research and development*—Find out what GE's working on now.

- *Find out about the GE Fund and get information on GE Fund grants*—Like many corporations, GE has a large fund from which it makes grants for purposes ranging from education to the arts and humanities. These sections detail what those grants have done, how they work, and how to apply for them.

- *Locate a GE employee*—Want to get in touch with someone who works at GE? While this link led to a couple of paragraphs of information rather than access to a database, many companies provide complete contact information—and even home pages—for their employees.

- *Find out about our corporate identity standards*—A large corporation like GE often produces hundreds of manuals, marketing pieces, and the like. A company usually develops an entire style manual for presenting and maintaining various corporate logos, typefaces, and preferred layouts. Since many times the production of printed items is outsourced, offering style information via the Web can make sure that contractors know how you want your company to be presented.

- *Locate GE pensioners information*—Do you run a 401k or other pension fund? How about stock options? Many corporate sites can offer information about these items via the Internet. While an internal network—that is, an intranet—might seem to be the best way to handle this task, people leave or retire and lose access to such networks. A secure site on the Internet can reconnect them to this vital information. For now, GE offers phone pointers to employees who want access to this info, but once security gets better, it could offer the information itself right on the site.

- *Get help from a GE customer service expert*—Need help with a GE product? GE gives out its customer service numbers, or you can send an email question to an expert.

Some Ideas for Corporate Identity Sites

- Think about all of the different people who will interact with your company, then design a site that assists them in doing so. Don't just say who you are when there is so much more your site can offer.

- Offer company contact information for employees and pointers to employee home pages (of course, check with your employees first).

- Does your company have partners or allies with their own Web sites? What other links might explain more about the company?

The Web Zine

I define a "Web zine" as an original publication that never existed prior to its debut on the World Wide Web. Zines tend to be among the Web's best sites, featuring tons of original content, excellent design, and widespread use of Web extensions, plug-ins, and Java. Of course, it's hardly surprising that these sites are so advanced, since most of the people behind them were among the Web's earliest and most devoted followers. Below are two zines that I check in on from time to time to see how the entire Web-publishing model is progressing.

Salon1999

http://www.salon1999.com

A joint venture between Apple and Adobe, Salon is an original magazine that is only available via the Web. Designed to be a cross between *Mother Jones*, the *New Yorker*, and the *Saturday Evening Post*, Salon is an amazing piece of work. If nothing else, it shows that a top-quality zine created especially for the World Wide Web is a whole new breed of publication.

Salon features original writers, as well as an amazingly well-run message section that can be a model for any site trying to create a bulletin board for users. Salon also features excellent layout and links to other content (as shown in Figure 8.4); overall, it's a joy to navigate and read (the use of larger-than-average text is a good way to make reading off the screen less strenuous).

Word

http://www.word.com

Like Salon1999, Word focuses on cultural, political, and cyberspace issues; makes skillful use of eye-catching graphics, font variation, and lots of original content; and features discussion boards (as well as RealAudio commentaries). One thing I like about Word is the graphics—the opening page, shown in Figure 8.5, packs a strong visual punch, but because the images are all fairly

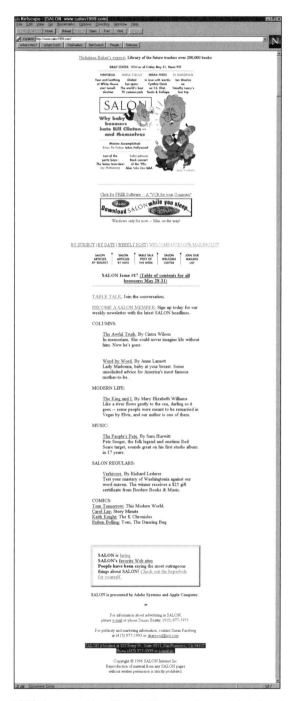

Figure 8.4 Salon1999, backed by friends like Apple and Adobe, has defined what an entirely Web-based magazine should look like.

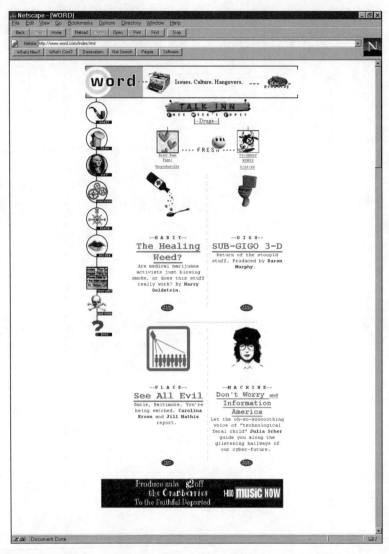

Figure 8.5 The hip Word zine is the East Coast cousin of Salon1999.

small (each less than 8 K in size), the page still loads quickly. This economy is accomplished through tables and by limiting each image to a small set of colors. Because each image uses a different set, however, the entire presentation seems colorful, even though the individual image isn't.

Word tends to be a bit more arty than other publications, so its stories are wrapped with graphics and a presentation style that tries to make the most of the Web without breaking the back of bandwidth restrictions. If you're looking to create artistic-looking yet Web-savvy layouts, Word is a nice benchmark to use.

Other Web Zine Benchmarks

Here are some other noteworthy zines for your perusal. Check them out.

Click

http://www.click.com.au

Click is a zine devoted to Web and multimedia developers that is produced in Australia. It makes clever use of tables for layout, and the graphics and articles are presented in a very crisp format.

Slate

http://www.slate.com

Slate, a brand new zine, is one of the most watched Web sites of 1996. Why? Because it's Microsoft's answer to Salon, Word, and other Web-based zines. In addition, the managing editor is Michael Kinsley, a former editor of the *New Yorker* and founder of the *New Republic*, as well as cohost of CNN's Crossfire for many years. How this publishing and media veteran, backed by Microsoft's mammoth resources, implements a Web zine will greatly influence the emerging world of original Web periodicals.

Some Ideas for Web Zine Sites

- Because Web zines are a new type of publication, with no past print legacy to protect, you should be very adventurous in defining this fledgling medium.

- Discussion groups and messaging seem to be key components of popular Web zines.

- Many zines are designed to be read offscreen, so make sure that you focus on the textual design of your site. Larger fonts, font variance, and careful use of graphics to add variety and space to the layout create a much more comfortable reading experience.

Newspapers on the Web

Newspapers are incredible things. Pick up a well-done newspaper (which, I admit, is increasingly hard to find these days) and instantly you can get a good feel for the city or area it serves. For about 50 to 75 cents, you get access to a wealth of information. The papers themselves include vast amounts of historical material, and newspaper organizations are experts about the life, culture, history, business, and people of their area. In short, newspapers are a lot more than the paper they're printed on.

Many people feel the World Wide Web will kill newspapers. But while newspaper readership has indeed dropped in the new-media age, the underlying mission of being an expert local information provider actually positions newspapers to be among the Web's most compelling sites. Some of the best newspaper sites bring to the Internet far more than just a duplicate of that day's headlines.

Los Angeles Times

http://www.latimes.com

There are well over a dozen major newspapers available on the Web, but in my mind one of the best is the *Los Angeles Times'* site (shown in Figure 8.6). Some of the things that make it an interesting benchmark are its use of Adobe Acrobat for downloadable versions of the paper rendered in major detail, a specialized news agent (called Hunter), an extensive archive with a search engine, and related-content links that include museum listings, city council minutes, local community news, and selected weekly publications.

The designers of the *L.A. Times* site used forms and list boxes to create a really easy-to-navigate table of contents covering all the paper's articles for that day. More importantly, the site draws on the *Times'* strength as a repository of information about the greater Southern California area. This depth, combined with the site's simple design and use of such cutting-edge features as Acrobat and downloadable content, make the *Times* an outstanding Web newspaper.

Portland Press Herald

http://www.portland.com

It might seem a little nepotistic for me to plug my hometown newspaper as a benchmark site, but the awards the *Press Herald* has won for its site to back up

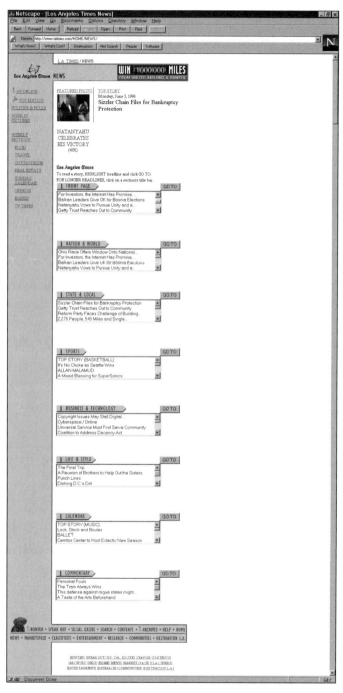

Figure 8.6   The *L.A. Times* is one of the nation's best newspapers, as well as one of the best newspaper sites.

my view that it truly is one of the better newspaper designs on the World Wide Web. The *Portland Press Herald*'s site (shown in Figure 8.7) exemplifies the idea that just as a printed newspaper can be the center of information for a community, so too can its Web site.

The opening page of a recent issue showed some of the special things the *Press Herald* has done to make its site worthy of frequent visits by Maine residents. First the page offers all of the regular stories from the day's paper, plus links to several days' worth of archived material. Other features include a dining and entertainment guide, as well as links to other sites related to current events and Maine in general. Rounding out the site are supplemental areas such as Baynet (which focuses on the greater Casco Bay area of Maine, including tide information, message boards, history, maps, and articles from the paper concerning Casco Bay).

This wealth of content is nestled in a stellar design (I find the opening black-and-white photo that sits atop each page to be an especially classy touch), and the print version of the newspaper reminds readers every day to check out online content that complements particular stories. More than many other newspapers' Web sites, the digital version of the *Press Herald* gives people who have never been to the local community (in this case, Maine) a detailed, well-rounded picture of the area.

Nando Times

http://www.nando.net

The Nando Times is consistently hailed as one of the best news sites on the World Wide Web. Born out of the efforts of the Raleigh, North Carolina–based *News and Observer* newspaper, Nando has grown so much that it is now a entity almost unto itself. The Nando Times includes many different news sources, including the Associated Press and other wire services.

The Times' front page (shown in Figure 8.8) is organized much like that of a typical newspaper, with a sample photograph and section headings across the top. Inside the site, stories are organized in summary fashion and presented in time order, much like a traditional wire service would do.

Nando also offers specialized presentations of its arts and entertainment news (called the Third Rave) and sports services, plus customizable news services for a fee. The entire site—especially the Third Rave section—is tightly organized

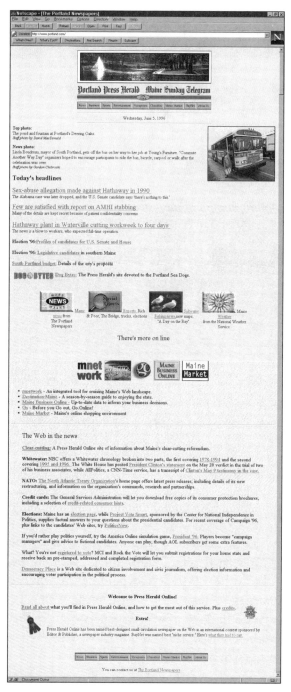

Figure 8.7   My hometown paper, the *Portland Press Herald,* has won awards for its informative Web site—it's better than the paper itself!

Figure 8.8 The Nando Times was one of the first innovative newspaper sites on the Web.

and uses just a smattering of graphics and presentation, since the copy is the star when it comes to news. NandoX, meanwhile, is a page that points browsers to other sites they might find interesting on the Internet.

One other interesting idea is NandoNext, which contains news stories of interest to young people written by high-schoolers around the North Carolina area. The paper and printing costs alone would have prohibited this kind of service in the regular paper, but on the World Wide Web it becomes possible. NandoNext is a great example of how newspapers can use their journalistic, presentation, and publishing skills in conjunction with Web sites to create whole new ways of reporting.

One of the first Web-based newspapers, the Nando Times still is one of the few sites really trying to figure out how the Web creates new opportunities for newspapers in this world.

Other Benchmark Newspaper Sites

Here's another newspaper site doing some interesting things.

The Washington Post

`http://www.washingtonpost.com`

The Washington Post has been building an extensive site that draws on its intended participation in the now-defunct Interchange project, which was based on SGML (the language that gave birth to HTML). While I haven't seen it at the time I write this, I am certain it will be a very comprehensive site that will set new standards for successful newspaper-based Web sites.

> ## Some Ideas for Newspaper Sites
>
> - Develop pages and content that draw on the wealth of local information and contacts most newspapers have.
>
> - Develop links to content on the Web that is relevant either to stories in the paper or to the area it serves.
>
> - Don't forget to promote the Web site in the print version by mentioning links in sidebars or at the end of as many stories as possible.
>
> - Explore new reporting options that are now feasible because such costs as printing and distribution aren't in the mix.
>
> - Create downloadable versions of the paper. The daily news is still something people like to read at the kitchen table or in a coffee shop, not off their computer screen.
>
> - Don't forget the amazing possibilities of all the archived material a typical newspaper can have. Things like old photos and historical information about people and places can be really useful to people.

Magazines on the Web

These sites are the Web versions of existing pulp-based magazines. Unlike their cousins, Web zines, these sites need to complement and work with the regular publication. If they are too much like the paper publication, readers will either view the site and stop buying the printed version or ignore the Web site because they've already read the magazine and know they won't find anything new. Thus, even more than is true for newspapers, Web versions of printed magazines need to make sure the sites aren't trying to occupy the same space as the original product. In addition, they need to maintain the high production standards that regular magazine readers expect while offering more interactive elements than just a letter-to-the-editors box. Below are several magazine sites that are trying to carve out such a symbiotic relationship with their printed counterparts.

Elle Magazine
http://www.elle.com

The *Elle* Web site showcases one of the cardinal rules of transferring an existing periodical to the Web: *Offer Web-specific content.* In fact, the first item on its opening table of contents links the user to Quicktime fashion shows, tours of top designers' studios, and more features they would never see in print.

Having created this niche for itself, the site also packages existing *Elle* content well, using excellent layout, several forms, and an extensive messaging center, as shown in Figure 8.9.

Inc. Magazine
http://www.inc.com

Inc. magazine has always been one of my favorites because of its consistently fresh layout and attention to content and resources. So it makes sense that if anyone would impress me with the Web version of their magazine, it would be *Inc.* Sure enough, they have.

Like *Elle, Inc.* immediately guides visitors to original Web content (here appropriately titled "Beyond the Magazine"). It also uses forms and scripts to provide interactive versions of worksheets that help entrepreneurs work out various business decisions with advice. There's a connection center to help match up people who can help each other, links to small business resources on the Web, and even a way to customize the site to your specific interests.

Thoughtful features like these make *Inc.* (shown in Figure 8.10) a great benchmark site. Over the years, special-interest magazines like *Inc.* build up knowledge until they become experts on the topic they cover—in *Inc.*'s case, small business. When they get to the Web, these magazines can capitalize on that knowledge by making their sites into central broadcasting points for all of

Figure 8.9   *Elle* Magazine is about style, but its Web site is about how a magazine can embrace multimedia to extend its content.

the information and wisdom they've collected. *Inc.*'s site certainly represents an excellent example of this type of migration to the Web.

Some Ideas for Magazine Sites

- A Web site shouldn't displace the use of the magazine (especially if the site cannot justify itself in terms of revenue), nor should a it be a rehash of magazine content. Original content that complements the printed version is the key to success.

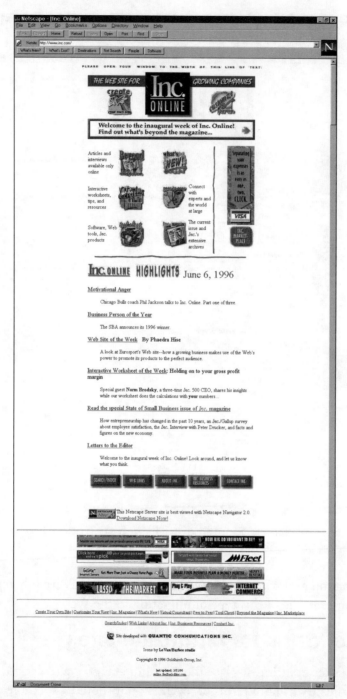

Figure 8.10 *Inc.* magazine's Web site is a powerful example of a magazine extending its editorial expertise to the Web.

- Build the site around the magazine's expertise on the topic, not the magazine's writing itself.

- Many major magazines have excess content or international versions with different stories that can be excellent complementary material.

- Make sure that the look of the Web site is similar to that of the printed magazine.

Narrowcasting

Almost every site on the Web engages in narrowcasting to some degree. Certain sites, though, really show off the incredible possibilities the Web offers in terms of catering to very specific audiences. A good narrowcasting site on the Web might involve nothing more than an audience of several thousand people.

Studio B

http://www.studiob.com

Studio B, a site devoted to computer book publishers, writers, editors, and readers, is narrowcasting at its finest. Run by a literary agency that specializes in representing book authors, the site is quite comprehensive and well designed (see Figure 8.11).

For very narrow sites such as Studio B, though, sometimes the benefit has to be as specific as the site. The advantage of Studio B is that by pulling together all sorts of computer book authors, the agency can more easily market its services to them, and by sponsoring discussions it gains valuable insights on the industry. Thus, the increased access to authors alone provides the agency with a welcome return on its investment in the site.

Some Ideas for Narrowcasting Sites

- Narrowcasting sites work well when you create ways for members to communicate with each other; list servers or message boards provide an excellent means to do this.

- In general, the narrower your focus is in terms of purpose or interest, the more expertise and detail your site needs to contain.

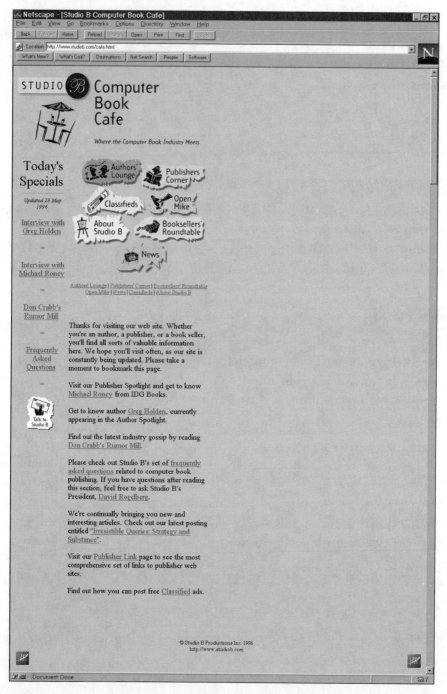

Figure 8.11 Studio B shows how the Web can open up even the narrowest of markets.

- The narrowest sites (such as Studio B) can't generate revenue through major advertising or by selling retail items, so other benefits will have to be evident in order to justify the cost of creating the site.

Archive Site

A Web archive site is an interface for retrieving content (such as documents or software) from a vast catalog of items. While some magazines offer recent back issues on their main site, archive sites might contain several years of past issues.

Many times larger sites are built around an archive. The idea is simple: By providing access to a large storehouse of material, these sites attract users of that content, to whom the site may then offer advertising or other services. Two major sites on the Web work very well with this model.

inquiry.com

http://www.inquiry.com

inquiry.com is quickly becoming a major resource for people who develop products for or work in the computer and software industry. One of the site's main attractions is its growing collection of past articles from several of the industry's major magazines and newsweeklies (such as *Communications Week*). Users can also search the archive in a variety of ways, as shown in Figure 8.12.

Over time inquiry.com has expanded to become a full-service stop by adding product literature listings and company information to its database of articles. An investment of roughly four million dollars by SoftBank when the site was several months old allowed inquiry.com to acquire the rights to even more articles to add to their database, thereby pushing the site even closer to becoming the top developer site on the Internet.

Viewpoint Labs

http://www.viewpoint.com

Another successful archive site is Viewpoint Labs (shown in Figure 8.13), which is the largest repository in the world for 3D object model files. Viewpoint offers not only its own custom models, but also several large public-domain model archives to which it has acquired the rights (such as the China Lake archive that some folks at the U.S. Air Force set up). By taking over the

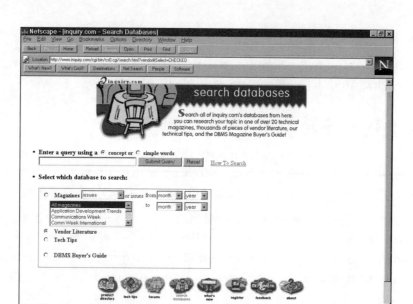

Figure 8.12 inquiry.com supports computer professionals with tons of archived magazine articles.

management and building a good interface to these free archives, Viewpoint attracts all kinds of modelers to its site, where they can purchase models from Viewpoint's for-sale library as well.

Other Benchmark Archive Sites

There are a number of other good archive sites on the Web. The following example is just one you might find while you're looking around.

Corbis

http://www.corbis.com

Sometimes referred to as "Bill Gates' other software company," Corbis is really much more. Realizing early on that a digital world would need to reproduce photographs and other visual works as easy and readably as the nonwired world does, Gates created Corbis. By combining online rights to famous art collections (such as the Ansel Adams photographs) with major stock photo archives (like the Bettman Archives), as well as creating original photos and drawings, Corbis is building one of the largest online archives in the world.

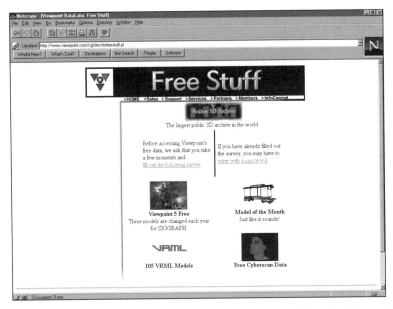

Figure 8.13 Viewpoint Labs recently bought and improved the Avalon archive to attract users to its commercial offerings.

A visit to the Corbis Web site allows you to browse through some of the archived offerings; you can also download special software to improve the viewing quality of the images. Each item is presented in slide view and also contains a brief synopsis of the photo's origin. Efficiently organized and managed, the Corbis archive is a useful benchmark for sites looking to offer similar benefits to users.

Some Ideas for Archive-Oriented Sites

- The interface for sorting through and retrieving archived content will make or break the site. All of the sites mentioned above offer excellent systems for retrieving content.

- Before a user downloads any material, offer him or her the ability to preview the content properly. (Viewpoint Labs offers a great example of this.)

- Build a robust site around an archive by surrounding it with other relevant materials.

The Search Engine

While I doubt many of you will be starting up a Web-wide search engine service, I'll discuss some of the best examples here, in part because the interfaces and directions some of them use are useful benchmarks if and when you set up a site search engine. As sites continue to grow, such site-specific engines can be a very useful addition.

The Web Spider: Lycos/Alta Vista/Excite

```
http://www.lycos.com
http://www.altavista.digital.com
http://www.excite.com
```

There are two types of search engine strategies. The first type of engine, the Web spider, is organized around text searches, and combs through a database of computer-indexed Web pages. These search engines will run through your site and index it for you, then provide the tools for your users to retrieve these pages based upon their search criteria. Unfortunately, even though these top-notch search engines are blazingly fast and thorough, they can be *too* thorough—bringing up every page that contains a link, even those that are irrelevant to the user.

The Indexed Site: Yahoo

```
http://www.yahoo.com
```

The second search engine option is to create your own summaries of each page on your site, index them according to publisher-defined keywords and summaries, then offer a detailed index to every page (and perhaps a search option that returns matches to keywords or text in the summaries). This is how Yahoo works. It's a bit more organized and precise, but it's success depends on your ability to summarize and keyword each page correctly and completely to offer the best searching functionality.

Some Ideas for Search Engine Sites

- Don't think in terms of one type of search engine. Only through a combination of both types of approaches—indexing *and* Web spiders—can you give users really good search abilities.

Advertising Site

Purely advertising-oriented sites are becoming increasingly common on the Web. Unlike with print or television advertising, though, Web users generally have to choose to visit and participate in an advertising site. This fact creates a special challenge: How do advertising sites build brand image or present product information in a manner that maintains user interest long enough to make a positive impression? Recently I've found a couple of companies whose exploratory efforts might serve as early examples of successful Web advertising sites.

Snapple

http://www.snapple.com

The makers of Snapple beverages have always been known for their quirky advertising style. Their Web site efforts, which are true to their familiar spirit, incorporate some key ideas that other advertising sites should consider.

Called the Snapplesphere, the current site is a series of pages devoted to exploring the world of Snapple. It works in conjunction with the company's current television and print advertising ideas, building on the theme that Snapple wants to be the number three soft-drink company (one of the site's sections includes a trivia contest about famous threes). Other pages on the site allow you to script plays about Snapple, learn various Snapple facts, and so on.

All of the elements are presented in an entertaining manner and try to build some interactivity between the browser and the site. Any advertising-oriented site is a tough sell, but Snapple is experimenting in the hope of creating a site that people want to visit, that they remember, and that improves the Snapple brand image in the mind of the visitor.

Some Ideas for Advertising Sites

- Make sure your site complements existing ad campaigns in other media.

- Consider going into more depth—sometimes products that need to be explained thoroughly are actually better suited to Web advertising.

- Think of various attractions to offer. Interactive games, contests, and other elements may be needed to pull people into a site about a product they may not feel compelled to check out.

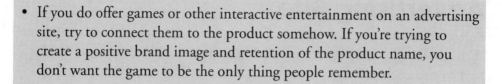

- If you do offer games or other interactive entertainment on an advertising site, try to connect them to the product somehow. If you're trying to create a positive brand image and retention of the product name, you don't want the game to be the only thing people remember.

Game and Entertainment Sites

Game and entertainment sites are already enormously popular, because people want to be entertained. The trick is to get users to keep coming back, and to get advertisers to realize that fun pays.

Riddler

http://www.riddler.com

The Riddler is one of the top Web gaming sites. It offers a range of trivia and word games where participants earn points toward prizes by answering questions correctly. (Throughout the entire experience, Riddler displays ads for other sites and products, as demonstrated in Figure 8.14.) The games are simple in design in order to support the Web's somewhat limited infrastructure, but still are presented in a very polished manner.

Riddler's site is an interesting benchmark for several reasons. One is how the site integrates the products and advertisements into the experience; players compete for "chips" that are offered in various product categories (for example, 500 Microsoft Visual C++ chips). Another is that the system is inherently designed for repeat visits, since it is hard to win anything substantive in one day. The Riddler designers are also embracing other technologies as they seek to expand their game offerings—the site recently launched crossword puzzles done with Java.

The Spot

http://www.thespot.com

While most sites seek to offer entertainment based on interactive gaming experiences, the folks at American Cybercast—taking their cue from daytime television and MTV—are offering a non-gaming entertainment site with The Spot, which is sort of a cross between a soap opera and MTV's "The Real World."

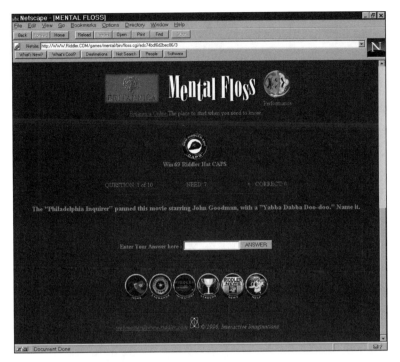

Figure 8.14   Fans of Riddler get hooked on the games, and then are exposed to
lots of Web advertisements.

Real people living in a house in Malibu, California, post narratives of their
daily lives and relationships to a site on the Web, some of it being triggered by
various activities that The Spot's producers set up on the site. Fans can learn
about the characters (see Figure 8.15) and what is going on by visiting every
day (and exposing themselves to various ads embedded in the site). They can
also send email to people living at The Spot, as well as view past episodes.

The Spot may seem a step back to some who see the World Wide Web as a
haven for more intellectually meaningful fare, but it does offer up excellent
production values, and it also helps to prove that entertainment on the Web
doesn't necessarily mean games.

Other Benchmark Gaming and Entertainment Sites

There are dozens of other gaming sites, including multiuser dungeons
MUDs) for role-playing games (see Yahoo's MUD listing at **http://
www.yahoo.com**). For the latest in games being created with Java, take a look

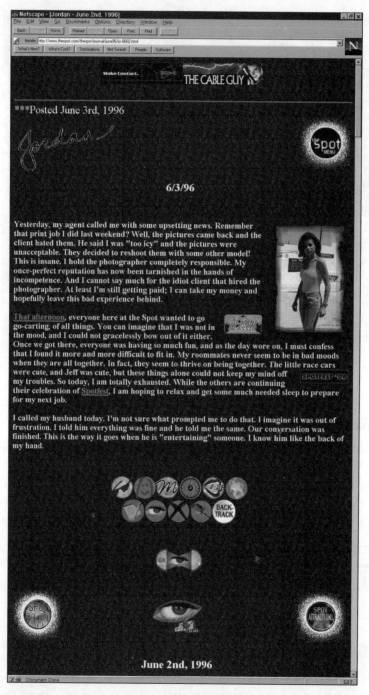

Figure 8.15 The Spot is trying to re-create the success of the TV soap opera in the next great mass medium—the Internet.

at Gamelan's Java Game listings (**http://www.gamelan.com**; see separate discussion below). Or check out Pop Rocket (**http://www.poprocket.com**), a company creating cutting-edge Shockwave games for the Web.

Another company to keep an eye on is AT&T's Downtown Digital (**http://www.dtd.com**), which has been experimenting with games and other forms of Web-based entertainment.

Some Ideas for Gaming and Entertainment Sites

- There are many ways to author Web games; research the various ways (I'll have more information on these later in the book) before you start working on one.

- If you're building a major site that might feature a gaming component, consider bringing in a seasoned game developer to help. Original game development, in both a technical sense and a design sense, is not as easy as it seems.

- Entertainment sites need not consist only of games. Web soap operas and other forms of entertainment (such as animated stories, music, and contests) might also be considered.

Comprehensive Site

When the World Wide Web began to explode in popularity, some people felt that comprehensive online services would disappear as dozens of specialized sites destroyed their reason for existing. This, however, has not been the case. Instead, online services are migrating to the Web, becoming major tour guides and organizers of what has become an incredibly large (and to many, unwieldy) universe.

In addition, site developers are finding that being big and comprehensive isn't so bad after all. Two sites that give you a complete picture on what's going on in the bigger-is-better department are outlined in the following sections.

Pathfinder

`http://www.pathfinder.com`

Pathfinder is Time Warner's comprehensive site for the World Wide Web. Being a large media conglomerate, Time Warner has a movie studio, a large publishing arm, several record companies, and both television and interactive game production divisions. The Pathfinder service tries to combine all of Time Warner's content into one large site. The giant corporation is also trying to embellish the site with a host of original Web-specific material, including games like SPQR and Web zines like Daily Spectrum and Seidman's Online Insider.

Pathfinder's organization is a little haphazard, and the navigation is a little tough. It's quickly becoming a huge site, however, and some of the stuff the designers are doing is somewhat innovative. They're also beginning to charge for certain services on a monthly basis, so Pathfinder can be seen as a major experiment in what people might be willing to pay for above and beyond access to the Web itself.

MSN
http://www.msn.com

The Microsoft Network (MSN) began life as an online service that was intended to compete with America Online and CompuServe. But as the Web began to be seen as the online service of the future—and Microsoft rushed to be a major component of the Web's future—the software behemoth began repositioning MSN as its comprehensive consumer site for the Web.

One of the major problems for comprehensive sites is how to help people find interesting content. This is an easy task when you're a simple Web site with a lot of focus, but not when you're trying to offer an enormous array of services. A key to the MSN interface is its customizable home page, where users can select particular links and information to greet them whenever they sign on to MSN (many times this becomes their Web browser's default startup page). Not only does Microsoft gain a lot of insight into their users' likes and dislikes this way, but they can use this information to present more customizable content throughout the site—causing items that a particular user would be interested in to "bubble up" where they might otherwise stay submerged.

Like Pathfinder, MSN is a work in progress. Also like Pathfinder, though, it promises to be one of the biggest, most diverse sites on the Web—and to charge for special access as well. If you're planning a large service (well, perhaps not quite as big as MSN), it might be worth your while to see

some of the things Microsoft is doing and check out the overall quality of
the site.

Other Benchmark Comprehensive Sites

Prodigy
http://www.prodigy.com

Prodigy is undergoing massive changes. After being sold by Sears and IBM,
the service is being totally rebuilt around the World Wide Web.

AOL's GNN
http://www.gnn.com

America Online recently purchased this service—which was started by Web
book developers O'Reilly and Associates—and is recasting GNN as its major
Web-based online service.

CompuServe
http://www.compuserve.com

CompuServe recently announced that in conjunction with Microsoft, it is
moving its entire online service to the World Wide Web via Microsoft's
Normandy online server system.

Some Ideas for Comprehensive Sites

- Navigation is key. For any site that gets big—and especially sites as large
  as the ones discussed in this section—creating easy-to-use navigation
  systems is essential. Things like customizable home pages, daily "what's
  new" pages, and email newsletters are important tools.

- Many of the above sites are being built by online services that learned
  they couldn't afford to ignore the World Wide Web. Thus the goal
  typically is to make these sites into the ultimate combination of new
  proprietary content providers and tour guides to the greater Web.

Hubs

Index sites such as Lycos and Yahoo are gigantic listings of all that the World
Wide Web has to offer. In trying to be all-encompassing, however, they leave

lots of room for sites that want to become mini-Yahoos for a particular area. I call these types of sites *hubs* because they act like hubs in the airline business —gathering passengers from other areas and then sending them back out to new destinations. With their specific coverage of one topic they can be extremely precise in their links, helping to weed out the large amount of irrelevant results that the larger search engines tend to generate.

Hubs are sort of a variation on narrowcasting. They tend to focus on a very defined segment of the Web, but they become hubs because their real draw is an extensive list of pointers to other sites. Once a hub site becomes established for a particular area, the amount of users passing through make it a prime location for Web advertising. A successful hub should ideally receive more hits than 95 percent of any of its target destinations. Following are a couple of examples of well-run World Wide Web hubs.

Gamelan
http://www.gamelan.com

Gamelan (shown in Figure 8.16) is the resource for Java applets on the World Wide Web. By indexing and providing links to all the major Java applets available on the Web, it is quickly becoming one of the most important sites to Java developers across the globe. The result is simple: Gamelan will have a lock on the major ad revenue that will be targeted toward this quickly emerging software development industry.

Yahoo San Francisco
http://www.sfbay.com

One of the hottest Hub business is one that AOL, Yahoo, and Microsoft have all said will be huge: digital cities. These online sites are essentially hubs to the Internet whose topic is a specific city. One of the first implementations of these that you should check out is Yahoo San Francisco, which is essentially a Yahoo-like site for the San Francisco Bay Area.

Some Ideas for Hub Sites

• A hub is concerned with navigation more than anything else. Building a comprehensive set of informative links to a specific set of sites is the first and foremost role of a hub.

Figure 8.16   Got Java? Gamelan is now an indispensable tool in the Java movement.

- Organization of these links is also essential. Look at Yahoo and other well-executed hubs for key ideas on how to organize large lists of links.

- Once the links and navigation are established, it pays to begin building other content around the links in order to create a more robust site.

9

Do one thing and do it very well—that attitude is what makes this chapter's benchmarks stand out.

Design Implementation Benchmarks: Specific Examples

In Chapter 8 I chose benchmarks based on the overall implementation of a site. I then provided an overview of the types of sites that are developed, then examined particular sites that seemed to succeed in each genre. But if looking at full sites is one way to discover secrets about good Web development, another is searching for benchmark implementations of either certain kinds of development or individual aspects of sites whose overall impact may not be as great. That's what we'll be doing in this chapter.

Pushing the Edge of Technology

For power users and developers, there's nothing like visiting a site that makes full use of what I call "bleeding edge" technology: all the special tags in a browser, applet technology, awesome graphics, streaming sound, and so on. About the only thing that's better is seeing this stuff used in a cohesive package. Checking out sites that attempt to blend various top-notch technologies is a great way to focus your thoughts on bringing whole new ideas to the Web, not just dressing up old sites with the latest gimmick.

Baseball Live
http://www.sportsline.com

Several sites have taken innovative approaches based on Macromedia's Shockwave technology. At Baseball Live, for instance, you can watch an animated version of a real major league baseball game as it happens. At any point you can call up a huge stat sheet on any player in the lineup, check other games that are in progress, or browse the box scores of games that have ended. While the graphics are fairly primitive, the effect is fascinating, and the sounds of the ballpark make you feel like you're sitting behind home plate. Can't make it to the game? Check out Baseball Live and see the future of Web sports broadcasting.

Enliven
http://www.narrative.com

Enliven is a state-of-the-art new multimedia streaming technology that I'll talk more about in Chapter 14. You've got to go check out the demos on Narrative's site, since they represent some of the most amazingly well done multimedia content on the Web. It's all enabled by Enliven, which can enable developers to create large multimedia content similar to what they put on

CD-ROMs (in fact the demos are of products that previously were CD-ROM games). If you want to see the cutting edge of multimedia on the Web, check out this site.

Combining Top Plug-Ins to Create Potent Sites

In the summer of 1996, a pair of sites (both of which should still be up when this book hits the shelves) demonstrated how you can put together several plug-in components—in these cases, Macromedia's Shockwave and Apple's QuickTime and QuickTime VR—to build high-impact sites.

Nissan's Pathfinder

`http://www.nissanmotors.com/pathfinder/gear.cgi`

The Nissan advertising site for its Pathfinder vehicle is listed by several review sites as one of the hottest-designed pages on the Web. Using Netscape 2.0, QuickTime, QuickTime VR, and Shockwave, it re-creates an entire African Safari which is both fun and informative. Most of all, you can't help but be reminded about the rugged, high-endurance off-road qualities of a Nissan Pathfinder, which is exactly what Nissan wants. Only through this high use of technological plug-ins could Nissan get me to stick around long enough or present such a cool impression.

The bottom line when it comes to using plug-ins is to make them worth the effort. Nissan's goals and success in meeting them with its Pathfinder site exemplify that design ethic.

Apple's *Mission Impossible* Game

`http://www.mission.apple.com`

Apple based its summer advertising on the blockbuster *Mission Impossible* film featuring Tom Cruise. To highlight its Internet technologies, like QuickTime and Apple Internet Servers, the firm commissioned a Web game site loaded with exciting multimedia content. While the *Mission Impossible* site is also burdened by the sometimes-lengthy downloads that go with the territory on the cutting edge of Web technology, such bandwidth-related issues will become less of a hang-up as modem speeds improve.

Note: One way to see which sites push Web technology to the limits is to check out the showcase pages of leading high-tech firms like Macromedia and Apple.

How Sites Can Push the Technological Envelope

1. Keep up on the breaking technologies and new versions of current products.
It seems that every day a new exciting product for Web developers is launched, and every three months an entire wave of new versions is released. As a result, it's easy to lose track of all the plug-ins, Java applets, and other technologies that are hitting the Web; but if you're going to push the bleeding edge you can't afford to fall behind. The best solution is to keep up with the trade publications (listed at the end of this book) and check in regularly on the major technology sites (listed at the end of this chapter and elsewhere in this book).

2. Make sure you offer "Web installation pages."
I've already said this at least once, but it bears repeating. If your site requires multiple plug-ins and special configurations of browsers, computers, and the like, include a page that helps users find, install, and use everything they're going to need to view your site at its best.

One useful idea is to explain up front what users will miss if they don't have a specific plug-in (for example, "Without [name of plug-in] you will miss all the commentary available for each painting on our site!" or "[Name of plug-in] is not a necessity, but without it you won't be able to view the Acrobat versions of our paper."). By using explanatory text, people can judge for themselves if the plug-in is really a requirement, or if it's just an embellishment to your site's content.

3. During design, assume everyone has fast connections.
When I'm trying to create a technologically superior site, I approach it from the standpoint that everyone has a T1 in their house. If you intend to push the limit, don't try to start with a constraint like a 14.4 modem. Once I've gotten as far as the initial design, then I add in the bandwidth constraints and figure out what features can make it through to the next phase. You have to assume that a major technology site is going to be

bandwidth intense, so don't commit to the bandwidth before you've committed to the technology.

The essential idea is the same as when you go out in cold weather—you overdress, because once you're outside you can always take off layers of clothes until you're comfortable, whereas if you underdressed, it's too late to add anything. By stripping your design ideas away from the highest possible ideal, you should end up with the most technology you could have possibly gotten through the pipe.

Getting the Most from a Minimalist Approach

Let's face it—many Web sites and pages are overdone, with too many graphics. Some great sites, in contrast, take a very minimal approach. They use just enough graphics to avoid a text-only look, and they make the text digestible instead of forcing users to download pages and pages of information all at once.

Developers can learn from these sites how to make a little go a long way. Below are some sites that keep things simple in terms of graphics and plug-ins, but still have a crisp, professional look to them.

Netscape and Microsoft

http://www.netscape.com
http://www.microsoft.com

Someone once joked that Netscape's site on the Web is one of the few sites that isn't "Netscape enhanced." The same could be said for Microsoft's site. Both avoid backgrounds and frames for the most part, and neither makes much use of their scripting languages, plug-ins, or applets. Even so, both are nice-looking sites, with small but effective graphics and excellent layout (often using tables). Perhaps as the browser wars heat up more they'll do more showcasing of their technologies and move away from this approach, but it's obvious that both companies are trying to keep their sites straightforward and let other companies push the envelope with customized features.

RealAudio
http://www.realaudio.com

RealAudio's site on the Web has never been one that stood out in the presentation category—after all, this is a site more interested in sound than in pretty pictures. But I continually find myself telling people whose sites are cluttered with too much eye candy to check out RealAudio's site. It doesn't fuss with tons of fancy content, and yet I think it has a distinctly good look to it. Go see for yourself.

Using Database Technology

Database technology is going to become the major engine behind most sites in the future. Marrying large archives of data directly to Web pages and applets will produce amazingly dynamic and informative sites. So far, not many sites are really taking advantage of database technology, but even so there are some powerful examples of what can be done.

MSN's Customizable Start Page
http://www.msn.com

One way that Web developers will use database technology is to customize sites to a user's tastes. For instance, Microsoft's MSN division lets users select from an array of options for a personalized home page. Users enter their preferences and other information on a form, which is then stored in a database that is referred to when they log onto the site. This is a nice example of how the ability to gather customer profiles can be translated into a more appealing and personally involving site.

Interesting Graphics

I'll devote more space later in this book to the entire realm of Web graphics, but the subject deserves some attention here. The criteria for "great" graphics are certainly situational—for some it's the absolute quality of the graphic, while for others the time it takes to display the image is a factor as well. Here I'd like to highlight certain sites that use graphics to heighten not just the look of their site, but its overall functionality.

Red Herring Magazine
http://www.herring.com

Red Herring's site doesn't try to compete with graphics powerhouses like SGI and Alias, but for me it's a benchmark all the same. The icons are well-drawn, nearly 3D objects that play with the shadowing made possible by a white background. Not only do they present a fine-looking home page for the site, they convey the information for the pages they lead to—the icon with the Rolodex takes me to a contacts page, the one with the microphone is clearly linked to an announcements page, and so on. Icons are nothing new to the Web or computers, but Red Herring's site seems to use them particularly well.

id Software
http://www.idsoftware.com

Rendering text as graphics is an excellent way to create distinctive layouts, as well as provide lots of control over layout options. Since text is delivered as a graphic form, it can take on any characteristics and positioning. This flexibility just isn't available in HTML. id Software's site is a great showcase for this approach. Keep in mind, though, that for large text-oriented sites this really isn't a great choice.

Companies oriented toward "new media" tend to have the most innovative sites in terms of graphics. For examples, check out the game giant Virgin at **http://www.vie.com** or 3D modeling software developers Alias|Wavefront at **http://www.alias.com**.

Well-Designed Navigation

In Chapters 5, 6, and 7, I spent a decent amount of time talking about navigation issues. Many large sites remind me of old New England farmhouses where each addition is simply slapped onto the old homestead with no planning or attempts at integration. In contrast, a site that is well structured and easy to get around in is a joy to encounter. You don't get lost, it's always easy to return to the home page or jump quickly to other pages of relevant interest, and every link is clearly defined and presented. Let's look at who's doing some cool things in the navigation department.

Yahoo

http://www.yahoo.com

Being a large archive of site summaries and listings, Yahoo needed a really well-defined navigation system so people can glide through its hundreds of pages to quickly find what they need. And so Yahoo turned to one of the most organized entities in the world—the library. The basic system is designed by someone with a degree in Library Science. Yahoo has applied a traditional organization scheme to its site and made it quite easy to jump around without losing site of where you are.

One thing Yahoo does that only a few other sites (such as C|Net) do is show the user how they clicked through to where they are. In the process they also provide an easy-to-manage backtracking system for users to navigate with. Look at Figure 9.1, which shows me buried within the Yahoo site. Note the topic 1: topic 2: topic 3: topic 4 link list at the top of the screen, which gives me an exact listing of the pages I moved through to get where I am. This is a great feature that many sites may want to implement, especially if their site contains a lot of branching.

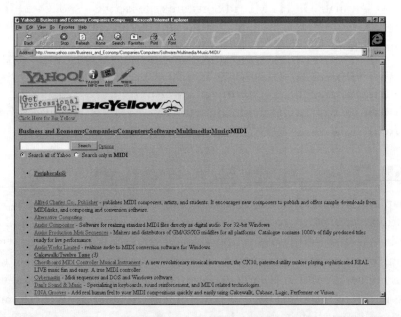

Figure 9.1   Note the long list of links near the top—this navigation system allows for quick backtracking in a highly layered Web site.

Apple Computer
`http://www.apple.com`

To be honest, I don't think Apple's site is among the best of the bunch, but a few navigational items that it has created are great examples. First look at Figure 9.2, which shows a common form of navigation on sites with a lot of content. It's a drop-down list of pages on Apple's Web site that allow users to quickly jump to a specific area without crowding the Web page with dozens of links. Also check out Figure 9.3, which is a complete overview map of Apple's Web site. Many companies are using this style of image map to help people quickly move around, but Apple's is especially well done.

Email Newsletters

The email newsletter is quickly rising in popularity as sites learn that even their most reliable users need reminders to visit and especially like to be informed of new content. Some sites send newsletters on a regular basis (weekly, biweekly, or monthly), while the rest wait until they have something new that is worth crowing about. In any case, the basic idea is

Figure 9.2   Apple isn't the first site to use drop-down lists—many sites are condensing long lists of similar links.

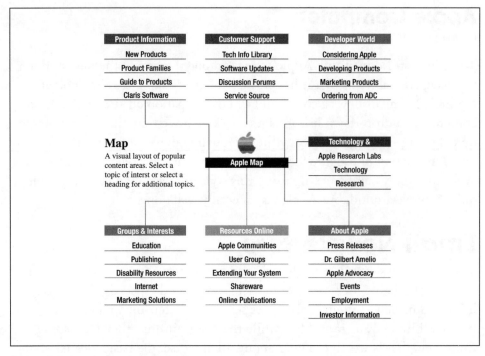

Figure 9.3 Lots of sites are adding clear overview maps of their Web sites.

simple—don't wait for people to think about you; send a reminder that you're thinking about them. A newsletter that does this can be a great asset to building a continuing community of browsers for your Web site.

C|Net

http://www.cnet.com

I subscribe to several email newsletters. The weekly C|Net dispatch is a well-organized newsletter that really gives a strong feel for what's going on at the site. Check out the sidebar to see a few things this newsletter does well.

To sample C|Net's newsletter, send email to **subscribe@cnet.com** with the following, and only the following, in the message body:

subscribe dispatch your_name

Of course, instead of "your_name", type your email address.

What Makes a Good Email Newsletter

The major job of most email newsletters is to drive people back to a particular site as soon (and as often) as possible. With thousands of sites to choose from, users can get pretty absentminded about coming back to your site—even if they want to come back. A good email newsletter not only reminds them, but helps them find their way back to your site. It also pays attention to the following principles:

1. Help users cut through the clutter of your site.
Structure your newsletter to help people navigate your site. Give them URLs so they can jump straight to pages that you highlight. Identify new content and upcoming additions, and give brief summaries about the site's features (including features that aren't new, as reminders). Don't just sing the standard praises of, "We're great, and check us out this week!"

2. Send it out on a regular basis.
People get lots of email, so do what you can to ensure they read yours. One way of getting people to read your newsletter is to send it on a regular basis. For instance, because C|Net's newsletter is weekly, every Monday I know to look for it. Another idea is to use things like all capital letters or special characters to make your email stand out in someone's in-box, such as:

ABCD'S WEEKLY UPDATE!!! 10/12/96

or

+++ ABCD Sites! — Email Newsletter 10/12/96 +++.

3. Add a quick highlights section or table of contents at the top of the document.
Many people won't scroll down to read an entire newsletter unless they know they'll find something worthwhile, so make sure to list the contents clearly in the first several lines.

4. Make those URLs stand out.
Don't bury URLs in a document; do like C|Net does and put them on their own line by themselves, using the full http:// prefix. This makes it easy for someone viewing the mail to click directly on the links (if they're using a Netscape mail program, for example) or cut and paste the URL

tags into their browser (if they're someone like me, who still uses the old
CompuServe mail program).

**5. Keep lines short so the document can be viewed in a small
window.**
Many people read their email in smaller-than-full-size windows. Margins
no wider than 50 to 65 characters will guarantee easy reading in most cases.

**6. Show how many subscribers you have, plus other interesting
information.**
Many newsletters list their current subscription level as a way to show off
the popularity of their site. For example, the C|Net dispatch goes out to
more than 480,000 people a week—an impressive figure that every
person reading the email newsletter sees.

Another item to include is subscription information so that people can
tell their friends how to get the newsletter. Also, it's always good manners
to include information about how to unsubscribe from the newsletter in
every issue.

Downloadable Content

Downloadable content is a key—and often underused—aspect for many Web
sites. Many archive sites are built on the idea of providing programs and files
to users. The primary purpose of Happy Puppy (**http://www.happypuppy.
com**), a site that serves gaming enthusiasts, is to let people download games,
demos, and shareware to play on their computers. As I pointed out in the
previous chapter, the *Los Angeles Times* offers an Adobe Acrobat version of its
newspaper for offline reading. With many people using the World Wide Web
to retrieve items for later use, you might ask yourself: "Since my users are
going to go offline at some point, what am I doing to stay in their minds
when their modems are turned off?"

Sony
http://www.sony.com

Sony is quickly becoming one of the most potent forces in computers and
interactive technology. Its comprehensive site contains information about the
company's extensive hardware and software offerings, including records,
movies, TV shows, and videogames.

One recent downloadable item at Sony's site was a screen saver for the movie *The Cable Guy*. In the past the site has offered desktop themes for Windows and, of course, an array of movie video and sound clips.

Nike

http://www.nike.com

They'll probably be gone by the time this book comes out, but Nike provided two 1 MB interactive versions of their wild print ads on their site. While the casual surfer probably wouldn't have downloaded them, many ekins (nike nutcases) might. The age of the downloadable ad is just in its infancy, but one of the world's most prolific advertisers is pushing the envelope once again. Figure 9.4 shows these offerings.

Tips for Downloadable Content

OK, so I've convinced you to offer up some cool stuff for people to download at your site. What sort of things can you do?

1. Offer programs for users' computers.
Think up useful utility ideas and adapt them to the theme or purpose of your site. This is an excellent approach for companies that are looking to promote something. You might create a screen saver, as Sony has done, or offer a simple address-book program that features ads for your company's products. How about a game that reminds people of your company or products (for instance, a driving game to support Ford Motor Company)?

Developing a customized program can be expensive, but it can be one of the best ways to attract users to your site and have them leave with something to remember you by. Among the ideas you might use are the following:

- Screen savers (these are among the easiest programs to create)

- Simple utilities like address guides, frequent flyer mile managers, world clocks, or schedulers

- Games

- Multimedia reference guides (for example, a guide to your hometown)

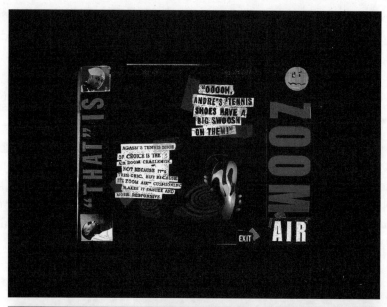

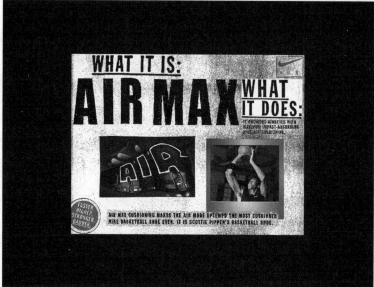

Figure 9.4 These are multimedia applets of Nike's print ads for its Air Zoom and Air Max shoes.

2. Provide desktop customization tools.

Microsoft Windows and the MAC OS allow people to customize their computers with "wallpaper" for their desktops, special system-event sounds, animated cursors, and more. Many sites are learning how to create these items for people to download. The basic idea is to become an everyday element of people's daily computer chores—which is almost better than being their default home page!

3. Offer multimedia files.

Lots of sites offer video clips of their products; others offer sound effects and audio highlights. People who download these items can view them as many times as they want offline. For example, I have a small clip from "Beavis and Butthead"—MTV posted it once, and now it's a permanent icon on my desktop to cheer me up. (Of course, if MTV was really smart, it would have embedded some text in the clip to remind me when the show airs.)

Multimedia files may seem like a waste of downloading time, but you'd be surprised at how many people keep and repeatedly view things like this.

4. Create Adobe Acrobat files of publications.

If you're producing a newsletter, book, or product guide, create an Adobe Acrobat version for users to print out and view offline. Because Acrobat files have higher resolution and better layout capabilities than HTML, you can give visitors to your site an attractive, magazine-like version of your Web documents.

Great Use of Sound

Sound is rapidly becoming a must-have element of top sites. This is true even though streaming sound (sound files which immediately start playing on download, such as RealAudio files) still has a ways to go, and the use of higher-quality samples requires a significant bandwidth. As these technological barriers are reduced, first-rate sound is only going to become more vital.

Slate

http://www.slate.com

Say what you will about Slate—some like it, some hate it—but the crew there is trying to break new ground and bring something innovative to the mix. One thing I particularly like is their use of sound within the context of their site. First, as shown in Figure 9.5, there's a RealAudio music file that sets up each issue; you activate it from a link in the corner. It's kept short (it's not meant to be theme music for an entire issue, just a nice opening touch) and usually is some sort of classical or jazz music. Another area where Slate uses sound (as shown in Figure 9.6) is in the RealAudio version of its weekly poem, narrated by the poem's author. All in all, Slate is making sure that even the more commonplace Web elements, such as sound, are being used to create a new look to the traditional *New Yorker*-style weekly that it's patterned after.

The typical use of RealAudio up until now has been for redoing radio broadcasts on the Web. While this is a great use of RealAudio, it's good to know places like Slate are utilizing it and other sound technologies in new ways.

 Check out the pages of sound technology companies to search out other creative uses of sound on the Web. You'll find a complete roundup of Web-based sound technologies in Chapter 13 of this book. Other sites I liked were: The DJ located at **http://www.thedj.com**, RealAudio's Timecast located at **http://www.timecast.com** and MSNBC's extensive use of sound clips and RealAudio (**http://www.msnbc.com**).

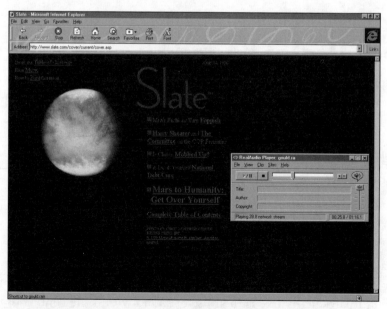

Figure 9.5 Slate's home page uses a RealAudio clip to spice things up.

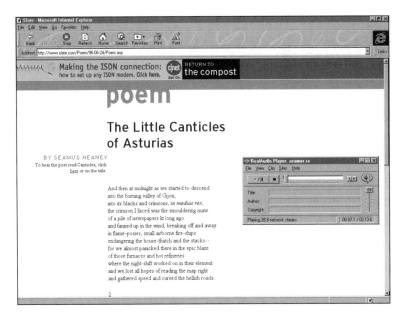

Figure 9.6 Each week Slate includes a poem recited by the author.

Awesome Forms

Finding forms that are truly well designed is not easy—forms are the neglected stepchild of all too many sites. Below, however, are some sites that are worth checking out.

MSN's Customized Start Page Form

`http://www.msn.com/choices.asp`

MSN's customized home page requires users to provide all kinds of information for its database, but this straightforward form makes the process a snap.

ZDNet's Registration Page

`http://www.zdnet.com/zdi/pview/register.cgi`

How many times have you filled out a form, just to be told that you forgot to answer a mandatory question? So users don't overlook these items, ZDNet places a big red star next to the registration questions it needs to have answered. Many form designers could learn from this simple, yet effective technique.

Some Benchmark Web Developers

Finally we come to benchmark Web developers. Many great developers are relatively nameless, working quietly away at their cutting-edge Web sites. Still others are emerging into influential shops that serve a worldwide array of major clients. I wish I could name them all—but I can't.

What I can do is highlight several developers who are producing some of the Web's top sites and, in some cases, have posted helpful information on their design philosophies as well. As I've said before, if your favorite developer isn't here, it's only because the Web is too big and my space to talk about them all too small.

Studio Archetype (formerly Clement Mok Designs)

http://www.studioarchetype.com

Clement Mok is one of the best-known designers—graphic or otherwise—in the San Francisco area. His company, now renamed Studio Archetype, has done work for such clients as Apple, Microsoft, and Nintendo. So it's no surprise that this firm, which has a lot of experience in the high-tech arena as well as in traditional forms of communication, would be a leader in Web design.

Studio Archetype's work for Rocket Science, the Microsoft Network, Sony, Adobe, HarperCollins, and Random House is top-notch.

Downtown Digital

http://www.dtd.com

Located in the trendy Tribeca district of New York City, Downtown Digital (often called DTD) is a new-media development firm specializing in Web development—especially Web-based games. The shop was founded from early work on interactive TV and is owned by telecommunications giant AT&T (though you wouldn't know that from visiting its site).

For the most part, DTD has focused on somewhat simple trivia games. These have been nicely done, however, considering that most were designed before the advent of Shockwave or Java.

Another of its creations is **http://www.herspace.com**, an interesting site aimed directly at women (who are a disproportionate minority on the Web).

Overall DTD has a two-part mission—build viable Web offerings, and explore the frontier of Web site development for AT&T. Combining the pragmatism needed to create viable sites with the visionary outlook of the long-distance giant, Downtown Digital is a developer worth watching closely.

Starwave
http://www.starwave.com

A bright new-media development company started by Microsoft cofounder and investor extraordinaire Paul G. Allen, Starwave is doing some of the best multimedia CD-ROM and Web site development around. Its sites on the World Wide Web include ESPN's SportsZone (one of the most popular sites on the Web), Mr. Showbiz (an entertainment-oriented site), Family Planet (a comprehensive site devoted to family issues), NBA.com (the official National Basketball Association site), and Outside Online (a comprehensive outdoors-information site developed in conjunction with Outside magazine).

All of Starwave's sites are aimed at broad consumer groups and designed to have large appeal. They are among the most polished-looking sites on the Web and typically show off the state of the art in layout, design, and implementation.

Recently Starwave hired Patrick Naughton, who was the original developer of Java at Sun Microsystems. His presence, Paul Allen's money, a savvy group of executives, and a wide-eyed vision of the Web and its impact for consumers combine to make Starwave a major benchmark developer to keep track of.

Microsoft
http://www.microsoft.com
http://www.msn.com
http://www.msnbc.com
http://www.slate.com

Whatever you may think of Microsoft, refusing to watch what they're up to is just plain stupid. Not only is this company the only remaining competition to Netscape in the browser wars, it's on its way to becoming a major site developer. It has a remarkably comprehensive site for its company and products (**http://www.microsoft.com**), has launched its own online service (now on the

Web) with Microsoft Network, recently broke new ground on a 24-hour news channel (MSNBC, a joint effort with NBC), and has given birth to a major Web zine (Slate, a sort of digital competitor to *Time* or *Newsweek* supervised by former *New Republic* editor and *Crossfire* host Michael Kinsley).

Microsoft's sites, optimized for its Internet Explorer browser, feature well-defined layouts, good use of forms, and an overall level of quality seen in only a few top sites. Whether you're watching them to guard your back or just to see where things are heading, Microsoft's efforts should be on anyone's short list of Web developments to track.

Finding Your Own Benchmarks

Please don't stop with the limited suggestions I've given you here! There are thousands of sites out there, and you need to be continually checking out the "state of the art" in various aspects of Web development. Fortunately, this is a fairly easy process, thanks to various services offered by some major technology developers and search engine sites. Here's a basic rundown of where I look to find the latest influential sites.

 ## Point Survey—Top 5% Sites

`http://www.pointcom.com`

This site, run by Lycos Communications, is an effort to identify the most compelling sites on the World Wide Web. Lycos reviewers grade sites on a scale of 1 to 50 in three categories—content, presentation, and experience—in order to arrive at a final point score. Sites that receive the "Top 5%" honor are allowed to place this logo on their site and are listed at **http://www. pointcom.com**, which is a growing database of all the winning sites. Although this is clearly a good resource for finding the best sites in various categories, it's not as comprehensive as it could be, and it takes some time for new sites to be given the Top 5% award. So be sure to look here, but be vigilant for other sources as well.

You can now even subscribe to their email newsletter to have the best site URLs sent directly to you. Subscribe at **http://point.lycos.com/subscribe/**.

MSN's Pick of the Week and Links Central

http://www.msn.com/access/links/other.htm

The Microsoft Network has an area where it bestows a "site of the week" award and points visitors toward what it considers to be some of the Web's best sites. MSN's weekly picks tend to be optimized for Internet Explorer (though not all of them are), so if you're doing work with MSIE this might be a good place to start.

 ## *USA Today's* Hot Sites

http://www.usatoday.com/life/cyber/ch.htm

USA Today presents its pulp and electronic surfers with lots of Web reviews with *USA Today's* Hot Sites, complete with an accompanying cool (I mean hot!) sticker for the bestowed to place on their site. Lots of the site truly are among the best.

 ## Magellan

http://www.mckinley.com/index_bd.html

Magellan is a combination search engine and review service. It ranks sites on a scale of one to four, so finding four-star sites in its search engines means they've deemed it the crème-de-la-crème of Web sites. This approach makes Magellan a great place to search out other benchmark sites, especially for specialized topic, such as the best site about rap music.

Magellan also keeps a list of what it calls "Stellar Sites," which it presents in topic form throughout the year (August happens to be the "best of Web travel sites" month). A complete backlist is also available.

If your site is reviewed by Magellan (visit them to find out how to request a review) and you do well, you can implement a sticker on your site to show off your achievement.

NetGuide's Site of the Day

`http://techweb.cmp.com/net/online/current/siteday/siteday.htm`

CMP's NetGuide is one of several major Web magazines with a pick of the day. You can also go to this page to submit your site for consideration.

 ## iWORLD's Site of the Day

`http://netday.iworld.com/poweruser/sotd/`

Mecklermedia's iWORLD is one of the top Internet news and information site around and they've been reviewing and handing out Site of the Day awards for some time. Surf here to check out the site of the day as well as see past sites or submit a site for consideration.

Yahoo's Cool Links, Yahoo for the Day, and New on the Net

`http://www.yahoo.com/Entertainment/Cool_Links/`

The Yahoo site offers several services to help you track down top-notch Web locations. Yahoo's Cool Sites is featured in daily and weekly doses, and archives for past weeks can be searched as well. New on the Net lists interesting new launches and is a good way to check out relatively high-profile new sites the second they're up and running.

Webreference.com's Cool List of the Day Sites

`http://webreference.com/cool/index.html`

Did you know there are dozens and dozens of similar "top pick" entities on the Web? What's a developer to do to find them all? Not much thanks to the folks at webreference.com. This site on the Web developer site, webreference. com, is a major listing of all the similar "top pick" sites around. It's pretty comprehensive (in fact so much so I wish I'd found it before I wrote this chapter). Well worth a check.

There's certainly more...

One thing about surfing the Web—you can't get to it all in one lifetime, let alone the time it takes to write a book. I really wish I could have gotten to every major site and added dozens of benchmark developers, sites, and examples. Unfortunately, I can't (maybe in another book!). Especially among developers, there are some really great benchmark companies and people out there doing cool stuff. Spend some time surfing to other Web developers and looking at their showcases (not just the places I've listed—check out the listings of other developers on Yahoo, Alta Vista, or Lycos). Check out the major ad agencies, too, like Chiat/Day, which made the Nissan Pathfinder site. Everywhere you look there are a lot of people and companies doing cool stuff.

The last two chapters were just to get you started—now you're on your own.

CHAPTER 10

There's lots of content to be served on the Web, and there are many ways to serve it.

Web Content Types: An Overview

As I noted in an earlier chapter, the World Wide Web is really a medium for delivering and interacting with various types of content. Indeed, the majority of Web development involves the creation of this content and the specific objects through which it is presented. The next section of this book will deal with the myriad of issues and resources related to the creation of Web content.

First, however, I want to talk about some overall issues that can affect all sorts of content. In later chapters I will focus on specific types of content, but for now I want to explore how they all relate to one another. Let's start by running through the nine major content types associated with the Web.

Text

The heart and soul of the Web, text content is fairly easy to produce—although there are ways to make it difficult, too. Most of this content is developed as straight text, edited, and then turned into HTML-formatted files for the Web. Many sites, however, are using text formatted as graphic images as well (for two examples, see **http://www.idsoftware.com** and **http://www. pythonline.com**). Text content can also be served up through Adobe Acrobat, Common Ground, or files in various word-processing formats; for instance, Microsoft has a Word helper program for viewing Word files found on the Web. Table 10.1 outlines the basic issues concerning text-based Web content.

Graphics

After text, the next most prevalent content type is static imagery, better known as graphics. Most people are familiar with the various GIF and JPEG formats, but experienced Web developers know there are many other formats to play with. Table 10.2 outlines several routes for displaying graphics on the Web. Many are available via plug-in technology like Corel's CMX files, Fractal Images, and a new format called Portable Network Graphics (PNG). And, of course, we shouldn't forget about ASCII art (cyberspace's answer to tattoos).

Digital Audio

Sound is an interesting content type because there are so many ways to deliver audio content to users over the Web. RealAudio may seem to be the only way, but that's only because they've done a great job delivering a really strong product.

Table 10.1 An overview of the options for delivering text content on the Web.

Content Solution	Advantages	Disadvantages	Future
HTML	Loads quickly, easy to develop.	Hard to get that perfect format text exactly how you want it. Little in the way of very creative layout and style options.	Better support for styles, fonts, and effects.
Portable Document Plug-Ins (for example, 999Envoy, Common Ground, and Adobe Acrobat)	Lots of formatting and creation options; platform-independent; high-quality output.	Large files sizes, users must have plug-in program to view field work.	Adobe, the leader, is working to integrate compression (lower file sizes) and build in more Web functionality, such as Web links to other sites.
Word-Processing Documents	Lots of formatting options; easy to edit (unlike files using portable document technology).	Large file sizes; users need plug-in for inline viewing. Not all file formats or platforms are supported.	More document formats to be supported.
Graphically Rendered Text	Lots of formatting options; keeps text from being copied directly to clipboard; wide platform support.	Large file size can be too big in many cases; users cannot copy, keeps text from being copied to clipboard.	Improved quality through programs like Web-3D is bringing high-quality text graphics to the Web.

Table 10.2 The basic ways to display graphical content on the Web.

Content Solution	Advantages	Disadvantages	Future
Browser-Supported Graphics	Wide support by platform and browser type.	Even with the different variants of GIF and JPEG, there is still a need for other types of graphic file support.	More in-browser/HTML support for other graphic file types, such as the new PNG format.
ASCII Art	The widest support for graphics, especially useful for email to site members.	Not exactly Rembrandt in terms of artistic quality.	ASCII art will always hold a special (if not always respected) place on the Web; the cyberspace tattoo.
Direct Plug-In Formats (such as, Corel's CMX, Autodesk Whip! or Macromedia's FreeHand)	Wide range of additional formats available for developers.	Plug-in needed for inline viewing; and of course not all platforms supported.	More document formats to be supported. Already some third-party plug-ins providing support for multiple graphic formats.
Indirect Plug-In Solutions (such as, Adobe Acrobat)	Portable document or word-processing file plug-ins let you incorporate many different graphic types.	Perfect if you want to include lots of text as well.	Not the best way to present graphics-only content. File sizes tend to be too big. Built-in compression will bring file sizes down for Acrobat.

Table 10.3 Various ways to deliver digital audio content for the Web.

Content Solution	Advantages	Disadvantages	Future
Browser/HTML-Supported Audio	Easy to include.	Slow; users must download the entire file before they can hear it.	Someday browsers will have built-in streaming technology.
Plug-In/Server Streaming Technology	Can play back audio streams in realtime; makes "live" broadcasts possible.	Large file sizes; both servers and users need plug-in software; audio quality is good, but not ideal.	Better sound quality; more multimedia functionality.
Plug-In-Only Formats	Plays back streams in realtime; no server technology needed.	Large file sizes; users need plug-in software for inline viewing.	Better sound quality; more multimedia functionality.
Digital Video Formats	Plays back streams in realtime; can be done without video, which can be useful to avoid mixing plug-ins.	Not exactly optimized for sound quality.	Xing's StreamWorks is a good example; expect digital video and digital audio.
Text-to-Speech	Excellent for providing handicap accessibility; low file size; numerous uses for dynamic Web sites.	Sound quality often leaves a lot to be desired.	Sound technology is quickly getting better.

While plain AU and WAV files (to name just two of a plethora of audio formats) don't offer "streaming"—realtime sound transmission, instead of downloading and later playback—or higher sound quality, there are other plug-in solutions, like TrueSpeech, Xing's StreamWorks, and Internet Wave.

You can also use your favorite digital video systems, like QuickTime or MPEG, to compress and deliver audio. Finally, new text-to-speech technologies will offer developers the chance to offer audio by simply sending text through a conversion system. All of this information is outlined in Table 10.3.

Musical Content

While many of the digital audio forms described in Table 10.4 are used to deliver musical content, the quality isn't always great, and special types of music content—like MIDI and Mod files—are on average far smaller than digital-audio tracks of songs.

MIDI files are especially welcomed by users because they provide excellent musical quality, yet tend to be relatively small and can thus download quickly. Developers can readily serve up MIDI content either by using HTML extensions to embed it into a document or by working with Crescendo, a popular streaming plug-in.

In contrast, Mod files still don't have an associated plug-in (although there are several helper applications to choose from), and they aren't as streamable as other audio types. As I will discuss later, however, these files have certain characteristics that can be very useful, depending on what you are developing. Table 10.4 looks at the distinct types of technologies for giving users musical content with their Web pages.

Table 10.4   Various ways to deliver musical content for the Web.

Content Solution	Advantages	Disadvantages	Future
Digital Audio	Only real solution for many situations, including recorded music and live broadcasts.	See solution-specific sections in Table 10.5	See solution-specific sections in Table 10.5
MIDI Files	High-quality output; mostly small file sizes.	Some browsers and platforms need plug-in software; streaming MIDI always requires a plug-in; final sound quality varies widely depending on users' local hardware.	Lots of interactive hooks (for example, multimedia cues to trigger local Web page events).
Mod Files	Hybrid format can create amazing songs using digital audio samples for great quality and wide options.	Occasionally large file sizes; many different formats;no streaming technologypossible; hard to author files.	More format expansion, bringing new features and possibili-ties; an inline plug-in seems certain at some point.
Koan Music	Hybrid system can create MIDI music on the fly based up-on a "musical expert system"; provides easy way to give variety and length to MIDI files; unique "ambiance"-style musical sound.	File sizes can be big; unique plug-in and authoring system needed.	Better musical system; further enhancement of its computer-generated music.

Animation and Video

Digital video on the Web may seem impossible, but it's being done. Lots of animation is also coming, too—and depending on the scheme you choose, it can be less taxing to bandwidth than digital video. Low-end examples like animated GIFs are a great way to jazz up a page with simple mini-animations, while Java and Shockwave applets can create programmed animations. Other plug-ins (like Sizzler) offer animation features, and systems like ActiveMovie from Microsoft, QuickTime from Apple, and VDOLive can play back streaming digital video. An interesting addition to this mix is Intel's Intercast technology, which offers developers the chance to merge TV signals with Web pages. This combination effort has created a whole new approach to interactive television. Table 10.5 looks at all the routes to merging digital video with the Web.

3D Graphics/VRML

Rob Glidden (who writes for *3D Artist* magazine and *WAVE*, a biweekly newsletter on 3D graphics) notes that 3D graphics are the first content type that can

Table 10.5 Various ways to deliver digital video content for the Web.

Content Solution	Advantages	Disadvantages	Future
HTML/Browser Supported Animation	Wide support for animated GIFs; easy to develop and distribute; AVI files (supported by Internet Explorer) can offer sound as well.	Server-push/client-pull system taxes server and client; animated GIFs are cumbersome for larger animations; AVI files can be especially large and slow to load.	More native browser inline support for animation formats.
Animation Plug-In Systems	Lots of creative options; integration into larger multimedia development is possible.	Large file sizes (even simple Shockwave applications can be over 150 K).	Better compression, more program and interactive ability.
Digital Video Server Plug-In Systems	Amazing technology streams MPEG, QuickTime, or hybrid formats like VDOLive to make live broadcasting possible.	Even with 28.8 Kbps modems, the video image can still be grainy and small; server packages can be expensive.	Faster, better video; built-in hooks and interactivity for triggered Web page events, transparency options, and more.
Intel Intercast	Utilizes specialized hardware and software to combine TV signals with Web content.	High cost (though not as expensive as you'd think); not compatible with all TV markets.	This is a very neat technology only now becoming advanced enough, but which offers exciting digital video /Web content possibilities.

be created only by a computer. So of course, something as computer-created as the Web contains numerous ways to distribute 3D graphics content.

VRML is the primary method of 3D graphic distribution for most developers, but it is just one specific technology; and even within the VRML universe there are many competing programs. All this is examined in Table 10.6.

Document-Oriented Content and Other Plug-Ins

Not all Web content centers directly around graphics, sound, and text—there are many highly specialized plug-ins and document-oriented content objects as well. For example, Microsoft has created Web-based viewers for PowerPoint and Excel documents, and SPC has a plug-in to view graphics from its Harvard Graphics software package. As the Web becomes a giant "hard disk"

Table 10.6 Various ways to deliver 3D content for the Web.

Content Solution	Advantages	Disadvantages	Future
HTML/Browser Supported VRML	Both Netscape and Microsoft have or are planning built-in VRML support offering wide user installed base.	May not be the top VRML systems available.	VRML standards are rapidly advancing.
Third-Party VRML Plug-Ins	Lots of formatting and creation options; platform-independent; high-quality output.	Some viewers might not be fully compliant or be beyond compliant, offering unnecessary special options.	Expect some third-party browsers to seek and gain acceptance by offering lots of different options beyond standard systems.
Non-VRML Plug-Ins	Might offer better solutions than VRML in some situations; there are several other non-VRML 3D systems of various types.	User base for non-VRML systems won't be nearly as large as that for a VRML user base, but might offer better solutions, depending on a given situation.	Even as VRML establishes itself as the basic 3D technology for the Web, don't expect hybrid formats to go away; there are many situations that will call for non-VRML 3D content solutions.

that stores, views, and exchanges files of various types, almost every program will include some sort of Web viewer for its specialized document types; if not, you can always download it and find the associated application that created it, and then load that content directly into the product that created it.

How specialized can plug-ins get? Well, consider Chemscape Chime, which allows you to view 3D representations of various molecular structures. Table 10.7 compares the use of applications to view specialized formats vs. a custom plug-in.

Programs

Many of the best Web sites are built around programmed content, which can range from simple scripts to "live" Java or Shockwave applets to downloadable programs. The Web is the ideal "virtual shelf-space" for programs to be available on. Rather than have limited shelf-space at retail outlets, more and more developers are delivering programs for us to use via the Web.

There are two key types of programmed content on the Web. The first are programs that in and of themselves represent a unique form of content—for example, a Java applet that helps you compute your taxes, or a downloadable

Table 10.7 A quick comparison between using plug-in formats and using applications to view Web content.

Content Solution	Advantages	Disadvantages	Future
Application Document Types	Can manipulate the content after download easily; loads fast, easy to develop.	Works great with very popular file types like Excel documents or PageMaker files, but not so great with files from programs people might not have as readily. Also not viewable in browser; hard to get that perfect formatting. Little in the way of very creative layout and style options.	Plug-ins and ActiveX controls are the future. Eventually expect entire applications to be able to work like plug-ins, providing manipulation and viewing directly from the browser. Better support for styles, fonts, and effects.
Specialized Plug-Ins	Viewable directly in browser. Lots of formatting and creation options, platform-independent. High-quality output.	Most likely can't do much more than "view" it. If you use a rare plug-in, can be hard to get users to view page. Large file size; need plug-in to work technology.	Expect more and more specialized plug-ins. Also expect "super plug-ins." Adobe is working to integrate compression to lower file size and build in more Web functionality; combine all kinds of file format viewing capabilities into one giant package.

word processor. The second are applets that deliver other content types—for example, a piece of animation created using Shockwave, or a Java program that scrolls text content.

The great thing about programmed content on the Web is that there are a lot of ways to deliver computer programs to users—either as Java applets, complete Web applications using scripts or as downloadable executables. The power of the Web to be a platform for extensive productivity programs, games, and multimedia programs is enormous. Table 10.8 shows the various ways to develop programs to deliver on the Web.

Table 10.8 Various ways to program content via the Web.

Content Solution	Advantages	Disadvantages	Future
JavaScript and VBScript	Load quickly; offer speedy development environment and native browser support.	VBScript is not yet supported in Netscape, while JavaScript is supported in IE; overall, neither is designed for "heavy lifting"; both can be tough to develop for, given the debugging process.	Expansion of both languages; wider platform support for VBScript.
Perl/CGI Scripting	Wide support among all servers, especially Unix server systems; server-side programming; wide availability of well-tested scripts and tools.	Slow; becoming outdated in wake of better server APIs and database back-ends.	Continued use until server and other more robust systems replace it.
Java	Offers incredible cross-platform solutions and robust development possibilities.	Still working out the kinks; requires a compatible browser; only works on 32-bit platforms; runs slowly. Faster speeds through native compiler systems, as well as embedding Java directly in the OS instead of the browser; a wider installed base; more bug-free solutions; increased development resulting from better programming environments like Borland's Latté and Microsoft's Jakarta. Specialized multimedia applets are perfect for this medium; lots of platform and browser support; good authoring environment.	In the future watch for the Java Virtual Machine to move from the Web browser to the operating system. Java will also be the main language for a host of Web appliance devices. In addition, expect more and more companies to program entire applications with Java-like word processors, spreadsheets, and other common applications.
Local Development Language	Lots of different languages and technologies to choose from; fast speeds are only possible with native application development.	Must create native applications for different platforms to ensure wide support; requires knowledge of TCP/IP socket libraries and knowledge of plug-ins or server programs.	Continued flow of new tools and libraries to develop Web applications with C/Delphi/VB and other programming languages.

A Special Note About Java and ActiveX

The current revolution in Web content is, of course, the rapidly growing popularity of Java and ActiveX. In almost every conceivable Web content situation, a Java/ActiveX solution can be used instead of a plug-in or other solution.

For example, Intel has released a special Java library for offering digital video, and another product (MidiShare) offers MIDI capabilities. I'll explore these Java-specific resources for delivering specialized content further a little later in this book.

Java is by no means for every Web developer; for instance, it's far easier to use a plug-in to give someone access to digital audio. However, as more people learn to use Java easily and as it becomes a more robust technology over the next couple of years, expect Java to become a catch-all content solution.

Matching Content to Solutions

Deciding on the right content to use in a particular situation is a two-fold process. First, because many object types can actually "cross over" and serve up different content types, you need to decide when this is to your advantage. For example, text rendered as a graphic image is really textual *content* but a graphical *solution*.

Second, there seem to be three possible answers for each specific content type. For example, you can choose from several different solutions for streaming audio, all of which offer different features and tradeoffs. In the following sections I'll explore some general issues related to selecting the right content solution for your needs.

Understanding Different Delivery Routes

As you start to become more familiar with lots of different object types, you will begin to see how comprehensive the process for building cutting-edge sites can become. There are many different ways to offer up the basic content types, and within each specific area there are even more choices to be made. Here are some factors that can help you narrow down the different options.

Cost

Some content types can be very expensive, especially those that require back-end servers. Products like VDOLive and RealAudio, in fact, make their money by selling the server systems needed to distribute content once its been developed. But associated costs for content types can show up in many other ways, including the cost to create the content (for example, Shockwave requires you to have Director to write the applications).

Support

Some specific types of content might have support-related issues. Plug-ins aren't always easy to install (in fact, I still can't get several of the ones I have to work quite right)—and, depending on how open your lines of communications are, guess who some of your product's users are going to call and ask for help? (Hint: It won't be the maker of the plug-in.)

Server Requirements

Many content solutions require specialized server software, an item that often doesn't come cheap for developers.

Platforms and Installed Base

Not all plug-ins work for all systems. Some are available only for Windows or only for Macintosh, and many content types are not available for Unix systems. As you expand your site to include things like digital audio, video, or multimedia content, be aware that the system you choose to bring these things to your users might actually shut out many of them.

Even if everyone can run a certain plug-in technology, don't expect them to *want* to do so. Lots of people can run Shockwave, but not everybody does; lots of browsers can use RealAudio but don't. Until someone starts to track who's using what regularly, you'll need to figure it out on your own.

Creation Terms and Tools

Just as there are multiple delivery options for each content type, each with its own idiosyncrasies, you will have to choose the tools you use to create the content in the first place—and, as the saying goes, an artist is only as good as his or her tools. Each option will come with its own restrictions or additional choices to be made. For example, creating multimedia content to be delivered via Shockwave requires knowledge of Director and its associated language, Lingo. In contrast, Java content can be created in a plethora of ways, from unique visual environments like Kinetix's Hyperwire to full-blast programming solutions like Borland's Latté. There are even more wide-open creation terms for other content types (for example, there are probably 100 different ways to create or obtain GIF graphics files).

Be sure to evaluate the tools available to create the content you want to make. Some may force you to buy expensive software and hardware, while others may require really specialized skills that may cause you to outsource the work or hire the needed talent. It's very easy to get stuck by assuming that all content is as easy to create as a simple text file—make sure you can create what it is you want to offer people!

Five Basic Rules for Staying Up on Content Options

1. Check in on BrowserWatch (**http://www.browserwatch.com**) to learn the latest info about plug-ins and browser-supported content variants.

2. Stay up on the latest in Java libraries and solutions by checking in on major Java publications. Even if you're not a Java programmer, there may be many ways for you to utilize Java applets to deliver specific content types to users.

3. Check in with the manufacturers of your favorite programs to see if they have Web content solutions related to their unique file structures and document types.

4. Always assume there is more than one way to deliver a specific type of content, and be familiar with each of them. Be especially aware of plug-ins and systems that can handle multiple file formats; these "super plug-ins" may include content types you haven't seen available in stand-alone situations.

5. Test out different processes—especially the more esoteric ones—because they may offer interesting ways to increase speeds, flexibility, or the availability of your specific content.

Where Do We Go from Here?

For many of you, the next several chapters will be the most useful ones in this book. That's because the bulk of resources of interest to Web developers are linked directly to the content creation and delivery tools that I'm about to cover in great depth.

Perhaps the biggest revolution in development has been the avalanche of programs to create different content. From products that even a novice could use to the amazing 3D animation systems capable of creating photorealistic effects, computer software now gives creative people tools that as little as five years ago either cost huge sums of money or simply didn't exist.

In addition, there are many new content types, some of which are growing in popularity as a result of the World Wide Web or were especially created to serve Web development needs. So where do we go from here? To the ins and outs of creating cool Web content—in other words, to the heart of the Web!

CHAPTER 11

Almost everything you could want to know about the fundamentals of creating Web graphics.

Web Graphics: Tips, Tricks, and Software

When I started planning this book, and especially this chapter, I knew I'd spend quite a bit of time talking about Web graphics—but I didn't realize just how much information I'd have to cover. The sheer volume of what's going on in the realm of computer graphics, especially as it relates to the Web, makes this a truly exciting time.

I'll start by covering what kinds of graphics you'll see on the Web and the overall techniques developers use to create them. After that I'll present a ton of resource information I've compiled, listing all the major commercial packages you might want to have in your tool chest.

What Types of Graphics Do We Regularly Create?

Below is a list of all the types of graphics that appear on the Web. This overview not only helps in terms of explaining the different ways to create (or obtain) these graphics, but you can also use it to gain a deeper understanding of the roles that graphics play on the Web.

- *Regular Pictures*—Of course, the most prevalent graphics on the Web are the millions of regular photos, drawings, charts, and other images that computers have been producing since before the Internet became a mass medium.

- *Banners*—If it seems like there are more banners on the Web every day, that's because there are. As the most common form of Web advertising, banners have become almost a standard item on most sites.

- *Icons*—The most common interface graphics are icons—small pictures that instantly convey to the user what feature will be launched when the icon is clicked. Common icons on Web sites include links to more pages (usually arrows of some kind), email icons (mailboxes or envelopes), and help icons (question marks).

- *Bullets and Link Bullets*—Lots of people use graphics instead of the common <LI> tags for bulleted lists. Some go one step further by making the bullet a mini-icon or link as well.

- *Bar and Line Dividers*—Developers often feel the plain <HR> tag just isn't jazzy enough to separate elements on their Web page, and so they use a custom graphic for the same purpose. Most of the graphics I see used for

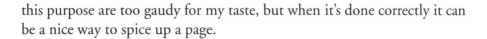

this purpose are too gaudy for my taste, but when it's done correctly it can be a nice way to spice up a page.

Stickers

I don't really know who can be credited with the name (or the actual idea) of Web "stickers," but it's too bad they don't get a royalty. Developers use these icon-like graphics—which are part advertisement, part link to needed software or other Web pages—to help users know what browsers their site supports, what plug-ins the user needs to get the most out of it, what tools were used to build the site, or what sort of ratings awards the site has won. Anyone who has seen the ubiquitous "Netscape Now" or "Top 5%" graphics has seen a sticker.

It seems there are hundreds of stickers sprinkled throughout various Web sites. They fall into four main types:

- *Best Browser/Needed Plug-In Links*—With the browser wars in full force, the major combatants are making sure that their stickers are everywhere. Many Web developers also use stickers supplied by software companies to display easy-to-recognize links to the various plug-ins that a user might also need (and there are more than you can shake a stick at).

   Just because you think your site favors one over the other, however, doesn't mean you can actually display a "Best Viewed" or "Plug-In" sticker. Make sure you check in on the following pages to learn the specific scoop about displaying these stickers:

  Netscape—http://www.netscape.com/comprod/mirror/netscape_now_program.html

  Microsoft Internet Explorer—http://www.microsoft.com/ie/logo/

- *Plug-In/File Format Identifiers*—Depending on the file format you're displaying, you might need to consider the use of plug-ins or ActiveX controls to be able to display it on the Web.

- *Toolset Indicators*—Some of the major tool companies—including Microsoft, Macromedia, and Adobe—have created stickers that indicate what back-end systems and tools you used to create your site. By using these stickers you're essentially advertising these products for the vendors, but you're also displaying your proficiency to site visitors who may wish to use your development skills.

- *Rating/Tie-In Indicators*—Among the more interesting stickers to obtain and use are the "Top Pick" or "Approved" rating labels given out by various entities in the Web universe. These stickers often double as links to an index of all sites that have received the same rating (including, of course, your site).

Plug-In Formats

If you've been a Web developer for a while, you probably think the only two graphic formats ever invented were GIF and JPEG. In fact, until the Web came along, even JPEG wasn't all that important. But now there are more graphic formats out there than anyone could possibly keep track of (at least not without a book like this), and with the advent of plug-ins and ActiveX controls, many of these formats can be accessed via the Web. While nine out of ten times you'll use the GIF/JPEG combination, there are good reasons to consider serving up some of the more specialized formats that are now available, as you'll see in the following section.

Corel CMX Viewer

Corel Corporation
1600 Carling Avenue
Ottawa, Ontario K1Z 8R7
Phone: 613-761-9176
Fax: 613-761-1146
WWW: http://www.corelnet.com

What is it?

Corel's CMX plug-in recognizes and loads the Corel CMX scalable drawing format. See Figure 11.1.

How do I create it?

Corel devised this format, of course, for its highly popular CorelDraw! product, which is a major art-creation package for the desktop publishing industry. CorelDraw! images can be scaled and rotated easily because they are not bitmapped.

Figure 11.1 Corel's CMX plug-in in action.

Whip!

Kinetix
111 McInnis Parkway
San Rafael, CA 94903
Phone: 415-507-5000
Fax: 415-507-5314
WWW: http://www.ktx.com

What is it?

Whip is a Netscape plug-in that allows users to view Autocad/DWG files. Users can scroll around the images, as well as zoom in and out.

How do I create it?

The DWG format was popularized by AutoCAD, the preeminent CAD package for computers, but it is used by other CAD and structured drawing programs (such as AutoSketch). If you're interested in presenting a CAD-like image on your site, but don't want to shell out the money for an expensive product like AutoCAD, look at some of Autodesk's lower-end packages that support the DWG format.

DWG/DFX Viewer and SVF Plug-In

SoftSource
301 West Holly
Bellingham, WA 98225
Phone: 360-676-0999
Fax: 360-671-1131
WWW: http://www.softsource.com

What is it?

SVF is an acronym for Simple Vector Format, a file format SoftSource developed jointly with NCSA. Both plug-ins work with scalable vector graphics, which allow the user to magnify portions of the drawing or toggle layer visibility without requiring multiple downloads. Thus the zoom, pan, and layer visibility controls of either plug-in make it easy for users to explore even the most complex CAD drawings online. The SVF plug-in also features navigation via embedded URLs.

How do I create it?

Several CAD packages, like SoftSource's own Vdraft product, support the SVF format.

FIGleaf Inline

Carberry Technology
600 Suffolk Street
Lowell, MA 01854
Phone: 508-970-5358
WWW: http://www.ct.ebt.com/figinline/

What is it?

FIGleaf Inline is a Netscape plug-in that allows you to view, rotate, zoom, and scroll around an image file within a Netscape Navigator window. It supports a variety of formats, including Computer Graphics Metafile (CGM), Tagged Image File Format (TIFF), Encapsulated PostScript (EPSI/EPSF), CCITT Group 4 Type I (G4), CCITT Group 4 Type II (TG4), Microsoft Windows

Bitmap (BMP), Microsoft Windows Metafile (WMF), Portable Network Graphics (PNG), Portable Pixmap (PPM), Portable Greymap (PGM), Portable Bitmap (PBM), Sun Raster files (SUN), Graphics Interchange Format (GIF), Joint Photographic Experts Group (JPEG), and Silicon Graphics RGB (RGB).

While its use as an Internet tool isn't as clear, FIGleaf Inline is certainly an excellent tool for intranets, where you might need to give users lots of access to files within the browser window.

How do I create it?

You'll need an art package that creates or converts graphics to the specific formats you're using. Most of the formats listed above are supported by programs like Photoshop, CorelDraw!, Fractal Painter, and a variety of conversion products.

Fractal Viewer

Iterated Systems
3525 Piedmont Road
Seven Piedmont Center, Suite 600
Atlanta, GA 30305-1530
WWW: http://www.iterated.com

What is it?

This plug-in can view and interact with standard fractal image files (also known as the FIF format).

How do I create it?

Iterated Systems offers a program that converts files to the more compressed FIF format. It's available for download from their Web site and is offered to users on a 30-day trial basis. The program can convert from a variety of graphic formats and works best with scanned photos or complex graphics, rather than a more precise computer illustration.

InterCAP InLine

InterCAP Graphics Systems, Inc.
Annapolis, MD
Phone: 410-224-2926
WWW: http://www.intercap.com

What is it?

InterCAP InLine supports inline viewing, zooming, dynamic panning and magnification, and animation of Computer Graphics Metafile (CGM) vector graphics within the Netscape Navigator 2.0 Web browser.

Because CGM supports hyperlinking of graphic objects within an illustration, authors can easily combine it with HTML to create interactive, graphics-driven documents that are compact and efficiently accessed via the Web. Because it can support high-quality vector graphics, CGM is also a natural format for publishing CAD data in a compact and efficient, yet interactive, form.

How do I create it?

A number of programs in the CAD vector drawing area support the CGM file format.

KEYView

FTP Software, Inc.
100 Brickstone Square
Andover, MA 01810
Phone: 508-685-4000
Fax: 508-794-4488
WWW: http//www.ftp.com

What is it?

This plug-in supports more than two hundred file formats for viewing over the Web. The formats supported include most of the popular application formats (such as Microsoft Word and spreadsheets), as well as a host of graphics formats, like TIFF and CorelDraw!. For a complete list of supported file types, visit the FTP Software Web site at **http://www.ftp.com/mkt_info/formats.htm**.

How do I create it?

There is no specialized file format supported. Depending on the file types you specifically want to create, you will need any number of graphics or basic application programs.

Lightning Strike

Infinop
P.O. Box 2562

Denton, TX 76201
Phone: 817-891-1538
WWW: http://www.infinop.com

What is it?

Lightning Strike is a new graphics format, invented by Infinop, that delivers very highly compressed graphic files.

How do I create it?

You convert any common graphic format using a special utility conversion program created by Infinop.

Electrifier & LightningDraw GX (Mac)

Lari Software Inc.
207 S. Elliott Road, Suite 203
Chapel Hill, NC 27514
Phone: 919-968-0701
Fax: 919-968-0801
WWW: http://www.larisoftware.com

What is it?

This Electrifier plug-in supports the GX format, which was developed by Lari Software for its vector-based LightningDraw GX program.

How do I create it?

Files are created with LightningDraw GX, which saves its files using this specialized format. This is a vector-based drawing program similar to CorelDraw! or Adobe Illustrator.

QuickSilver

Micrografx, Inc.
1303 E. Arapaho Road
Richardson, TX 75081
Phone: 214-234-1769
Fax: 214-234-2410
WWW: http://www.micrografx.com

What is it?

Micrografx has been a leading supplier of graphics-creation and charting products for as long as Windows has been around. Its new QuickSilver plug-in allows inline viewing of files created with its ABC Graphics Suite to the Web.

Among the features of the QuickSilver format and plug-in are rotation and resizing (as these are vector-based graphics) as well as embedded URLs in the drawings. The format also allows some animation and interactive features, because designers can attach small action programs to objects in the graphic files (a user can trigger events when a mouse is dragged over an object, or when the object is clicked on, and so forth).

How do I create it?

To create files for this plug-in you will need to employ the Micrografx ABC Graphics Suite package, which includes Micrografx Designer, ABC FlowCharter, Picture Publisher, Instant 3D, and ABC MediaManager. The programs also support the ActiveX architecture, and their documents can be viewed and edited within Internet Explorer.

The scripting language inside the QuickSilver suite is quite similar to either Visual Basic Script or JavaScript, and so programmers familiar with these products should find the language pretty easy to implement.

RapidVue

Pegasus Imaging Corporation
4010 Boy Scout Boulevard, Suite 400
Tampa, FL 33607
Phone: 813-875-7575
Fax: 813-875-7705
WWW: http://www.jpg.com

What is it?

RapidVue allows you to view Pegasus's new PIC format, a high-speed JPEG derivative.

How do I create it?

Pegasus has created a slew of tools to allow you to create, convert, and manipulate this new file format, including Photoshop plug-ins and standalone software.

Shockwave/FreeHand

Macromedia, Incorporated
600 Townsend Street
San Francisco, CA 94103
Phone: 415-252-2000
Fax: 415-626-0554
WWW: http://www.macromedia.com

What is it?

The FreeHand vector drawing program was originally offered by Aldus, but it was sold to Macromedia when Aldus merged with Adobe. This plug-in allows users to view and manipulate FreeHand drawings in the native file format.

How do I create it?

It's simple—just order a copy of FreeHand software from Macromedia and start working.

Wavelet Image Format Plug-In

Summus, Ltd.
950 Lake Murray Blvd.
Irmo, SC 29063
Phone: 803-781-5674
Fax: 803-781-5679
WWW: http://www.summus.com

What is it?

A new graphics format that uses cutting-edge wavelet compression to deliver highly compressed images.

How do I create it?

Summus provides a command-line program for converting common graphics file formats to its proprietary format.

ViewDirector Imaging

TMSSequoia
206 W. 6th Avenue
Stillwater, OK 74074

Phone: 405-377-0880
Fax: 405-377-0452
WWW: http://www.tmsinc.com

What is it?

This plug-in supports viewing of a wide array of graphic file formats within your browser. Among the formats supported are TIFF (uncompressed, modified Huffman, G3 1&2D, and G4), CALS Type 1, JPEG, PCX/DCX, and BMP. You can manipulate images with panning and zoom; simple image-processing functions such as rotation, gray scaling, and color pixel smoothing are also possible.

How do I create it?

Almost every graphics-creation package supports one of this plug-in's supported file formats.

PNG Plug-In Solutions

http://quest.jpl.nasa.gov/PNG/pngapbr.html

What is it?

The PNG (Portable Network Graphic) format was created when Unisys said that the GIF format violated their patents on certain compression algorithms. In reaction, a group of graphic wizards and programming gurus got together over the Internet and on CompuServe and created a whole new and better format called PNG. The PNG plug-in lets users view the PNG format. It's eventually hoped that PNG will become a native format for both Netscape and Internet Explorer.

How do I create it?

The PNG format is poised to gain wide acceptance in the coming years and may even enjoy widespread native browser support in the next year or so. In the meantime, check out the Web page I listed for the most comprehensive and up-to-date ways to view PNG-formatted graphics on the Web.

What Tools Do We Use to Create All This Stuff?

There are more ways to create graphics than you can imagine. Here, though, is a good attempt at categorizing the different products a Web developer needs in his or her toolbox.

Paint and Imaging Packages

Not too long ago, paint packages were thought to be very different from imaging packages. Now that paint packages have begun to add a lot more imaging functionality (and vice versa), however, it's easy to find products like Adobe's Photoshop and Corel's PHOTO-PAINT that straddle both zones. The advent of the World Wide Web has helped Photoshop become perhaps the most popular graphics tool in computers today. There are also a few paint-specific programs, such as Fractal Design Painter, that I'll cover in the software resources section of this chapter.

3D Rendering and Animation

Rob Glidden, who writes for *WAVE* and *3D Artist* magazines, has referred to 3D graphics and animation as "the computer's first native media type," and he's right. The 3D art seen in the latest computer games and Hollywood movies was simply impossible to create before the advent of computers.

Unfortunately, bandwidth considerations have always placed a chokehold on the heavy use of 3D graphics on the Web. Behind the scenes, though, developers are already rendering lots of static, two-dimensional imagery with cutting-edge 3D tools, and others are getting ready for the tidal wave of 3D graphics that will follow bandwidth expansion and the soon-to-come VRML explosion. All in all, 3D is quickly becoming as major a force for Web developers as it recently became for the game development industry.

Since their development is already way ahead of the playback capabilities, the tools won't be lagging at all as the Web becomes more supportive of 3D graphics. Later in this book I've listed a number of useful contacts and information sources about 3D tools and products to consider. While VRML is covered in Chapter 14 of this book, just take a look at either **http://www.softimage.com** or **http://www.alias.com** for an example of how even two-dimensional graphics exported as a rendering from a 3D package can create graphics that leap off the screen, and you'll see why even today a good 3D package can be a very useful resource.

Digital Video and Animation Programs

When VDOLive debuted at the October 1995 Internet World in Boston, it showed the world that what one company did with streaming audio, another

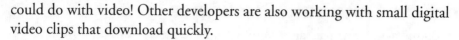

could do with video! Other developers are also working with small digital video clips that download quickly.

Meanwhile, there is a whole section of Web technology, like Shockwave and mBED, that can deliver great computer animations. As you'll see in the chapter on digital video and animation (Chapter 14), a majority of the technologies that enable animation over the Web are tied to some form of specialized authoring environment. That's not always the case, however, and in many cases you still need a strong fundamental background in Web graphics and production packages.

Special Utilities

In addition to the three groups of products listed previously, there are always those special programs and utilities that become the figurative glue in any graphics production toolbox. Every good Web developer needs helpful products like an image-map creator, a handy conversion program, and perhaps something to provide better file-management functionality. I'll list many of these types of products throughout this chapter.

Palettes: A Secret to Good Web Graphics

I'm convinced that someone could make a living in the computer industry solely as a consultant on graphic palettes. There are major palette issues in every type of computer software development I've ever encountered, especially multimedia forms. Not surprisingly, Web development is no different.

Following is a quick roundup of the general types of palette issues that you'll encounter, followed by some deeper coverage of issues specifically related to Web development.

- *Application Palettes*—Some applications, such as Netscape, work best with graphics that are optimized for a palette it supports.

- *Palettes and Digital Video*—Palettes are extremely important when it comes to digital video. There are several palettes for which various codecs are optimized; among the most notable of these are the palettes for Intel's Indeo and Radius' Cinepak. Refer to your favorite guide on how to digitize quality video for more information.

- *Palettes and File Size*—The biggest issue with palettes is how they affect file size—there's nothing like a huge palette to send those sizes soaring. Later on I'll list several major tools that help you strip out as much unwanted palette information as possible.

The Aesthetics of Color Selection

Good Web sites will have a unified look to them, and perhaps one of the biggest unifying forces is a well-designed palette. The pages for Sun Microsystems (**http://www.sun.com**), for instance, employ a purplish palette for backgrounds, with shading and different hues within the same overall color range used to define separate elements. Other companies, like Softimage (**http://www.softimage.com**), work a white/silver palette against a black background, creating a key contrast within their palette that works nicely.

So, as you work out the technical issues, don't forget that you should also choose a palette that creates a unique and unified color scheme for your entire site.

The Netscape Palette

Netscape uses a specific palette to render graphic images it finds on the Web. Until developers discovered this, they couldn't understand why sometimes their graphics didn't look exactly as planned in Netscape. There are several resources available to help you understand this issue better, and to make sure your graphics coordinate with the Netscape palette.

Victor Engel's No Dither Netscape Color Palette

`http://www.onr.com/user/lights/netcol.html`

This page does a great job of explaining the Netscape palette and how it affects developers. A great first place to check, it has lots of great links to even more information and resources.

The 256, Oops, 216 Colors of Netscape

`http://www.connect.hawaii.com/hc/webmasters/Netscape.colors.html`

Another excellent tutorial about the Netscape palette.

Image Maps

Image maps are collections of bitmapped graphics that contain links to other pages or objects. Server-side maps, the first kind to be developed, respond

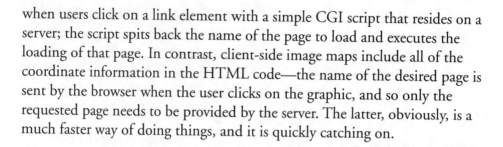

when users click on a link element with a simple CGI script that resides on a server; the script spits back the name of the page to load and executes the loading of that page. In contrast, client-side image maps include all of the coordinate information in the HTML code—the name of the desired page is sent by the browser when the user clicks on the graphic, and so only the requested page needs to be provided by the server. The latter, obviously, is a much faster way of doing things, and it is quickly catching on.

How to Make an Image Map

Making an image map isn't too hard, and several good programs make it even easier. Here are several tools that I found to be used most often by other developers, as well as some others I use and like.

Web Hotspots (Windows)

1Automata
WWW: http://www.cris.com/~automata/order.htm

This is one of the most popular image-map programs. It supports client-side and server-side image maps, multiple file formats (GIF, JPEG, BMP, TGA, TIFF, and PCX), zoom editing, live testing, and multiple image editing.

Mapedit (Windows and Unix)

Boutell.Com, Inc.
P.O. Box 20837
Seattle, WA 98102
Phone: 206-325-3009
Fax: 206-325-3009
WWW: http://www.boutell.com/mapedit/

This is perhaps the most commonly used program for editing image maps. There are literally dozens of versions for Windows 95, 3.1, and NT, and about ten Unix versions for every popular Unix platform. It handles client-side image maps, a variety of image formats (JPEG, PNG, and GIF), and supports frames.

WebMap (Macintosh)

Rowland Smith
219 Old Roper Rd.
Plymouth, NC 27962
WWW: http://home.city.net/cnx/software/webmap.html

This Macintosh program for editing image maps includes support for GIF and PICT files, as well as support for both CERN and NCSA image-map formats.

Convert Your CERN/NCSA Map Files into Netscape Client-side Maps

`http://www.popco.com/popco/convertmaps.html`

This great Web-based utility helps you convert server-side image maps to client-side files. Just enter in the URL or the image-map data, and then run the program—it will spit back to you the HTML code to copy into your document.

Image Map Scripting Programs

The server package you bought or the provider you're using will probably already have a CGI script for processing image maps. Just in case, though, here are some URLs you can use to get some of the most common CGI scripts for your server.

NCSA Image Maps

`http://hoohoo.ncsa.uiuc.edu/docs/tutorials/imagemapping.html`

CERN Image Maps

`http://www.w3.org/hypertext/WWW/Daemon/User/CGI/HTImageDoc.html`

MAC HTTP Script

`http://home.city.net/cnx/software/webmap.html`

Web Pages and Tutorials

Got all the pieces, the graphic, the program, and the script you need—but still aren't sure how to pull it all together? Here is the best tutorial I found for learning about image maps.

The Imagemap Help Page (IHIP)

`http://www.hway.net/ihip/`

The IHIP is a very good, comprehensive tutorial on both server- and client-side image maps. It's well organized and has links to lots of different editors (more than just the ones I've mentioned above), as well as links to the main server script sites.

Backgrounds

When Netscape first introduced backgrounds, people got a little crazy—it seemed like backgrounds ended up on every site. Occasionally the result was fine, but many times it was a mess. I myself like to use a basic white or black background: It's simple, it loads fast, and it lets you use shading options to make graphics "leap" crisply off the screen.

Other backgrounds are acceptable to me as long as they complement the foreground and don't overwhelm the site. Backgrounds also work best when they tile seamlessly.

There are a host of programs (ranging from Photoshop to a variety of texture makers) that make creating backgrounds easy. In addition, a host of Web-based resources contain hundreds of backgrounds; these are included in Table 11.1 in the next section.

Web-Based Resources for Web Graphics

One of the best places to start when you're creating Web graphics is the World Wide Web itself. Many sites offer up either free imagery for your site or scripting programs (using Java) that actually help you create your own cool graphics. I've tried to list as many as I can in a table for you.

When you visit any of the sites listed in Table 11.1, make sure to read any fine print they may have about providing credit or any other form of compensation in exchange for using their work.

Graphics Creation Sites

The following sites are truly amazing. Go to them and watch as cool, useful Web graphics are created for you, tailored to your desires based on the answers you give to simple questions. Table 11.2 shows sites that can help you create graphics.

Optimizing Your Web Graphics

Information about Web graphics optimization is important for any developer. Images, of course, are the most common reason for slow Web page access, and most people either don't optimize their images at all or have no clue how much more optimizing they can do even after they're satisfied with the look of the image itself.

Table 11.1 Graphics resources on the World Wide Web.

Name of Site	URL	Description	Usage Issues
A+ Art Gallery	http://www.netset.com/~wyatt/user/art/index.html	A large gallery of art, including balls, bullets, backgrounds, animated GIFs, icons, clip art, bars, and borders.	Free to use.
Aim's Graphics	http://firstnations.ca/~aim/graphics/disclaim.htm	A collection of bars, background, and buttons, all original works by Aim artists.	Aim asks that you include a special logo and link to their page somewhere on your home page.
An Archive of H's Seamless Background Tiles	http://www.whitenoise.com/champ/background/index.html	A collection of more than 30 seamless backgrounds, both color and greyscale.	Create a link from your site to http://www.jezebel.com
Ball Boutique	http://www.octagamm.com	Wild collection of orbs, cubes, and other imagery. All of these are quite original and of high quality.	May use in non-commercial sites, but must link back and give credit to the author.
Baylor University Icons	http://www.baylor.edu/icons/	A collection of buttons and icons, many with a 3D relief look.	Free to use.
Button World	http://www.demon.co.uk/Tangent/buttons.html	Variety of blank buttons optimized for Web transmission.	Notify Tangent by email: buttons@tangent.demon.co.uk
Clip Art—Formerly known as Sandra's Clip Art Server	http://www.n-vision.com/panda/c/	One of the largest free clip art servers on the Internet. It takes a while to find anything truly useful, but there is a lot of stuff here. Also a good collection of links to other clip art archives.	Free to use (as far as I could tell), unless noted.
Custom Textures	http://home.ptd.net/~mcturner/textures/	A collection of more than 65 abstract textures.	Free to use, but author would like credit mention on page.
Daryl's Image, Ball, Line & Background Archive	http://www-engr.uvic.ca/~dstorey/Icons/	A large collection of icons, bullets, and lines.	None that I could find, yet some of the items are certainly of copyrighted materials (such as the cartoon character icons).
Decorative Initials	http://www.psy.uwa.edu.au/iconsfnt.htm	A nice collection of decorative fonts useful for headlines, initial caps, or other uses where a standard font just won't cut it.	Some fonts are copyrighted and have usage rules, while others don't. Check out the specific instructions included with each one.
Dr. Bob's Interesting 3D and 2D Textures!	http://home.ptd.net/~drbob/textures.html	A collection of textures, mostly 2D but some with 3D relief looks.	Free to use.
GIF World	http://www.starnet.com.au/~graphics/	A large collection of originally designed rules, backgrounds, buttons, and bullets.	Free to use in your Web pages, do not add to any collections.
HTML Writers Guild Graphics Page	http://www.hwg.org/archives/graphics/graphics.html	A nice set of images ranging from bars to icons, bullets, and link indicators, all in a non-interlaced transparent GIF89a format.	Free to use.

(Continued)

Table 11.1 Graphics resources on the World Wide Web. (Continued)

Name of Site	URL	Description	Usage Issues
Icons Etc.	http://www.mtnlake.com/icons2/	A collection of the usual Web graphics, balls, bars, lines, arrows, and stars.	Free to use, as far as I could tell.
Images: Index of Icons, Images and Graphics	http://osiris.colorado.edu/GIF/	One of the best—an excellent archive of all sorts of imagery from arrows and direction buttons to lines, bars, and backgrounds.	Free to use. Some images are copyrighted, but these generally require you only to provide a link or give credit to the author.
Laurie McCanna's Free Art Site	http://www.mcannas.com	Illustrator Laurie McCanna is the author of *Creating Great Web Graphics,* and this site has a bunch of artwork she is making available for other designers. The free art here is of awesome quality, and a lot of the icons are quite good as well.	The creator asks for a link back to http://www.mccannas.com if you use any of the artwork, and you are NOT allowed to redistribute this artwork.
Lem Con One's Graphic Vault	http://www.lemcon.ml.org/lemcon/graphicsindex.html	A large collection of clip art, including many of the usual Web graphic types.	Images have been collected from other sites and seem free to use, but check to make sure.
Leo's Icon Archive	http://fsinfo.cs.uni-sb.de/~leo/trans.html	A collection of the icons, backgrounds, and buttons, some of which are from other areas on the Web. The best things here are the initial-caps graphics.	Free to use, as far as I could tell.
Matterform Media Qbullets—Hinted Links	http://www.matterform.com/mf/qbullets/aboutqbullets.html	A terrific interface tool, Qbullets are tiny icons meant to sit next to links on your page and give further clues about where the links lead.	Matterform asks that you give them credit and link to their page. A README file dictates copyright restrictions (and provides a helpful style guide), but other than that Qbullets are free.
Media Links Free Graphics	http://www.erinet.com/cunning1/tiles.html	A site featuring over 725 free graphics, GIF animations, and AVI animations as well.	Don't alter the imagery, give author credit, and provide a link.
Microsoft's Multimedia Clip Art Gallery	http://www.microsoft.com/workshop/design/mmgallry/	A very good selection of all kinds of imagery for many different styles of Web sites.	The work is royalty-free and is selected by Microsoft from PhotoDisc, Inc. There is a license agreement you should read first, though.
Netscape's Gold Rush Toolkit	http://www.netscape.com/assist/net_sites/starter/samples/index.html	Netscape has several pages or links to clip-art, including the infamous Mozilla artwork of its underground mascot.	Free to use, but double-check the copyright information provided on the page.

(Continued)

Table 11.1   Graphics resources on the World Wide Web. (Continued)

Name of Site	URL	Description	Usage Issues
Pardon My Icons by Jeffrey Zeldman	http://www.zeldman.com/icon.html	Not your usual icons, many of these are Andy Warhol-style headshot prints of various people, both famous and infamous.	Even though I couldn't find a formal request, these deserve a credit on your home page and a link back to them.
Quick Clips	http://www.blue.aol.com/images/public/index.html	One of the more original and well-done collections of icons, lines, and bullets. Also present is a nice collection of graphical fonts.	Free to use, as far as I could tell.
Randy's Icon and Image Bazaar	http://www.infi.net/~rdralph/icons/	A large collection of imagery collected from various Web sites, including many of the usual bars, icons, and backgrounds, but also a nice collection of other clip art not normally found on other sites (the miscellaneous, flowers, fractals, and stars groupings in particular are excellent).	This imagery is collected from other sites, so it's ultimately up to you to recognize any copyright violations (though none are evident at this site). The author asks that you limit yourself to using 20 or fewer pieces of work from his site.
Realm Graphics	http://www.ender-design.com/rg/	A great site of custom imagery, including bullets, backgrounds, buttons, and more.	Images are free, but credit to the author and a link are requested. Users are asked to fill out a graphics survey to help the author author create new images, and there is a FAQ to read as well.
Terry Gould's Graphics Page	http://www.vol.it/mirror/Graphics/list1.html	A large archive of backgrounds, lines, bars, horizontal rules, bullets, and icons.	Free to use.
Texture Land	http://www.meat.com/textures/	A collection of 196 textures for use in Web pages. Features Abnormal Textures, a collection of 160 textures you might not have encountered in other collections.	Free for individual use or for non-profit companies, but commercial sites need to pay a modest fee. Email yyz@meat.com for more info on pricing.
TextureWorld	http://www.demon.co.uk/Tangent/texture/index.html	Variety of textures optimized for Web transmission.	Notify Tangent by email: textures@tangent.demon.co.uk
The Icon Browser	http://sunsite.unc.edu/gio/iconbrowser/	Tons of icons, all in a 32 ¥ 32 format. As you click on huge tables of icons, the service eventually zooms in until you get to the individual icon you want.	Free to use.

(Continued)

Table 11.1   Graphics resources on the World Wide Web. (Continued)

Name of Site	URL	Description	Usage Issues
The Imaging Machine	http://www.vrl.com/ Imaging/index.html	The cheapest imaging program in the world. Give it the URL of any image you want to work with, and then apply a number of different effects to that image.	Free to use.
The MIT KPT Background Archive	http://the-tech.mit.edu/ KPT/bgs.html	A large collection of backgrounds, many of which have been made with Kai's Power Tools.	Free to use. There is a visitor contribution link, and several tutorials to check out as well.
Ventana Communications Clip Art	http://www.vmedia.com	A sister company to The Coriolis Group, Ventana has been producing lots of books about desktop publishing for a long time. This archive is a collection of useful clip art with lots of great stuff, especially the Crazy Original Clipart feature!	Free to use.
Virtualibrary	http://www.mindspring .com/~phaeton/Vsteve.html	A collection of original art by the author, including backgrounds, bars, buttons, icons, separators, all very well done.	All images are copyrighted by Steven Thomas, the author. He asks that you publish a credit for him and a link back to his page some-where on your Web site.
Washington State University, IEEE Image Library	http://www.eecs.wsu.edu/ ~ieee/gifs/image.html	A collection of 587 backgrounds, as well as bullets, arrows, and more.	Free to use.

Someone could probably write an entire book about things you can do to optimize graphics for the Web. Since I don't have that kind of space to devote here, however, I'll just give you a quick rundown of a couple of the best tutorial sites that explore how to create small, fast-loading graphics.

The Bandwidth Conservation Society
http://www.infohiway.com/faster/

This is a great page, set up by a group of Web developers to provide a one-stop shop on tools, techniques, and tips for reducing the time it takes to access a Web page. Naturally, a lot of attention is devoted to cutting down the size of graphics. There are articles here about bit depth, GIF images, JPEG imagery compression, how to optimize with Adobe Photoshop, and more.

Table 11.2 Sites that help you create your own custom graphics.

Name of Site	URL	Description	Usage Issues
RulesMark's Bevelizer	http://cartoon.ecn. purdue.edu/~mmatthew/ button/	Input a GIF's URL and then choose the size of the bevel you'd like; the program finds the GIF and then applies the bevel.	Free to use.
Kansas State University, Department of Electrical and Computer Engineering: Interactive Graphics Renderer	http://www.eece.ksu. edu/IGRNEW/	Create cool-looking 3D geometric shapes shapes with different characteristics (color scheme, lighting options, and more).	Free to use for generation of graphics for personal and non-commercial uses; email for any other permissions.
The Background Generator	http://east.isx.com /~dprust/Bax/index.html	A great site that allows you not only to choose from a variety of well-done backgrounds but also change their color scheme using a Java applet.	Free to use; authors submitting tiles to the site can get a link back to their own page.

Optimizing Web Graphics

http://www.webreference.com/dev/graphics/

This article on all the things you can do to optimize Web graphics is very comprehensive. A good set of links to additional resources makes it a must-read.

The Great GIF vs. JPEG Debate

Even veterans of Web development still disagree on one of the most fundamental Web graphic issues: when and where to use either the GIF format or the JPEG format, as well as such derivative formats as GIF89a, animated GIFs, interlaced graphics, and the progressive JPEG format. Here's some information to help clear this all up.

All About GIF in 20 Seconds

The GIF format was created in 1987 by CompuServe. The format specification, called GIF87a, defines the basic scheme and structure of GIF graphics. The GIF format supports resolutions up to 64K × 64K and 256 colors. It's a great format for providing sharp imagery (there is no loss of data), especially

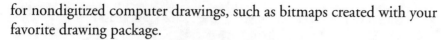

for nondigitized computer drawings, such as bitmaps created with your favorite drawing package.

An update to the GIF format in 1989, called GIF89a, allowed users to store multiple pictures and specialized text information in one file. GIF89a spawned the now-infamous animated GIF format, which languished for quite a while, until someone pointed it out to the browser companies and they built browser support for it.

GIF file data is normally stored as consecutive lines from top to bottom (which, for the most part, is how GIFs load into your browser). There is also the interlaced format, where data is stored on every eighth row; such GIFs are rendered in a progressive manner when loaded.

Most major imaging programs, like Photoshop and Paint Shop Pro, allow you to save images in either interlaced or normal fashion. For animated GIF89a files you may need to use a simple construction program, as detailed in the section on animated GIFs in Chapter 13.

All About JPEG in 20 Seconds

Needing a highly standardized format for compressed high color images, the International Telecommunications Union (ITU) and International Organization for Standardization (ISO) created the Joint Photographic Experts Group (JPEG), which defined the compression specifications for this format.

JPEG images are stored in what is called a "lossy" compression, which means that information may be discarded as the size of the picture file is compressed, though the overall representation is maintained. As a result, JPEG is great for complex color images (24-bit ones especially), but not necessarily for detailed graphics where every single pixel may count.

JPEG is very good for photographs and is the only native format in browsers that support more than 256 colors. JPEG may also be more useful than GIF files for less than 256-color systems, but be careful, because text imagery and other graphics that are produced perfectly by GIF might not be handled as well with JPEG. Many artists recommend storing images in the uncompressed TIFF format when digitizing or taking a digital camera image of a picture, then saving it in JPEG only after you're done working with it. Progressively re-imaging and saving JPEG imagery is like making copies from a copy—the quality eventually worsens over time.

A newer variant of the JPEG format, called progressive JPEG, renders the file in several phases, with each pass sharpening the image until it's perfectly viewable. Most major imaging programs, like Photoshop and Paint Shop Pro, allow you to save images in either JPEG or progressive JPEG.

 Do your own tests. Play around with all the formats, and see for yourself what you like. Some people love progressive or interlaced rendering, but others don't. Some people use JPEG for almost everything, while some purists don't like what JPEG will do with certain sub-256 color images.

Sites with More Graphic Help

Here are a couple additional sites which help you sort through the various graphical display options that are native to Netscape and Microsoft Internet Explorer.

Creating High Impact Documents by Netscape

`http://www.netscape.com/assist/net_sites/impact_docs/index.html`

This page on Netscape's site does a great job of explaining the various formats and basics of adding graphics to your Web page. It covers interlaced GIFs, JPEGs, JPEG versus GIF, low- to high-resolution flipping (where you first load a low-resolution version of your graphic quickly, then replace it with a high-resolution version), and more.

The JPEG Playground

`http://www.cclabs.missouri.edu/~c675830/jpeg_tests/testgrnd.htm`

This site has everything you ever wanted to know about JPEG but were afraid to ask—including lots of links and information, and good coverage of the progressive JPEG format.

 Don't forget the customized formats some plug-in technologies offer. Earlier in this chapter, I outlined several plug-ins that can be used to develop very highly compressed imagery. While users will need to get the plug-in to view the files, in an intranet or highly specialized setting this approach can be the perfect solution.

The Major Web Graphics Packages

What follows is a comprehensive listing with summary of all the best commercial, shareware, and freeware graphic packages that are relevant for Web developers. In some cases I've also tried to dig up useful resources for the programs themselves, searching out Web tips, newsletters, and other resources for products like Photoshop. After all, it's one thing to have these programs—it's quite another to know how to use them well.

Asymetrix Web 3D

Asymetrix Corp.
110 - 110th Avenue N.E., Suite 700
Bellevue, WA 98004
Phone: 206-637-1600
Fax: 206-637-1504
WWW: http://www.asymetrix.com

With Asymetrix Web 3D, you can turn ordinary, flat-looking Web pages into dazzling 3D marvels with eye-popping logos, bullets, and other images that are limited only by your imagination. Asymetrix Web 3D is an affordable graphics tool that lets you create professional 3D images and animations with ease and speed.

This is a great product for graphical text headers and banners. It also has some animation functionality, as you can spin, rotate, and move models over customized animation paths. Web 3D supports JPEG, GIF, and animated GIF, and it can import metafiles, 3D Studio, and AutoCAD DXF files as well.

Fractal Design Painter 4.0 (Windows and Macintosh)

Fractal Design Corporation
P.O. Box 2380
Aptos, CA 95001
Phone: 408-688-5300
Fax: 408-688-8836
WWW: http://www.fractal.com

Fractal Design Painter (shown in Figure 11.2) was first released in 1991. Since then it's gotten rave reviews and found widespread use among all kinds of artists throughout the computer industry.

The program provides a feature called "Natural Media" painting, which lets you simulate the processes of artists using traditional art tools and media. For example, you can paint on the screen as if you were using charcoal on a sheet of paper, or you can apply oil paints to different types of "paper." This amazing feature helps many artists make the transition to using a computer.

The newest version improves on all the features, and it even brings back a useful feature that was discontinued. Once again, you can create shapes by drawing vectors (lines), then perform bitmap editing techniques on the lines to fine-tune your images. This is like having the features of Deluxe Paint and CorelDraw! combined in one program.

Painter 3.1 brought users the ability to create Web graphics in GIF and JPEG formats with support for interleaved and transparent GIF images. Painter 4 expands these capabilities by providing the ability to create image maps for use in Web page designs.

Figure 11.2 An object in Fractal Design Painter.

If you are a Fractal Design Painter user, you'll want to check out a useful newsletter called *Artistry,* published by a couple of independent computer artists from New York City. You can get a copy by visiting CompuServe's GO GRAPHICS forum or by visiting **http://www.delta.com/peter/paint/tools/ tools.htm** on the World Wide Web.

Adobe Photoshop (Windows, Macintosh, and SGI)

Adobe Systems, Inc.
1585 Charleston Road
P.O. Box 7900
Mountain View, CA 94039-7900
Phone: 415-961-4111
Fax: 415-967-9231
WWW: http://www.adobe.com

Perhaps the most well-known and most awesome image-processing product is Adobe Photoshop (see Figure 11.3). Originally a Macintosh-only product, it's now available for both Windows and Mac platforms. Photoshop really does so much it's hard to label it: It's a drawing package, a file conversion product,

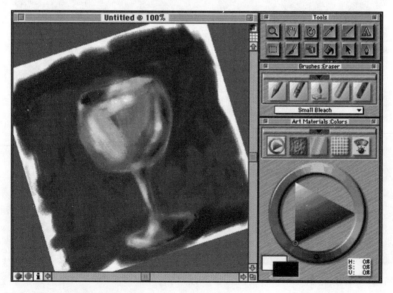

Figure 11.3   Photoshop in action.

and a digital effects product, and it has extensive photo-imaging capabilities and supports plug-in extensions. If you can buy only one product for your Web art toolkit, Photoshop should be that product.

Check out **http://www.adobe.com/prodindex/photoshop/addingon.html** and **http://www.imageclub.com/aps/** for Adobe's own listing of all the major Photoshop plug-ins, including its new free plug-in to support the GIF89a format.

JAG II (Windows and Mac)

Ray Dream Inc.
1804 N. Shoreline Boulevard
Mountain View, CA 94043
Phone: 415-960-0768
Fax: 415-960-1198
WWW: http://www.raydream.com

Available for both Macintosh and Windows, this is an interesting utility that automatically smoothes the jagged edges in digital images and animations. JAG can improve the quality of images created in painting, photo retouching, and video applications after you've done everything else to modify the image.

Kai's Power Tools (Windows, Macintosh, and SGI)

MetaTools, Inc.
6303 Carpinteria Avenue
Carpinteria, CA 93013
Phone: 805-566-6200
Fax: 805-566-6385
WWW: http://www.metatools.com

Several years ago, Kai Krause, a leading computer artist, began designing a line of computer graphics tools that today is widely known as Kai's Power Tools (KPT). Versions are available for Windows, Macintosh, and Silicon Graphics. KPT is a set of powerful utilities that operate as plug-ins for products like Adobe Photoshop, Fractal Design Painter, Autodesk Animator Studio, and other programs that implement Adobe's plug-in technology.

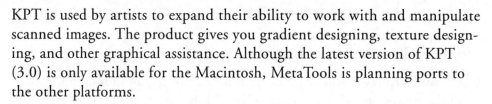

KPT is used by artists to expand their ability to work with and manipulate scanned images. The product gives you gradient designing, texture designing, and other graphical assistance. Although the latest version of KPT (3.0) is only available for the Macintosh, MetaTools is planning ports to the other platforms.

An additional KPT Web site you'll want to check out is Kai's Power Tips and Tricks for Adobe Photoshop, (**http://the-tech.mit.edu/KPT/**). This is a reprint of 23 tips and tricks that were developed by Kai Krause.

Autodesk Animator Pro and Animator Studio (Windows)

Autodesk
111 McInnis Parkway
San Rafael, CA 94903
Phone: 800-879-4233
Fax: 206-860-2196
WWW: http://www.autodesk.com

Autodesk Animator Pro, which recently was put through a major update, is probably the best PC-based animation package available. Animator handles 24-bit color with 8-bit alpha-channel transparency, and it works with Photoshop-compatible plug-ins like Kai's Power Tools. You can even paint on a multiframe animation using video sprites. (For example, suppose you've got one animation running; you can run another animation and create a composite animation from both of them.)

Animator's animation features include a full set of graphics functions, including airbrush, lines, fill, and the other usual characters. This program also supports onion skinning to help you do great line art animation.

With its newest release, Autodesk has added an integrated studio for recording, editing, and synchronizing audio from sources such as CDs, tapes, and external microphones. Sophisticated editing features include the ability to modify pitch and tempo independently, to stretch or "squeeze" a sound track to fit an animation without changing its pitch.

Overall, if you're not dealing with a major SGI package and you need animation capabilities, you're going to have to search far and wide to find a better animation package than either Animator Pro or Animator Studio.

Deluxe Paint IIe (DOS)

Electronic Arts
1450 Fashion Island Boulevard
San Mateo, CA 94404
Phone: 415-571-7171
Fax: 415-570-5137

Deluxe Paint is still considered one of the best pixel-pushing editors around. Its suite of tools and easy-to-use interface allow artists to get down and dirty, editing at the pixel level. EA discontinued production of this product in spring 1995, although you may still find copies. Pick it up if you see it!

DeBabelizer Toolbox 1.6 and DeBabelizer Lite (Mac and Windows)

Equilibrium Technologies
3 Harbor Drive, Suite 111
Sausalito, CA 94965
Phone: 415-332-4343
Fax: 415-332-4433
WWW: http://www.equilibrium.com/Welcome.html

For many users, this major image-processing and palette manipulation program is indispensable. This award-winning product includes dozens of essential editing tools for automated image processing while also providing extensive translation for more than 60 bitmapped graphics and animation formats. DeBabelizer runs native on any Power Mac or 68000-series machine.

Its biggest and most praised feature is its 24-bit to 8-bit color reduction and palette controls. Among them is a feature called SuperPalette, which automatically creates the best palette for a series of images. It can even modify effects over time on a series of QuickTime frames, still images, or other animation files.

The DeBabelizer Lite package is less expensive and translates among more than 55 different cross-platform bitmapped formats. It does *not*, however, offer internal scripting, image processing, or palette manipulation as the full version does.

 The folks at Equilibrium have created some specific utilities for users of the DeBabelizer toolkit who are also developing imagery for the Web. Check it all out at **http://www.equilibrium.com/ SoftwareScripts.html**.

Amazon Paint/Amazon 3D Paint/ Piranha Animator (SGI)

Interactive Effects, Inc.
102 Nighthawk
Irvine, CA 92714
Phone: 714-551-1448
Fax: 714-786-2527
WWW: http://www.webcom.com/~ie/

These three packages offer a complete high-end graphics paint system for SGI workstations. All three packages list for $3,000. Let's look at the features that you get for this steep price tag:

- *Amazon Paint*—In development for over four years, Amazon Paint is a leading paint system for Silicon Graphics workstations. This package has more than 50 image-processing tools, plug-in architecture support for products like Kai's Power Tools, more than 20 special brush effects, and advanced texture mapping, as well as support for any Type 1 PostScript fonts.

- *Amazon 3D Paint*—Using Amazon's 3D Paint, you can paint directly onto the surface and across the seams of multiple 3D models with all the functionality of the 2D version of Amazon Paint. Support exists for model files created in Wavefront, Alias, and Softimage.

- *Piranha Animator*—Piranha Animator is Amazon Paint with advance scripting and keyframe animation support. Among its features are rotoscoping, advanced editing, matte animation with a range of different composing functions, and compatibility with a number of external rendering and output devices for digital video production.

Shareware

Are you on a shoestring budget? No problem! Here's one of several quality shareware paint packages:

Paint Shop Pro (Windows)

JASC, Inc.
P.O. Box 44997
Eden Prairie, MN 55344

Phone: 612-930-9171
Fax: 612-930-9172
WWW: http://www.jasc.com

Available for just a $69 registration fee, this is one of the best bargains in art tools. Paint Shop Pro is a Windows paint package with a lot of power. It has seen numerous enhancements over the years and no doubt will see more. It offers the usual array of drawing options, as well as support for numerous file formats (making it an excellent conversion utility). In addition, it features an array of image-processing options, including plug-in architecture compatibility for Kai's Power Tools. In fact for $99, JASC will send you both Paint Shop Pro *and* a special version of Kai's Power Tools!

Modeling Software

There are a number of really good software products available for helping you with animation. I've included a few of the best in this section.

Poser (Windows and Macintosh)

Fractal Design Corporation
P.O. Box 2380
Aptos, CA 95001
Phone: 408-688-5300
Fax: 408-688-8836
WWW: http://www.fractal.com

The company that brought us the incredible Fractal Design Painter has a really neat solution for creating animated figures. This package, called Poser, allows you to create an infinite variety of human figures that can be posed, rendered with surface textures and multiple lights, and easily incorporated into artwork. Poser works closely with all kinds of products, including Photoshop, Director, and, of course, Fractal's own Design Painter.

Both male and female base models—from infants to children to adults to superhero-like characters—are supplied, and each can be moved, modified, and shaped into any pose and viewed from any angle. If you grab the hand of a figure and move it, Poser knows exactly what to do with the rest of the arm. Once you've created the wire-frame look you want, you can add light sources, texture and bump maps, and render the image. You can export the models as graphic images or as DXF files for use in other 3D packages.

Poser comes with a slew of libraries featuring lots of examples, body shapes, lighting schemes, and textures. For creating fast human models Poser is tough to beat.

LightWave (Amiga, Windows, Windows NT, and SGI)

NewTek, Inc.
1200 SW Executive Drive
Topeka, KS 66615
Phone: 913-228-8000
Fax: 913-228-8099
WWW: http://www.newtek.com

Ever since NewTek came into existence as a top-flight creator of Amiga software, it has constantly amazed people with awesome products produced at an extremely low price. Its modeling package, LightWave (which works with Amiga, Windows, Windows NT, and SGI) is no exception. It sells for under $1,000 and it offers excellent modeling capabilities, inverse kinematics for character animation, plug-ins, and simple creation of organic and aerodynamic objects with metaforms, which transform rough geometry into organic-looking objects.

LightWave allows you to render full ray-tracing graphics, and you can output your creations in a number of file formats. In addition, it features key-framing animation capabilities; LightWave also comes packed with license-free objects, images, and textures.

LightWave Pro Magazine
Avid Media Group
1308 Orleans Drive
Sunnyvale, CA 94089
Phone: 408-743-9250
Fax: 408-743-9251
WWW: http://www.portal.com/~amg/

This magazine's designed to help you get the most out of LightWave. It offers a regular assortment of tips, tricks, news, and companion products for NewTek's LightWave 3D. The magazine comes in both printed and Web versions.

Martin Hash's 3-Dimensional Animation (Windows, Mac, and SGI)

Hash Inc.
2800 East Evergreen Boulevard
Vancouver, WA 98661
Phone: 360-750-0042
Fax: 360-750-0451
WWW: http://www.hash.com

While Animation Master is Hash's flagship product, the company continues
to push forward in developing low-cost, 3D animation packages. Martin
Hash's 3-Dimensional Animation, which is available for Windows, Mac, and
Power Mac platforms for a list price of $199, is just one more example of this.
Hash's 3D experience and downright cheap price tag provide every reason to
investigate this package, which rolls modeling, animating, and rendering into
one bundle.

Beginners will find this package extremely helpful, with its comprehensive
online help, a training video, and a CD-ROM full of sample actors, props,
scenery, and images. Among its standard features are such major 3D staples as
spline-based modeling, character-based motion, inverse kinematics, patch
modeling and animation, skin, materials, skeletal morphing and bending, ray
tracing, and lip-synch keyframing.

Ray Dream Studio (Windows and Mac)

Ray Dream Inc.
1804 N. Shoreline Boulevard
Mountain View, CA 94043
Phone: 415-960-0768
Fax: 415-960-1198
WWW: http://www.raydream.com1

Ray Dream Studio is available for both the Mac and Windows platforms.
Priced under $500, it seamlessly integrates four components: Ray Dream
Designer 4, Ray Dream Animator, Dream Models, and Extensions Portfolio.
These four products offer a complete 3D modeling and animation package
that is priced just right for small individual developers. The Extensions Portfolio component allows customers, VARs, consultants, and developers to create
product extensions and enhancements to the product.

The modeler, Ray Dream Designer 4, offers a full range of features, such as perspective, subtle shadows, lighting effects, textures, and reflections. It also incorporates "wizards" that simplify the process of creating 3D images or scenes; this feature makes the package especially well-suited for beginners. The shader allows users to specify properties in several channels, including color, highlight, shininess, bump, reflection, transparency, refraction, and a glow channel that makes objects appear to emit light. Finally, the package includes more than 500 textures and 500 models.

The Animation model gives you access to inverse kinematics, rotoscoping, tweeners, object deformation, and object behaviors. These are all features that are supported in packages costing hundreds (if not thousands) of dollars more.

Incidentally, Ray Dream was just setting up its home page as I was finishing this book. This user-created site by David Ramirez (**http://www.webcom.com/ ~dram/rdd/welcome.html**), however, is so good that it almost fooled me into thinking it was the official Ray Dream site.

Softimage 3D and Softimage TOONZ

Microsoft Corporation
1 Microsoft Way
Redmond, WA 95082
Phone: 206-882-8080
WWW: http://www.softimage.com

Softimage, creators of high-end animation tools, found themselves thrust into the spotlight when Microsoft plunked down a whopping $135 million to buy the company. What's really cool about Softimage is that it replicates—in software—the techniques of traditional, hand-crafted cel animation.

In its role as a supplier to Sega for Saturn Development Tools, Softimage is incorporating a set of extensions in Softimage 3D. This toolkit includes Saturn file output filters, color reduction tools to move down from 24-bit images, and an online viewer to preview images as they would look on a Saturn.

Version 4.0 of Softimage incorporates such cutting-edge features as pencil testing, palette editing, an ink and paint module, and a flip module, and it can be further customized by adding separate modules for scanning and rendering. And if you're disappointed because you don't use an SGI platform, you'll be happy to hear that a Windows NT version of Softimage's product line is in production.

Softimage's users page can be accessed at **http://delphi.beckman.uiuc.edu/softimage/**. Check out this comprehensive unofficial Softimage Web page for complete information on the Softimage community.

POV-Ray (DOS, Mac) and Associated Modelers (DOS, Windows, and Mac)

Walnut Creek CD-ROM
4041 Pike Lane, Suite D
Concord, CA 94520
Phone: 510-674-0783
Fax: 510-674-0821
Email: info@cdrom.com
WWW: http://www.povray.org

Much of the shareware 3D modeling market revolves around a product called POV-Ray. (POV is short for Persistence of Vision.) This highly capable rendering program was written for the public domain; the developers even allow you to have access to the program's source code.

The problem with POV-Ray is that it renders scenes, but it doesn't construct them. For modeling, you'll have to use another program that works in conjunction with POV-Ray. Several major POV-Ray–compatible modelers are available, along with the latest version of the program itself, at the POV-Ray Web site or CompuServe's graphics forum (GO GRAPHICS).

You can also visit your local bookstore for one of many books dedicated to teaching you everything there is to know about POV-Ray and its associated modeling programs.

Autodesk 3D Studio (DOS) and 3D Studio MAX (Windows NT)

Autodesk
111 McInnis Parkway
San Rafael, CA 94903
Phone: 800-879-4233
Fax: 206-860-2196
WWW: http://www.autodesk.com

When the Atari ST and Amiga were shipped, each included a major art package: DEGAS on the ST, and Deluxe Paint on the Amiga. The two programs' respective creators, Tom Hudson and Dan Silva, went on to play critical roles in the development of 3D Studio, one of the best 3D rendering products for IBM/DOS-based systems. 3D Studio has been in use by a majority of top-notch game and multimedia development shops for many years. Even with the move by the larger publishers to Silicon Graphics–based workstations, many still use 3D Studio.

In the life of 3D Studio, 1995 was an important year: The product was split into two distinct product lines. The Yost Group, the actual programmers of 3D Studio, have totally redesigned it into a new product called 3D Studio MAX. Since 3D Studio MAX is for Windows NT only, Autodesk has committed to releasing further upgrades of the current 3D Studio product, which runs in a DOS environment.

How long this strategy lasts is probably based on customer demand. Rest assured, though, that 3D Studio users, while seeing amazing advanced features implemented in 3D Studio MAX, will see further work and functionality in 3D Studio as well.

3D Studio MAX has been built around object-oriented programming, giving it exceptional plug-in architecture and allowing for quick updates in addition to more esoteric abilities like human modeling, various platform support, and facial expressions. Additional 3D Studio MAX features include:

- A developer API document

- A multitasking, multithreaded environment

- Multiple processor and 3D acceleration hardware support

- Advance time editing, which allows you to synchronize animation with sound

 Check out a good unofficial Autodesk Products users page, **http:// www.opencad.com/Magic_Mirror/**, for comprehensive information about using Autodesk products—especially 3D Studio— from the pros who use them daily.

trueSpace2 (Windows)

Caligari Corporation
1933 Landings Drive
Mountain View, CA 94043

Phone: 415-390-9600
Fax: 415-390-9755
Email: sales@caligari.com
WWW: http://www.caligari.com

trueSpace originally started out as a 3D rendering package for the Amiga in the late 1980s. While the demise of the Amiga really killed trueSpace, the program has had a kind of glorious rebirth as the major competition to Autodesk's 3D Studio.

This package's basic drawing features include drawing spline shapes into 3D objects, constructing a 3D object from any 2D shape, creating 3D beveled text with any TrueType font, rendering up to 24-bits with alpha channel, and the ability to include transparencies and shadow and fog effects. trueSpace also offers powerful animation capabilities, which include field rendering and animated textures, motion blur and depth of field, support for FLC (Autodesk) and AVI (Microsoft Video) video formats, morphing, frame-by-frame animation, and easily definable 3D animation paths for objects.

trueSpace2 is entirely icon-driven and works with Photoshop-compatible plug-ins, so you can use products like Kai's Power Tools directly in the program. trueSpace2 also uses Intel's 3DR to provide realtime solid rendering. This eliminates the need for mesh frames in edit mode. (The mesh mode is still available if you prefer to use this feature.) trueSpace2 also comes with a CD-ROM of 600 3D clip objects and hundreds of textures and materials like wood, glass, stone, and more.

Animation:Master (Windows)

Hash Inc.
2800 East Evergreen Boulevard
Vancouver, WA 98661
Phone: 360-750-0042
Fax: 360-750-0451
WWW: http://www.hash.com

Animation:Master is quite a powerful and inexpensive 3D modeling and animation package. It's specifically designed for character animation, providing a very powerful spline-based modeling system and including such features as character morphing, facial movements, and direct support for the Polhumus motion capture system.

Animation:Master takes a full 3D character animation system—Playmation's 3D—and adds all kinds of major rendering features, as well as several new high-end features like inverse kinematics, motion blur, field rendering, shadow buffers, and depth buffers.

This product is available in versions for Windows and Windows NT workstations (Alpha, MIPs, and Intel), and all object and motion files are completely portable. With the Windows version, you can use a Windows network to increase rendering times and flexibility.

Extreme 3D

Macromedia, Incorporated
600 Townsend Street
San Francisco, CA 94103
Phone: 415-252-2000
Fax: 415-626-0554
Email: info@macromedia.com
WWW: http://www.macromedia.com

Extreme 3D began life as a 3D creation product known as MacroModel. The reborn Extreme 3D uses spline-based modeling and includes some new features (such as surface trim) and user interface improvements. Most notable is that Macromedia has replaced its rendering module, which used to be Pixar's RenderMan, with its own renderer. One other significant improvement is that all object and scene animations are now time-based and frame-based.

Specular Infini-D

Specular International
479 West Street
Amherst, MA 01002
Phone: 413-253-3100
Fax: 413-253-0540
WWW: http://www.specular.com

Infini-D is a powerful spline-based modeler with photorealistic rendering. Infini-D features excellent texture flexibility with a built-in texture generator, animated textures, and much more. Another cool feature is the ability to take any Adobe Illustrator or Macromedia FreeHand file and turn it into a 3D object. Also, you can use any Adobe Photoshop file as a texture, lighting gel, or background. Visit the Specular Web site and download a working demo copy of the program.

Strata StudioPro

Strata, Inc.
2 West George Boulevard
St. George, UT 84770
Phone: 801-628-5218
Fax: 801-628-9756
WWW: http://www.strata3d.com

Strata has perhaps one of the best advertisements available for its 3D rendering product—it was used by the Miller brothers to create Myst, a spectacular display of 3D animation. This product offers all of the major 3D animation features, including metaballs, 3D sculpting, extrude along path, photo-realistic ray tracing with atmospheric effects, and much more.

Strata recently received an equity investment from computer graphics stalwart Evans & Sutherland that is bound to enhance future upgrades of this package. Rumor also has it that there is a Windows version in the works.

Power Animator (SGI)

Alias|Wavefront
110 Richmond Street East
Toronto, Ontario, Canada
M5C 1P1
Phone: 416-362-9181
Fax: 416-362-0630
WWW: http://www.aw.sgi.com

Alias and Wavefront were once major competitors in the high-end 3D graphics software market—until Silicon Graphics decided to purchase both companies and merge them together as Alias|Wavefront. The resulting alliance promises to be an important force.

For now, though, developers "only" have access to the current incarnations of some mind-bogglingly awesome graphics software. Specifically, among the products both companies offer are Alias' Power Animator and Wavefront's GameWare.

In creating GameWare, Wavefront has combined traditional artistic principles with the technical specs used in games. For example, this product has a powerful 3D graphics rendering engine that takes into account the color and geometry limitations of consoles and various PC platforms. Thus you can render a really high-resolution person with all kinds of textures, and GameWare will redraw that graphic to work as well as possible for the desired platform by rendering new reduced palettes or creating 2D graphical versions of its 3D renderings.

Additionally, because this is high-end technology, Wavefront offers training and assistance in the entire GameWare process. The trainers and support techs are knowledgeable about game development and the industry, not just 3D rendering and artwork creation.

Overall, this software might be out of your reach—technically and financially— but like everything in this business, you can expect that the features and ideas here will trickle down over time. I advise you to be as familiar with this product (and other such products) as possible; if you sign on with a bigger company or publisher, you may find yourself with access to this high-end suite of tools. And when you're interviewing with one of these large companies, of course, it's best to sound knowledgeable about the latest technological trends.

You can access to get the latest information and tips on these products at **http://www.uni-uppertal.de/computer/software/grafik/Alias/welcome. english.html**. This well-run unofficial Web home page includes lots of links and some software as well.

Texture Creation Products

In researching this book, I talked to several 3D artists and I heard the same thing from all of them: You can never have enough textures when doing 3D work. With that in mind, I searched out the best texture libraries and texture creation products.

What's amazing is that each of these products offers a different approach or a different set of textures. From wild geometric patterns to alien skin textures to all kinds of takes on wood and fabrics and surfaces, you might find yourself in the poorhouse if you invest in all of these products. Even so, each one is worth the investment.

Alien Skin Textureshop

Virtus Corporation
118 Mackenan Drive, Suite 250
Cary, NC 27511-3625
Phone: 919-467-9700
Fax: 919-460-4530
Email: info@virtus.com
WWW: http://www.virtus.com

Everybody loves a good slimy (or scaly, smooth, or metallic, for that matter)
alien. Alien Skin Textureshop is a neat product that allows you to create cool
alien skin for your 2D and 3D products. It runs either as a Photoshop plug-in
or as a standalone product.

Adobe TextureMaker

Adobe Systems, Inc.
Mountain View, CA
Phone: 415-961-4400
Fax: 415-961-3769
Email: info@adobe.com
WWW: http://www.adobe.com

This Macintosh-only package is Adobe's entry into the texture creation
business. TextureMaker excels at creating staple textures like wood, marble,
and sandstone, and you can also use it to create different skin surfaces (though
not like Alien Skin) and other organic textures. In addition, TextureMaker
offers various animation effects.

Xaos Tools' Terrazzo

Xaos Tools, Inc.
600 Townsend Street, Suite 270
East San Francisco, CA 94103
Phone: 415-487-7000
Fax: 415-558-9886

This product uses various mathematical algorithms, many based on symmetrical routines, to create simple but really cool textures.

TextureScape

Specular International
479 West Street
Amherst, MA 01002
Phone: 413-253-3100
Fax: 413-253-0540
WWW: http://www.specular.com

Just for starters, TextureScape comes with 750 textures. That number alone is worth the price of admission. This product isn't just a library of textures (of which you can purchase more), but an entire new texture-generation system. *MacUser* called it "unsurpassed in the level of control it provides over texture composition."

TextureScape allows you to create all kinds of amazing textures and output them in a variety of graphics formats (PICT, TIFF , EPSF, and QuickTime, among others). You can even create animated textures by choosing key frames and then letting TextureScape morph them from frame to frame, outputting the result as a QuickTime movie.

Texture Libraries

The demand on 3D artists is growing dramatically, and so rapidly building a kick-butt texture library for 3D production should be one of your primary concerns. The following libraries can serve as excellent foundations for such an endeavor.

Texture Universe

Autodesk
111 McInnis Parkway
San Rafael, CA 94903
Phone: 800-225-6106
Fax: 206-860-2196
WWW: http://www.autodesk.com

This CD-ROM contains more than 400 ready-to-use textures and backgrounds. The collection is pretty broad, ranging from wall surfaces to animal skins. A utility is included for browsing and searching the textures in either DOS or Windows.

Fractal Design's Really Cool Textures— The Sensational Surfaces CD-ROM

Fractal Design Corporation
P.O. Box 2380
Aptos, CA 95001
Phone: 408-688-5300
Fax: 408-688-8836
WWW: http://www.fractal.com

The makers of Fractal Design Painter have five texture libraries, all modestly priced. One, known more specifically as The Sensational Surfaces CD-ROM, contains five libraries of 20 natural textures each, including wood, paper, stone, stone tiles, and other surfaces. The CD-ROM contains both the Macintosh and Windows versions of the textures, which are derived from the textures created by Artbeats Software, Inc., a premier supplier of textures for computer art and multimedia. Most of these textures are photographic in origin and bring a further sense of reality to natural-media capabilities.

Artbeats Texture Collections

Artbeats Software, Inc.
2611 South Myrtle Road
Myrtle Creek, OR 97457
Phone: 541-863-4429
Fax: 541-863-4547

Artbeats Software, Inc., is a leading developer and publisher of background and digitized images for pre-press and multimedia users. The company's products include Prelude, Seamless Textures Collection Volume I, Marble & Granite, Wood & Paper, and Marbled Paper Textures. Artbeats has also created some specific bundled packages, including Backgrounds for Multimedia Bundle, Volumes 1 and 2, and the Full Page Images EPSF Library.

Wild Tiles!

Cameo Graphics
3400 Jackson Street
Oxnard, CA 93033
Phone: 805-486-5591
Fax: 805-486-5591

Wild Tiles! is a collection of more than two thousand 300 × 300 tileable designs rendered in various file formats. None of these textures is of the run-of-the-mill photo-realistic type, which makes this collection a great alternative.

Wraptures Volumes 1 & 2 and Page Overtures Volumes 1 & 2

Form and Function
1595 Seventeenth Avenue
San Francisco, CA 94122
Phone: 415-664-4010
Fax: 415-664-4030

Wraptures is a collection of 250 seamless tileable photographic textures. Each set costs about $120 and contains more than 100 textures. You can request free literature from Form and Function, which gives you a thumbnail description of every texture in the collection. Each texture comes in multiple-bit depths and sizes, and all are royalty-free.

Page Overtures is another two-volume set of textured images. Unlike Wraptures, these textures are not designed for the 3D market. The images are more or less sized and at a color depth for page layout and paint products. Still, this is a great-looking collection of photo-realistic textures that any good artist could bring into Photoshop, resize, and then drop the bit depth to make use of the texture in 3D work.

Three-Dimensional Libraries

As 3D worlds become constantly more complex, the use of 3D clip art is going to increase. There are many reasons to use 3D art, and just as many reasons to not use it. There are, however, some quality 3D libraries and 3D model "brokers" that you can use to cut down on the time and cost associated with in-house 3D model production.

Three-Dimensional Object Stock Libraries

The libraries listed here should provide you with an abundance of images for your projects.

Viewpoint DataLabs International

625 South State Street
Orem, UT 84058
Phone: 801-229-3000
Fax: 801-229-3300
WWW: http://www.datalabs.com

Viewpoint DataLabs is best described as a 3D modeling brokerage. This company manages a large database of 3D models that, when converted, can be used in a wide variety of top programs. Artists can actually submit 3D models (via the Web) for Viewpoint to resell.

As this database grows and catches on, it will become an awesome resource for those out-of-the-way models—like spacecraft, human figures, and such. As VRML expands in importance on the Web and as more graphic stills are really 3D rendered scenes, this will become as important a source of help to Web developers as it already is for computer animators and game developers.

Viewpoint bought the rights to the Avalon's online 3D database, which was the leading Internet site for public-domain 3D models. Viewpoint took over management of the old China Lake free 3D model archive some time ago. If you go to their Web site, you can access all the cool models that were available at China Lake—for free!

The Mesh Mart
http://cedar.cic.net/~rtilmann/mm/index.htm

The Mesh Mart is another online 3D object broker being developed by Richard Tilmann. While Viewpoint is larger, The Mesh Mart will provide a source of 3D mesh object files for the growing number of 3D modeling artists and developers.

The UK VR-SIG 3D Object Archive
http://www.dcs.ed.ac.uk/~mxr/objects.html

Yet another 3D model archive, but with a slight twist—it focuses on free models that are optimized for VR applications. These models are often compact, simpler representations, making them excellent for games. Criterion, maker of the 3D game library RenderWare, is a supporter of the site, which is maintained on behalf of the United Kingdom Virtual Reality Special Interest Group (UK VR-SIG).

CD-ROM-Based Libraries

The libraries listed here are all collected on various CD-ROMs.

3D Props CD-ROMs

Autodesk
111 McInnis Parkway
San Rafael, CA 94903
Phone: 800-879-4233
Fax: 206-860-2196
WWW: http://www.autodesk.com

Autodesk, which recently entered the 3D model library arena, currently has two CD-ROMs, each containing more than 300 models.

Replica 3D Libraries

Specular International
479 West Street
Amherst, MA 01002
Phone: 413-253-3100
Fax: 413-253-0540
WWW: http://www.specular.com

From the developer of the Macintosh-based modeling software Infini-D, comes 13 volumes of 3D models. Among the various categories are furniture, transportation, dinosaurs, starships, and human forms. You'll find several texture volumes to use as well.

Three-Dimensional Conversion Products

Unfortunately, not every developer uses the same packages to produce Web sites; even some of your own packages might not offer compatible file formats for you to move among products. Here is one piece of conversion software that is sure to help you.

InterChange

Syndesis Corporation
235 South Main Street

Jefferson, WI 53549
Phone: 414-674-5200
Fax: 414-674-6363
WWW: http://www.webmaster.com/syndesis/

InterChange, available as a plug-in to 3D Studio or as a standalone for Windows, translates between more than 20 different common 3D file formats, including 3D Studio, LightWave Objects & Scenes, Wavefront, Alias polysets, RenderWare, AutoCAD DXF, and POV-Ray 2.0. InterChange preserves geometry, surface information, hierarchy, rotational centers, and more.

Additional Hardware

You can input artwork into a computer using either scanners or digital cameras. Both have specific uses, so I'll wrap up my product reviews with these two pieces of hardware.

Scanners

The best bet for introducing handmade artwork into a computer is to use a scanner. Here's all the contact information you need to find out about their latest and greatest models from the three major scanner manufacturers:

Hewlett-Packard

3000 Hanover St.
Palo Alto, CA 94304
Phone: 415-857-1501
Fax: 415-857-7299
WWW: http://www.dmo.hp.com/peripherals/scanners/main.html

Hewlett-Packard makes a complete line of excellent flatbed scanners under its ScanJet brand name.

MicroTek

3300 NW 211th Terrace
Hillsboro, OR 97124
Phone: 503-645-7333
Fax: 503-629-8460

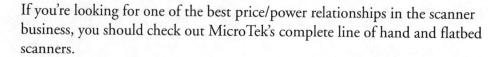

If you're looking for one of the best price/power relationships in the scanner business, you should check out MicroTek's complete line of hand and flatbed scanners.

Agfa

200 Ballardvale Street
Wilmington, MA 01887
Phone: 508-658-5600
Fax: 508-658-8982
WWW: http://www.agfa.com

After Xerox, German-based Agfa is one of the biggest professional printing and graphic arts hardware manufacturers in the world. They make a complete line of awesome scanners. Check out their Web site (which is, by the way, unusually excellent) for more information.

3D Scanners

3D scanners scan an object and then construct a 3D mesh representation. While these can generally be considered equipment for a "dream" graphics studio, it's good to know what's out there.

Cyberware, Inc.

2110 Del Monte Avenue
Monterey, CA 93940
Phone: 408-657-1450
Fax: 408-657-1494
WWW: http://www.cyberware.com

Maybe you have a rich uncle who will die and leave you a ton of cash, or perhaps your latest Web product will be a gold mine. Whatever lighting bolt of luck strikes you, if you've got the cash to spend, add this company to your Rolodex.

Cyberware manufactures a variety of hardware devices to enable 3D scanning. Using lasers, the hardware scans an object in seconds and from that scan constructs a 3D mesh representation. Cyberware has standard devices that are desktop and full-body size (the latter model retails at over $400,000!). They'll even custom design equipment for you.

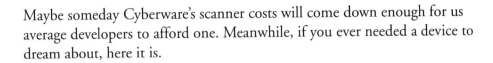

Maybe someday Cyberware's scanner costs will come down enough for us average developers to afford one. Meanwhile, if you ever needed a device to dream about, here it is.

Digital Cameras

Digital cameras are useful for creating natural-world 3D images for your computer. They're also awesome for capturing real-world textures digitally (a brick right off a wall, for example). Here is the contact information for the three major creators of digital cameras and accompanying software.

Agfa

200 Ballardvale Street
Wilmington, MA 01887
Phonc: 508-658-5600
Fax: 508-658-8982
WWW: http://www.agfa.com

Agfa has created a line of digital cameras based on Nikon lens technology for highly accurate and detailed digital photography.

Kodak

Eastman Kodak Company
343 State Street
Rochester, NY 14650-0518
Phone: 716-724-4000
Fax: 716-722-1178
WWW: http://www.kodak.com

Kodak makes two types of digital cameras. Both are self-contained units and can function as attachments for common SLR cameras.

Apple Computer

1 Infinite Loop
Cupertino, CA 95014
Phone: 408-996-1010
Fax: 408-996-0275
WWW: http://www.apple.com

Apple markets the Apple QuickTake, a sister series to Kodak's digital cameras.

Tablets

Many artists prefer to create art by hand. For them, working with one of the many cutting-edge graphics programs that use tablets is a necessity. Here is the contact information for the three most common tablet manufacturers.

Kurta

3007 East Chambers
Phoenix, AZ 85040
Phone: 800-445-8782

Summagraphics

8500 Cameron Road
Austin, TX 78754-3999
Phone: 512-835-0900
Fax: 512-339-1490
WWW: http://www.summagraphics.com

Wacom

501 S.E. Columbia Shores Boulevard, Suite 300
Vancouver, WA 98661
Phone: 360-750-8882
Fax: 360-750-8924
WWW: http://www.wacom.com

Art Magazines

I have found several really great magazines that I think will help any Web site developer in the art arena.

3D Design

Miller Freeman, Inc.
600 Harrison Street
San Francisco, CA 94107
Phone: 415-905-2200
Subscription: $29.95
Newsstand: $3.95
Publishes: Monthly
Pages: 100

3D Design focuses on the issues professional 3D designers face every day. Within a mere 100 pages, you'll find hands-on, how-to feature articles, product news and evaluations, and analysis of design-oriented issues and trends.

Computer Artist

Pennwell Publishing Co.
10 Tara Boulevard, 5th Floor
Nashua, NH 03062
Phone: 603-891-0123
Fax: 603-891-0539
Subscription: $24.95
Newsstand: $3.95
Publishes: Bimonthly
Pages: 100

This magazine covers a wide range of computer artwork creation, including illustration and 3D modeling. You'll also find a lot of news articles about new products and developments.

Computer Graphics World

Pennwell Publishing Co.
10 Tara Boulevard, 5th Floor
Nashua, NH 03062
Phone: 603-891-0123
Fax: 603-891-0539
WWW: http://www.lfw.com/WWW/CGW/cgwhome.htm
Subscription: $50.00
Newsstand: $4.95
Publishes: Monthly
Pages: 100

Also published by Pennwell, *Computer Graphics World* focuses on a wider range of graphical issues beyond traditional artwork, including digital video and high-end imaging. Of course, you'll still find discussions on SGI-type products, animation packages, and more for the traditional artist.

Digital Video Magazine

ActiveMedia, Inc. (IDG)
600 Townsend Street, Suite 170

San Francisco, CA 94103
Phone: 415-522-2400
Fax: 415-522-2409
Email: letters@dv.com
Subscription: $24.97
Newsstand: $3.95
Publishes: Monthly
Pages: 112

You may recall that I mentioned this magazine in Chapter 10, when we discussed digital video in depth. *Digital Video* magazine is the undisputed king of digital video, but this great magazine doesn't stop there. You'll find information on 3D animation and modeling, multimedia authoring, and audio. With lots of tutorial and in-depth coverage on how to produce video and how to make models that you can integrate into multimedia and interactive products, *Digital Video* magazine will surely keep you interested.

3D Artist Magazine

Columbine, Inc.
P.O. Box 4787
Santa Fe, NM 87502-4787
Phone: 505-982-3532
Fax: 505-820-6929
Email: info@3dartist.com
WWW: http://www.3dartist.com
Subscription: $33.00
Newsstand: $3.95
Publishes: Monthly
Pages: 100

These guys at Columbine are 3D maniacs; they don't just write about this stuff, they live it night and day. Before Miller Freeman introduced *3D Design*, this was the only major 3D-specific magazine around.

What I really enjoy about this magazine is the extensive Web site, which (among other things) allowed me to sign up for its newsletter, *The Tesselation Times*. Every two weeks via email, I get a complete news breakdown of new products and announcements and general happenings in the world of 3D graphics and design. If you haven't subscribed to *The Tesselation Times,* you should!

Planet Studio

120 Bedford Center Road, Suite 4
Bedford, NH 03110
Phone: 603-924-0100
Fax: 603-924-4066
Email: planet_studio@dv.com.
Subscription: $59.95 (Charter)
Newsstand: N/A
Publishes: 6/yr
Pages: N/A

An offshoot from the folks at *Digital Video* magazine, *Planet Studio* is a bimonthly newsletter covering all the multimedia products produced by Autodesk and any affiliated plug-ins. This means you get dedicated high-end coverage of 3D Studio, Animator Pro/Studio, and more.

Books

Here is a breakdown of some of the better books around to help you with Web art creation tasks.

Web-Specific Art Books

A slew of new books can really help you learn the ins and outs of creating Web graphics. A lot of these involve using Photoshop, but the ideas and techniques presented are applicable to other imaging and drawing packages as well.

Creating Great Web Graphics by Laurie McCanna (published by Henry Holt & Company, 1996, ISBN 1-558-28-4796)

Deconstruction Web Graphics by Lynda Weinman (published by Macmillan Computer Publishing, 1996, ISBN 1-562-05-6417)

Designing Web Graphics by Lynda Weinman (published by Macmillan Computer Publishing, 1996, ISBN 1-562-05-5321)

Web Workshop on Graphics and Web Page Design by Laura Lemay (published by Macmillan Computer Publishing, 1996, ISBN 1-575-21-1254)

Web Publishers' Design Guide for Windows 95 by Mary Jo Fahey (published by The Coriolis Group, 1995, ISBN 1-883-57-7616)

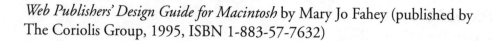

Web Publishers' Design Guide for Macintosh by Mary Jo Fahey (published by The Coriolis Group, 1995, ISBN 1-883-57-7632)

Siggraph Book Reference

`http://www.siggraph.org/artdesign/publications/bookshelf.html`

There's some overlap between what I list here and what this page has, but for the most part this is a great source of coverage to find books (both old and new) to help you create cool art and animation.

Computer Art/Painting Books

Fractal Design Painter 3.1 Unleashed by Denise Tyler (published by SAMS, 1995, ISBN 0-672-30707-3)

Denise Tyler is a freelance computer and game artist who wrote the art how-to section for Andre Lamothe's *Tricks of The Game Programming Gurus* book, also published by SAMS. In her book she shows you the ins and outs of Fractal Design Painter. An accompanying CD-ROM includes all of the samples as well as demo software.

3D Modeling and Animation Books

Animation and Modeling on the Mac by Don and Melora Foley (published by Peachpit Press, 1995 ISBN 0-201-88420-8)

Although this is a Macintosh-focused book, there is a ton of information here relevant to any 3D artist. The book has tips and examples for all sorts of cool Mac graphics products, including Premiere, Photoshop, Infini-D, After Effects, Paint Alchemy, Ray Dream Designer, Electric Image, form*Z, DeBabelizer, and more.

Becoming a Computer Animator by Mike Morrison (published by SAMS, 1994, ISBN 0-672-30463-5)

This book, which covers all the basics of computer-based animation, has interviews with industry experts and covers both 2D and 3D animation. The companion CD-ROM (a dual Mac/PC product) comes with several animation program demos. It also covers job information for the most common computer animator jobs, including interactive entertainment.

3D Studio IPAS Plug-In Reference by Tim Forcade (published by New Riders Publishing, 1995, ISBN 1-562-0543-17)

There are more than 200 different plug-ins for 3D Studio—how do you figure out which ones might be useful for your special needs? Get this book, that's how. If you're a major 3D Studio user, this book will help you get even more out of the program by explaining and showing you the variety of products that extend and supplement it. The accompanying CD-ROM includes more than 100 plug-in demonstration programs, such as Schreiber Instruments' Fractal Bouquet and Positron Publishing's MeshPaint 3D.

3D Studio MAX Design Guide by Anthony Potts, David Friedel, and Anthony Stock (published by The Coriolis Group, 1996, ISBN 1-883577-83-7)

This book gives designers graphic tutorials they can put to use immediately to create professional animations for cartoons, multimedia games, presentations, and more. Offers step-by-step tips for bouncing balls, object tracking, high realism, cartoons, character animation, motion tracking, and morphing. It also gives instruction on effectively using materials, such as metals, glass, wood, skin, animated textures, smoke, and reflections.

Inside 3D Studio Release 4 by Steven D. Elliot and Phillip L. Miller (published by New Riders Publishing, 1995, ISBN 1-56205-415-5)

If you want a cover-to-cover tome on 3D Studio, this is a good place to look. The companion CD-ROM contains more than 200 megabytes of meshes, utilities, textures, and bump maps.

Adobe Photoshop 3 Filters and Effects by Gary David Bouton (published by New Riders Publishing, 1995, ISBN 1-56205-448-1)

This book covers all the various Adobe and third-party filters for use with Photoshop. An accompanying CD-ROM includes all demo versions of plug-in filters and several custom design filters, as well as sample images.

Adobe Photoshop Creative Techniques by Denise Salles, Gary Poyssick, and Ellen Behoriam (published by Hayden, 1995, ISBN 1-56830-132-4)

Basically, this book is a step-by-step guide that covers Version 3 for Macintosh.

Kai's Power Tools Filters & Effects by Heinz Schuller (published by New Riders Publishing, 1995, ISBN 1-56205-480-5)

A step-by-step guide with a CD-ROM containing a demo version of the product. This book covers how to work with KPT within popular products like Fractal Design Painter and Adobe Photoshop.

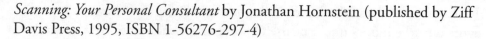

Scanning: Your Personal Consultant by Jonathan Hornstein (published by Ziff Davis Press, 1995, ISBN 1-56276-297-4)

Real World Scanning Halftones by David Blatner and Stephen Roth (published by Peachpit Press, 1994, ISBN 1-566-0909-38)

These two books will show you how to get the highest-quality reproduction out of your scanner. Both cover halftones, scanner tips, adjusting scans, scanning software, and more.

More Art-Oriented World Wide Web Listings

I've presented some vendor-specific Web sites throughout this chapter to help you locate more information about the products discussed. This section includes some of my favorite Web sites for locating general information, tips, techniques, and resources on Web art and animation topics.

General Art and Animation Sites

Brian Leach's Digital Illusions
http://www.mcs.net/~bcleach/illusions/

This is one of my favorite sites on the Web. It features a complete self-published online magazine devoted to cutting-edge computer animation and art. Check out this Web site as you explore the various art resources available to you on the Web.

Animation Site
http://www.cam.org/~pawn/ANIMRES.html

Animation Spots on the World Wide Web
http://laotzu.art.niu.edu/~asifa/animspot.html

Both of these sites are good jumping-off points for locating information on computer animation tools, tips, and techniques.

General 3D Art and Animation Sites

3D Site
http://www.3dsite.com/3dsite/

Devoted to the creation and animation of 3D computer graphics, 3D Site contains an unbelievably complete list of links to information about your favorite art programs.

GWeb—An Electronic Trade Journal for Computer Animators

http://www2.cinenet.net/GWEB/index-text.html

GWeb is an informal trade journal for people in the computer animation industry, as well as those pursuing a career in computer animation. Some of the main highlights of GWeb include an up-to-date job listing section and insightful, behind-the-scenes interviews with the people leading this industry.

Organizations

ACM/SIGGRAPH—The ACM Special Interest Group on Graphics

http://www.siggraph.org

Siggraph is the organization for graphic artists, programmers, engineers, and researchers. Tune in to this site to catch up with cutting-edge topics and examples concerning computer graphics.

International Animation Association

http://laotzu.art.niu.edu/asifa.html

The ASIFA is a leading organization for professional animators around the world. Check out this Web site to find out more about becoming a member and to explore its resources for traditional and computer-based animators.

Awesome List of Animation Schools

http://samson.stud.hivolda.no/~asifa/

This list is absolutely amazing. It features detailed summaries about the courses and resources of every major art/animation school in the world. You've got to see this to believe it.

Motion Effects Web Site

http://www.tiac.net/users/motionfx/

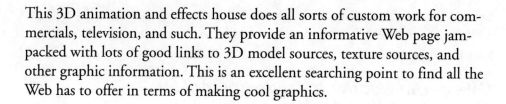

This 3D animation and effects house does all sorts of custom work for commercials, television, and such. They provide an informative Web page jam-packed with lots of good links to 3D model sources, texture sources, and other graphic information. This is an excellent searching point to find all the Web has to offer in terms of making cool graphics.

CHAPTER 12

From WAV files to streams, the Web is alive with sound and music.

Web Music and Sound

Common Web Sound Formats

Last time I counted, there were 24 different audio file formats—and that was before the Web came along! Now, some of you may be scratching your head and saying, "Wait, there's only one fundamental set of math concerning the re-creation of a sound. Why are there so many formats?" Well, it seems to boil down to new formats being specifically tailored to new technologies (for example, a more capable sound card) or to create new hybrid features like RealAudio's streaming-on-demand format, which sacrifices sound quality for realtime play over slow Internet connections.

Following is a basic rundown of the formats you should be most concerned with.

Digital Audio File Formats

- *AIFF and AIFC (Apple Interchange File Format and Apple Interchange Format Compressed)*—This format was created by Apple, and it's also commonly found in SGI circles. The AIFC version of the file introduced compression capabilities.

- *AU*—This is perhaps the second most prevalent standalone sound format found on the Web (the first being WAV files). It's the sound format found on Sun systems, which of course are the platforms for numerous Web servers. Netscape and several other browsers support this format without any need for additional plug-ins.

- *QuickTime*—Apple's video playback engine also has an accompanying sound format. The format supports an unlimited number of tracks and up to six different compression schemes. QuickTime also supports the AIFF format, as well as a more native format to integrate sound and music directly into a movie file.

- *RIFF (Rich Interchange File Format)*—This format, invented by Microsoft, is specific to the Windows platform. It supports both 8-bit and 16-bit resolution, multiple sample rates, stereo, embedded text, markers, and playlists.

- *VOC*—This format from Creative Labs is the original native format of its Sound Blaster PC sound cards. The main difference between the two available versions is in the resolution of the formats; the older version supports only 8-bit resolution, while the newer VOC supports 16-bit resolution.

- *WAV*—This is the most common form of sample sound file on Windows, and it's becoming the most common sample format on the Web as well. It was designed by Microsoft and supports 8-bit and 16-bit resolution, multiple samples, and stereo and mono playback. WAV files can support a wide variety of audio compression algorithms.

Musical Formats

There are two major formats for delivering scored music on computers (and the Web). While some people prefer to digitize music into a common sound format, other developers use musical file formats to create synthesized scores. The files can be far smaller and of higher sound quality than most digitized music, especially on the Web, where bandwidth can wreak havoc on sound quality.

MIDI

I'll discuss MIDI in greater depth later in this chapter—for now, I'll define it as a universal musical scoring format. MIDI files contain note-by-note information, which defines the note played, the length of the note, the effect, and the instrument being used (from a defined set of instruments). When all of this is read and played back by compatible sound cards and synthesizers, users can re-create entire scores just as they were originally composed. MIDI files are relatively small considering the amount of information they contain, and they will produce even better listening experiences as sound cards improve. MIDI has been slow to take hold on the Web because everyone is so caught up with digital audio streaming systems, but expect it to get much more popular in the near future.

MOD

As I will also discuss in more detail later in this chapter, MOD files are a specialized sort of hybrid format for reproducing musical scores. Essentially, a MOD composer takes a series of digital audio samples of different instruments (or voices, or whatever catches their fancy), then adds timing, pitch bends, and other effects to create wild musical experiences. A warning, though: MOD files can be much larger than MIDI files for musical pieces of similar length. They also can be far closer to digitized versions of those songs, too.

Web-Specific Formats and Plug-In Sound Technologies

RealAudio

Progressive Networks, Inc.
1111 3rd Ave, Suite 2900
Seattle, WA 98101
Phone: 206-674-2700
WWW: http://www.realaudio.com and http://www.timecast.com

If you haven't heard of RealAudio (Figure 12.1), then you've only been on the Internet for an hour or two. Even developers who don't have any need for the product on their sites have heard of this, the top dog of realtime audio technologies.

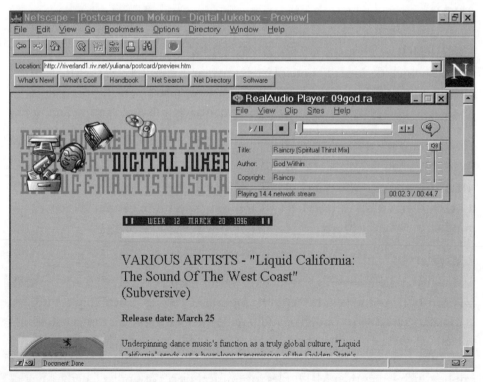

Figure 12.1 The RealAudio Player in action.

While in my opinion there are some other technologies that sport slightly superior sound, RealAudio got out of the gates first with a solid product, a great interface, and far and away the most complete all-around plan for realtime Web audio—so it's no surprise that RealAudio has the largest user base. Progressive feels that at 14.4 Kbps modem speeds, RealAudio's sound quality is roughly that of AM radio, and at 28.8 Kbps it is closer to FM radio. Users who crank their audio up, however, might suggest otherwise. My own feeling is that while RealAudio certainly has good quality at 28.8 Kbps, it doesn't sound FM-like until you lower the volume level so that the hisses and pops aren't as audible.

In order to incorporate synchronized multimedia elements, RealAudio 2.0 allows you to embed URLs and other multimedia hooks into your audio streams. One product taking advantage of this is Progressive's own Timecast, which I'll discuss in a later section.

Because of its king-of-the-mountain status and mature implementation, I'll take some time here to document as much I can about RealAudio.

RealAudio Player Options
There are several ways to offer end users access to RealAudio content. First and foremost are Progressive Networks' player software applications, which include versions compatible with many different browsers on the PC and Macintosh platforms. The biggest dilemma for developers is whether to offer 14.4 or 28.8 Kbps modem support, which should be based on how the content is encoded. For musical content, a 28.8 Kbps modem is the minimum to get what many users consider acceptable audio quality (though I've listened to a few 14.4 Kbps sites with musical content that wasn't awful). Whatever you decide, make sure your users understand how their connection speeds will correlate directly to their ability to access your RealAudio files.

Users can download directly from RealAudio all the software they need to experience realtime streaming audio from your sites.

Encoder Information
To create RealAudio files for your site, you'll need to run your digital audio files through RealAudio Encoder 2.0, which will compress the files properly for broadcasting over the Web. RealAudio Encoder supports many common audio file formats.

As I noted before, RealAudio Encoder 2.0 supports better sound if it is set for broadcasting over 28.8 Kbps or better connections. Make sure you do your own series of tests to decide if the 28.8 encoding optimization is worth the reduced pool of users; unless your sound content is mostly music with a lot of variance and instruments, then encoding for 14.4 Kbps and better should be fine.

RealAudio Encoder 2.0 is available for Microsoft Windows 95, Microsoft Windows NT, Microsoft Windows 3.1, Mac OS, and Unix platforms. You can get the encoding product for free by filling out a form on RealAudio's site, where you will also find a document that explains how to get the best-quality audio out of the entire process. Once your files are encoded, you'll need to place and configure them on your server, but you'll also need a compatible RealAudio server subsystem to send the files out over the Web.

You can also order a special Live Encoder product that (in conjunction with a RealAudio server) allows you to broadcast live events to other users. This is a great product for sites that feature interviews, concerts, speeches, and the like.

Server Details

There are many varieties of the RealAudio Server package, all using the same technology but differing greatly in terms of pricing and some basic features.

Essentially, the server package orchestrates the simultaneous broadcasting of a certain number of streams—for example, a low-end package (priced between $500 and $1000) may support five streams going out at any one time. High-end server packages, in contrast, may offer support to hundreds of simultaneous users. Your needs for support and upgrades will also affect the price and type of the package you choose.

Your overall connection speed will ultimately determine how many streams you can offer. For instance, a 56 Kbps frame relay can support up to 4 simultaneous streams, while a T1 can support up to 100 streams, and a T3 connection can send out more than 3,000 streams at the same time.

The RealAudio Server package is compatible with many leading Web server packages, including Netscape Netsite, O'Reilly Website NT, Mac HTTPD, NCSA HTTPD (v1.3 or v1.4), Emwac HTTPS 0.96, CERN HTTPD (v3.0), and WebStar for Macintosh. It also supports a broad range of hardware platforms, from PCs to Macs to many flavors of Unix workstations. Check with the folks at Progressive Networks for exact requirements about your specific hardware setup.

Expect your RealAudio files to require between 1.1 and 2.4 K of storage space per second of audio, depending mostly on whether you encoded for 14.4 or 28.8 resolution.

For all you nonprofessionals out there with home pages or perhaps a simple site, Progressive offers the RealAudio Personal Server, which will support two realtime streams with delay. The Personal Server runs on Windows 95 and Windows NT platforms, and it includes the RealAudio Encoder as well. A complete interface gives you a window that tells you who's accessing your site and specifically what they're listening to.

 You might not need to get your own RealAudio Server package, since a lot of major Web page hosting services offer access to RealAudio-capable servers. If you want to spend less time managing Web sites and more time developing them, consider looking for one of these services. Progressive Networks keeps a list of such companies on its site at **http://www.realaudio.com/products/server/isp.html**.

RealAudio Software Development Tools

Progressive Networks has introduced a number of tools to help Web developers create custom applications that use RealAudio technology. One eager developer has used these tools to create a novel Web-based radio station at **http://www.thedj.com**.

RealAudio Software Development Kit for Windows C/C++

RealAudio has recently expanded its technology to include a software development kit (SDK) that allows you to build RealAudio into your own software creations. In order to get the SDK, you must apply for it by visiting the RealAudio SDK page at **http://www.realaudio.com/products/sdk/index.html**.

Available for Windows only, the SDK lets developers embed or create their own RealAudio controls as needed. The kit contains a complete API that gives you access to all of RealAudio 2.0's features, or you can obtain a low-level API that enables access to the core RealAudio technology.

RealAudio ActiveX

If using the C/C++ library isn't your forte, then check out RealAudio's complete ActiveX implementation. With the RealAudio ActiveX control, you can create custom RealAudio products using Visual Basic or any other product that supports ActiveX programming.

RealAudio Xtra for Macromedia Shockwave

RealAudio is also available as an Xtra—that is, a special development addition to the Macromedia Director environment that creates Shockwave files. With this Xtra, developers can create Director movies that open and play RealAudio files.

RealAudio Programs

Timecast
http://www.timecast.com

Progressive Networks has built a major site devoted to RealAudio content on the Web. If you're developing with RealAudio, you might want to talk to Progressive Networks about becoming part of the Timecast family, or simply obtaining a listing on this site that will become the major jumping-off point for RealAudio users.

StreamWorks

Xing Technology
1540 West Branch Street
Arroyo Grande, CA 93420
Phone: 805-473-0145
Fax: 805-473-0147
WWW: http://www.xingtech.com

Essentially, Xing's StreamWorks 2.0 is a streaming MPEG system, which means that it's video and audio capable. Some sites deliver MPEG video files with it, while others just transfer MPEG audio files at a higher resolution.

The current version of StreamWorks works just like RealAudio, in that development requires distribution of a player application, a specialized encoder program for creating the files, and a back-end server system designed for simultaneous streaming of the files. All of this is based on Xing's MPEG compression technology.

StreamWorks Player Options

The player component of StreamWorks is a simple program that users download and install as a helper application to their favorite Web browser. The program handles such things as volume, download statistics, and setting of modem speed. For developers, though, the most important feature is that users can set options for files to be downloaded with audio quality highest to video quality highest; for the undecided, there is also a mixed option. (Note: You may want to alert users as to what you feel is the best setting for your content, to ensure they get the best quality.)

Xing hasn't followed RealAudio by producing any specialized player toolkits of custom controls, but it may begin to do so in the near future.

Encoder Information

Before you place a video or audio file on your server, you need to run it through Xing's MPEG encoding process. While there are also hardware MPEG encoding systems (which help tremendously with speed), Xing offers an entirely software-based system. Xing MPEG Encoder creates fully compliant MPEG-1 streams for use on the Web and can work with a number of video capture and editing packages.

Server and Back-End Options

At the center of the StreamWorks system is the StreamWorks Server, which has a number of options. As with other streaming products, prices vary based on the number of simultaneous users, ranging from a few hundred dollars for a small number to thousands of dollars for several hundred (or more) simultaneous users.

Xing's server technology also has several extension packages, which Xing markets under its StreamWorks Server PlusPACK. These packages allow you to add capabilities for live broadcasts, delivering the same streams simultaneously at different data rates (cool!), and feeding streams out through multiple servers. In the long run, this last technique is the only system that will be able to handle multiple streams going to thousands of high-bandwidth users (in fact, this is the system most interactive TV trials are using).

Xing's StreamWorks player is available for Windows, Macs, and some Unix platforms. To the best of my knowledge, the server package is only available in Windows and Unix versions.

Shockwave Streamed Audio

Macromedia, Inc.
600 Townsend
San Francisco, CA 94103
Phone: 415-252-2000
Fax: 415-442-0200
WWW: http://www.macromedia.com

This is a relatively new streaming audio technology which is delivered via Macromedia's Shockwave. Using a special Director Xtra program (Xtras are programs which extend Director's capabilities), developers can add streaming audio files to their Shockwave programs or simply add a play button and just offer the streaming audio directly. Director's streaming audio doesn't require a server and the quality is very good (in my limited experimentation, the sound quality was better than almost any non-server software backed system, and gave both RealAudio and Streamworks a run for their money). Macromedia claims the sound technology can compress at ratios from 11:1 all the way to 176:1.

Developers can compress sound files using Macromedia's own SoundEdit 16 digitization package, or they can download the free Xtra needed to compile Shockwave programs with the streaming audio option. Developers should also be aware that their users will have to upgrade their Shockwave client to experience this new feature—make sure to warn them about that need.

The cool aspect of this technology is that you can design your own interfaces in Director for your sound content. Macromedia developed a really nice CD-style interface (shown in Figure 12.2) as a demo of the technology, but you can create different styles. The drawback is that users will have to wait for the Shockwave applet to download before getting access to the sound (which means you'll probably want to keep these apps really small).

RapidTransit

Fastman, Inc.
1613 Capitol of Texas Hwy South, Suite 222
Austin, TX 78746
Phone: 512-328-9088
WWW: http://www.monsterbit.com/rapidtransit/

Figure 12.2   A Shockwave streaming audio demo in action.

RapidTransit works by encoding Web sound files with a compression ratio that can obtain up to 50:1 results. Users will need to have installed the RT Player to read the files.

RT uses a method of wavelet compression, a very hot new type of compression technology. Unlike other sound technologies, though, it's not yet a realtime system. After the WAV files are compressed, the player downloads the compressed format and expands it back into a WAV file onto the user's hard drive. The user can then play the file back with either the RapidTransit plug-in or another WAV player.

The sound of the resulting file is quite good. If some distinct, tinny pops and hisses had been fixed, the RapidTransit beta version I used would have produced the clearest, best-quality sound I've heard. Fastman also is working on a realtime system.

In order to develop content with this technology, you'll need to get the encoder product from Fastman (which wasn't available at the time of this writing). The beta version I used was a Win95 product, but packages for other platforms are planned.

TrueSpeech

DSP Group, Inc.
3120 Scott Boulevard
Santa Clara, CA 95054
Phone: 408-986-4300
Fax: 408-986-4323
WWW: http://www.truespeech.com

TrueSpeech, a sound codec, produces WAV files that can be transmitted in realtime without specialized server software.

Although TrueSpeech is supported in the Windows 95/NT system as a codec, users will still need the TrueSpeech player plug-in to access files in realtime over the Web. Developers will also need to convert any digitized WAV file to one that is digitized with the TrueSpeech codec; as long as the codec is on your Win95 system, you can use just about any Win95-compliant sound editor (like the Cool Edit shareware application) to do this.

The TrueSpeech codec is designed to support 16 bits of resolution and an 8 kHz sampling rate, producing sound that may not be of CD quality but is still fairly clear (especially if you've engineered the sound itself for this rate before converting it to TrueSpeech format).

Visit **http://www.truespeech.com/webpage.htm** to learn how to support TrueSpeech, download TrueSpeech icons, and register your site with the DSP Group.

As of the time I wrote this, TrueSpeech was a Windows-based sound technology, but there are plans to release an encoder product for the Macintosh and to move the player and encoder to other platforms as well.

Internet Wave

VocalTec
35 Industrial Parkway
Northvale, NJ 07647
Phone: 201-768-9400
Fax: 201-768-8893
WWW: http://www.vocaltec.com

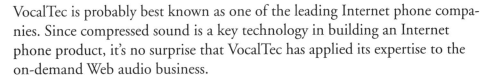

VocalTec is probably best known as one of the leading Internet phone companies. Since compressed sound is a key technology in building an Internet phone product, it's no surprise that VocalTec has applied its expertise to the on-demand Web audio business.

Its audio streaming product, called Internet Wave, consists of a player applet, an encoding scheme, and some special server utility software. You use the encoder software to convert audio files to the Internet Wave format, then place them on the server. Once the utility software is added, you're all set up.

Currently the server utility and encoder are both free, and a live audio encoding package is available for a charge. If Internet Wave takes off, you can probably expect the other components to be priced to sell as well.

The IWave package is built for Windows and supports a variety of browsers, with a nice-looking interface to boot. So far I've yet to see any new announcements concerning other versions.

Echo Speech

Echo Speech Corporation
6460 Via Real
Carpinteria, CA 93013
Phone: 805-684-4593
WWW: http://www.echospeech.com

Echo Speech is a streaming sound technology that is optimized for speech sound files. It does not require a server application—developers only have to encode the files and place them on the Web. Users, of course, will need to download Echo Speech's Netscape plug-in, which is available for Windows but will soon debut for the Macintosh as well.

Because Echo Speech claims compression ratios of 18.5 to 1, it can take 16-bit sampled speech at 11025 Hz and shrink it enough for realtime delivery over a 14.4 Kbps or faster modem.

The cost to use Echo Speech for commercial purposes is a one-time $99 fee per Web site (not per stream); noncommercial uses are free. While other streaming technologies might be better for more complex audio files or offer more robust features, if all you want is to add narration or other speech-type features to a Web page, Echo Speech is one of the easier and cheaper ways to go.

Apple Speech Technology Plug-Ins

Apple has pushed speech technology forward with its PlainTalk product, which allows for text-to-speech, Mexican Spanish text-to-speech, and English speech recognition. Some industrious programmers have followed up with Web-based plug-ins that enable Macintosh-based developers to incorporate speech technology into their sites.

Talker 2.0
http://www.mvpsolutions.com/PlugInSite/Talker.html

Talker 2.0 allows you to embed speech files into your Web pages. You create a text file with a specific speech extension, then place the file on your page to be accessed by people with the Talker 2.0 plug-in. You can embed specific commands that allow you to accentuate certain words and phrases, switch voice styles, and more.

ListenUp!
http://snow.cit.cornell.edu/noon/ListenUp.html

ListenUp! by Bill Noon utilizes the speech-recognition aspect of Apple's technology to let users' voices activate Web browser commands embedded in HTML files. For example, a user might say "Home" to go to a site's home page.

Apple's Speech Web Site
ftp://ftp.info.apple.com/Apple.Support.Area/Apple.Software.Updates/US/
Macintosh/System/PlainTalk_1.4.1/

In order to use these plug-ins, your users will need to find and install Apple's PlainTalk technology. Help them out by pointing them to this site, as well as the sites for Talker or ListenUp!

Microsoft's Speech API
http://www.microsoft.com/mediadev/audio/mspeech1.htm

While Apple clearly has the lead in voice technology, Microsoft is, of course, trying to catch up. At the above Web address you can learn more about the Microsoft Speech API, which all Windows-based speech technology will revolve around.

Speech Recognition Update
TMA Associates
P.O. Box 17598
Encino, CA 91416

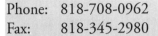

Phone: 818-708-0962
Fax: 818-345-2980

This is a monthly newsletter that provides excellent coverage of the entire speech-recognition market and technology.

ToolVox

Voxware, Inc.
305 College Road East
Princeton, NJ 08540
Phone: 609-514-4100
Fax: 609-514-4101
WWW: http://www.voxware.com

This product is similar to Echo Speech in that it, too, concentrates on compressing and playing back speech-only audio files on demand. ToolVox claims a 53:1 compression ratio with excellent quality. As with other similar speech streaming technologies, there is no server back-end software needed; the compressed files are treated like any other standard file on your server.

Unlike Echo Speech, which charges a token $99 usage fee, ToolVox is absolutely free. (Voxware feels it can gain more money through licensing to major companies.) Users have to download a Netscape plug-in to access the files, and developers need to run audio files through a specialized encoder before the content can be made available.

Voxware has announced plans to release an enhanced version of ToolVox, called ToolVox Gold; check in on the company's Web site for up-to-date release information.

Sound Editing Tools

Whether you're digitizing for a sound file format, for a Java or multimedia plug-in format, or just doing some re-engineering before converting an audio file to a streaming audio format, a good sound editing package is crucial. The same is true when you create sound effects from CD-ROM libraries. Although those libraries provide brilliant sound effects, it will usually be up to you to edit and experiment with your files to get the exact sound you're after.

All of the packages listed below are top-notch. Personally, I like Sound Forge and Gold Wave, both of which are PC packages. However, you'll find advocates for every package presented here.

Sound Forge (Windows)

Sonic Foundry, Inc.
100 South Baldwin Street, Suite 204
Madison, WI 53703
Phone: 608-256-3133
Fax: 608-256-7300
WWW: http://www.sfoundry.com

This very useful application includes all kinds of effects and makes editing a breeze. You can see for yourself by downloading the demo (the option to save files is disabled) from the Sound Forge Web site.

Sound Designer II (Macintosh)

Digidesign
1360 Willow Road
Menlo Park, CA 94025
Phone: 415-688-0600
WWW: http://www.digidesign.com

Sound Designer II is one of the best and most popular sound editors available for the Mac. It features tons of effects and professional editing capabilities. It also supports "plug-in" technology, allowing other companies (specifically the 3D sound companies) to create new sound effects packages and use them within Sound Designer II.

SoundEdit 16   (Macintosh)

Macromedia, Inc.
600 Townsend
San Francisco, CA 94103
Phone: 415-252-2000
Fax: 415-442-0200
WWW: http://www.macromedia.com

This longtime Macintosh sound editing package is available as a standalone tool or in one of the multimedia authoring bundles Macromedia offers.

Alchemy

Passport Designs
100 Stone Pine Road
Half Moon Bay, CA 94109
Phone: 415-726-0280
Fax: 415-726-2254
WWW: http://www.passportdesigns.com

Passport Designs is one of the leading music software companies around. Its high-end sound editing package, Alchemy, is a great choice no matter what your needs are.

Disc-To-Disk

Optical Media International
51 East Campbell
Campbell, CA 95008
Phone: 408-376-3511

Disc-To-Disk is one of those odd little utilities that makes you say, "Why didn't I think of that?" Disc-To-Disk captures CD audio digitally right off a CD-ROM, bypassing the need to run it through your sound card's digital-to-analog converter. The results are crystal clear. You can store the results in any one of several popular sound formats, then go to town with your favorite sound editing program.

Shareware Sound Editing Packages

In the shareware arena, two products—Gold Wave and Cool Edit—stand head and shoulders above the rest. Both handle a wide range of sound files and offer tons of digital editing effects. I prefer Gold Wave, but I could give you a long list of colleagues who swear by Cool Edit, so the choice is yours.

Cool Edit

Syntrillium Software Corporation
P.O. Box 60274
Phoenix, AZ 85082-0274

Phone: 602-941-4327
Fax: 602-941-8170
WWW: http://www.netzone.com/syntrillium/

Cool Edit is the most popular shareware sound editor, which is no surprise given all of the features and power it has. Three registration schemes are available: $25 (Lite), $50 (Basic), and $100 (Preferred).

Gold Wave

Chris Craig
P.O. Box 51
St. John's, NF
Canada A1C 5H5
Email: chris3@garfield.cs.mun.ca
WWW: http://www.cs.mun.ca/~chris3/goldwave/home.html

Gold Wave is a digital audio editor, player, and recorder. It supports and converts several RIFF formats; WAV formats such as PCM, MULAW, and ADPCM; and other file formats such as VOC, Amiga 8SVX, Sun, and NeXT. It can also display and edit separate channels of stereo sounds. You can register Gold Wave on a standard ($30) or deluxe ($50) basis.

Don't Forget the Basics

If you're going to do your own digitizing, the first thing you need to do is go to a music store and get a top-rate microphone. Unfortunately, most of the microphones provided with regular sound cards are not of professional quality. Recently, I came across the following potential resource for information about microphones:

Allen Sides Microphone Cabinet
Cardinal Business Media
Available from Electronic Musician Magazine
Phone: 800-233-9604

This CD-ROM provides a complete run-through of everything you ever wanted to know about microphones. You'll have to shell out $69.95, but if you're looking for the right microphone plus information on recording techniques, this is your source.

If you really want to explore sound, you might want to look into some of the other equipment you can get to improve your sound effects, like portable DAT recorders for field recording. If you want to get the ultimate in audio equipment, check out magazines like *Electronic Musician* and *Keyboard* for the complete scoop on major audio gear.

More About MIDI

To talk about the full array of MIDI-oriented products would take me into the next millennium. While it's fairly easy to narrow down the key sound editing packages, sorting out the best MIDI sequencing software and other utilities is an absolute headache. I do, however, want to point out a couple of packages that could be helpful to small developers who plan to generate their own music.

Shareware and Commercial Packages

I use the following shareware and commercial packages to play around with MIDI files.

WinJammer

WinJammer Software Limited
69 Rancliffe Road
Oakville, Ontario
Canada L6H 1B1
Phone: 905-842-3708
Fax: 905-842-2732
Email: 72662.3021@compuserve.com

WinJammer is a great MIDI sequencer product that's available as shareware. While you can find more extensive packages, this is a good program for small developers who need a simple product to rework MIDI files, change instruments, experiment, and so on. The company also offers WinJammer Pro, which is a substantial upgrade for those who need to go to the next level.

You can find WinJammer at **http://www.shareware.com** or in the MIDI forum on CompuServe.

SuperJam

The Blue Ribbon SoundWorks, Inc.
1605 Chantilly Drive, Suite 200
Atlanta, GA 30324
Phone: 404-315-0212
Fax: 404-315-0213

From one of Microsoft's latest acquisitions, Blue Ribbon SoundWorks, comes the perfect tool for those of us who are less musically inclined but want to generate some simple tunes. SuperJam is available on a wide range of platforms, including Windows, Macintosh, and even Silicon Graphics. This tool is best used to generate music on a temporary basis until you can hire a professional composer.

SuperJam uses some of Blue Ribbon's automatic composition technology to generate music on the fly. It incorporates more than 25 different musical styles, such as classical, jazz, reggae, and rock.

Autoscore

Wildcat Canyon Software
1563 Solano Avenue #264
Berkeley, CA 94707
Phone: 800-336-0983
Fax: 510-527-8425
WWW: http://www.wildcat.com

If you are creating music simply for the fun of it, check out this product. As a hobbyist, you might not be much of a musician, nor have enough money to hire one. If you can hum a tune or a rhythm, though, you can make music with Autoscore, which takes whatever you sing into a microphone and translates the pitch of your voice to music. It also takes input from live musical devices, so if you play a little clarinet or guitar, you'll be well on your way.

Using Autoscore isn't exactly a professional way to generate original music, of course, but it does work. (I fully tested it, but I'm not going to let you hear me sing.) A demo copy is available on the company's Web site, so you too can test it and see if it works for you.

Commercial MIDI Software

Here is a general listing of the heavyweights in MIDI software, plus a few interesting resources. For a more complete breakdown, subscribe to the magazines listed at the end of this chapter, which will help you get on the road to becoming a MIDI software and hardware expert.

Artic Software

P.O. Box 28
Waterford, WI 53185
Phone: 414-534-4309
Fax: 414-534-7809
WWW: http://www.execpc.com/~artic/

Artic Software is a great MIDI software resource for Visual Basic programmers. Its founder, Arthur Edstrom, sells a large range of useful tools for VB programmers (such as MIDI Cool Tools) and a number of useful utilities, including a great database management product to keep track of MIDI files.

Cakewalk Music Software

P.O. Box 760
Watertown, MA 02272
Phone: 800-234-1171
Fax: 617-924-6657

Cakewalk makes a whole range of MIDI and digital audio tools. Its MIDI sequencing product, Cakewalk Pro, is one of the most popular sequencers around.

Mark of the Unicorn, Inc.

1280 Massachusetts Avenue
Cambridge, MA 02138
Phone: 617-576-2760
Fax: 617-576-3609
WWW: http://www.motu.com

Mark of the Unicorn was founded in 1980 and is best known for its Performer product, a longtime benchmark MIDI package. Today the company has an extensive line of products for Macs and PCs; its Web site features demos and extensive literature on these products.

Opcode Systems

3950 Fabian Way
Suite 100
Palo Alto, CA 94303
Phone: 415-856-3333
Fax: 415-856-3332
WWW: http://www.opcode.com

Opcode is one of the oldest and best music software companies around. It has extensive MIDI product lines for both the Macintosh and PC platforms. Its Web site is quite comprehensive and features downloadable demos of some products.

Passport Designs

100 Stone Pine Road
Half Moon Bay, CA 94019
Phone: 415-726-0280
Fax: 415-726-2254
WWW: http://www.passportdesigns.com

Passport makes not only the Alchemy sound editor I mentioned earlier, but a nice range of MIDI sequencing software. Its most notable lead products for MIDI are MusicTime (a nice entry-level package) and MasterTracks Pro for Macintosh and Windows (its key sequencing product).

Voyetra Technologies

5 Odell Plaza
Yonkers, NY 10701
Phone: 914-966-0600
Fax: 914-966-1102

If you've bought a sound card in the last 18 months, chances are you're familiar with Voyetra. This company supplies a lot of the simple music utilities that come bundled with PC sound cards these days.

The Unique MOD File Format

MOD files could easily be considered a type of digital audio file, but they've got such a peculiar history and structure that they are really a format unto themselves.

MOD files got their start on the Amiga and have now migrated to the PC, the Macintosh, and even workstations. The files contain not only samples, but playback information that indicates which sample is played at which time. The approach is kind of like combining WAV files and MIDI. Although the samples are called "instruments," they don't have to be actual instrument sounds; you can use voices, sound effects, or even the screams of a crowd.

How do MOD files work? Well, most music—in terms of the stuff musical groups produce—is comprised of four distinct tracks: drums, bass, rhythm, and a "lead" track. Programmers applied this concept to the Amiga and utilized all four of the Amiga's "voices" to replay digitized samples of instruments on these tracks. By looping and switching instruments on the tracks, programmers created a software reproduction of some really amazing sounds. In addition, lyrical snippets could be added because the playback technology was all based on digital audio and not FM synthesis.

On the downside, MOD files can have tinny popping noises, which occur as a result of poor sample quality and the type of sound card used.

Unlike MIDI, no one controls the MOD file format, so new versions have appeared often. You can find new MOD file formats with up to 32 simultaneous channels, a maximum of 255 instruments, possible sample rates of up to 48 kHz, and 16-bit source samples of (almost) unlimited size. Although these newer formats can be useful, you should investigate their effect on the speed of your Web site, as they can be quite taxing. See the associated sidebar for more information.

Web Developers' Guide to MOD Files

MOD files, or modules, are made up of a set of samples (the instruments) and sequencing information that tells a MOD player when to play a particular track at a specified pitch. Thus, MODs are different from pure sample files such as WAV or AU, which contain no sequencing information. MODs are also different from MIDI files, which do not include any custom samples or instruments. MODs are extremely popular in the demo world because they offer a way of making music of an acceptable quality rather cheaply. With the advent of high-quality sound hardware, new generations of MODs may even improve to nearly professional quality sound.

Sequencing information is based on patterns and tracks. A pattern is a group of tracks with a certain length, usually 64 rows. The tracks are independent of each other, meaning that a four-track MOD can play four voices or notes simultaneously. The patterns can be sequenced in a playlist, so that repeating the same sequence of patterns doesn't require rewriting them. This makes MODs a hybrid between pure sample data files such as WAV, VOC, or IFF/8SVX and pure sequencing information files like MIDI.

As I've mentioned, the MOD world is riddled with all kinds of different formats, some of which are getting incredibly fancy. There are three main components to the major formats:

- Number of instruments that can be programmed into the file

- Frequency range of the samples

- Number of channels or digital streams that can be played at one time

Let's take a quick look at each of the popular MOD formats that are in use today:

- *MOD*—This is the main type of MOD file in use today. It was the first standard and it is based on the original Amiga format. There are several slight variations offering more instruments, but the basic capabilities of this format support 31 instruments (with 4 playing at any one time) at an 8-bit resolution.

- *S3M and MTM*—S3M and MTM are somewhat similar in their format. Both offer 8- and 16-bit samples, and both are capable of supporting 32 simultaneous channels of music. S3M can support up to 99 available instruments. To build MOD files, you should use the ScreamTracker formats editor for S3M and the MultiTracker editor for MTM. S3M also apparently can mix in some FM instruments—up to 9 on SB and SB PRO cards.

- *XM*—This is the latest and greatest format on the scene. It supports up to 32 tracks, 128 instruments, multisampled intruments, an extremely large sample size, and lots of MIDI support. Samples can be 8 or 16 bits. The FastTracker editor can be used to create files of this format.

Creating MOD Files on the PC

Creating a MOD file requires a MOD writing program, commonly called a tracker. So far I have heard of only one MOD tracker for Windows, and try as a I might I couldn't actually get my hands on it. The other major trackers are all DOS-based. The ones used most often include the following.

ScreamTracker

`ftp://ftp.cdrom.com/pub/demos/music/programs/trackers/scrmt32.zip`

This MOD editor, created by a member of the European demo team Future Crew, is a full-featured MOD maker that supports the S3M format as well as many other former MOD formats.

FastTracker II

`ftp://ftp.cdrom.com/pub/demos/music/programs/trackers/ft203.zip`

This MOD editor supports S3M and all kinds of samples and several other MOD formats.

MultiTracker Module Editor 1.01b

`ftp://ftp.cdrom.com/pub/demos/music/programs/trackers/mtm101b.zip`

This application is not as full-featured as the previous two, but each MOD editor is different enough from the others to warrant playing with several to find your favorite.

MacMod Pro

`ftp://wuarchive.wustl.edu/systems/mac/info-mac/snd/util/mac-mod-pro-322.hqx`

This is a complete player and tracker for the Mac, capable of creating MODs from 4 to 32 channels.

Conversion Tools

In addition to creating and editing MOD files, you'll need a way to convert them. Unfortunately, converting between different formats, and especially to non-MOD formats, is a difficult process. Converting from one of the later MOD formats to an earlier format is not for the faint of heart; going from an earlier format to one of the latest incarnations is far easier, however, and there are a couple of products to help you out.

PT-MID 0.3 for the PC

`ftp://x2ftp.oulu.fi/pub/msdos/programming/convert/ptmid3.zip`

This program converts general MIDI files to a couple of MOD formats. The converted MODs still require some tweaking and re-editing using a MOD editor.

PT-MID 0.3 for the Mac

`ftp://ftp.mm.se/playerpro/PtMid_0.3_Folder.sit.bin`

This program has the same functions and shortcomings as its PC sibling.

Key Mac MOD Resource at Opcode

`http://www.opcode.com/omn/mac_mod.html`

This page on the Opcode systems site contains a large collection of all the known Mac-related MOD programs.

More MOD Information

To obtain more information about MODs, check the ever-updating MOD FAQ that Matt Behrens maintains on the Web at **http://www.csis.gvsu.edu/~behrensm/absm-faq/index.html**.

Here Comes 3D Sound

The current wave of innovation in music and sound types is the notion of "3D sound." The title, though, is something of a misnomer because it's used to describe everything from simple "beyond-the-speaker" sound to full 3D aural experiences. Here are the more common classifications:

- *Spatial enhancement*—This technique adds depth and space to existing sounds. Using a spatial sound algorithm, a sound can be given a wider field of playback on a speaker system. This technique is known as "going beyond the speakers."

- *Stereo spreading*—This technique is basically advanced panning. Using simple techniques and shifting sound playback timing between left and right speakers (and thus the listener's ears), sounds can be "placed" in a 180-degree space facing the listener. For optimal use of this technology, listeners need to position their speakers (headphones will not work) to find the "sweet spot" that enhances the use of this process.

- *"True 3D" sound*—The technique takes a mono input and then attempts to "place" the sound through algorithmic modifications and timing techniques. Unlike the previous two techniques, the object is to make the sound truly 3D with a range of 360 degrees, around as well as above and below the speaker and at any "distance." Listeners will need four speakers or headphones. Again, speaker placement is key for optimal performance. Microsoft is working on a "True 3D" standard to promote as its Direct3D Sound technology. Products claiming to be "True 3D" will conform to a specification that offers 360-degree surround sound.

Is 3D Sound for You?

3D sound, for all the hoopla, is simply another mixing technology that you can employ to heighten the intensity of your Web site experience. The sound can be unbelievably good, but until consumers are able to get more advanced sound hardware into their homes—better sound cards and additional top-quality speakers (true surround-sound 3D technology requires more than two speakers)—this technology may have to take a back seat to your other options. In addition, you need to consider the work involved in creating the sound. Just because a Web product has a "3D Sound" label doesn't mean the sound is good.

Music and Sound Production Resources

You can always count on an industry generating several quality resources for its followers, and the music industry is no exception. The following magazines do not necessarily devote their pages to how electronic music fits into the World Wide Web, but the technology is the same.

Sound Effects Libraries

Most major publishers work either with established musicians and sound technicians or build in-house musical capabilities. Either way they give their developers access to major archives of professional-quality sound effects libraries.

For most developers, building a library is fairly easy. It may take some money, but if you look, you can find extensive collections of sounds. These should provide you with so many selections that you can develop an original library just by spending time with one of the sound file editors described earlier.

Here are some of the most popular libraries around. Most of these companies charge between $50 and $150 for a single CD, depending on the specific CD and other circumstances (such as a CD-ROM version versus an audio CD). Some package their CD collections in sets that cost several hundred dollars, while others are converting their Web sites into download services so you can buy sound effects a la carte. However you slice it, though, among the following four companies you can find an amazing array of sound effects to use and modify.

The Hollywood Edge

7060 Hollywood Boulevard, Suite 1120
Hollywood, CA 90028
Phone: 213-466-6723
Fax: 213-466-5861
WWW: http://magicnet.net/~drport/sdx/net/hwedge.html

This is one of the most famous and most commonly used sound effects libraries in existence. The entire library (which includes CDs) was created by Soundelux, a longtime coalition of recording studios that have done extensive movie work. The coalition works to obtain sounds directly from the original DAT recordings its member companies used in major Hollywood films.

To date, Soundelux has compiled some 3,000 hours of sounds into CDs and online archives that you can purchase. The current complete set spans more than 50 CD-ROMs. Both complete and partial sets are available directly, as well as through many major stock music and sound companies.

Sound Ideas

105 West Beaver Creek Road, Suite #4
Richmond Hill, Ontario, Canada L4B 1C6
Phone: 905-886-5000
Fax: 905-886-6800
WWW: http://www.sound-ideas.com

Looking for a zillion different sound effects? Look no further. This company, which has aggressively promoted itself to the game development community, offers tons of sounds and many well-packaged sound libraries.

Sound Ideas is currently working to set up online distribution as well as move its libraries from regular audio CDs to CD-ROMs. You can order a free demo and a full catalog from them at any time by sending email to **info@sound-ideas.com**.

Network Music, Inc.

15150 Avenue of Science
San Diego, CA 92128
Phone: 800-854-2075
Fax: 619-451-6409

This library contains more than 5,500 sound effects compiled on 72 compact discs. On the company's Web page, you can request a demo CD and browse through its catalog.

Valentino Sound Effects Libraries

TV Music
500 Executive Boulevard
Elmsford, NY 10523
Phone: 800-223-6278
Fax: 914-347-4764
WWW: http://www.tvmusic.com

The Valentino Sound Effects Library covers 44 CDs and is a complete library pulled from television, radio, and feature films. You can order a CD demo and 80-page catalog by sending email to **info@tvmusic.com**. (I actually downloaded an Acrobat file from their Web site that had a complete listing.)

There is also a CD-ROM for Windows and Macintosh that includes demos for every selection in the library.

Search Leading Sound Effects Libraries

`http://www.rpmseattle.com/rpm/efx/efx_the.html`

This comprehensive site actually allows you to search through the above libraries. If you want to see whether a particular library has a really obscure sound—for example, a particular type of weapon—then you can go here, search through the library, and find out which specific CD has it, if any. That way, you can buy just what you need.

Other Resources

Stock Sound Companies

There are dozens of stock sound companies around that can assemble digital files or tapes of sounds you might need. You may pay for custom stock like this, but sometimes it's a quick way to find that special sound effect you want. *Interactivity* magazine recently published a long list of such companies.

Major Record Chains

Whenever I'm in Tower Records or some similar large chain, I always try to check out the sound effects sections. You have to be careful to see if these are useful libraries; sometimes they tend to have CDs like the *Star Trek* sound-effects disc, which isn't meant for use on a Web site. Still, I found an animals CD-ROM once for $9.95 that gave me some good grunts and snorts to use for monsters in an RPG game.

Magazines

Electronic Musician
6400 Hollis Street #12
Emeryville, CA 94608
Phone: 510-653-3307
Fax: 510-653-5142
Subscription: N/A
Newsstand: $3.95
Publishes: Monthly
Pages: 110

Along with *Keyboard* Magazine, *Electronic Musician* is the major magazine covering all the issues of making music using computers. Each edition is jam-packed with information about MIDI, digital sound, and the latest electronic music equipment.

Future Music Magazine
Future Publishing
30 Monmouth Street
Bath, England BA1 2BW
Phone: 44-1225-822511
Fax: 44-1225-446019
Subscription: £87
Newsstand: N/A
Publishes: Monthly
Pages: 100

From England-based Future Publishing—which publishes a number of major computer, game, and other special-interest magazines—comes a wonderful magazine on high-tech music and computer music production. I bet you're wondering how much £87 is, right? Depending on exchange rates, it's roughly $130.

Keyboard Magazine
Miller Freeman
600 Harrison Street
San Francisco, CA 94107
Phone: 415-358-9500
Fax: 415-358-9527
WWW: http://www.mfi.com/keyboard/
Subscription: N/A
Newsstand: $3.95
Publishes: Monthly
Pages: 150

This magazine covers everything related to computer and music technology. It's read religiously by professional musicians and audio people, and it has feature articles about creating music in the interactive multimedia and games environment. If you're creating music for Web sites or just interested in electronic music as an industry, and you aren't reading this magazine, you're absolutely crazy.

Music and Computers
Miller Freeman
600 Harrison Street
San Francisco, CA 94107
Phone: 415-358-9500
Fax: 415-358-9527
WWW: http://www.music-and-computers.com
Subscription: $18.00
Newsstand: $4.95
Publishes: Bimonthly
Pages: 80

Miller Freeman, which publishes more magazines than I can name, has debuted this exciting new magazine that focuses solely on the bond between music and computers. Articles cover Web issues, production issues, samples, programming, and much more. A must-read for anyone with even a passing interest in sound or computer music.

Web Sites

http://ac.dal.ca/~dong/music.htm

This is a good site for information on music and sound file formats, as well as shareware tools.

http://ally.ios.com:80/~midilink/

An excellent site for all sorts of MIDI authoring tools and resources.

ftp://mitpress.mit.edu/pub/Computer-Music-Journal/CMJ.html

This site is home to MIT's *Computer Music Journal,* a leading technical journal on music and sound as it pertains to computers.

http://www.eeb.ele.tue.nl/midi/index.html

An excellent site for good MIDI links.

http://www.xraylith.wisc.edu/~ebrodsky/

This site by Ethan Brodsky is a good site for programming sound resources.

http://www.futurenet.co.uk/music/futuremusic.html

Future Music Magazine is a UK-based magazine that covers all sorts of computer and music issues—from scoring to playing, this magazine covers a lot of good material. This Web site contains much of the material found in the magazine's pulp-based version.

http://interact.uoregon.edu/MediaLit/FC/WFAETechnical

Yet another excellent site for more links to explore musical Web resources.

13

Make your Web pages come alive with animated GIFs, specialized plug-ins, and the wonderful world of digital video!

Web Animation: From Pageflips to Digital Video

Animation on the World Wide Web has moved quickly in the last year. At first, everyone thought it was kind of scary—indeed, the idea of using schemes like server push/client pull for animation seemed to be indicative of the Web's many problems. With the debut of animated GIFs, the Java language, and plug-ins like Shockwave and VDOLive, however, there is a growing amount of animated content on the Web. As many developers have discovered, even a few small animated GIFs can liven up a static-looking page in no time.

File Formats or Animation Systems

First, let's get familiar with the major animation file formats you'll find on the Web. Once I've worked through the various file formats, we'll examine each one a little more closely concerning how to develop content for the Web.

Browser/HTML-Supported Formats

There's a lot you can do to liven up your Web pages with animation without ever touching an ActiveX control or a plug-in. Here's a rundown on the technologies native to Internet Explorer and Netscape that can add animation to your Web pages.

Animated GIFs

This format—also known as GIF89a, which is the name of the specification for multi-image animated GIF files—is becoming the primary type of animation on the Web. Animated GIFs are easy to produce, and most don't take up much space. It's truly amazing to see how four or five simple animated GIFs can really add a spark to your Web page.

Server Push–Client Pull

In the early days of browser development, Netscape introduced the idea of server push/client pull, which would create Web pages that would automatically make a call for updated information from the server as soon as they were loaded by the user. This system, which works on a timing mechanism, allowed savvy Web developers to create animation by constantly requesting new pages with different graphics. Although it still works, this method isn't nearly as useful for animating Web pages as it once was—and that's a good thing.

Java Animation

Java applets are a very good way to deliver animation to users, because Java gives you a wider user base than any typical plug-in. Sophisticated Java animations, though, aren't easy. Fortunately, as referenced in the chapter on Java later in this book and in a few instances in this chapter, tools are available to help even novice developers create some forms of Java animations. Some of them, like Sausage Software's Egor Animator, are extremely easy to use, so creating Java animation doesn't mean you need a computer science degree.

Plug-In Variants

A massive variety of specialized file formats exists primarily because of the equally wide array of plug-in systems. Many of these plug-ins are multimedia systems tied to a particular file format produced by a specific authoring package. Here's what was available when I was writing this chapter.

Enliven by Narrative Communications

Narrative Communications Corp.
204 Second Avenue
Waltham, MA 02154
Phone: 617-290-5300
Fax: 617-290-5312
WWW: http://www.narrative.com

Enliven is a very comprehensive system that uses a specialized development suite (discussed in a later section) to create files viewed via a plug-in control. Enliven can produce very sophisticated animations—in fact, the demo on its Web site features copies of some scenes from Broderbund/Random House's excellent Living Books series.

Multimedia Emblaze

GEO Interactive Media Group
Phone: 972-3-573-4288
Fax: 972-3-573-3290
WWW: http://www.geo.inter.net

The specialized Emblaze animated file format requires developers to use the Emblaze Creator authoring environment (see later section), and users must have the plug-in control to utilize it.

Multimedia mBED

mBED Software
San Francisco, CA
Phone: 415-778-0934
WWW: http://www.mbed.com

Multimedia mBED is a unique type of plug-in file format that lets developers use a specialized HTML-like scripting language to author dynamic Web animations. In order for users to view the object they will need the mBED plug-in control.

Shockwave

Macromedia
600 Townsend
San Francisco, CA 94103
Phone: 415-252-2000
Fax: 415-442-0200
WWW: http://www.macromedia.com

Developers can use Shockwave to convert Director files (compressed using the Afterburner engine) for distribution over the Web, where they can be viewed by users who have the Shockwave player. Due to its widespread use and the amount of resources available, I have devoted a whole chapter later in this book to Shockwave resources.

Multimedia RadMedia

RadMedia
Palo Alto, CA
Phone: 415-617-9430
Fax: 415-473-6826
WWW: http://www.radmedia.com

RadMedia has developed an extensive high-end Web animation and multimedia development system utilizing its RadMedia authoring environment and a plug-in client for browsers.

Sizzler

Totally Hip Software Inc.
1224 Hamilton Street, Suite 301
Vancouver, BC V6B 2S8
Phone: 604-685-6525
Fax: 604-685-4057
WWW: http://www.totallyhip.com

A Sizzler file is similar to an animated GIF file, but with more options. Using Totally Hip's WebPainter package (which is explained later), animators can create snappy-looking "pageflip" animations. Files are then compressed using Sizzler's specialized technology for rapid transfer over the Web.

Vivo

Vivo Software, Inc.
411 Waverley Oaks Road
Waltham, MA 02154
Phone: 617-899-8900
Fax: 617-899-1400
WWW: http://www.vivo.com

Video files stored in the format created by Vivo's digital video codec can be placed on a Web server for download via a specialized plug-in. No special server software is needed.

Digital Video Formats and Codecs

Aside from some new Web-based digital video files, many forms of video on the Web will come in formats and codecs that many computer developers are already intimately familiar with. Even so, some of these formats have taken on new features as the speed of computers has dramatically improved and as digital video technology has become more sophisticated. Don't assume you know everything you need to, especially in the context of how these formats and codecs fit together for your Web developments.

AVI

This is the main format found for digital video on the Microsoft Windows platform.

ClearFusion

Iterated Systems
3525 Piedmont Road
Seven Piedmont Center, Suite 600
Atlanta, GA 30305-1530
Phone: 800-437-2285
Fax: 404-264-8300
WWW: http://www.iterated.com

Iterated Systems is an imaging company that has worked extensively with a form of fractal compression. ClearFusion uses this fractal technology to deliver AVI files in a streamed manner. For optimal performance, Iterated recommends that you create a specialized AVI file using a 1:1 audio interleave, no key frames, and an audio track.

Note that this system doesn't guarantee realtime playback—the codec specs you use and the speed of your client-server connection will matter as well. Iterated (see later section) is developing an optimal AVI codec for ClearFusion or other similar plug-ins, and it is also working on supporting ActiveMovie and QuickTime.

MPEG

MPEG is a widely accepted standard for compressing and transmitting digital video and audio. For a while MPEG languished because of the amount of computing power needed to encode and decode the files, but the advent of Pentium-level machines has caused the format to get a lot more attention. Developers can use several distinct plug-in programs to distribute MPEG video over the Web.

Action

Open2u
http://www.arasmith.com/action/

The Action plug-in allows you to embed movie clips into your Web pages. Action uses the latest MPEG routines and offers scalability from regular telephone lines to a T1 or LAN connection. Action can also capture the data and allow you replay it at a later time.

InterVU

201 Lomas Santa Fe Drive
Solana Beach, CA
Phone: 619-350-1600
Fax: 619-793-2525
WWW: http://www.intervu.com

InterVU's MPEG player plug-in can stream MPEG files off the Web and shows you the first frame before you download the entire video. Full-speed replay is available once the download is finished.

ActiveMovie

Microsoft
One Microsoft Way
Redmond, WA 98052
Phone: 206-882-8080
Fax: 206-883-8101
WWW: http://www.microsoft.com

Microsoft's ActiveMovie technology can handle MPEG files.

QuickTime

Apple Computer, Inc.
1 Infinite Loop
Cupertino, CA 95014
Phone: 408-996-1010
WWW: http://www.apple.com

Apple's QuickTime format is available for both Mac and PC platforms. Several systems that can work with QuickTime files directly over the Web are:

Apple QuickTime Plug-In
http://quicktime.apple.com

Apple has its own QuickTime plug-in for several platforms—most notably Netscape, which has been distributing the Apple plug-in as part of the extended download of Netscape Navigator.

Microsoft ActiveMovie Control
http://www.microsoft.com

Microsoft's ActiveMovie can also play QuickTime files, but not QuickTime VR.

MovieStar QuickTime Plug-In
Intelligence At Large Software
3508 Market Street
Philadelphia, PA 19104-3316
Phone: 215-387-6002
Fax: 215-387-9215
WWW: http://www.beingthere.com

TEC QuickTime Player
TEC Solutions, Inc.
19672 Stevens Creek Boulevard, Suite 169
Cupertino, CA 95014
Phone: 408-973-8855
Fax: 408-973-8979
WWW: http://www.tecs.com

MovieStar and TEC player are not as polished as Apple's plug-in, but they do offer some advantages in supporting a wider array of browsers.

QuickTime VR

Apple Computer, Inc.
1 Infinite Loop
Cupertino, CA 95014
Phone: 408-996-1010
Fax: 408-974-2113
WWW: http://quicktime.apple.com

This hybrid version of the QuickTime digital video system is used to display interactive 3D environments (which are large 3D photographs played back through the QuickTime engine). So far, only Apple's QTVR player is able to distribute QuickTime VR files over the Web.

 Looking for lots of help with your QTVR development? Check out **http://w3.qtvr.com/qtvr**, a full-service site that can help you find experienced QuickTime VR developers, as well as products to help you with your own QTVR development.

Surround Video

Black Diamond Consulting
195 Hanover Street, Suite 22

Portsmouth, NH 03801
Phone: 603-430-7777
Fax: 603-430-7778
WWW: http://www.bdiamond.com

This is Microsoft's answer to QuickTime VR. Microsoft is letting Black Diamond take the lead in promoting the format, as well as the plug-ins and controls necessary for people to be able to use it. Currently, only Black Diamond's Surround Video ActiveX control is able to distribute Surround Video over the Web.

VDOLive

VDOnet Corp.
4009 Miranda Avenue, Suite 250
Palo Alto, CA 94304
Phone: 415-846-7700
Fax: 415-846-7900
WWW: http//www.vdolive.com

VDOLive is a specialized format that allows for the playback of realtime digital video over the Web. Regular digital video is converted to the VDOLive format by software supplied to VDOLive developers. Users must have the VDOLive plug-in to receive the converted files.

A Codec Primer

Digital video can get a little confusing. Not only are there both file formats and codecs, but sometimes a file format is a codec in and of itself (MPEG, for example). In many cases, however, you can work with a separate specialized codec that can deliver different types of digital video. For instance, AVI may be the format of the file your users see, but within that file there is a specialized format—the codec—that you use to define the digital video contained within. It pays to be very informed about specific codecs, so here's a quick rundown on the most often-used resources.

SuperMac Cinepak

Radius, Inc.
215 Moffett Park Drive
Sunnyvale, CA 94089-1374

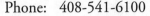

Phone: 408-541-6100
WWW: http://www.radius.com

Cinepak is one of the granddaddies of video-compression technology. Microsoft, 3DO, Sega, Atari, and Creative Labs, to name just a few, have all been on the Cinepak bandwagon at one point or another. Although Cinepak is still popular because of its excellent cross-platform capabilities, newer products like Indeo Interactive and TrueMotion are moving in. Rumor has it that Radius is introducing an update soon; check the Cinepak Web site for more information.

Intel Indeo

Intel Corporation
2200 Mission College Boulevard
Santa Clara, CA 95052
Phone: 408-765-8080
WWW: http://www.intel.com

Intel Indeo, the dominant video codec on the PC platform, comes standard with Video for Windows. It is also available for OS/2 and QuickTime (Mac and Windows versions), making it an excellent cross-platform solution. The latest release (3.2, V3.24.01.01) continues to build upon the excellent playback performance and image quality Indeo is known for. On a Pentium processor-based PC, Indeo can support full-screen digital video.

Later in the chapter I'll discuss Indeo Video Interactive, another Indeo codec that Intel has introduced. This codec is not a replacement for Intel Indeo; rather, it is an interactive addition to the Intel family of codecs.

MPEG (Motion Pictures Expert Group)

http://www.mpeg.org

MPEG was formed to draw up a scheme for enabling full-screen motion video with a high compression rate. The system is originally based on the JPEG (Joint Photographic Experts Group) uniform standard for compressing and rendering still-image files.

The MPEG codec can achieve transfer rates of up to 30 frames per second by storing a full screen at the beginning and every four frames thereafter, then working out the differences between each stored frame of video. This very neat idea has some drawbacks. First, you can't cut to any frame automatically, because you can only look at the stored images in the file (every fourth frame). In addition, only really fast Pentium systems or special MPEG-equipped accelerator boards can handle the complicated mathematical process that MPEG uses. (The other codecs discussed here are software-only systems.) Encoding MPEG also requires specialized hardware, some of which can be quite expensive.

There is a small discussion of MPEG encoding resources later in this chapter.

TrueMotion-S

Duck Corporation
Tribeca Film Center
375 Greenwich Street
New York, NY 10013

and

Horizons Technology
3990 Ruffin Road
San Diego, CA 92123
Phone: 619-292-8331
Fax: 619-292-7321

TrueMotion-S is currently one of the best digital video codecs in the business. According to Duck, TrueMotion is "the only video frame-specific, software-only video compression solution available today that provides true television quality across multiple platforms. Content developers can compress video images once and play them back on a variety of computer platforms."

TrueMotion features a compression rate of 20:1 and full-screen playback. Duck Corporation has designed TrueMotion to compete directly with MPEG, which requires a lot more throughput than TrueMotion to achieve the best results.

Getting a handle on TrueMotion's capabilities has been tough. Until recently you had to deal directly with Duck, which is more of a development shop than a distributor of products. Now there is a package out on the market for developers featuring the TrueMotion-S technology. The product form of the TrueMotion CODEC is available from Horizons Technology, while Duck itself concentrates on building the technology and licensing it for other important DV areas like broadcasting and games.

Smacker!

RAD Software
307 West 200 South, Suite 1003
Salt Lake City, UT 84101
Phone: 801-322-4300

If you locked some really smart developers in a room and told them to write a flexible and useful digital video codec and playback library that was especially oriented for game development, as soon as you left they'd pick up the phone and order Smacker! from RAD Software. Then they would hide Smacker! in a desk drawer for three months, look busy whenever you opened the door to check on them, and spend their abundant spare time playing games.

Most digital video codecs work to please a huge group of developers, some of whom couldn't care less about making games. Smacker! concentrates on the key aspects of digital video essential for today's game developer:

- It's optimized for only 256-color files. Most codecs have to account for 24-bit color and scalability. This means their compression schemes and speeds aren't always optimal for the 256-color images that make up 99 percent of games these days. Smacker! is fully optimized for 256-color mode, which results in better playback speeds and quality, plus tighter file compression.

- It's designed for developers, not end users. Smacker! includes lots of goodies for developers, including support for FLC and FLI files, AVI files, and sequentially numbered image files. Smacker! also supports Smacker! calls from your code with a full API you can order. In addition, Smacker! provides a script language that offers a ton of interactive scripting features.

- It allows you to touch up compressed files with Animator Studio. Once files are compressed, you can touch them up to improve their quality. Smacker! specifically works well with Animator Studio, a popular animation product from Autodesk.

- It increases playback speed. For some codecs and their users, compression speed is often a major concern. Game developers, however, often look first for maximum performance on the playback end. Smacker! doesn't let them down.

Smacker! has a number of pricing schemes, and while some might seem expensive, they're quite cheap considering the overall gains you make from a shipped product. The basic package runs approximately $195. If you want your shipped product to have playback of an anonymous capability (that is, without any pop-up displays), you need to order a redistribution license, which will cost around $1,000. C-callable APIs for DOS, Windows 3.1x, Windows 95, and Macintosh run from $3,000 to $15,000, depending on the number of products you will ship and whether you require source code.

For complete details and updates (coming attractions include a Sega Saturn playback library, VB OCX, and Windows MCI extensions), you should definitely call RAD Software.

Indeo Video Interactive

Intel Corporation
2200 Mission College Boulevard
Santa Clara, CA 95052
Phone: 408-765-8080
WWW: http://www.intel.com/pc-supp/multimed/indeo/

Indeo Video Interactive is an entirely new version of Intel's original Indeo codec. This version uses a hybrid wavelet-based software video that enables realtime interaction and control of video and graphics, with emphasis on sprites over video and video on top of other video.

Not only do you get this increased interactive focus, but the new codec features improved image quality, especially at lower data rates (great for animation playback), and a new scaleable quality feature that optimizes performance on Pentiums (after all, this is an Intel product). Indeo Video Interactive boasts several cool features:

- *Transparency*—This feature allows you to display video or graphics of different shapes on a video or graphics scene, then interactively control the playback on the fly.

- *Local Windows*—This feature allows you to create independent, simultaneous video-playback windows with a large video playback or a graphics scene. This technique is especially useful for creating panned video. For example, imagine a car chase scene in which you actually pan from right to left during the video feed on the fly!

- *Random Keyframes*—Many video codecs place keyframes at specific intervals in the video—not the most flexible way to provide fresh image quality. Indeo Video Interactive allows placement of keyframes anywhere in a movie.

- *Change Saturation/Contrast/Brightness Controls*—This feature allows you to change all these specifications on the fly. Now you can send brightness up to pure white in a car crash or "black out" in a steep dive in an airplane!

- *No Cost*—Intel will license Indeo Video Interactive to any software developer for free and without royalties.

Iterated System Low-Bit-Rate Codec

Iterated Systems
3525 Piedmont Road
Seven Piedmont Center, Suite 600
Atlanta, GA 30305-1530
Phone: 800-437-2285
Fax: 404-264-8300
WWW: http://www.iterated.com

The folks who brought you the CoolFusion digital video format are working on a low-bit-rate codec that should be useful for many Web digital video file formats. Check with Iterated for more information as this product develops.

Creating Animation and Digital Video for the Web

Knowing what file formats exist and how to plug this stuff into your Web pages is fairly straightforward, but what about *creating* animated imagery? Ouch! That's not nearly as simple, especially when it comes to digital video and 3D animation (which I covered a little bit in Chapter 11).

Creating quality animated content isn't easy, and squeezing the most out of small file sizes isn't any easier. The following sections include as many helpful resources as I could find concerning each of the file formats I've discussed, followed by a list of general resources that can help any Web developer working with animation or video.

Animated GIF Resources

There are several programs that support developers who are putting together animated GIF files. Here are the ones that are mentioned most often.

GIF Construction Set 1.0

GIF Creation Programs
Alchemy Mindworks, Inc.
P.O. Box 500
Beeton, Ontario, Canada, L0G 1A0
WWW: http://www.mindworkshop.com/alchemy/alchemy.html

GIF Construction Set (GCS for short) is a Windows application that takes separate GIFs and helps you assemble them and other animated GIF animation items like timing and loop information. GCS also handles transparency and palette issues, and it can even produce simple animated-text GIFs automatically.

GIFBuilder

Yves Piguet
Email: piguet@ia.cpfl.ch
WWW: http://iawww.epfl.ch/Staff/Yves.Piguet/clip2gif-home/GifBuilder.html

I haven't used it, but GIFBuilder by Yves Piguet seems to be the best-liked Mac program for creating animated GIFs. It will produce GIF89a-compliant animations and handles palette management, dithering, and transparency as well.

There are many sites where you can download premade animated GIFs, get more information on techniques and tips, and download GIF construction utilities. Here's a roundup of the best places to check out.

Yahoo Animated GIF Listing

http://www.yahoo.com/Computers_and_Internet/Graphics/Computer_Animation/
Animated_GIFs

GIF Animation on the World Wide Web

http://members.aol.com/royalef/gifanim.htm

Run, don't walk, to this site—it was created by Royal Frazier, the best Web-based expert on the animated GIF phenomenon. His site is packed with a book's worth of information and resources!

The Animated GIF Gallery

http://members.aol.com/royalef/galframe.htm

In this attachment to Royal Frazier's awesome animated GIF site, Royal points you to all the various animated GIF samples he's found or collected on the Web.

Server Push-Client Pull

If you're still interested in doing server push/client pull animations, you can find all you need to know at the following site.

Yahoo's Server Push-Client Pull Page

```
http://www.yahoo.com/Computers_and_Internet/Internet/World_Wide_Web/
Programming/Server_Push_Client_Pull/
```

Enliven

Narrative Communications Corp.
204 Second Avenue
Waltham, MA 02154
Phone: 617-290-5300
Fax: 617-290-5312
WWW: http://www.narrative.com

Delivery Specifics

Users can download the Enliven viewer application or inline plug-in from the Narrative Web site. There is also an Enliven server package that is designed to deliver multiple realtime streams—and download subsequent portions as well in the background.

According to Narrative Communications, the viewer/server combination can ensure playback that is comparable to CD-ROM levels, even at 28.8 Kbps.

File Construction Specifics

In order to create Enliven animations for your site, you have to use the Enliven Producer program, a scene-based drag-and-drop program that can import existing digital content from programs like Macromedia's Director.

Multimedia Emblaze

GEO Interactive Media Group
Phone: 972-3-573-3288
Fax: 972-3-573-3290
WWW: http://www.geo.inter.net

In order to author for Multimedia Emblaze, you will need their Emblaze Creator authoring tool. Emblaze can create a full-motion, full-screen animation with sound. As of this writing, the full Creator package is still under development, but a for-sale version should be ready by the time this book is out. Check out the GEO Web site for more information.

Multimedia mBED

mBED Software
San Francisco, CA
Phone: 415-778 0934
WWW: http://www.mbed.com

Delivery Specifics

mBED has created both a plug-in and an ActiveX control to play back mBED animations. You may download both from the mBED Web site.

File Construction Specifics

The file construction process for Multimedia mBED is unique—using an HTML-like markup language, you program your animations with tagged commands. This can be done with nothing more than a text editor and their MDB language specification, which is available for free at their Web site (and worth a download).

mBED Software has created a series of utilities and an editor that you can purchase from them to speed up the process; but unlike other systems, developers don't require you to buy the authoring environment. Their marketing of the authoring package as an optional advantage to the entirely free format is faithful to the concept of open technology that the Web has always promoted.

PowerMedia

RadMedia
Palo Alto, CA
Phone: 415-617-9430
Fax: 415-473-6826
WWW: http://www.radmedia.com

Delivery Specifics

Users download the PowerMedia plug-in, which is available for a variety of platforms.

File Construction Specifics

You will need the specific PowerMedia authoring package, available from RadMedia's Web site for Windows, Macintosh, or Unix platforms. With it you create, import, and link various animation files (and other multimedia files) into a final form complete with timing, cues, and so on—and then compile the final product into a form ready for distribution on the Web.

The cost of the authoring environment runs around $495 to $2,395, depending on the platform and/or support package you buy, with the Unix version being the most expensive.

Sizzler

Totally Hip Software Inc.
1224 Hamilton Street, Suite 301
Vancouver, BC V6B 2S8
Phone: 604-685-6525
Fax: 604-685-4057
WWW: http://www.totallyhip.com

Delivery Specifics

Sizzler is available as a plug-in or (soon) an ActiveX control. Both are freely distributed from the Totally Hip Web site.

File Construction Specifics

In order to author for the Sizzler format you need Totally Hip's WebPainter program, an easy-to-use package that combines painting tools with a cel-animation package. WebPainter has unique animation features like onion-skinning, multiple-cel editing, and foreground/background drawing cels. There is also a library full of animations to use. WebPainter supports PICs, QuickTime Movies, GIF89a, and GIF (and perhaps Java when the final version ships). Artists using the program can produce a Sizzler animation file when the artwork is complete.

WebPainter is a Macintosh-only program right now, but there is a Windows conversion program for Sizzler-formatted files.

Vivo

Vivo Software, Inc.
411 Waverley Oaks Road

Waltham, MA 02154
Phone: 617-899-8900
Fax: 617-899-1400
WWW: http://www.vivo.com

The first great thing you'll notice about Vivo4's approach to digital video over the Web is that it doesn't require special server software. Although it is a little slower than VDOLive on average, the difference is significant only with slow connections.

The key component of Vivo's system—aside from its freely available plug-in—is the VivoActive producer program, which takes AVI files and turns them into VIV files. This is the program from which Vivo makes its money. Developers wishing to use the Vivo technology can purchase the VivoActive producer once its final version has shipped, which should have occurred by the time this book is available.

AVI Files

An AVI file can have many characteristics and can be delivered in many forms because of its native support in the Windows environment.

Delivery Specifics

- *HTML Tags*—AVI files can be embedded in Web pages by Internet Explorer just by using HTML tags (see CD-ROM). Of course, this is a pretty simplistic way to deliver video content, because the entire AVI file has to be downloaded before it can be played. I've seen it best used with very small AVI files that are more like mini-animations than full-fledged digital movies.

- *ActiveMovie Control*—Microsoft's ActiveMovie control can download and play an AVI-compatible movie in a much more robust fashion than the HTML tags, and it will soon become a much more prevalent way of playing AVI movies.

Creation Specifics

There are already a number of programs (many listed later on) that can create and output an AVI file, with QuickTime being perhaps the most widely supported movie format. However, be aware that many different codecs can change the nature of the AVI file you send to your users. (For more information, see the background information provided earlier on many codecs.)

QuickTime & QuickTime VR

Apple Computer, Inc.
1 Infinite Loop
Cupertino, CA 95014
Phone: 408-996-1010
WWW: http://www.apple.com

Delivery Specifics

http://qtvr.quicktime.apple.com

There are QuickTime and QuickTime VR plug-ins available for Macintosh and Windows platforms. In addition, some other programs (such as Microsoft's ActiveMovie control) can support the playback of QuickTime files. Apple does have some licensing agreements to follow, which are not very demanding, but nevertheless are worth surfing over to their site to read before you get started.

File Construction Specifics

QuickTime files may be created by a number of leading digital video tools described below, and Apple has a suite of development tools to assist you in the creation of QuickTime VR files. For the moment, however, you can only author QuickTime VR movies on the Macintosh platform. You might also need a special "panoramic" camera that can take special photos of 360-degree environments, though a 3D file may work as well.

QuickTime VR Authoring Tools Suite
Apple Developers Catalog Online
http://www.devcatalog.apple.com

This suite of tools includes a number of items you need to process and put together a QuickTime VR movie. Here are the exact catalog item numbers:

QuickTime VR Authoring Tools Suite 1.0 R0629ZB (NTSC) $495.00
R0637ZB (PAL) $495.00

Photographing QuickTime VR Scenes Video R0646LL/B (NTSC) $29.95
R0645LL/B (PAL) $29.95

QuickTime VR Developers' Site
`http://qtvr.quicktime.apple.com/Develop.htm`

This page features a number of additional QuickTime VR development resources. There are several articles from Apple's developer magazine, as well as a pointer to additional utilities and new techniques people are using.

The QuickTime VR Mailing List
`http://www.solutions.apple.com/ListAdmin/`

This Web site makes subscribing to the developers' mailing list a cinch.

The QuickTime VR Samples Page
`http://quicktimevr.apple.com/Samples.htm`

Don't forget to check out Apple's page of links that showcase QuickTime VR technology!

Surround Video

Surround Video is a new competitor to QuickTime VR that is authorable on Intel platforms (QuickTime VR, while playable from Intel-based computers, isn't authorable on them).

Black Diamond Consulting

195 Hanover Street, Suite 22
Portsmouth, NH 03801
Phone: 603-430-7777
Fax: 603-430-7778
WWW: http://www.bdiamond.com

After an extended period of "vaporware" rumors, Surround Video has finally reared its head. Microsoft has licensed the technology and development of Surround Video to Black Diamond Consulting, which has Webified it as an ActiveX control with a complete SDK.

Delivery Specifics

Browsers that can read ActiveX controls download the Surround Video ActiveX control and then are able to interact with Surround Video environments. This player is available on Black Diamond's Web site or can be placed as a control on your server.

File Construction Specifics

You can create Surround Video files using the Surround Video Editor (available as part of the overall Surround Video SDK for $495, the same price as QuickTime VR) and the Surround Video Link Editor, which can embed URL links into the files. Scenes can be created within the editor by either using a panoramic cameras or by importing from a 3D rendering package.

Surround Video vs. QuickTime VR

There are certainly a lot of questions concerning which of these two major Video VR formats to use, and I'm still sorting out some of them. In general, it seems that QuickTime VR is a little more robust, but Surround Video is nice as an ActiveX control and with its API. The other major difference is that QuickTime VR authoring kits are only available for the Macintosh, while Surround Video editing tools are only available for Windows. The players exist in cross-platform versions; hopefully in the end there will be cross-platform authoring tools as well.

So which one should you use? Since I'm a Windows person and dabble in programming, Surround Video seams to be the way to go for me. Because so many people are already familiar with the ins and outs of QuickTime VR, though, I expect it to be the more popular product for at least a while longer.

Surround Video and QuickTime VR Hardware Resources

I think that the QuickTime VR and Surround Video formats are really going to take off as more people discover how these items work and how to prepare the content for them. Part of making content for these systems, however, is knowing about the specialized hardware that you can use. Here's one manufacturer of this type of hardware and a good Web resource to find out more.

Globuscope Camera

44 West 24th St.
New York, NY 10010
Phone: 212-243-1008

WWW: http://www.everent.com/globus/

This company sells panoramic cameras.

The Panoramic Imaging Zone!
`http://ourworld.compuserve.com/homepages/radia/`
Check out this great all-in-one resource on the entire panoramic imaging
scene. It includes pointers to books, groups, multimedia programs like
Surround Video and QuickTime, and much more.

MPEG

MPEG video files can be downloaded and run using ActiveMovie or other
MPEG-compliant video players. For streaming MPEG video to users in realtime,
however, you'll need a product like Xing StreamWorks (see the upcoming section).

Creating MPEG video files will require an encoding system. This is a specialized software and hardware setup that helps to compress the raw digital video
file quickly into the MPEG format. Since there are many different types of
MPEG development systems, here are some links to Web-based reviews and
key MPEG technology companies.

MPEG.ORG
`http://www.mpeg.org`
The Web site for the MPEG consortium is an excellent place to start building
more knowledge about MPEG. You could spend days researching MPEG files
and information from this site.

MPEG 4.0 FAQ
`http://www.powerweb.de/mpeg/mpegfaq/`
MPEG involves many more things than I could possibly present here. If you
want to really dig into the subject, this excellent HTML page will point you
to a lot of the right places to go.

New Media Magazine
`http://www.hyperstand.com`
Some of the best articles I've seen on MPEG have been in New Media Magazine, and you can search their archives easily here. One recent article had a
very strong roundup of all the major encoding systems, including those from
3DO, Sony, ReelMagic, and Sigma.

Visible Light's MPEG Products Mall

Visible Light MPEG Products Division
P.O. Box 162024
Altamonte Springs, FL 32716
Phone: 407-786-5693
Fax: 407-786-2167
WWW: http://www.visiblelight.com/mall

This site contains a ton of information about MPEG products and software, including FAQs and company links. It's a store, too, so you have the ability to purchase everything from software to hardware encoders online.

Even More Sites...

```
http://www.optibase.com/primer2.html
http://www-plateau.cs.berkeley.edu/mpeg/mpegptr.html
```

With these two and the earlier listed sites, I expect you all to be MPEG experts by the time I write a revised version of this book!

VDOLive

VDOnet Corp.
4009 Miranda Ave., Ste. 250
Palo Alto, CA 94304
Phone: 415-846-7700
Fax: 415-846-7900
WWW: http//www.vdolive.com

The VDOLive system consists of three main products to deliver and produce the video format:

- The VDOLive Video Player, which is a plug-in/ActiveX control that users download and install into their browser.

- The VDOLive Video Server, which provides the bandwidth compression and delivery to clients.

- The VDOLive Tools, which help developers with the capture, encoding, and compression of digital video files into the specialized VDOLive format.

The VideoLive server system is available for wide variety of servers, including Windows NT, Sun Solaris, SunOS, SGI Irix, IBM AIX, Linux, FreeBSD, BSDI, DEC Alpha NT, and Unix.

There is also the VDOLive Personal Server, which is a smaller version of the VDOLive server system that typical sites will use. The personal server allows users to create two simultaneous "streams" of video of up to one minute in length. Since you can upgrade to a larger version at any time, the personal server is an excellent way to get familiar with the VDOLive technology.

The current version of Adobe Premiere includes the VDOLive personal server, which can also be downloaded from VDOLive's Web site.

VDOLive 2.0, the newest version of the platform features improved video quality and an increased viewing resolution (now up to 352×288). The Storybook mode lets you use the VDOTools to synchronize images to an audio track, creating your own storybook Web sites—the VDO content doesn't even have to be present; it can be just stills and voice.

Xing StreamWorks

Xing Technology Corp.
1540 West Branch Street
Arroyo Grande, CA 93420
Phone: 805-473-0145
WWW: http://www.xingtech.com

Xing StreamWorks builds on Xing's experience with MPEG and brings streaming MPEG video to the Web. The system consists of four main products:

- StreamWorks Network Stream Generator, which converts video streams into MPEG-1/MPEG-2 files capable of Internet transmission for live broadcast.

- StreamWorks Network Servers, which are available for a wide range of Unix servers and Windows NT. Once installed, these allow you to stream MPEG compressed video to users of the StreamWorks Network Client, although you'll need the StreamWorks Network Stream Generator to offer up live streams.

- StreamWorks Network Manager, which helps provide remote management capabilities for StreamWorks server databases.

- StreamWorks Network Client, which is available for Windows, X-Windows, and Macintosh platforms. Users may register for technical support for $29, and there is a specialized versions for LAN users.

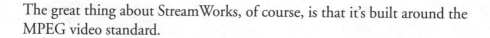

The great thing about StreamWorks, of course, is that it's built around the MPEG video standard.

ActiveMovie

Microsoft
One Microsoft Way
Redmond, WA 98052
Phone: 206-882-8080
Fax: 206-883-8101
WWW: http://www.microsoft.com

ActiveMovie is a new technology from Microsoft that replaces its previous video-playback engine, Microsoft Video for Windows. One thing that makes ActiveMovie particularly inviting is that it can handle a wide variety of digital video formats, including MPEG audio, WAV audio, MPEG video, AVI video, and Apple QuickTime video. And because it's an ActiveX control, ActiveVideo handles the playback over the Internet as well. (ActiveX is also a very programmable component, as I will discuss in later programming sections.) Web developers creating custom applications will appreciate ActiveVideo's ability to be hooked directly into their Internet plans.

Intel's Intercast Technology

Chip giant Intel has recently begun promoting its Intercast technology, which is a hybrid of the World Wide Web and broadcast video.

Users of PCs equipped with Intercast technology receive standard antenna or cable television signals directly into their computer. Encoded with the signal are various Web pages, which are downloaded alongside the broadcast stream and stored locally on the computer. Users can then simultaneously watch the broadcast and interact with the Web content.

The possibilities with this technology are quite interesting: for example, a national news network could broadcast Web pointers to various in-depth reports on a subject being mentioned during a newscast. A sports broadcast could download statistics on various players, plus updates on other games. During commercials, advertisers could send Intercast users their Web site's home page.

Intercast-equipped PCs will be shipping from major manufacturers like Gateway 2000 sometime in late 1996 or early 1997. MTV (a Viacom subsidiary) is already using Intercast for its new video channel, M2, and NBC is planning on using it as well.

For more on Intercast technology, check out these great resources:

Intel Corporation
2200 Mission College Boulevard
Santa Clara, CA 95052
Phone: 408-765-8080

The Intercast Industry Group
P.O. Box 10266
Portland, OR 97210
http://www.intercast.org

You can actually join the Intercast organization by sending a letter or visiting its Web site. Membership costs around $2,500.

Digital Video Construction Resources

Up until now I've focused on a lot of Web-specific discussion topics, but those are only half the story. The other part of this resource guide—which starts here—concerns how to make the video in the first place!

Composing Digital Video Files: Software Considerations

Purchasing the software to compose your files is just one more crucial decision in the world of digital video technology. In this section, I've listed both low- and high-end editing packages for your perusal.

Adobe Premiere

Adobe Systems, Inc.
P.O. Box 7900
Mountain View, CA 94039-7900
Phone: 415-961-4111

Fax: 415-967-9231

WWW: http://www.adobe.com

Premiere is aptly named, because it is indeed at the top of the heap of various digital video editing products on the market today.

Premiere is available for both Windows and Macintosh platforms. As with almost any artwork-related production package, you want to get the most powerful computer and memory setup you can afford to allow the full power of this program to shine through.

Asymetrix Digital Video Producer

Asymetrix Corporation

110 110th Avenue, NE #700

Bellevue, WA 98004

Phone: 206-637-5828

WWW: http://www.asymetrix.com

Although Premiere is the benchmark product against which other digital video editing products are judged, I would be doing you a disservice if I listed only that package. Asymmetrix's DVP, a drag-and-drop video editing product for Windows, is one competitor worth mentioning.

in:sync Razor and Speed Razor Pro

in:sync Corporation

6106 MacArthur Boulevard

Bethesda, MD 20816

Phone: 301-320-0220

Fax: 301-320-0335

WWW: http://www.in-sync.com

This digital video editing package is another nice alternative to Adobe Premiere. in:sync Razor comes in two distinct flavors: The regular Razor is for Windows 3.1 and Windows 95, while Speed Razor is a 32-bit Windows NT application. As far as I know, the latter is the only native NT digital video software package around.

What's also cool about the in:sync folks is their Web site (**http://www. in-sync.com/in-sync**), where you'll find a fully capable demo of their lower-end product, in:sync Razor. Unfortunately, the demo only works with black-

and-white video, but for evaluation purposes (or that "film noir" Web site you've been planning) you'll find it useful.

Autodesk Animator Pro and Animator Studio (Windows)

Autodesk
111 McInnis Parkway
San Rafael, CA 94903
Phone: 800-879-4233
Fax: 206-860-2196
WWW: http://www.autodesk.com

Autodesk Animator Pro, which recently received a major update, is probably the best PC-based animation package available. Let's take a look at some of its more interesting features.

Animator handles 24-bit color with 8-bit alpha-channel transparency, and it works with Photoshop-compatible plug-ins like Kai's Power Tools. You can even paint on a multiframe animation using video sprites—for example, if you've got one animation running already, you can run another animation and create a composite animation from both of them.

Animator's animation features include a full set of graphics functions, including airbrush, lines, fill, and the other usual suspects. This program also supports onion-skinning to help you do great line-art animation.

With its newest release, Autodesk has added an integrated studio for recording, editing, and synchronizing audio from sources such as CDs, tapes, and external microphones. Sophisticated editing features include the ability to modify pitch and tempo independently, so you can stretch or "squeeze" a sound track to fit an animation without changing its pitch.

Higher-End Editing Systems

The average Web developer doesn't need much more than Adobe Premiere to help capture and edit digital video. If you want to move up a step to a more robust process, however, there are several major systems that you can evaluate. It takes a large block of complex digital video needs to warrant investment in these systems (some cost more than $20,000), but many companies are making the investment. Beyond these products are even more powerful and expensive set-ups, but you're not trying to be Spielberg—or are you?

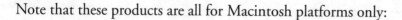

Note that these products are all for Macintosh platforms only:

Avid Media Suite Pro

Avid Technology
1 Park West
Tewksbury, MA 01876
Phone: 508-640-6789
Fax: 508-640-9486
Email: 71333.3020@compuserve.com

Media Suite Pro is one of Avid's lower-end, nonlinear editing packages. It offers a wealth of features and comes with its own proprietary editing software.

Media 100

Data Translation
100 Locke Drive
Marlboro, MA 01752
Phone: 508-460-1600

Media 100 is Avid's biggest competitor in the midrange, nonlinear editing category. It's a popular system that uses its own proprietary editing software.

Telecast

Radius, Inc.
215 Moffet Park Drive
Sunnyvale, CA 94089
Phone: 408-541-6100

Telecast, one of Radius' top-of-the-line products, uses a special version of Adobe Premiere as its editing software. The specialization is mainly to support some proprietary time coding information, but apart from that it should be easy for any Premiere junkie to use.

More Resources for Digital Video

This section contains some basic books, magazines, and Web sites to help you create good digital video files.

Magazines and Newsletters

Several magazines offer good help to the digital video enthusiast. Besides the hardcore digital video periodicals listed here, check out the great computer art magazines, including *Digital Video* (which despite the title covers more than just digital video), *New Media*, and *Computer Graphics World*. These magazines are listed elsewhere as overall graphics resources.

Digital Video Magazine's Full Motion Newsletter

ActiveMedia, Inc., (IDG)
600 Townsend Street, Suite 170
San Francisco, CA 94103
Phone: 415-522-2400
Fax: 415-522-2409
Email: letters@dv.com
Subscription Fax: 603-472-2419
Subscription: $49.95
Newsstand: N/A
Publishes: 6/Year
Pages: 20

Digital Video Magazine

DV Full Motion
120 Bedford Center Road, Suite 4
Bedford, NH 03110

This newsletter comes from the producers of *Digital Video* and focuses on using Adobe Premiere, After Affects, and other Adobe digital video and related products. I haven't actually read this newsletter, but I have heard that it is very helpful.

Videography

Miller Freeman PSN Inc.
2 Park Avenue, Suite 1820
New York, NY 10016
Phone: 212-779-1919
Fax: 212-213-3484
Email: videography@psn.com
Subscription: $30.00

Newsstand: $3.95
Publishes: 12/Year
Pages: 170

Videography is the leading magazine for high-end video/digital video production. If you're serious about putting together the proper digital video resources, you should be reading it. You'll find information on computer digital video, as well as all the latest and greatest hardware.

Video Magazine

Hachette Filipacchi Magazines
1633 Broadway
New York, NY 10019
Phone: 212-779-1919
Fax: 212-213-3484
Email: videography@psn.com
Subscription: $30.00
Newsstand: $4.95
Publishes: 10/Year
Pages: 110

Video is decidedly lower-end in nature—it's most useful for that home-theater freak you might know. Even so, it covers a lot of good equipment from the nonbroadcast-quality spectrum, which for many hobbyists/shareware/lower-end developers may be more than adequate. I recommend that you get *Videography* first.

Books

The Digital Videomaker's Guide by Kathryn Shaw Whitver (Michael Wiese Productions; ISBN 0-941188-21-3)

This handy guide starts with an overview of digital video terms, formats, and studio requirements. It also deals with how to get the production process rolling, as well as specifics on marketing, copyright, and distribution. *The Digital Videomaker's Guide* includes a complete bibliography and a resource guide.

Web Sites

I found some really useful stuff at the various codec-related Web sites. SuperMac and Intel, makers of two of the most popular digital video codecs, have a lot of great information on their sites, as well as pointers to additional tools and services.

Cinepak Information and Digital Video Tips
`http://www.radius.com`

SuperMac invented Cinepak—but Radius bought SuperMac, so visit the Radius site. It has a specific page of information and contacts for the Cinepak codec, as well as general digital video information.

Indeo Information and Extensive Digital Video Tips
`http://www.intel.com/multimedia/indeo`

Intel has been a key pioneer in interactive digital video. This site has a ton of useful information on capturing, editing, and programming digital video.

Adobe Premiere and After Effects Information and Tips
`http://www.adobe.com`

As noted earlier, Adobe Premiere is the leading digital video editing package for both Windows and Macintosh. Check here often to see what new products and extensions Adobe is adding to its growing line of digital video applications.

Digital Movie News
`http://spider.lloyd.com/~dmnews/`

This is a really cool site with lots of help for people making full-length movies with only a camera and their PCs. There's good basic information here on almost every aspect of digital video production.

Northwestern University Library
Marjorie I. Mitchell Multimedia Center
`http://www.library.nwu.edu/media/resources/`

This site is an excellent source of links to all kinds of film, video production, and digital video information on the Web.

Digital Video Magazine Web Site
`http://www.dv.com`

Digital Video has a ton of useful information for the digital video enthusiast, as well as information on all sorts of graphics products.

CHAPTER

Multimedia authoring tools can add significant flash to your site development!

Multimedia Content Solutions

The World Wide Web can be thought of as the world's largest multimedia application. Of course, a Web site itself also can be seen as a single multimedia application, and the same goes for a page, since they can contain separate elements of sound, music, graphics, animation, and text. There is also a direct need, however, to create self-contained multimedia objects to be distributed via the Internet. In this chapter I'll discuss the tools and options you can use to build these multimedia programs and integrate them into your Web pages.

The most famous multimedia Web technology (and certainly one of the best) is Macromedia's Shockwave, which compiles Director programs for the Web. As important as Shockwave is, though, it's not alone. There are some new kids on the block with some unusual features, some alternative ideas that fit well in particular situations, and of course Java, which I'll discuss as well. As we've seen in the preceding chapters for graphics, sound, and animation, there are lots of ways to approach multimedia on the Web.

What Qualifies as a Multimedia Content Solution?

Before we get ahead of ourselves, let's define the exact characteristics of a multimedia content product. First, it should allow for some combination of sound (perhaps including music) and graphics to be presented according to a script created by the developer. Second, it should allow for user interaction.

Some relatively primitive products don't completely meet these criteria, but still qualify as multimedia. In the upper echelon of multimedia solutions, though, interaction and programmatic presentation are at the heart of the system.

Things to Remember When Developing Multimedia Content for the Web

For the most part, CD-ROM multimedia has failed to deliver on its initial promise—instead, the World Wide Web is where multimedia has truly come into its own, combining media forms and adding interactive experiences to give ordinary text-with-pictures displays new life. The irony is that developers who cut their teeth on the input-output performance of CD-ROM drives or even fast hard drives have literally had to reinvent themselves in order to cope with the limited bandwidth the Web can handle. This is how multimedia developers find themselves with unparalleled opportunities, but being challenged technically like never before.

As a result, probably no one understands how bandwidth issues affect software development more than multimedia developers. And it's no surprise that the technology gurus who can write compression schemes are among the most sought-after engineers today. I've already noted that even when compressed, digital video and audio file sizes can bulk up quickly—now imagine the trouble involved in handling multimedia, which is trying to deliver not one, but all of those media types in one integrated package! This raises a set of issues to consider that I'll try to address as I discuss the options and resources available to multimedia developers for the Web.

Why Create a Multimedia Application in the First Place?

It's almost guaranteed that if you're going to include a Shockwave or Mirage program in your Web site, it's going to be the most time-consuming and expensive part of the site—so are you sure you need to do it in the first place? For example, if you want to have text that interacts with pictures, why not use a synchronized RealAudio system?

Of course, I'm not trying to scare you off—if it's done well, even a small multimedia application can be just the thing to make your site stand out. Just be aware that multimedia can suck you in like a black hole; make sure it really adds a benefit before you commit to using it.

Matching Bandwidth with Multimedia Need

The biggest problem in creating a multimedia Web application is making one that downloads quickly enough to keep users from clicking to go elsewhere, yet is exciting enough to be worth even a short wait. While other single media forms (digital video and audio, for instance) have helped span the bandwidth gap with streaming technologies, multimedia over the Web is just getting around to working with streams. Even Enliven, the best solution so far, has a 30- to 40-second waiting period before the first material hits the user's screen, and that requires a major server back-end to help the process along.

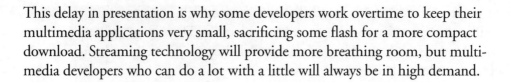

This delay in presentation is why some developers work overtime to keep their multimedia applications very small, sacrificing some flash for a more compact download. Streaming technology will provide more breathing room, but multimedia developers who can do a lot with a little will always be in high demand.

Integrating the Application, the Page, and the Site

Just because you can create a super multimedia game for your Web site doesn't mean you should do it. Lots of site developers fall into the trap of placing a really cool application on a page even if it doesn't really fit in with the page or the overall site. Some companies and advertisers consider games as attractions for their sites, even if the game has nothing to do with the product they're trying to sell.

Java and ActiveX Solutions

Although specialized multimedia authoring solutions are the focus of this chapter, Java and ActiveX technology can also handle multimedia. While Java is furthest along in this regard, expect ActiveX scripting and Microsoft's J++ (a combination of ActiveX and Java) to become major players in the creation of specialized multimedia content for the Web.

Already several companies—including Intel—are building specialized tools or libraries to help developers create multimedia applications in Java. Kinetix Hyperwire is a visual environment for Java development geared especially toward multimedia content creation. (For more about Java and its capabilities for multimedia development, see the chapter on Java later in this book.)

Store and Forward

Many Web sites that have games and other multimedia content don't present it as inline content on the page—instead, they offer it as a separate file to be downloaded and run on your computer. There are several reasons to do this, the first being that Web surfers tend to tolerate longer download times when they view the program as an offsite experience. Second, this method allows developers to create applications in non-Web-oriented environments, especially with programming languages like C++, Visual Basic, or Delphi. Third, these application can be distributed further through other means (for example, via disk or reuploading elsewhere on the Web). Figure 14.1 (which I

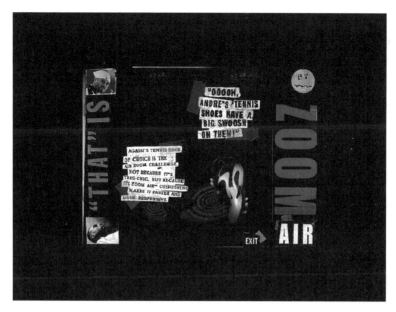

Figure 14.1   Nike is using downloadable multimedia for added punch to their site.

mentioned earlier in this book) is a multimedia interpretation of a Nike ad downloaded from the shoe company's Web site (the 1.2 MB files are "perfect for disk distribution," claims Nike).

The Major Multimedia Web Technologies

The best-known Web animation technology, the Shockwave system from Macromedia, is very impressive, but if you do a little research you'll find that there are a host of other products worth a look. I'll explore Shockwave at the end of this section—but when it comes to multimedia on the Web, don't limit your choices.

Astound

Astound, Inc.
3160 West Bayshore Road
Palo Alto, CA 94303
Phone: 415-845-6200
Fax: 415-845-6201
WWW: http:// www.astound.com (trial version of authoring package at
           http://www.golddisk.com/awp/trial.html)

Astound provides lots of predesigned templates for quick creation of presentations, but it also offers several multimedia content editors to customize and perfect your work. The current version, Astound 2.0, is available for Windows and Macintosh platforms, as is the plug-in player to distribute Astound files over the Web. Multimedia support exists for simple animations, transitions, QuickTime movies, MIDI files, and WAV files. Interactive elements include hotspots, digital video control, and a great deal of control over timeline functions to synchronize events with one another and with user actions.

The Astound package includes six editors to help you create content for your presentations: Astound Draw, Astound Image, Astound Video, Astound Actor, Astound Animator, and Astound Sound. While more robust content-creation products exist in each category, having all these editors in one package makes Astound a solution that is especially suited for small intranet developers on tight budgets.

Studio M

Astound, Inc.
3160 West Bayshore Road
Palo Alto, CA 94303
Phone: 415-845-6200
Fax: 415-845-6201
WWW: http://www.astound.com

Studio M, a less robust package than Astound, is aimed more toward the home market. It bills itself as "the fun and easy way to create your own personalized multimedia greeting cards, invitations, family albums, and more." In short, Studio M is like a multimedia printshop, with lots of easy-to-use templates to help users combine graphics, photos, text, video, voice, and music and distribute the results via the Web.

Certainly Studio M is not a high-level or powerful multimedia solution, but it doesn't claim to be one. It seems to be an especially nice package for novices looking to create multimedia content for personal Web pages.

Enliven

Narrative Communications Corp.
204 Second Avenue

Waltham, MA 02154
Phone: 617-290-5300
Fax: 617-290-5312
WWW: http://www.narrative.com

I was impressed by Enliven from its very first demos, which took segments from two of Living Books' most popular multimedia CD-ROM edutainment products and made them work over the Web as if they were coming off a CD. Wow!

Enliven is a powerful system that turns finished products from existing Macromedia Director environments into offerings that are fully streamable over the Web. While it doesn't handle digital video components, all other aspects of the Director package are streamable, and Narrative is working to expand to other authoring environments. (Macromedia is planning to add streaming capabilities to Shockwave soon, but not the server-backed streaming that enables Enliven to handle very complex and robust multimedia files.)

The complete Enliven package consists of Enliven Producer, Enliven Server, and the Enliven Viewer, a plug-in/helper application for users to download. The system's proprietary technology allows Narrative to manage the simulta-neous delivery of large volumes of content to lots of users, especially the mixed content types found in multimedia files.

Enliven Producer

Like an encoding system, Enliven Producer processes Director files into a form that can be distributed via Enliven's server as a streamed piece of con-tent. The people at Narrative, however, explained to me that Producer also compresses each object separately in an optimized manner and then orders them in such a way as to maximize the streamability of the product. So Producer is more than just a typical compression technology.

Enliven Server

Enliven uses a powerful server component that you will need in order to manage the throughput, provide quality streaming of files, and especially to support multiple simultaneous users. One key feature of the client-server approach is the tight work between the two products to stream down more information in the background as the user interacts with the program (in other words, as the user thinks about his or her next hotspot selection, the client and server are busily loading in more data).

Enliven Viewer

The Enliven client-side viewer can be implemented as a Netscape Navigator plug-in, as a helper application to any Mosaic browser, or as a standalone application for displaying content in the Enliven format.

~mirage/MediaForge

Strata, Inc.
2 West Street
St. George, UT 84770
Phone: 801-628-5218
Fax: 801-628-9756
WWW: http://www.strata3d.com

MediaForge (Figure 14.2) is a Windows 95/NT-based package that offers full 32-bit, event-driven, multithreaded multimedia authoring. It comes with more than 100 distinct special effects and an embedded Visual Basic editor called MediaBasic. With support for OLE/ActiveX controls and custom DLLs, it's highly extendable as well.

MediaForge also offers built-in sprite controls, smooth animation, digital video, MIDI, WAV, and CD sound support. The ~mirage component is a

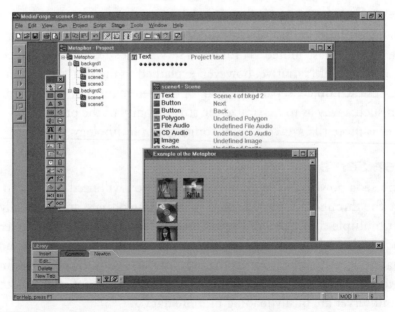

Figure 14.2   MediaForge in action.

plug-in player (1.5 MB when compressed) that users download in order to access MediaForge titles posted on the Web.

I downloaded a 30-day trial of MediaForge from the Strata Web site and was impressed with how simple it was to use in development. Of course, I'm quite familiar with Microsoft's Visual Basic, which seems quite close to MediaForge in terms of how the editing environment works. If you're a Visual Basic pro, you might find MediaForge useful for developing multimedia applications for World Wide Web sites.

QuarkImmedia

Quark, Inc.
1800 Grant Street
Denver, CO 80203
Phone: 303-894-8888
WWW: http://www.quark.com

QuarkImmedia is an extension that uses the power of the Quark XPress desktop publishing program to build multimedia applications. The system consists of the QuarkImmedia Design Tool (which requires Quark XPress) and separate downloadable viewer programs available for Windows and Macintosh platforms (though both were still under final development when I wrote this).

According to Quark, typical Immedia Web titles take no longer than about one minute to download the first page via a 28.8 Kbps modem, and no more than 15 to 40 seconds for each subsequent page. Of course, this estimated speed can vary depending on the application's complexity and the speed of the connection.

QuarkImmedia supports digital video, sound, animation, and hotspots, and it includes a comprehensive scripting language, database connectivity, and an XTension technology that allows you to add your own custom features.

The QuarkImmedia authoring environment is only available on the Macintosh.

PowerMedia

RadMedia
Palo Alto, CA
Phone: 415-617-9430
Fax: 415-473-6826
WWW: http://www.radmedia.com

With the PowerMedia authoring package—available for Windows, Macintosh, or Unix platforms—you create, import, and link various animation files (and other multimedia files) into a final form complete with timing, cues, and so forth, then compile that into a format ready for distribution on the Web. Users view the file by downloading the PowerMedia plug-in, which is available for a variety of platforms. The authoring environment costs between $495 and $2,395, depending on the platform and/or support package you buy; the Unix version is the most expensive.

mTropolis

mFactory
1440 Chapin Avenue, Suite 200
Burlingame, CA 94010
Phone: 415-548-0600
Fax: 415-548-9249
WWW: http://www.mfactory.com

Once mTropolis was the zippy new rookie on the multimedia authoring block, but it's rapidly becoming a seasoned pro. Many major game developers are using this product, including Cybersights, Rocket Science, Cyan, and Warner Inscape.

The core technology behind mTropolis is mFusion, which is billed as a scaleable core technology that delivers true object orientation to multimedia applications. The resulting object-oriented environment is tailored to take advantage of reusable components (for example, you could create a clock object that could be placed anywhere in a program with a simple drag-and-drop procedure).

mTropolis is also quite fast, because hundreds of objects can be responding to events and messages while animation and sound are being processed. In fact, mTropolis features a multithreaded kernel designed specifically for synchronous multimedia, which improves playback performance.

The folks at mFactory tell me that by the time this book is out they'll have a Netscape plug-in available, and that they're working to add streaming features and Internet Explorer support to the mTropolis environment. Another new feature will allow various mTropolis programs to send messages back and forth to each other—in other words, an mTropolis product on a CD-ROM could communicate with other titles sitting on the Web!

Until the plug-ins and ActiveX controls ship, users can download the base player for mTropolis titles and then download and run individual titles from the Web. While some mTropolis files (like those of any authoring environment) can be quite large, you can create some cool products that are 512 K or smaller.

Some early developers were put off by the lack of an mTropolis development program for Windows (at first, it was Macintosh only) and by a rather high product cost. mFactory has since gotten far more aggressive in terms of pricing (check for the latest prices on the company's Web site) and supporting added platforms for the authoring environment.

IconAuthor 7.0

AimTech
20 Trafalgar Square
Nashua, NH 03063
Phone: 603-883-0220
Fax: 603-883-5582
WWW: http://www.aimtech.com

Now available in version 7.0, IconAuthor is a longtime multimedia development system that recently added Internet content creation (and the requisite plug-in) to its repertoire. The latest version is only available for Windows 95 as of this writing, as is the Netscape plug-in.

IconAuthor is more of a corporate multimedia authoring package—it features lots of database and corporate training hooks—than Director, mTropolis, or TopGun, which are aimed at creators of end-user applications. For business-oriented Web multimedia applications, it may be the best way to go.

TopGun

7th Level, Inc.
1110 E. Collins Blvd., #122
Richardson, TX 75081
Phone: 214-498-8100
Fax: 214-437-2717
WWW: http://www.7thlevel.com

If a leading game developer took its entire game engine, turned it into a major multimedia development system, and then created a Web version of it, you might think they'd done something pretty cool. Well, what if they went one step further and made the authoring environment available to other developers? Would you think they were crazy?

Perhaps their close work with Monty Python's Flying Circus has made the crew at 7th Level temporarily insane, but that's exactly what they're doing. Their internal development engine, TopGun, is expected to be available for other developers sometime soon (it's not out as I write this).

Until then, you can see TopGun in action by visiting the Kidsworld site that 7th Level created at **http://www.kidsworld.com**. TopGun is a full multimedia development environment, with a real emphasis on delivering quality interactive animations. It's the power behind many of 7th Level's games, including the GameBreak series the company created for Disney.

Based on the power of the products I've seen created with it, TopGun could be a really great multimedia content creator for Web developers. Keep an eye out for it!

Macromedia Director

Macromedia, Inc.
600 Townsend Street
San Francisco, CA 94103
Phone: 415-252-2000
Fax: 415-626-0554
WWW: http://www.macromedia.com

I saved Macromedia's top-notch Web multimedia product for last because I felt strongly that there are other products out there worth considering. I've included a separate chapter later in this book on resources for Shockwave, which has Director authoring roots.

Director (shown in Figure 14.3) is the benchmark program for multimedia authoring. Even though some newcomers—most notably mTropolis— offer some new forms of power, the fact that everything in this market is compared to Director indicates the latter program's reach and stature.

Now available in version 5.0, Director is a full-fledged development tool. It can animate text and graphics, create hotspots, and display video. It also includes an extensive scripting language, called Lingo, that makes it a very robust development environment. Director has a very large base of loyal users (estimated at more than 400,000). In combination with Shockwave, which

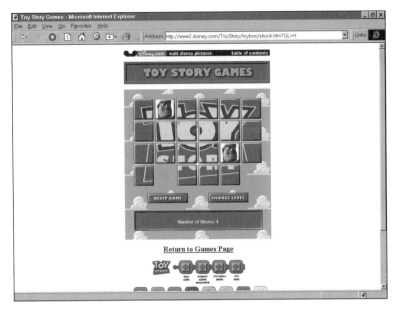

Figure 14.3 Director on the Web—a Shockwave!

allows users to play Director files directly from Web pages, it is become one of the most important Web authoring tools around.

Multimedia Web Content Resources

Your first stop for multimedia Web content information should be the home pages of the companies described earlier in this chapter. Their showcase pages (where they point you toward hot examples created with their products) and their authoring help will be your most invaluable resources. Beyond that, however, there are a few other sites that help multimedia developers looking to work specifically on the Web; the most useful ones are listed in the following paragraphs.

Don't forget, though, that other resources related to Web multimedia can be found throughout this book (for instance, in the previous three chapters).

Key Developers

By no means is this an exhaustive list of the best Web multimedia developers. If nothing else, however, the work of these shops (mostly using Director) is worth seeing as a gauge of what good Web multimedia applications can do.

Pop Rocket
http://www.poprocket.com

Pop Rocket is one of the premier Director developers in the world. It concentrates mostly on game development, including the hit game Total Distortion and a number of cool Shockwave games that really show off the creativity you can release with Director/Shockwave Web content. Pop Rocket also has a subsidiary, RocketShop, that assists other Web sites in developing Shockwave games.

M/BInteractive
http://mbinter.com

This development shop does a lot of Shockwave work—including the site for one of my favorite musical groups, Deep Forest. The Deep Forest site is a really nice example of quality multimedia design for the Web.

Web Sites

Right now the overall pickings on the Web for multimedia can be considered either plentiful or sparse, depending on what you're looking for. If you're looking for help on general multimedia development, there are numerous sources; but for Web multimedia in general, the pickings are a little more exclusive. Here are some of the more essential spots on the Web concerning Web-based multimedia.

Mecklermedia's Weekly Multimedia Web Archive
http://netday.iworld.com/devforum/multimedia/mw-archive.shtml

Each week on its awesome iWORLD site, Mecklermedia posts a new article about what's going on in the Web multimedia scene. This URL will point you directly to the current and past issues.

Yahoo's Multimedia Authoring Services List
http://www.yahoo.com/Business_and_Economy/Companies/Computers/Software/
Multimedia/Authoring_Services/

Developers Listing
http://www.visdesigns.com/developers.html

Often, when a developer or company wants to add a multimedia application to its Web site, it hires a specialized developer or multimedia shop to do the work. While there are hundreds—if not thousands—of developers out there to choose from, you can find many good leads right on the Web. These two URLs will help you explore your options.

Sun's Guidelines for Multimedia on the Web
`http://www.Sun.COM/951201/columns/alertbox/`

SunWorld: Delivering Multimedia on the Internet
`http://www.sun.com/sunworldonline/swol-03-1996/swol-03-multimedia.html`

Sun has produced numerous white papers and articles to help Web developers create better, cooler Web products. These two articles, written by Sun employees, were excellent reading for me as I put this book together; any seasoned or rookie developer should find them worth checking out as well.

The Web Multimedia Tour
`http://ftp.digital.com/webmm/fbegin.html`

A person at Digital Equipment Corporation put together this site, which leads you through a myriad of Web multimedia technologies. It's a neat resource to see what's possible, and it does give you a good idea of how to proceed with your own Web multimedia developments.

Multimedia Links
`http://www.cdmi.com/Lunch/multimedia.html`

There are many listings of multimedia development resources on the Web. While this one, prepared by the folks at Cambridge Digital Media, is by no means exhaustive, it's a very good starting place.

A Note About Books and Organizations

Because so many books, organizations, and conferences that are useful to multimedia developers apply to the entire realm of Web developers, I've listed them in a separate appendix at the end of this book. Rest assured that there are many good resources to take advantage of in these areas.

The MBONE

One of the most exciting multimedia developments on the Internet is the MBONE, a virtual network that uses special protocols and software to broadcast live audio and video more quickly (and therefore more usefully) than ever before. Essentially the MBONE is a virtual network; it works directly over lots of existing Internet infrastructure but the protocols and software it uses allow it to move its data faster through the pipes, which is really useful for multimedia broadcasting.

How Does It Work, and What Do I Need?

The MBONE consists of a special infrastructure that recognizes data traveling the Internet in the IP (Internet Protocol) Multicast format and routes it directly to destination computers.

In order to receive MBONE broadcasts, machines will have to be very fast in terms of both their own speed and power and that of their connections. While some lower connection speeds have been considered (such as ISDN), a T1 line is the standard connection for MBONE reception. Most MBONE receiving computers are workstation machines such as SGI Indigos and Sun SPARCstations. You will need to add some software to those machines so they can receive the specialized IP packets that are MBONE transmissions. Information for this software is provided by the resources listed after this section.

You will also need to be connected to a network provider that is properly configured for the MBONE. Network providers need to implement a specific set of OS improvements and infrastructure changes to support MBONE transmission to their clients. Again, all of this information is provided in the resources listed after this section.

What Will It Mean for Me?

There is no question that the MBONE is still far away from widespread use, but nothing has characterized the Web more than its ability to convert experiments quickly to everyday use. MBONE represents the rise of specialized systems for transmitting high-end multimedia functionality; its video and audio pipeline could become the backbone system for high-end multimedia applications on the Web. As the software becomes more widely available and high-speed lines become more common, we could see a lot more computers with the capacity for MBONE output and input.

MBONE Resources

If you've got the power, you might want to check out the MBONE today. If you don't, you might spend some time now getting familiar with this system, as it could easily become very important in the next few years.

The MBONE is still in its infancy, but already there are two major books, as well as several major Web sites and FAQs. Here are some of the best places to (pardon the pun) "bone up" on the MBONE.

MBONE FAQs

Any hot new Internet technology that doesn't have at least one or two accompanying sites for FAQs probably doesn't exist yet. The MBONE does exist, so here are two really good sets of FAQs to read right away.

The MBONE FAQ
`http://www.mbone.com/techinfo/mbone.faq.html`

Everything you wanted to know about the MBONE and then some. This FAQ is a must-read for anyone looking to utilize the MBONE for their own Web broadcasts.

Dan's Quick and Dirty Guide to Getting Connected to the MBONE
`ftp://genome-ftp.stanford.edu/pub/mbone/mbone-connect`

Want a no-frills six pages that will get you up on the MBONE? Look no further than this FAQ. If you've read The MBONE FAQ and are looking to jump on as quickly as possible, this FAQ can help you do just that.

Books

Already there are two excellent books on the MBONE. Unlike most early-technology books, both are excellent, in-depth tomes that can really help you explore the possibilities of the MBONE today.

MBONE: Interactive Multimedia on the Internet by Viany Kumar (published by Macmillan Publishing, 1996, ISBN 1-56205-397-3)

This first major book on the MBONE is filled with all sorts of technical information, a review of the MBONE initiative, and details of getting connected and software for MBONE capabilities.

MBONE: Multicasting Tomorrow's Internet by Kevin Savetz, Neil Randall, Yves Lepage (published by IDG Books, 1996, ISBN 1-56884-723-8)

This book (which has a Web page that includes several free chapters at **http://www.northcoast.com/savetz/mbone**) is a wonderfully written account of the MBONE and its capabilities (and possibilities). It includes a section on how to get hooked up, background on MBONE initiatives and developments, and lots of pointers to MBONE software.

MBONE Web Sites

mbone.com
http://www.mbone.com

As you might expect from a site named mbone.com, this is a really strong site with lots of information and pointers to the original papers that outlined the construction of the MBONE itself.

VRML: 3D Graphics and Multimedia Meet the Web

I'll be honest: This book is going to give short shrift to VRML. I'd love to detail all of the many resources and issues at play, but I just don't have enough time or space to pull it off in this edition.

Even so, I won't leave you completely empty-handed. While many in the Web community are wondering exactly where VRML is going to go, there is no doubt that standardized 3D graphic interfaces will eventually be a huge part of how we navigate and interact with one another on the Web.

For the last two years, though, VRML has been very much a stepchild to the rest of the Web. At first it was thought of as a separate entity; then people wondered if it would ever really work. Then more saw the need to make it work, especially as an integrated system with existing Web development.

Now, after much speculation, some of the recent VRML work has finally started to pay off. The VRML 2.0 standard is light-years ahead of the first excuse for VRML, and the tools are finally catching up to the spec. Lots of the major 3D packages I outlined in Chapter 11 have VRML output capabilities. What I've gathered for you here is a roundup of the key information and resources that can put you on the road to being a VRML expert. I've also outlined as many of the major VRML software packages as I can.

VRML Primer

VRML is essentially a programming language that can define 3D worlds—
and, more importantly, characteristics of the objects and structures in those
worlds that allow for things like animation, collision detection, responses to
clicks, time, sound, and more.

VRML got its start in 1994 when Mark Pesce and Brian Behlendorf from
Wired magazine began trying to get people involved in coming up with a
common format for 3D files on the Web, just as HTML is a common document format. A group of developers at Silicon Graphics responded by proposing its Open Inventor 3D technology as the basis for VRML (almost like
HTML was based largely on SGML). After much haggling, VRML 1.0
debuted—and with it, a host of startup companies like Paper Software,
Dimension X, and SGI began building Web browsers and plug-ins to view the
first VRML files.

As with most first tries, VRML was interesting, but many people knew a lot
more work needed to be done—and so the work on VRML 2.0 began quite
quickly. In the meantime, major companies like Microsoft, Sony, and SGI
began developing their own plans as to what would make up this more robust
VRML standard. In some cases, startup VRML experts like Paper Software
were bought by larger companies (in Paper's case, Netscape).

Microsoft charged forward with its ActiveVRML standard, and SGI (with
help from many others, like Sony) proposed its robust Moving Worlds specification. The haggling got fierce; in the end, it was decided that Moving Worlds
would be adopted in full, with some additional input as the spec officially
moved toward VRML 2.0.

Today VRML 2.0 is causing a lot of excitement; my spies report that at the
1996 Siggraph, it was the talk of the show. Perhaps the stepchild of the Web is
about to explode into a major multimedia content type, with features that
truly deliver on the promise suggested by the word "cyberspace."

VRML 2.0

The biggest problem with VRML 1.0 was that it was really rudimentary—in a
word, it was static. VRML 2.0, though, is definitely *not* static. In addition, as
VRML 2.0 comes in the wake of other rising Web technologies like Java,

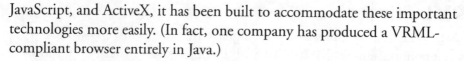

JavaScript, and ActiveX, it has been built to accommodate these important technologies more easily. (In fact, one company has produced a VRML-compliant browser entirely in Java.)

Here's an overview of what VRML 2.0 offers:

- *A very comprehensive 3D definition system*—3D objects can be quite complex, with texturing, characteristics, and more. Most major 3D packages now have a utility to output their object creations in formats that make them ready for VRML production.

- *Lots of interactive features*—VRML worlds can have sensors in them that set off events when the user clicks on or travels near them. There is a timing sensor to trigger "events" in VRML worlds based on time, and collision detection keeps users from walking through walls.

- *3D objects can be animated*—In addition, built-in interpolation can accomplish morphing, path animation, or automatic movement of users through the world. Developers can tell VRML browsers the starting and end points and positions of objects, and the browser will accomplish the rest on its own!

- *Extensive scripting features*—Objects (such as creatures that might inhabit your worlds) can be programmed to do things like walk a path, retrieve other objects, and so on.

Essentially, you have an entire 3D system at your disposal, with all kinds of Web functionality built in. Users can press 3D links to go to other sites on the Web (VRML or HTML), launch Java programs, and anything else that comes to mind.

The Uses of VRML

The amazing thing about VRML is that it really does let you build a 3D world. Because it's such a wide-open technology, there are numerous applications.

Many companies will use it to create 3D entertainment—such as a museum exploration where the user can actually walk through and look at paintings by clicking on links, or a 3D city complete with chat capabilities. But VRML has uses beyond mere entertainment; for instance, developers could preview products in 3D, or provide walk-throughs of real estate. In addition, as researchers have shown, sometimes data displayed in 3D (or 3D interfaces) can be even more intuitive than 2D displays.

VRML also promises to provide the final piece of the puzzle of multimedia content: realtime 3D graphics. As developers learn to integrate this last piece of multimedia power, amazing things will happen.

So what tools and resources can get you working with VRML technology? Well, you've got a whole scripting language to learn, 3D modeling software and hardware to get, and at least a half-dozen different browser or plug-in modules that you can point your users to. I've tried my best to outline all the major products, sites, and sources that you could possibly want to know more about. All I can say is that you had better budget some serious time to explore all this stuff, because VRML is a whole new world of Web development.

Software: Plug-Ins and Development Tools

Cosmo

SiliconGraphics
2011 North Shoreline Boulevard
P.O. Box 7311
Mountain View, CA 94039
Phone: 415-960-1980
Fax: 415-390-6220
WWW: http://www.sgi.com

SiliconGraphics's VRML tools revolve around its Webspace servers and Cosmo development technology. SGI has built a Cosmo VRML 2.0-compliant player (shown in Figure 14.4) that runs on SGI and Windows 95/NT and is available for download at **http://webspace.sgi.com/cosmoplayer/ download.html**.

Live3D

Netscape Inc.
501 E. Middlefield Rd.
Mountain View, CA 94043
Phone: 415-937-3777
Fax: 415-528-4124
WWW: http://www.netscape.com

Live3D is the VRML viewer that comes with Netscape. Netscape purchased Live3D's creator, Paper Software, and has incorporated this product into the

Figure 14.4 Cosmo in action.

larger Netscape Navigator software suite. Live3D is at the center of Netscape's plans to build VRML functionality into its entire framework. Already a few companies are working to build their VRML products using Live3D as a base, and Black Sun Interactive (listed a little later) has created servers and client software for 3D chat worlds that work with Live3D.

With a large installed base on the back of Netscape's browser, Live3D will be a major force in the VRML world.

Liquid Reality

Dimension X, Inc.
181 Fremont Street, Suite 120
San Francisco, CA 94105
Phone: 415-243-0900
Fax: 415-243-0997
WWW: http://www.dimensionx.com

Liquid Reality is a toolkit for VRML 2.0 authoring done completely in Java. It includes support for 3D sound and multiple servers, 250 Java classes for 3D content (which can allow developers to build their own branded VRML 2.0 browsers), and full access to the low-level 3D graphic engine (allowing them to modify it for specialized applications such as games). This is a powerful way for hard-core developers to approach presenting VRML content on their sites, and is well worth a look.

MAX VRML2 and Topper

Kinetix
111 McInnis Parkway
San Rafael, CA 94903
Phone: 415-507-5000
Fax: 415-507-5314
WWW: http://www.ktx.com

For users of 3D Studio MAX, Kinetix (a new subsidiary of Autodesk that focuses on 3D graphics) has created MAX VRML2, a 3D Studio MAX plug-in that can create 3D VRML 2.0 files compatible with browsers such as Silicon Graphics's Cosmo player plug-in for Netscape. MAX VRML2 takes any 3D file created in 3D Studio MAX and converts it to Moving Worlds VRML 2.0.

Kinetix also makes a Netscape plug-in called Topper, which supports VRML 1.0 and VRBL (Virtual Reality Behavior Language), a Kinetix addition to VRML 1.0 with many functions that are now part of VRML 2.0. VRML 2.0 support will be in the next major release of Topper (though one might expect Kinetix to just support SGI's Cosmo player).

OZ Virtual

Soft2vrml (Softimage to VRML converter)
OZ Interactive, Inc.
1250 Arlington Avenue
Los Angeles, CA 90019
WWW: http://www.oz-inc.com

Reykjavik, the capital of Iceland, isn't exactly known as a hotbed of software technology, but OZ Interactive is changing that perception very quickly. It's been a leading 3D graphics developer for some time, and now it's really bursting out with good products. One product of concern to VRML developers is Soft2vrml, an SGI IRIX-only utility that lets you convert Softimage 3D files to VRML WRL (World) files.

Figure 14.5 OZ Virtual in action.

OZ also recently took the wraps off OZ Virtual (Figure 14.5), an extended VRML browser with high resolution and frame rate that really looks hot. It's set up for multiuser servers and allows for chat and other Avatar features. (Avatars are VRML "life forms" that represent users.) The audio is full 16-bit stereo, and there is support for MPEG audio and 3D sound as well. OZ Virtual also features the OZ MotionLib, which helps to create virtual actions and expressions on the Avatar figures.

All in all, OZ Virtual embraces VRML and then turns it into a powerful 3D world system very much geared toward chatting and other multiuser interactions. OZ even has a sample OZ Virtual site for children in the works.

Pioneer and Pioneer Pro

Caligari Corporation
1935 Landings Drive
Mountain View, CA 94043
Phone: 415-390-9600
Fax: 415-390-9755
WWW: http://www.caligari.com

Pioneer is a VRML modeling and authoring environment that builds on Caligari's original trueSpace modeling product. Authors can add scripts, sounds, and other VRML-like features. If you're already familiar with trueSpace (an awesome interface that many people have come to appreciate), Pioneer could be a really good choice.

WIRL

VREAM, Inc.
2568 North Clark Street, Suite 250
Chicago, IL 60614
Phone: 312-477-0425
Fax: 312-477-9702
WWW: http://www.vream.com

VREAM is another major VRML startup company. Its major browser product is called WIRL, and it also has an authoring environment called VRCreator. A special VRCreator Toolkit gives programmers low-level access to VREAM's API, allowing them to create their own specialized browser creations.

WIRL follows the original VRML 1.0 spec; it has since added more than 100 extensions to that spec and should be delivering on 2.0 compatibility soon.

WIRL is available as a Netscape Navigator plug-in or a Microsoft Internet Explorer ActiveX control, both of which can be downloaded by users from VREAM's Web site.

WorldView 1.0

Intervista
303 Sacramento Street, Second Floor
San Francisco, CA 94111
Phone: 415-434-8765
Fax: 415-434-3734

WorldView is a Windows 95/NT VRML viewer. Intervista has worked closely with Microsoft, and there is also a plug-in version for Internet Explorer available from Microsoft now in its Internet Explorer download area at **http:// www.microsoft.com/ie/download/ieadd.htm.**

Cyber Passage/Cyber Passage Conductor/ Cyber Passage Bureau

Sony Corporation of America
9 West 57th Street, 43rd Floor
New York, NY 10019
Phone: 212-833-6849
Fax: 212-833-6923
WWW: http://vs.sony.co.jp (or http://www.sony.com)

Sony is quickly jumping on VRML, which it sees as a major technology for its future; the company was a major backer of the VRML 2.0 Moving Worlds spec with SGI. Its software Cyber Passage is a VRML 2.0-based system consisting of three major components: Cyber Passage, the main browser product; Cyber Passage Conductor, which lets people create their own VRML worlds; and Cyber Passage Bureau, a server setup for complete VRML chat worlds with full Avatar action.

CyberHub

Black Sun Interactive
50 Osgood Place, Suite 330
San Francisco, CA 94133
Phone: 415-273-7000
Fax: 415-273-7001
WWW: http://www.blacksun.com

German-based Black Sun makes several VRML product under the brand name of CyberHub for a variety of platforms (Windows 95, Windows NT, Macintosh, and Unix).

The lead product is CyberHub, a VRML server product that lets you incorporate 3D multiuser worlds into your Web site. Users will need the CyberHub Client, which is a VRML plug-in for Netscape that works in conjunction with Netscape's own Live3D VRML browser and adds to this the multiuser capability of CyberHub servers (which can handle from 10 to 1,000 users). CyberHub works with any VRML-compliant world, and the client works with users who have at least a 14.4 Kbps modem. Complete motion technology lets users see other users' Avatars in full animation, much like OZ Virtual does.

A full API called CyberSockets is available and it's based on VRML and Java. This API gives a wide range of development tools to programmers looking to add multiuser capabilities to their applications or games.

Finally, there is CyberKit, which is Black Sun's VRML authoring product. It allows designers to create the their own VRML worlds.

Books

Advanced VRML Techniques by Jeff Sonstein (published by New Riders, 1996, ISBN 1-562055-89-5)

VRML, Flying Through the Web by Mark Pesce (published by New Riders, 1996, ISBN 1-562055-21-6)

Virtus VRML Toolkit by David Smith (published by Hayden, 1996, ISBN 1-568302-96-7)

VRML 2.0, The Next Step in Cyberspace by Mark Pesce (published by New Riders, 1996, ISBN 9-996922-07-3)

VRML: Browsing and Building Cyberspace by Mark Pesce (published by New Riders, 1995, ISBN 1-562054-98-8)

Creating 3D Worlds for the Web by Rory O'Neill and Eden Muir (published by Wiley, 1996, ISBN 0-471159-44-1)

The VRML 2.0 Sourcebook by Andrea L. Ames, (published by Wiley, 1996, ISBN 047-114159-3)

Building 3D VRML Worlds by Sebastian Hassinger (published by Osborne-McGraw Hill, 1996, ISBN 007-882233-5)

Exploring Moving Worlds: Mapping the 3D World Wide Web by Ed Dille (published by Ventana, 1996, ISBN 1-566044-67-7)

VRML: Exploring Virtual Worlds on the Internet by Walter Goralski (published by Prentice Hall, 1996, ISBN 0-134869-60-5)

Instant VRML Worlds by Rich Sherwin (published by Ziff Davis Press, 1996, ISBN 1-562764-21-7)

VRML Power Publishing with Caligari Fountain (published by Ventana, 1996, ISBN 1-566044-50-2)

60 Minute Guide to VRML by Sebastian Hassinger (published by IDG Books, 1996, ISBN 1-568847-10-6)

VRML: Bringing Virtual Reality to the Internet by John Vacca (published by Ap Professional, 1996, ISBN 0-127099-10-7)

Web Publisher's Construction Kit with VRML/Live 3d: Creating 3d Web Worlds by David Fox and Philip Shaddock (published by Waite Group Press, 1996, ISBN 1-571690-68-9)

Web Workshops on VRML 2.0 & 3D Graphics by Laura Lemay (published by Sams, 1996, ISBN 1-575211-43-2)

Magazines

While lots of the Web and general multimedia development periodicals will also cover VRML, many of the general VR community publications will provide the most exclusive coverage. For this reason, I've listed some specific VR reading materials that give coverage to VRML as well.

ZD3D's VRMLSite

Ziff Davis Publishing
WWW: http://www.zdnet.com/zdi/vrml/
Subscription: Free
Publishes: constant updates

Presented as an online magazine, this Web site publication focuses on VRML issues, software, and much more. It's got an awesome set of links and tons of information on VRML. Well worth bookmarking!

VRMLSite Magazine

Aereal, Inc.
11 Brush Place, Suite 1
San Francisco, CA 94107
Phone: 415-522-0975
WWW: http://www.vrmlsite.com
Subscription: Free

Another well-done online magazine with loads of information. Be sure to sign up for the mailing list to be alerted when new issues appear.

VR World Magazine

Mecklermedia Inc.
20 Ketchum Steet
Westport, CT 06880
Subscription: $29.00/yr
Newsstand: $4.95
Publishes: Bimonthly
Pages: 1100

VR World Magazine may have stopped publishing, as their Web site is no longer part of Mecklermedia's iWORLD, and I don't remember seeing a new version in a while. Hopefully it's just retooling to debut as *VRML World* later on. If you manage to find some back issues, they won't have a ton of stuff on VRML, but their coverage of VR in general is worth checking out.

CyberEdge Journal

1 Gate Six Road, Suite G
Sausalito, CA 94965
Phone: 415-331-3343
Fax: 415-331-3643
WWW: http://www.pomo.nbn.com/home/www/6.html
Subscription: $129.00/yr ($249 if ordering as a business)
Publishes: Bimonthly

CyberEdge Journal, like *VR World*, covers cutting-edge consumer- and business-oriented VR news, articles, and reviews.

VR News

P.O. Box 2515
London, N4 4JW, UK
Phone: 44-181-292-1498
Fax: 44-181-292-1346

I couldn't track down all the information on this London-based newsletter/magazine. I did find out, however, that it was launched in 1991 and has an average monthly readership of around 10,000 in some 40 countries. Again, like the other magazines listed here, it covers the whole realm of virtual reality rather than VRML alone.

FAQs

VRML FAQ

http://vag.vrml.org/VRML_FAQ.html

This is a light FAQ that lets its links do the talking. A great place to get right to the heart of VRML, it points you to many relevant Web pages.

Organizations

VRML Architecture Group

http://vag.vrml.org

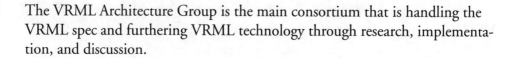

The VRML Architecture Group is the main consortium that is handling the VRML spec and furthering VRML technology through research, implementation, and discussion.

Web Sites

While there are dozens of sites devoted to the burgeoning VRML industry, the following two are very comprehensive and especially worthy of mention.

The VRML Repository

`http://www.sdsc.edu/vrml/`

The folks at the San Diego Supercomputer Center (SDSC) have built a large Web site filled with links that lead you to most, if not all, of the very best VRML and VRML-information sites on the Web.

3DSite's VRML Web Site

`http://www.3dsite.com/3dsite/cgi/VRML-index.html`

This is a very large and comprehensive listing of the key products and sites in the VRML world. Along with the VRML Repository, ZD3D's VRML Site (listed earlier in magazines), and VRMLSite Magazine (listed earlier in magazines), it gives VRML developers access to more information than they could ever dream of.

Not for the Beginner

Multimedia, VRML, the MBONE—we're not in Kansas anymore. Technologies like these are not for the casual developer, and while the tools are getting better, they're far from easy to master. Additionally, the faster that bandwidth, compression, and technologies like Enliven hit the market, the more multimedia skills are going to be essential—not just putting together small snippets or the simple applet, but creating full-blown applications comparable to today's multimedia CD-ROMs.

So, the true context of multimedia as it pertains to the Web is that it stands as the great divide between Web developers with lots of hardcore previous development experience, and the slew of new developers who've been brought to the world of computers because of the Web. Depending on the camp you feel you're in, you either have a great competitive advantage or a lot of learning to do. I hope this chapter has helped you, no matter which camp you're in.

CHAPTER 15

Serving up the basics about serving the Web.

An Overview of Web Serving

As the title says, this chapter is just an overview of Web servers—if you're looking for a full list of products and resources, turn to Chapter 16. A solid overview is important, because servers are getting more and more complex every day. While many content developers will never actually deal with them, every developer should have a strong understanding of what putting together a server entails.

The server aspect of your site can either be really complicated or really simple, depending on your needs. As the Web tools market has become much more mature, there have been a lot of advances made in server software that make it possible for even complete novices to launch their own sites. Ironically, just as servers are getting even more simple, lots of large sites and major companies are choosing to outsource their Web serving to large computer services companies like EDS or AT&T. Outsourcing is really a more robust form of Web hosting, and it will probably become the dominant form of Internet serving in the future for many companies.

This chapter takes a peek at all these top level issues and helps to sort through the basics. I've tried to list major resources for you throughout the chapter, so you'll have a reference on issues such as turnkey server systems, Web outsourcing places, and even information on where to get your own domain name.

The Makeup of a Server

What exactly is a Web server? It's not just some typical computer and some software. Figure 15.1 outlines the components that come together to make up a class-A Web server system.

Each of the elements of the figure are described briefly in the following paragraphs.

HTML and Content

At the top of the figure are HTML code and content, which together make up the actual pages and objects you're trying to place on the Web. Note that content includes VBScript, JavaScript, and Java programs, which are all items you deliver directly to the user.

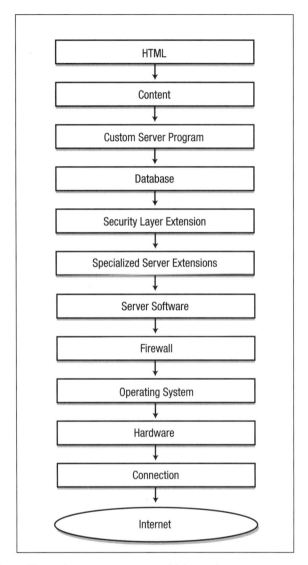

Figure 15.1 An outline of server component hierarchy.

Custom Server Program

This program would contain any of the behind-the-scenes code you've written to customize the framework of your site. For most sites these programs are CGI scripts or specialized server applets designed to pull content out of databases, process transactions, or assemble on-the-fly HTML and content.

In terms of languages used, most programmers of top-quality sites are switching from CGI scripting using Perl or Visual Basic (not to be confused with VBScript) to custom programs written in C (where you work directly with the server's code or associated API). Of course, the latter requires extensive knowledge of C and the various server APIs, like Netscape API or IIS API, as well as the operating system that the server is running on.

Database

More and more top developers are learning how to utilize back-end databases to create killer sites. Either by providing access to really powerful databases (for example, a database of products for sale) or by databasing component objects and HTML for on-the-fly Web pages, these systems are becoming an integral part of most Web server setups and sites. The technologies at play here include both the actual database products (such as Oracle, Informix, or Microsoft Access) and the system used to retrieve and build the pages in conjunction with the database (such as NeXT's WebObjects, or a custom program you write yourself).

Security Layer Extension

Protecting access to your site is a major component (and headache) that every server setup has to deal with. There are essentially three major components of Web server security. The first element, user authentication, attempts to regulate access to the content on the site by password and user-ID protection. There is also secure transaction/encryption technology, which servers use to ensure information is transferred to and from the client in such a manner that no other person can read it without proper authority. The third component, firewalls, will be discussed in a later section.

Specialized Server Extensions

Server extensions and *co-servers* are any prepackaged programs you add to your original server software to extend its features. These include items like chat systems, message boards, or the ability to stream a particular type of content (such as RealAudio, VDOLive, and Enliven).

Server Software

The heart of all this is your server software, your bare-bones HTTP system for distributing content and dealing with requests from the client browsers. It's your combination traffic cop and gofer, deciding who gets what, when, where, and how. Later on in this chapter I'll explain most of the major choices you'll have to make involving server software.

Firewall

As I said earlier, the firewall is part of the trio of major Web server security components. A firewall does essentially what the name suggests—it blocks anything or anyone coming between your server core and the rest of the Internet. There are several major firewall systems, which I will describe in Chapter 16.

Operating System

Essentially, three major operating systems offer Web server software packages: Mac/OS, Windows NT—you can use Win95, but NT is the way to go—and Unix. (There are also some minor operating systems, along with the usual array of Unix derivatives.) Some companies, such as Netscape, have created versions of their software for both Unix and NT; however, many others, like Microsoft and O'Reilly, have concentrated on just one specific platform. If you're going to mix and match operating systems, you'll probably want to go with server software that is available on multiple platforms.

The origins of the Web are Unix based, so it's no surprise that the majority of servers in use are Unix based as well. As Microsoft has tweaked and upgraded Windows NT, though, more server software has debuted for that platform. Expect NT to become a strong second-place contender to Unix in the Web operating-system market, or even overtake it, as time goes by.

Hardware

Depending on your choice of operating system and server software, there is a host of different hardware options available to run your Web server. A good half-dozen systems run particular flavors of Unix (DEC, SGI, HP, and Sun) and various server products. Other choices include Macintosh PowerPC systems and Intel-based PCs (which can run a Unix product like Linux, too).

The leading server hardware is made by Sun, with Intel-based PCs bringing up the rear. SGI's systems are getting lots of attention, especially as they also are becoming major systems for content creation (particularly VRML).

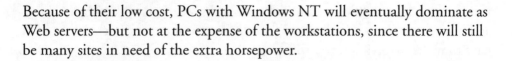

Because of their low cost, PCs with Windows NT will eventually dominate as Web servers—but not at the expense of the workstations, since there will still be many sites in need of the extra horsepower.

Connection

Got your server all ready? It's still useless unless you're plugged in. For now, at least, the choices here are fairly straightforward: ISDN, leased lines, T1, T3, fractional T1, or fractional T3. The pricing and exact information about each connection follows later in this chapter.

The Major Server Options

There are four main ways to serve up a site on the Web. Let's take a moment to explore each of them in some detail.

ISP and Online Service Personal Home Pages

This fall, I'm finally going to post a home page on the Web via one of the online services I subscribe to. As more and more people join the Web, there will be more home pages cropping up through the likes of America Online, CompuServe, and Prodigy. Lots of ISPs also offer this as a free service, and many people get their first taste of Web publishing through this route.

For most developers, though, this is not a serious outlet for publishing a site. Nevertheless, I'll present a quick roundup of what's available, just in case you're interested, or if you've bought this book as your first Web development guide and want a cheap place to experiment.

CompuServe

http://www.compuserve.com

On CompuServe, type GO HPWIZ to arrive at the Home Page Wizard. You're allowed up to 1 MB of hard disk space, which is enough for several simple pages. Home Page Wizard leads you step by step through the creation of a simple home page. You can edit and upload your own work as well.

America Online
http://www.aol.com

The keyword HTML within America Online sends you to the Web Page Toolkit and Personal Publisher program. Personal Publisher shows you everything you need to do to make your own home page, and it also leads you to tools you can download in order to do fancier work. This section of AOL, though, has nothing to do with the company's business of hosting larger-scale Web sites; see my later section on "Top Outsourcing Options" for more on this.

Prodigy
http://www.prodigy.com

Use the Jump command and enter Personal Web Pages (PWP) to get to Prodigy's home page service. There you can download the Hippie HTML editor or go through Prodigy's fill-in-the-blank tools. Members are given 1 MB of space; for added fees, more room and advanced options are available.

Local ISP Hosting

Most Internet service providers also host Web sites for customers in their local area. For many developers, this is the fastest way to get on the Web for the first time, and it is a common step to take before setting up one's own server. Some people even combine these steps by buying all the equipment and software and asking the ISP to build and manage the server directly from the developer's site.

One advantage of using a local ISP is that they may have people who know your local area markets and economy—something useful for merchants looking to create a site—and they are certain to be knowledgeable about local area Web developers who could help you if you needed it. Local ISPs that are flexible about their service might be in a better position to add such features as RealAudio and VDOLive, and many have built up a rich library of scripts and utilities to help you as well.

On the downside, a local ISP might not be the most robust service available, and it also might be more expensive than some of the national firms. While giants like AT&T and America Online sometimes "go down" and lose service, local ISPs are far more likely to have technical problems or be susceptible to things like storms and blackouts.

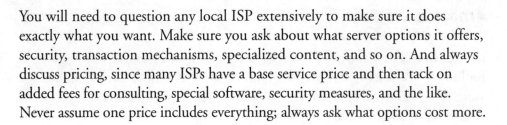

You will need to question any local ISP extensively to make sure it does exactly what you want. Make sure you ask about what server options it offers, security, transaction mechanisms, specialized content, and so on. And always discuss pricing, since many ISPs have a base service price and then tack on added fees for consulting, special software, security measures, and the like. Never assume one price includes everything; always ask what options cost more.

The List
http://thelist.iworld.com

Mecklermedia publishes this huge directory of more than two thousand local ISPs. Remember, though, that a good access provider may not be the best ISP for hosting a Web site. Check here first, then call around to all ISPs in your local area.

Web Outsourcing

Outsourcing, a step beyond the local ISP, is the fastest-growing segment of the Web services market. The differences between these services and your local ISP are the companies involved and the depth of service these companies offer. Some of these companies have been in the telecommunications, Internet, or computer services outsourcing business for quite some time, and they offer very complete programs for Web site creation.

Typically these packages are aimed at small businesses and corporate customers. They usually include excellent server access, development tools like FrontPage or Navigator Gold, around-the-clock security and maintenance, and access to all kinds of connection options (all the way up to T3 accounts).

Some other plans (those marked with an asterisk in the resources that follow) also have set up formal designer recommendation and location programs. In these schemes, the outsource provider screens and then recommends various independent Web development people or companies that can help you with the design and construction of your site.

Web Advantage
BBN, Inc.
150 Cambridge Park Drive
Cambridge, MA 02140

Phone: 617-873-2000
Fax: 617-873-5011
WWW: http://www.bbnplanet.com

BBN is one of the largest hosting and Internet service companies around. Web Advantage, their main product for high-end Web outsourcing, is sold in three forms—Gold, Silver, and Bronze. BBN uses Unix servers running Netscape software and offers a range of connection schemes, plus other options depending on the level of service you choose. The Bronze category is a special form of outsourcing where you supply the server hardware of your choice and BBN hooks it up to its farm of servers, giving you even more control over exactly what your server options will be.

UUNet Technologies, Inc.

3060 Williams Drive
Fairfax, VA 22031
Phone: 703-206-5600
Fax: 703-206-5601
WWW: http://www.uunet.com

UUNet is one of the biggest Internet service companies in the world. It was recently acquired by MFS Communications; before that, it was partially owned by Microsoft. UUNet offers a straightforward Web hosting service, run on servers on its network. UUNet will also provide reports on service and offers its customers Web authoring help via access to NetObjects Fusion and Microsoft's FrontPage.

PSIWeb

Performance Systems Intl (PSINet), Inc.
510 Huntmar Park Drive
Herndon, VA 22070
Phone: 703-709-0300
WWW: http://www.psi.com

PSINet, a major nationwide Internet provider, offers Web hosting under its PSIWeb brand name. PSIWeb offers servers hooked up to shared T1, 10 Mbps, or T3 connections.

AT&T EasyCommerce*
http://www.att.com/easycommerce/easywww/

EasyCommerce works much like every other typical Web outsourcing system—except that it's run by AT&T, which provides for a few wrinkles. AT&T has been aggressive in setting up a developer referral system, and it is also leveraging its other telecommunication products for EasyCommerce customers—such as offering you ways to reach customers dialing in via 800/888 toll-free service, and links from AT&T's 800 directory.

AT&T EasyCommerce is using FrontPage as its distributed authoring tool.

PrimeHost*
America Online
http://www.primehost.com

AOL may be an online service to most people, but it has expanded heavily into the Internet/Web field; its efforts include GNN, a Web-only online service, and PrimeHost, its full-service Web outsourcing company. PrimeHost uses a suite of powerful tools (gained from AOL's acquisition of NaviSoft) and offers a Web site developer referral service as well.

Ready-To-Run Server

Many developers want their own server, but they don't like the idea of installing it themselves—installing the operating system, setting up the server system, and so on. What they want is a plug-and-play setup. Thankfully, companies like Compaq, Sun, SGI, MCI, and Intel have responded with special package deals that give you a "server-in-a-box." This is a particularly good solution for small companies, or companies installing intranets with multiple Web servers.

Here's a rundown on the major packages out there. Since the type of companies likely to go this route are apt not to be very Unix-savvy, I've concentrated mostly on NT-based systems. (In Chapter 16, I'll list all the contacts for specific products of this type.)

One note, though—prepackaged Web servers are a market that is getting bigger every day. One year from now, the list that follows will probably be 30 times as large. If you have a favorite company (especially in the PC/NT arena) that's not shown here, by all means check to see what it has to offer.

Easy Web Server (NT/Unix)

Digital Equipment Corp.
146 Main Street
Maynard, MA 01754
Phone: 508-493-5111
Fax: 508-493-8780
WWW: http://www.digital.com/info/internet/resources/servers

Digital has used its Alpha chip technology to build some of the best-reviewed and fastest Web server hardware in existence. The Easy Web Server project, created to leverage the Alpha chip technology, can run Windows NT and Unix.

InterServe Web Servers (NT)

Intergraph Computer Systems
1 Madison Industrial Park
Huntsville, AL 35894
Phone: 205-730-2000
Fax: 205-730-6188
WWW: http://www.intergraph.com

Intergraph is a major workstation manufacturer best known for high-end CAD systems. It has recently become a big player in the high-end Windows NT hardware market for both 3D imagery creation and network/Web servers.

WebFORCE Indy (Unix)

Silicon Graphics Inc.
2011 N. Shoreline Blvd.
Mountain View, CA 94043
Phone: 415-960-1980
Fax: 415-961-0595
WWW: http://www.sgi.com/Products/WebFORCE/

The WebFORCE series of ready-to-run Unix-based servers has gotten highly positive reviews for its speed and content authoring tools (which should be expected from SGI).

Netra Servers

Sun Microsystems
2550 Garcia Avenue

Mountain View, CA 94043-1100
Phone: 415-960-1300
Fax: 415-969-9131
WWW: http://www.sun.com/products-n-solutions/hw/servers/netra.html

All Netra servers contain software optimized for a specific application area. An intuitive HTML graphical user interface makes it easier for non-Unix users to operate the server. All the software and tools you need to get up and running are already installed and configured for you straight from the factory, making rapid deployment in your environment that much easier.

WebMaker

MCI Communications
1801 Pennsylvania Ave. NW
Washington, DC 20006
Phone: 202-872-1600
Fax: 202-887-3140
WWW: http://www.webmaker.mci.com

MCI has teamed up with chip giant Intel to produce Windows NT/Pentium Pro servers for small business and corporate clients. Combined with MCI Internet access service (MCI was a critical builder of the Internet infrastructure), it is a great one-stop solution—users get not only the hardware and software, but the telecommunications infrastructure as well.

Custom-Developed Servers

For many Web developers creating end-user-oriented sites on the Internet, the only choice is to build an in-house server from scratch. That means purchasing all the components separately—the computer, the software, special server options, security products, and so on—then handling all of the installation, configuration, security measures, and more.

This is certainly the hardest route, and it can be particularly costly if you're going to need a Webmaster constantly tinkering with the setup. Still, the flexibility and control you get with your own server is unparalleled, especially if you're going to be handling sensitive customer information, which is the main reason developers take this route.

The Connection Primer

One thing to consider in any aspect of Web serving is the connection you establish between the server and the Internet. While users can get 28.8 connections with unlimited usage for as little as $19.95/month, higher-end connections for Web serving are considerably more expensive. There are four types of costs associated with a permanent Internet connection: the equipment cost, the connection startup fee, the monthly costs, and local phone company costs (which may or may not apply, depending on your location and local Bell company).

In terms of equipment costs, you should contact your ISP to get the best advice on routers and other required items. Web outsourcing systems save you from worrying about this in detail, but their connection startup fees will pass on the cost.

Here, then, is a concise rundown of the type of connections you will be offered.

56 K Frame Relay and ISDN

Depending on the ISP and your local phone company, the low end for Web connections would be a 56 K leased line or ISDN service, which can offer you a bandwidth of 56 to 128 Kbps. If you're setting up your own server at your own location, however, make sure you examine your costs carefully. In some parts of the country ISDN is cheap, but in others it's quite expensive.

T1/Fractional T1

Most industrial-strength Web sites are being set up on dedicated T1 lines, which offer 1.5 Mbps of bandwidth and are strong enough to support dozens of simultaneous surfers and decent multimedia. Some ISPs offer fractional T1 service; if your needs aren't as heavy as a typical corporate customer, this may be a good money-saving route. Typically you'll pay somewhere between $1,000 and $2,000 a month for T1 service.

T3/Fractional T3

For the most demanding sites—those receiving major amounts of visitors, or trying to deliver lots of graphics and multimedia applications—a T3 connection offers big-time bandwidth. Very few sites will need the full 45 Mbps of a

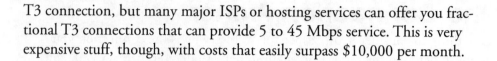

T3 connection, but many major ISPs or hosting services can offer you fractional T3 connections that can provide 5 to 45 Mbps service. This is very expensive stuff, though, with costs that easily surpass $10,000 per month.

Domain Names and IP Addresses

Perhaps even more visible than your home page is the domain name your site uses. Domain names are simply aliases for your site's IP address (the set of numbers that uniquely identifies you on the Web, just like your telephone number identifies you at home).

The first thing you need to do is come up with a name for your site that hasn't already been taken. This is pretty simple to do; just go to the InterNIC directory (located at **http://rs.internic.net/cgi-bin/whois**), which will tell you if your domain name has already been registered.

Once you've decided on a domain name, contact whoever is providing your Web access—chances are they can take your name suggestion and do all the dirty work for you. Always try to pawn this stuff off!

If you can't get someone else to do it, then you'll need to go through the InterNIC registration process yourself by logging onto the Web and going to **http://rs.internic.net/rs-internic.html**. From there you'll be able to access all the information and services you need to register your IP address and domain name with InterNIC, the body that governs domain names.

Although it used to be free, there is now a $50/year fee to process and hold onto your domain name. Failure to pay or keep up subsequent payments will mean that your domain name gets placed back into the pool of available names.

 Remember, courts are siding with companies and other owners of certain trade names that people have been using as personal domain names. For example, if you name your site **www.exxon.com** you might find yourself in court against the oil giant, claiming it owns the rights to use of that name (and the same goes for something like **www.john-wayne.com**). An original domain name search isn't always a guarantee that it's all right to use a particular name.

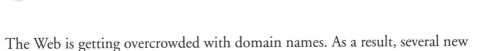

The Web is getting overcrowded with domain names. As a result, several new things are taking place in the domain name game:

- InterNIC soon won't be the only game in town for getting domain names. Several other startups are working to become domain name registrars. These startups have petitioned the Internet Assigned Numbers Authority (**http://www.isi.edu/iana/**) to become full-fledged DNS registrars. The names and sites of some of these companies are:

  Alternic
  http://www.alternic.net

  Macro Computer Solutions
  http://www.mcs.com

- Look for new domain types to be offered, such as .idv for individual home sites, .biz for businesses, and many more. Most of these new names will be spawned by the previously mentioned new registrars.

- Look for new sites that are starting a sort of stock market for buying and selling already approved and registered domain names. In fact, a few such sites are already up on the Web:

  Domain Mart
  http://www.domainmart.com

  Internet Domain Exchange
  http://domains.wanted.com/

 Want to see what's up in the world of domain name disputes? Many legal issues surround the domain name game. George Washington University law school maintains a page devoted to all the legal issues and stories about domain names, visit it at **http://www.law.georgetown.edu/lc/internic/domain1.html**.

Which to Choose: ISP, Outsource, or In-House

There are a number of questions you need to answer before you can decide what the best option is for your Web endeavors, including:

- *Cost*—On average, what are the overall costs associated with this option?

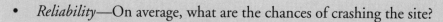

- *Reliability*—On average, what are the chances of crashing the site?

- *Control*—What kind of control over the server do I have?

- *Ability to change quickly*—How fast can new changes be implemented?

- *Staff/Expertise*—What level of staff will be needed to worry about the site management?

- *Options*—How likely is it that I'll be able to implement options like VDOLive?

- *Performance Options*—Which option has the most flexibility in terms of boosting performance options as needed?

- *Connection*—How easy is it, and what options do I have in the connections arena?

Table 15.1 shows how I feel the different server options rate in response to these questions.

No Half-Steps

Perhaps the biggest question concerning Web servers is this: Do you buy or build your own server, or go with hosting?

Table 15.1 How the different server options stack up.

Item to Consider	Local ISP	Outsource	Turnkey Server	In-House Server
Cost	Decent	Better	Cheaper than in-house	Most expensive
Reliability	Decent	High	Good*	Good*
Control	Least	Less	Much more	Most
Ability to change quickly	Worst	Better	Good	Best
Staff/Expertise	Basic	Basic	Good	High
Options	Small	Small	Better	Best
Performance	Least	Good	Better	Best
Connection	Decent	Best	Good	Good

*Note that in this case it depends on your staff skills and the connection company.

My personal feeling is that there is no easy answer. As with every other part of Web development I've discussed so far, there are many options to sort through, and the options change daily. Larger companies are finding that it makes sense to go with a major hosting service or build an expensive, fully staffed in-house team. That seems like good logic. If you're going to go the in-house route, commit yourself to doing the job right. If you're at all worried that you don't have the resources (technically or financially) to go all the way, then go for the hosting service. When it comes to in-house servers, a half-step is more likely a step backwards.

CHAPTER 16

Serving up server information.

Web Server Details

What's Here, and Why

A wealth of information about server products can be found on Serverwatch, an indispensable Web site (listed near the end of the chapter). In an effort to complement that fine site, I've limited my comments to just the few things I felt were particularly interesting or special about each product, focusing on the specific niche it fills better than its competitors (for example, Netscape's servers are more widely available over many platforms, and O'Reilly's WebSite is a particularly great tool for Visual Basic programmers, because it uses VB extensively).

I've also included full snail mail and phone/fax contact information, which Serverwatch doesn't readily provide. So be sure to consult other resources in combination with this chapter to get the most in-depth coverage of the server products that are available.

Remember, Try Before You Buy

Of course, hands-on personal experience is usually the best resource. Fortunately, the Web market is so cutthroat and crowded that the "try before you buy" marketing method commonly found in the shareware world is becoming the de facto method for distributing Web server products. You can download a full copy of almost any product mentioned in this chapter and use it for 30 or more days before you need to pay for it. I've pointed you to every URL you need to get your hands on the software you want to try out.

Windows NT-Based Servers

Windows NT 4.0 debuted in the summer of 1996 to great reviews. It married the Windows 95 interface with a slew of improvements designed to enhance Windows' already-powerful networking and Web serving capabilities. While Unix dominates the Web server OS market, NT is picking up lots of steam.

Windows NT Varieties

The critical accomplishment of Windows NT, designed for Microsoft by the amazing programmers who developed VMS for Digital Equipment, is that the operating system is powerful and capable of being ported to new hardware platforms, yet maintains a lot of backward compatibility with the existing Windows API. As a result, NT comes in a variety of platforms and flavors.

The two main versions, NT Server and NT Workstation, are intended to operate the opposing halves of client-server computing. While the pair are almost identical, NT Server is more expensive and comes with additional software to run the server side; NT Workstation is designed to be run on the client end.

Windows NT is also available as an operating system for MIPS (SGI), Alpha (DEC), and Pentium/Pentium Pro–based platforms. There is no NT for SPARC (Sun), PowerPC, or HP-RISC platforms, nor are there any plans that I know of to develop such systems. Digital has been especially aggressive about embracing NT, and its Alpha-based systems running NT are popping up everywhere—the extremely fast Alpha chip is perfect for intensive Web serving or high-end 3D graphics.

The NT Workstation/Server Controversy

In the summer of 1996, an important controversy arose as Microsoft began trying to enforce its intention that NT Workstation not be used for either network or Web server purposes. Although it did not allow customers to run its Web server package (Internet Information Server) on NT Workstation, the software giant claimed that companies such as O'Reilly (with WebSite) and Netscape (with its NT-based servers) were allowing and even encouraging their customers to use the Workstation version, which was priced considerably lower than NT Server. Microsoft went to court over the issue.

Needless to say, the accused companies accepted neither the logic nor the threats and lawsuits from Redmond, and they retaliated heavily both in the press and with complaints to the U.S. Department of Justice about monopolistic practices. The issue is the main point of contention in many firms' ongoing battles with Microsoft, and may be for some time.

The implications are substantial. If the courts agree with Microsoft and tell Netscape and others to stop allowing people to run servers this way, customers could be the next target. Microsoft could then charge users with wrongful execution of its licensing agreement for running a Web server with Windows NT Workstation. On the flip side, the courts could tell Microsoft that it cannot control what software is or isn't allowed to be run on its operating systems, and that it can only limit customers who buy its server.

The most likely resolution, though, is that Microsoft will lower the price of Windows NT Server to a point that makes the entire spat moot. Even then,

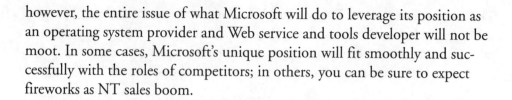

however, the entire issue of what Microsoft will do to leverage its position as an operating system provider and Web service and tools developer will not be moot. In some cases, Microsoft's unique position will fit smoothly and successfully with the roles of competitors; in others, you can be sure to expect fireworks as NT sales boom.

Software

Remember that there are many forms of server software you might want to take note of. What's listed in this section are not just the main server software packages, but all the various extensions you can add to improve your site's capabilities.

WebSite (Win95/NT)

O'Reilly & Associates
101 Morris Street
Sebastopol, CA 95472
Phone: 800-889-8969
Fax: 707-829-0104
WWW: http://www.ora.com

WebSite, an excellent package that The Coriolis Group uses for its Web site, is available in "regular" and "professional" versions. The latter includes enhanced security (with secure SSL) and commerce features, a full Web-site API that is compatible with Microsoft's IIS API-ISA, and excellent database connectivity.

One thing that makes this server especially interesting is its excellent support for VB4 programmers, who can use that language as well as Perl 5 and Java to write to the WebSite API. This has made WebSite one of the top servers for VB-savvy Webmasters.

The documentation for WebSite is among the best you'll find, which isn't surprising since O'Reilly is one of the top publishers of Internet development books. Everything you need to know about WebSite is located at **http://software.ora.com**.

Internet Information Server 2.0 (Windows NT)

Microsoft Corporation
One Microsoft Way
Redmond, WA 98052-6399

Phone: 206-882-8080
Fax: 206-883-8101
WWW: http://www.microsoft.com

When Microsoft debuted its Web server at Internet World in the fall of 1995, it caused a real stir by promising that all copies of Windows NT Server would include the product. This caused Web server pricing to drop dramatically as other companies cut prices to compete.

Of course, the major selling point of IIS is that since Microsoft wrote it, it is well integrated with the existing NT Server framework. Anyone who is familiar with NT Server will find working with IIS easy, because many components of the server management system overlap from NT Server.

Microsoft has also created a full server API (dubbed IIS API) that you can use to create extensive custom server programs with many different Microsoft programming languages. The company has also recently released the Microsoft Index Server, a major search engine product, and the Microsoft Proxy Server, which helps integrate the Web with existing corporate networks and intranets.

Another aspect of IIS worth noting is its integration with the BackOffice product line, Microsoft's full-service corporate computing and database solution. IIS is now an integral component for that line's application within corporate intranets.

All the info you need about IIS is located at **http://www.microsoft.com/ workshop/admin/default.htm**.

Netscape Server (Win95/NT)

Netscape Communications Corp.
501 East Middlefield Road
Mountain View, CA 94043
Phone: 415-937-3777
Fax: 415-528-4124
WWW: http://www.netscape.com

Netscape markets so many different server products that it's tough to sort through them all. The major server package, Enterprise Server, offers SSL 3.0 security, full support for Java and JavaScript, and a full API component (known commonly as NS API). You can find a full rundown on this server package at **http://www.netscape.com/comprod/server_central/product/ enterprise/index.html**.

Netscape also offers a Mail Server for messages, a News Server for creating private and public discussion groups, a Catalog Server for setting up and maintaining indexed material, and a Proxy Server that helps companies integrate the Web with corporate networks and intranets.

A major attraction of Netscape servers—aside from their fine construction and speed—is that they are available for many Unix variants, as well as Windows NT. Large corporations mixing Unix servers with PC servers throughout the organization may find this a particularly useful advantage.

One interesting new addition to Netscape's suite is FastTrack, a scaled-down server product for individuals, small businesses, or small intranets. It features a full server system with an entry-level interface and a bundled version of the Navigator Gold HTML editor. The product is simple to install and includes lots of templates and page wizards to help companies develop Web sites quickly. FastTrack is also quite inexpensive, costing only a few hundred dollars as opposed to thousands for a full-service Enterprise Server setup.

You can find a full rundown on FastTrack server at **http://www.netscape.com/ comprod/server_central/product/fast_track/index.html**.

Another advantage of Netscape servers is that the company is solely devoted to Internet development. Microsoft is serious about the Internet, too, of course, but Netscape has used its focus to build a larger all-around set of server products and other Web tools to support very advanced situations.

Purveyor (Win95/NT)

Process Software Corporation
959 Concord Street
Framingham, MA 01701
Phone: 800-722-7770
Fax: 508-879-0042
WWW: http://www.process.com

Purveyor is available in versions for Windows 95 and NT; the latter version supports IIS API and includes indexing, courtesy of Verity's search engine.

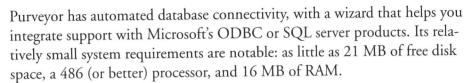

Purveyor has automated database connectivity, with a wizard that helps you integrate support with Microsoft's ODBC or SQL server products. Its relatively small system requirements are notable: as little as 21 MB of free disk space, a 486 (or better) processor, and 16 MB of RAM.

Purveyor also has Web server products available for Netware and DEC's OpenVMS platform.

Open Market (Win95/NT)

Open Market, Inc.
245 First Street
Cambridge, MA 02142
Phone: 617-577-3820
Fax: 617-679-0360
WWW: http://www.openmarket.com

Open Market has servers for several platforms. Its NT server, now in version 2.0, includes FastCGI, a new high-performance CGI gateway that is said to combine all the speed and power of proprietary server APIs with the compatibility of common CGI. Another interesting feature is its built-in support for page-at-a-time viewing of PDF files (that is, instead of serving up the entire file, it can send down just one page) if clients are using Adobe Acrobat Reader 3.0.

Hardware

Although they are the only ones that I'll discuss here, DEC, Alpha, and Intergraph systems are not the only NT Web server hardware platforms around. Longtime PC vendors like Compaq, Dell, Gateway, and Hewlett-Packard should be considered as well, and most of the top-tier producers have full systems (using Pentium or Pentium Pro chips) configured specifically for Web serving.

Alpha

Digital Equipment Corporation
111 Powdermill Road
Maynard, MA 01754
Phone: 508-493-5111
Fax: 508-493-8780
WWW: http://www.digital.com

One of the world's most incredible computer companies, Digital, spawned the minicomputer market and rode that to billions of dollars from the 1960s to the 1980s. As more and more companies turned to fast PCs and workstations, though, Digital saw the writing on the wall. Its answer was to create a new chip architecture to propel it into the workstation market and fuel new growth—the Alpha chip.

The Alpha chip is arguably the fastest, most powerful PC/workstation CPU around. Microsoft noticed this and ported NT to it (which is ironic, since the NT workstation was developed largely by the former head of OS development for Digital). At first the expected Alpha-NT synergy didn't take place, but with the rise of 3D graphics and the World Wide Web, PC developers everywhere are talking about Alpha-based NT workstations.

Digital has leveraged NT and the Web beautifully to push Alpha sales, and part of that effort is its specific line of Alpha-based NT servers. If you're developing a major Web site that will need maximum NT power, then heavily consider Alpha-based systems. You'll find all the information you need at **http://www.digital.com/info/alphaserver/webalpha/webalpha.html**.

Intergraph

Intergraph
One Industrial Park
Huntsville, AL 35894
Phone: 205-730-2000
Fax: 205-730-7898
WWW: http://www.intergraph.com

NT has encouraged several major companies to hit the market with extremely powerful but low-cost workstation performance systems. While Digital offers the highest performance among NT-based servers, Intergraph has been hitting the middle to lower end of this market with its Interserve workstations (many of them multiprocessor-based systems), which are powered by Pentium Pro chips.

Intergraph also has several turnkey-based solutions; check with the company for more information.

Unix-Based Servers

The majority of Web servers in use today are Unix-based systems running on either advanced RISC-based workstations or Intel systems running FreeBSD

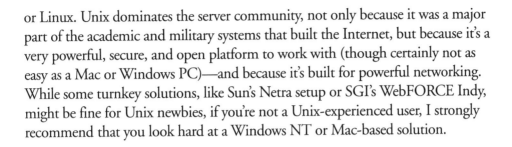

or Linux. Unix dominates the server community, not only because it was a major part of the academic and military systems that built the Internet, but because it's a very powerful, secure, and open platform to work with (though certainly not as easy as a Mac or Windows PC)—and because it's built for powerful networking. While some turnkey solutions, like Sun's Netra setup or SGI's WebFORCE Indy, might be fine for Unix newbies, if you're not a Unix-experienced user, I strongly recommend that you look hard at a Windows NT or Mac-based solution.

Software

There are too many Unix server options to list even in a book as comprehensive as this one. The most serious contenders for commercial use, however, are mentioned here. If you're looking for every last server available for your particular favorite version of Unix, again I point you toward **http://www.serverwatch.com**, which maintains a large list of available servers—no matter how good or bad.

Netscape

Netscape
Netscape Communications Corp.
501 East Middlefield Road
Mountain View, CA 94043
Phone: 415-937-3777
Fax: 415-528-4124
WWW: http://www.netscape.com

I described the Netscape server product line briefly in the NT section, but the full line also exists for many Unix systems. Netscape has software that supports IRIX (SGI), SPARC (Sun), and several other flavors of Unix. Its extensive support of Unix-based operating systems has been one of Netscape's strongest selling points.

Open Market

Open Market, Inc.
245 First Street
Cambridge, MA 02142
Phone: 617-577-3820
Fax: 617-679-0360
WWW: http://www.openmarket.com

Open Market, which I also covered earlier in the NT section, has servers for several Unix platforms.

Apache

http://www.apache.org

Apache was created as an outgrowth of developers who were constantly providing patches (hence the name "Apache") for NCSA's original Web server product. Rather than constantly fixing that product, the Apache Working Group created this very well-received and capable public domain server. You can find all the necessary information to download, install, and maintain the Web server on the Apache site.

Stronghold Apache

Community ConneXion, Inc.
WWW: http://www.us.apache-ssl.com

This is a special version of the Apache public domain server with increased functionality for secure communications with SSL. Community ConneXion has created a commercialized version of Apache with full support and a more robust implementation of the entire Apache program. Apache is a very strong server, but if you're looking to use Apache as a full product with company support, then Stronghold Apache is for you.

At the Web site you can download a demo, check out the information about how this is a commercialized version of Apache, and learn what specific features and changes are different from the public domain version.

Both Stronghold and regular Apache are the most popular servers on the Net.

Hardware

The first two options listed here are Intel-based systems, which are actually very capable in terms of running the Unix OS as a platform for various Web servers.

FreeBSD

http://www.freebsd.org

FreeBSD is a spinoff of the Berkeley version of Unix for the Intel platform. It's available in its latest state for free, and source code is available for any midnight engineers. FreeBSD was written by many people working in collaboration to expand and improve the overall Berkeley system; many sites use it, especially in the academic community.

A version of the powerful, free, and popular Apache Web server is available for FreeBSD. For the tinkerer—or individual/business on a tight budget—this is a great way to go. Inexperienced users, however, shouldn't try this solution unless they don't have any other choice.

Linux

`http://www.linux.org`

Linux was originally written by Linus Torvalds in Helsinki, Finland. Like FreeBSD, Linux is a freeware Unix solution for Intel platforms, created and maintained by a committee of developers. Unlike FreeBSD, though, Linux is available for a number of different hardware platforms, including Motorola 68 K, Digital Alpha, and Motorola PowerPC machines. Several servers exist for Linux, including the NCSA-HTTPD server.

WebFORCE/IRIX

Silicon Graphics Inc.
2011 N. Shoreline Boulevard
P.O. Box 7311
Mountain View, CA 94039-7311
Phone: 415-960-1980
Fax: 415-390-6220
WWW: http://www.sgi.com

SGI is known around the world for its amazing 3D graphics workstations— if you've seen a blockbuster special-effects movie in the last three or four years, you've been a witness to SGI's prowess. Now SGI is leveraging the power of its systems and MIPS CPU to deliver high-end Web server hardware and software.

The effort has taken the form of SGI's WebFORCE product line. This line of servers includes the low-end WebFORCE Indy; the WebFORCE Challenge S for high-performance situations; and the WebFORCE Challenge DM, L, and XL, which are multiprocessing systems for extreme power.

All SGI servers come with a ton of software and the IRIX (SGI's version of Unix) operating system. Most SGI software packages are built around Netscape server software, but versions of other Web server software packages (like Open Market and NaviSoft) also can be run on the systems.

Alpha

Digital Equipment Corporation
111 Powdermill Road
Maynard, MA 01754
Phone: 508-493-5111
Fax: 508-493-8780
WWW: http://www.digital.com

While Alpha is best known for its compatibility with NT, it is a major Unix
solution, too. Digital markets Digital Unix (its flavor of Unix) for the Alpha
platform, and several server solutions are available, including Netscape. The
complete suite of Digital's impressive AltaVista Internet tools is available for
this platform as well.

Sparc/Solaris/SunOS

Sun Microsystems
2550 Garcia Avenue
Mountain View, CA 94043-1100
Phone: 415-960-1300
Fax: 415-969-9131
WWW: http://www.sun.com

Every major Unix workstation manufacturer has its own distinct flavor of Unix
and an associated chip architecture. Sun's SPARC chip technology is one of the
most mature workstation CPU technologies around, and its Solstice and Solaris
Unix variants are extremely popular (Solaris even exists for Pentium).

The many different Sun servers are perhaps the most commonly used systems
on the Web, although Intel-based systems are quickly catching up. In particular, Sun's line of Netra servers integrate the SunOS with a slew of server
software and utilities to create an excellent (and quite popular) setup for Web
serving. You can find out more about Netra at **http://www.sun.com/prod-
ucts-n-solutions/hw/servers/netra.html**.

HP-3000/9000

Hewlett Packard
3000 Hanover Street
Palo Alto, CA 94304

Phone: 415-857-1501
Fax: 415-857-7299
WWW: http://www.hp.com

One of the largest computer companies in the world, HP is also one of the last few successful companies that offers computers for the PC, workstation, and minicomputer markets. HP has a significant Intel-based computer line, but also markets a major Unix workstation line with Web serving solutions. The HP-3000 and HP-9000 series are HP-RISC-based Unix Web servers that can run any of several software packages, including Netscape or Open Market.

For more information on the HP-9000 series Web servers, check out **http://www.hp.com/gsyinternet/products/hp9000.html**, and to learn more about the HP-3000 series go to **http://jazz.external.hp.com**.

Macintosh Servers

Despite Apple's recent setbacks, it's still a potent player in the world of computers—and if anything, the Internet promises to help the Macintosh. Because it's still arguably the best system for digital video, graphics, and sound development, the Mac is a killer Web development platform.

Software

The Macintosh lags somewhat in server software (this is one of the few platforms Netscape doesn't support), but there are some capable examples.

MAC HTTP-D

Apple Computer, Inc.
One Infinite Loop
Cupertino, CA 95014
Phone: 408-996-1010
Fax: 408-974-2113
WWW: http://www.apple.com

Apple created this server product to ensure that there was at least some semblance of a server product available for its systems.

WebStar

Quarterdeck Corporation
2550 Ninth Street, Suite 112
Berkeley, CA 94710
Phone: 510-649-4949
Fax: 510-548-0393
WWW: http://www.starnine.com

Made by StarNine, a new Quarterdeck subsidiary, WebStar is the only third-party commercially available Web server for the Macintosh. Fortunately, WebStar is a very good product.

Hardware

One of the knocks against Apple was that it never licensed out its OS so that clones could offer people greater availability of products, more options, and potentially better pricing. This is no longer true, however, as there are now two major Mac clone manufacturers worth checking out. While Apple remains the premiere Mac product developer, these two companies certainly make things interesting.

Apple PowerMac Servers

Apple Computer, Inc.
One Infinite Loop
Cupertino, CA 95014
Phone: 408-996-1010
Fax: 408-974-2113
WWW: http://www.apple.com

Apple has a whole suite of server products based on its PowerPC chip architecture. Apple even can provide servers with AIX (Apple's version of Unix) as the operating system. For more specifics about Apple's server hardware, visit **http://www.solutions.apple.com/Servers**.

Power Computing

2555 North IH 35, Suite 200
Round Rock, TX 78664-2015
WWW: http://www.powercc.com

Power Computing is to Apple what Dell was to IBM—a high-quality mail-order clone manufacturer. (In fact, Power Computing's ads look just like Dell's, and both firms are based in Texas.) Offering a full range of systems at very attractive prices, Power is quickly becoming a major player in the Mac hardware field.

BeBox

Be, Inc.
800 El Camino Real, Suite 300
Menlo Park, CA 94025
Phone: 415-462-4141
Fax: 415-462-4129
WWW: http://www.be.com

The BeBox is an exciting new computer platform that was created to compete in those niche markets—graphics, digital video, and digital audio—that have been dominated by computers like the Macintosh, Amiga, and Atari ST. The company was founded by former Apple R&D chief Jean-Louis Gassée, and the system has won rave reviews for its focus, technology, and overall capabilities.

While it still needs more tools and software, BeBox has awesome potential as a Web server and development platform. Its OS is a completely new object-oriented operating system, and the architecture is built for multiprocessing PowerPC architecture, which means it can really fly in that configuration. Best of all, the BeBox is being engineered to deliver all this exciting power for a very, very low price (relatively, anyway).

As I said, the BeBox is a new platform, and the final touches are still being put on the first round of Web tools. Many people, though, are keeping their eyes on this product based on its potential alone—and you should, too.

Server Software Stuff

As I pointed out in Chapter 15, a server is constructed from many parts. What follows is a decent roundup of the other major software packages you need for your server.

Commerce Tools

"As soon as we have good commerce technologies..." has been an oft-repeated phrase at Web-related trade conferences around the world. Well, much has happened to bring this holy grail of Web commerce within reach. The rise of key secure transaction technologies like Netscape's Secure Sockets Layer (SSL) and RSA Data Security's encryption algorithms encouraged companies like Netscape, Microsoft, and Open Market to build the server systems needed to do all the other work (such as building catalog sites).

Things began to get dicey, though, as different groups of companies lined up behind competing standards for secure transactions with credit cards. MasterCard, IBM, and Netscape backed a system known as SEPP (Secure Encryption Payment Protocol) which was based on Netscape's SSL. Meanwhile, Microsoft and Visa had developed a technology dubbed STT (Secure Transaction Technology), and S-HTTP (Secure Hypertext Transfer Protocol) had been developed by Terisa Systems.

Following an outcry from users and merchant banks who didn't like the idea of dealing with or choosing among multiple technologies, the two main sides called a truce and worked out a universal technology that became SET (Secure Electronic Transactions). Although SET is the system you should be seeing for credit card transactions, expect a lot of competition in the many complementary technologies involved in this very important Web business. Various so-called ecash schemes promise to create a system for "microtransactions" at prices that could be a fraction of a penny (and thus are not large enough to justify the cost of processing credit card transactions).

CyberCash Merchant

CyberCash
2100 Reston Parkway, Suite 430
Reston, VA 22091
Phone: 703-620-4200
Fax: 703-620-4215
WWW: http://www.cybercash.com

Lots of companies are working to bring us the equivalent of digital money, but CyberCash is perhaps farthest along. It has a very robust system and lots of key partnerships with major financial and software companies. If you're a developer, you must fill out a form on the CyberCash site to request downloading of its merchant system, which works with your server software. Then you need to hook up with a bank that accepts CyberCash's system (if you can't find one, CyberCash will help you either convert your bank or find a CyberCash-friendly institution).

Once you are hooked up, customers using CyberCash's system will be able to purchase items directly from you. CyberCash's software handles all the necessary encryption and security measures.

Entrust

Northern Telecom
Northern Telecom Plaza, 200 Athens Way
Nashville, TN 37228-1397
Phone: 615-734-4000
Fax: 615-734-5190
WWW: http://www.nortel.com

Entrust is network security software backed by RSA Data Security. Now available in version 2.0, it offers encryption and digital signatures and can work with many different applications you might use on your site, including popular email packages such as cc:Mail or Microsoft Mail. It is available for a variety of leading platforms: Windows (3.1, NT, and 95), Macintosh, HP Unix, SunOS, and Solaris.

Entrust can support tens of thousands of users; Entrust Lite provides security for sites with smaller user bases. The latest version incorporates an ability to certify entire domains, making it easy to establish certification across a whole company (perfect for purchase-ordering systems, such as for an office-supplies distributor). For more about Entrust, check out **http://www.nortel.com/ entprods/entrust/main.html**.

vPOS and vGATE

VeriFone
Three Lagoon Drive
Redwood City, CA 94065-1561
Phone: 415-591-6500
Fax: 415-598-5504
WWW: http://www.verifone.com

VeriFone is one of the largest credit card verification companies in the world, so it's no surprise to see them become a major player in the secure Web commerce market. One thing VeriFone can provide is reassurance to many stores and businesses that already use its existing services and might otherwise

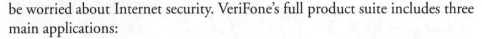

be worried about Internet security. VeriFone's full product suite includes three main applications:

- *vWALLET*—The payment application users install to interact with the system.

- *vPOS*—Used by your site to accept payment; check credit; process reversals, voids, and settlement/reconciliation; and send out a receipt. vPOS also does all the back-end work with reports on inventory, daily transactions, and sales reports.

- *vGATE*—Used to move the transactions securely over the Internet from your site to the actual processing organization (in other words, your bank).

All of VeriFone's software is compatible with the SET standards set forth by the Visa-MasterCard alliance. Microsoft is also incorporating the vPOS system into its Merchant Internet Retailing software, so this will be a major system many companies will use.

Search Engines

As sites grow exponentially, and documents and content build up faster than you can create links or organize any of it, a search engine component can be the difference between a site where people can find what they want and one that is just a big mess. The following is a rundown of major search engine technologies to consider.

Excite

Excite, Inc.
1091 North Shoreline Boulevard
Mountain View, CA 94043
Phone: 415-934-3611
Fax: 415-934-3610
WWW: http://corp.excite.com

Excite is one of the top search engine companies around; its software is used by a number of sites around the Web, including Netscape's site. Excite is available for a variety of platforms, including SunOS, HP-UX, Solaris, IBM AIX, SGI IRIX, BSDI, Windows NT, and more to follow (such as DEC OSF and Linux).

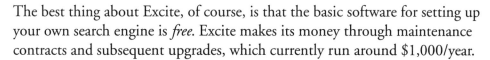

The best thing about Excite, of course, is that the basic software for setting up your own search engine is *free*. Excite makes its money through maintenance contracts and subsequent upgrades, which currently run around $1,000/year.

One drawback for intranet-oriented users is that Excite only indexes text and HTML files (PDF support is promised soon). If you want to have indexing for other document types, like Word files, you'll need to go elsewhere. For most sites, though, HTML, text, and PDF file indexing will be just fine.

Fulcrum SearchServer and SearchBuilder

Fulcrum
785 Carling Avenue
Ottawa, Ontario K1S 5H4
Phone: 613-238-1761
Fax: 613-238-7695
WWW: http://www.fulcrum.com

Fulcrum SearchServer is a Windows-based search engine with support for the most common Windows file formats (like text, HTML, Word, Excel, and PowerPoint). This concentration on Windows and extensive support for multiple file formats makes it a great system for corporate intranets. The SearchServer technology is extremely open, with a full API and support for custom database technology and report building.

SearchBuilder is a series of products that help programmers using either VB, Visual C++, or PowerBuilder create customized search solutions. There is also a full SearchServer SDK available for programmers using C that provides direct access to the SearchServer engine.

Glimpse

University of Arizona
Department of Computer Science
WWW: http://glimpse.cs.arizona.edu

Glimpse is available for a variety of platforms, including Linux, IBM AIX, SGI IRIX, Sun Solaris, SunOS, DEC OSF, HP-UX, DEC ULTRIX, and NeXT Mach. You can download a version of the Glimpse engine, called WebGlimpse, for use as a general search utility for your site. Best of all for techies, you can also download the source code to the Glimpse search engine and experiment in order to learn what goes into creating such a tool.

Livelink Search

Open Text
180 Columbia Street West
Waterloo, Ontario N2L 3L3
Phone: 519-888-7111
Fax: 519-888-0677
WWW: http://www.opentext.com

The Livelink product line is a full suite of applications to build high-power corporate intranets with complete groupware and other features. The Livelink search engine is available for Windows NT, SUN Solaris, SunOS, HP-UX, IBM AIX, SGI, and DEC OSF/1; it works with HTML, SGML, PDF, and Microsoft Office file formats.

OpenText also offers the option of Livelink Spider, which will crawl over your site(s) and continuously index new content.

PLWeb

Personal Library Software
2400 Research Boulevard, Suite 350
Rockville, MD 20850
Phone: 301-990-1155
FAX: 301-963-9738
WWW: http://www.pls.com

PLWeb is a search engine available for Sun Solaris, HP-UX, IBM AIX, SGI IRIX, and DEC OSF/1. The system supports ASCII text, HTML, and Acrobat (only on the HP and Sun Solaris systems so far). A free evaluation copy of the software is available on the PLS Web site. America Online recently invested in Personal Library.

One cool aspect of the PLS software line is a product called Personal Agent, which works with the search engine to find new documents that fit a defined profile and then notifies the user about their existence.

RetrievalWare Web Server

Excalibur Technologies
1921 Gallows Road, Suite 200
Vienna, VA 22182

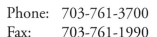

Phone: 703-761-3700
Fax: 703-761-1990
WWW: http://www.excalib.com

CMP's Techweb uses Excalibur's search engine for its extensive site. The extensive RetrievalWare line of software—which is available for a variety of Unix platforms and Windows NT—includes support for a variety of formats, and there are special versions for niche markets (such as companies that use imaging extensively). There is also a full SDK available for creating custom applications with a variety of ways to build tools that work with the search engine, including through Microsoft's Visual Basic.

Tecumseh Scout

Tippecanoe Systems, Inc.
5674 Stoneridge Drive, Suite 119
Pleasanton, CA 94588
Phone: 510-416-8510
Fax: 510-416-8516
WWW: http://www.tippecanoe.com

Tecumseh is a Windows NT-based search engine primarily intended for small businesses using NT Server. The basic version of Tecumseh is free to download and use, but can only handle up to 4,000 documents in its indexed database; more expansive versions are available at a cost from Tippecanoe Systems. Tecumseh supports searching through HTML, text, and various Windows files like Word and Excel.

Topic Internet Server

Verity
1550 Plymouth Street
Mountain View, CA 94043
Phone: 415-960-7600
Fax: 415-960-7698
WWW: http://www.verity.com

Topic is one of the more popular search engines in use on the Internet today. Compatible with systems running Microsoft's Internet Information Server or Netscape's Enterprise Server, it is available on a huge range of platforms (from NT to Unix, OS/2, and Macintosh). The system is incredibly extensive, depending on the ultimate software that you purchase. There are several databasing tools, an SDK, and a personal agent development kit as well.

Many data formats are supported, including ASCII, Adobe Acrobat PDF, SGML, HTML, and more than 50 file formats related to word processing, spreadsheets, and desktop publishing.

You can also set up the search engine to work extensively with topics that you select. This form of searching helps users quickly search areas of particular interest, and it lets developers automatically fit in cross-referenced information. (For example, a user's topic search concerning Microsoft might be set up to find documents not containing "Microsoft", but still containing "Bill Gates".)

AltaVista

Digital Equipment Corporation
111 Powdermill Road
Maynard, MA 01754
Phone: 508-493-5111
Fax: 508-493-8780
WWW: http://www.digital.com

Since its debut in 1995, AltaVista has been the most complete and powerful search engine on the Internet (sometimes too powerful, if you ask me). Now Digital is moving the technology into a product line to provide AltaVista's search power to individual systems and corporate intranets. Find out more directly at **http://altavista.software.digital.com**.

Security and Firewalls

As more companies connect their private networks to the Internet—and more countries and individuals (not just teenage thrillseekers) turn hacking into a serious effort—strong firewalls have become critical. The firewall business is booming as a result; several of the leading options are listed here.

Understanding Internet Firewalls

Firewalls have improved considerably in the last few years, as the growth of the Internet has fueled lots of work in the network security business. Aside from just pointing out the leading packages, I wanted to list a few resources to help you decide which one is right for your needs.

NCSA Certification

`http://www.ncsa.com/fwpg_pl.html`

The NCSA has done a lot of work in the firewall development industry, and it recently began establishing standards both for software and for people implementing security on their servers. All of that information is found on their Web page; also look for the NCSA Seal of Approval on various security packages.

Serverwatch

`http://www.serverwatch.com`

I told you at the beginning of this chapter to review all of Serverwatch's information. Its comments section on firewalls is especially important and useful.

Gauntlet FAQ

`http://shadowplay.hq.tis.com/docs/products/gauntlet/gauntletfaq.html`

I am not an Internet security expert by any means, so I really appreciated this well-written FAQ on what Internet firewalls are. While it's also an ad for how Gauntlet (by Trusted Information Systems) works, it's excellent reading for anyone only vaguely familiar with Internet security.

ANS InterLock

ANS CO+RE
100 Clearbrook Road
Elmsford, NY 10523
Phone: 800-456-8267
Fax: 703-758-7717
WWW: http://www.ans.net

ANS is one of the oldest Internet companies around. In its original non-profit state, it was crucial in building the NSF backbone that spurred the Internet's growth; now it's a major component of America Online's Internet services division.

The ANS InterLock firewall product supports HTTP, Telnet, FTP, SMTP, Gopher, NNTP, X-Windows, NTP, and generic TCP and UDP Internet protocols. It is available for Sun Solaris and IBM AIX-based systems. Full information about this product is available at **http://www.ans.net/InterLock**.

Black Hole

Milkyway Networks, Inc.
2055 Gateway Place, Suite 400
San Jose, CA 95110
Phone: 408-467-3868
Fax: 408-441-9152
WWW: http://www.milkyway.com

Black Hole is a very extensive firewall system for Intel systems; I spent an hour just reading about its numerous features. One thing it does very well is help you set up various private networks to keep unprivileged users out.

ON Guard

ON Technology
One Cambridge Center
Cambridge, MA 02142
Phone: 617-374-1400
Fax: 617-374-1433
WWW: http://www.on.com

In April 1996, ON Technology—the makers of DaVinci eMAIL and Meeting Maker—purchased neTrend, a developer of firewall security software. Shortly thereafter it released ON Guard, its first firewall product.

ON Guard is aimed at corporations with IP and IPX networks that need complete firewall protection for those two fundamental network protocols. ON Guard also specializes in providing firewall security for remote hookups to corporate LANs and intranets.

Eagle

Raptor Systems, Inc.
69 Hickory Drive
Waltham, MA 02154
Phone: 617-487-7700
Fax: 617-487-6755
WWW: http://www.raptor.com

Eagle runs on the major Unix platforms of Sun, HP, and IBM workstations, and there is a version for Windows NT as well. Eagle sells the product in license form with separate levels for small, medium, and large corporations.

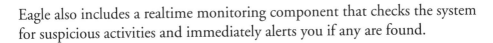

Eagle also includes a realtime monitoring component that checks the system for suspicious activities and immediately alerts you if any are found.

Digital Firewall

Digital Equipment Corporation
111 Powdermill Rd.
Maynard, MA 01754
Phone: 508-493-5111
Fax: 508-493-8780
WWW: http://www.digital.com

Firewall is an NT product that is part of Digital's AltaVista family of Internet software and is based on the company's years of experience with network security issues. Specific information and demo downloads are available at http://altavista.software.digital.com.

Gauntlet Internet Firewall 3.1

Trusted Information Systems, Inc.
3060 Washington Road (Rt. 97)
Glenwood, MD 21738
Phone: 301-854-6889
Fax: 301-854-5363
WWW: http://www.tis.com

This product (which was *PC Magazine*'s Product Pick in its roundup of Internet firewall products) is available for Intel, BSD, SunOS, HP-UX, and soon Solaris and NT. An IRIX version of Gauntlet is available directly from SGI.

Gauntlet provides a wealth of security features to prevent users from intruding on your system, as well as to prevent employees from doing things that could jeopardize the system. One feature, Java Guard, blocks Java programs from being retrieved and run on users' machines, even if the users haven't disabled Java at the browser level.

Interceptor 2.0

Technologic, Inc.
4170 Ashford Dunwoody Road, Suite 465
Atlanta, GA 30319

Phone: 404-843-9111
Fax: 404-843-9700
WWW: http://www.tlogic.com

While Interceptor 2.0 is a firewall for Windows and Sun-based servers, its RADAR management system allows any user with an SSL-configured browser to do the administration right from their desktop. This makes the system easy to use and allows the Webmaster to control it from whatever machine he or she is using.

Another neat feature is Technologic's attack simulation process, which checks more than 100 common security snafus and alerts you to potential problems before they occur. Support exists as well for RealAudio, which can have trouble dealing with other firewalls. Interceptor also has realtime monitoring for suspicious activities.

PrivateNet Secure Firewall Server

NEC
8 Corporate Center Drive
Melville, NY, 11747
Phone: 516-753-7000
Fax: 516-753-7041
WWW: http://www.nec.com

PrivateNet is a turnkey-based system that gives you a fully configured Pentium machine running BSD-Unix with complete firewall security. For companies looking to avoid setup hassles, PrivateNet may be the way to go.

SunScreen

Sun Microsystems
2550 Garcia Avenue
Mountain View, CA 94043-1100
Phone: 415-960-1300
Fax: 415-969-9131
WWW: http://www.sun.com

Like the NEC product, SunScreen is a turnkey firewall system. It works with a SPARCstation computer configured with lots of security software and uses an Intel PC to configure and administer the system on a remote basis.

Messaging and Chat

These chat systems are mostly text-based server systems, some of which work with specialized client plug-ins. None of these, however, are VRML-based chat systems (I profiled some of those in Chapter 14; please look there for virtual-worlds chat products).

AltaVista Forum

Digital Equipment Corporation
111 Powdermill Road
Maynard, MA 01754
Phone: 508-493-5111
Fax: 508-493-8780
WWW: http://www.digital.com

Forum 2.0 is more than just simple "chat" software—it's a complete workgroup system featuring chat, document sharing, and markup, as well as a calendar. Meetings can be set up on private or public sites, and Forum includes support for realtime IRC chat and CU-SeeMe teleconferencing software. There is also full support for post-and-reply bulletin boards, making this a very complete solution for organizing Web-based conversations.

Forum is available for a variety of Unix platforms and Windows NT under Netscape or Purveyor server setups.

Livelink

Open Text
180 Columbia Street West
Waterloo, Ontario N2L 3L3
Phone: 519-888-7111
Fax: 519-888-0677
WWW: http://www.opentext.com

Open Text's Livelink product line is particularly geared toward intranet setups, as it supports discussion bulletin boards, document sharing and project task lists, and collaboration, but not realtime conferencing.

PictureTalk Conference Server

PictureTalk, Inc.
4234 Hacienda Drive, Suite 200
Pleasanton, CA 94588-2721

Phone: 510-467-5300
Fax: 510-467-5310
WWW: http://www.picturetalk.com

PictureTalk is a graphics-oriented chat and conferencing system. A specialized server facilitates communications between users who have the PictureTalk client installed in their browser. (The client, which is available for Mac, PC, and various Unix flavors, can be downloaded directly off PictureTalk's Web site.) Once a meeting is established, a group presenter is selected, and all information from the presenter's screen is sent to the other users—a process that makes showing off presentations a snap. Each presenter can transfer "presenting" status to another user when he or she is finished.

The server software is available for Sun SPARCstations running Solaris, Windows NT systems, and Digital Alpha servers running NT. In fact, Digital has signed on with PictureTalk to promote this system.

Allaire Forums

Allaire Corporation
7600 France Avenue South, Suite 552
Minneapolis, MN 55435
Phone: 612-831-1808
Fax: 612-830-1090
WWW: http://www.allaire.com

Allaire Forums is an elegantly done Web bulletin board system that doesn't require any special plug-in. It was developed, and can be extended, with Allaire's Cold Fusion Web development product. With Allaire Forums you can create extensive threaded topic discussions, much like those found on CompuServe or AOL. All of this is run through a database system that stores, organizes, and quickly retrieves messages for users on your server. Users can send private messages to one another and can also set custom preferences that are instituted each time they visit, via a "cookies" technique.

ChatBox

Emerald Net
4003 E. Speedway, Suite 123
Tucson, AZ 85712

Phone: 520-318-1993
Fax: 520-670-1922
WWW: http://www.emerald.net

ChatBox works entirely without any special software, using server push-pull and a special server. Emerald provides ChatBox Lite for free, which allows up to ten participants to converse. ChatBox Pro allows for multiple rooms and many more participants, while ChatBox ISP offers an unlimited number of rooms and conversations, as well as an "amphitheater" room with rows to support guest sessions.

Podium 2.0

Proxima, Inc.
1749 Old Meadow Road, 6th Floor
McLean, VA 22102
Phone: 703-506-1661
Fax: 703-506-4797
WWW: http://www.proxima.com

Proxima, a major builder of top-tier Web sites, developed Podium to add excellent discussion capabilities to the sites it was creating for companies like L'eggs and MCI, and the film *Independence Day*.

Podium 2.0, to put it bluntly, is really slick. I tested the example with optional frames and graphics icons on the Proxima Web site, and it was one of the more impressive bulletin board solutions that I have come across. You can find the demos I tested on their site at **http://www.proxima.com/podium**.

Web Crossing

Lundeen & Associates
Phone: 510-521-5855
Fax: 510-522-6647

In Chapter 8, I wrote about Salon1999, the Web-based publication from California. One of the items I liked best about this site was its very lively and well-done message boards. Salon1999 uses Web Crossing for its bulletin board systems.

Web Crossing is available for many different platforms (including Macintosh, Windows NT, AIX, AlphaOSF, FreeBSD, BSDI, HP-UX, IRIX, Linux, Solaris, and SunOS), making it perhaps the most wide-ranging product of the

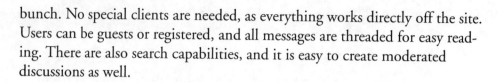

bunch. No special clients are needed, as everything works directly off the site. Users can be guests or registered, and all messages are threaded for easy reading. There are also search capabilities, and it is easy to create moderated discussions as well.

Focus

UK Web, Ltd.
46 The Calls
Leeds, LS2 7EY
United Kingdom
Phone: 44-113-222-0046
Fax: 44-113-244 8102
WWW: http://www.ukweb.com

UK Web's Focus is available for Solaris, SunOS 4, IRIX (SGI), and Linux. It is a threaded bulletin board system that is very simple to use, but not nearly as flashy as Podium. No special client extensions are needed.

Focus provides lots of administrative functions, and fully moderated discussions are possible. Java capabilities are also used to extend the system and add additional outlining functionality for users, allowing them to quickly find posts they want to read or respond to. Users can also register and select preferences, and security allows administrators to limit conferees and set levels of access and capabilities.

ichat

ichat
8303 North Mopac
Austin, TX 78759
Phone: 512-349-0339
Fax: 512-349-0005
WWW: http://www.ichat.com

ichat is one of the best and most popular realtime chat systems for Internet sites; Time Warner and the Democratic National Commitee are among its users. ichat works as a plug-in to Netscape Navigator or with an ActiveX control for Microsoft Internet Explorer, and there is also a new Java-built client.

ichat supports event moderation and provides the ability for the site moderator to screen questions for guests. Audio and video are also possible through ichat's own plug-in architecture. Another unique feature is the ability to take users on "Web trips," guiding them to other pages on the site or other sites altogether.

The product also supports IRC connectivity directly within the user's Web browser—if a user clicks on an IRC link, ichat automatically switches into IRC client mode. The company also offers a standalone application product for developers of MUDs or other online products that might have specialized needs.

Web Sites

The sheer number of server packages and programs which extend server capabilities is growing enormously. Here are the best sites on the Web to help you stay on top of what's going on with server software and hardware.

Serverwatch
`http://serverwatch.1world.com`

Serverwatch is the number one Web-based resource for information about anything related to serving the Web. Run by the same folks who gave us BrowserWatch (at **http://www.browserwatch.com**), this resource is an indispensable bookmark for any Webmaster or developer. It contains information about almost every server package and many accessories.

While I've tried to outline most of the major tools here, Serverwatch covers almost everything. One particularly important feature is that the designers of this site solicit and then integrate comments from Webmasters about each and every tool.

WebCompare
`http://webcompare.iworld.com/compare/chart.html`

Looking for a simple comparison of various Web server solutions? Well, look no further than this page, which lists every known server (including a link to the associated home page), the operating systems it's available for, and the price range for the software.

PC Magazine's Internet User: Web Server Listings
`http://www.pcmag.com/IU/INTRANET/intranet.htm`

This site is an excellent listing and rundown of some of the best servers and server tools around.

WebMaster Magazine's Home Page
http://www.cio.com/WebMaster/

An awesome collection of links that list and examine a number of the products I've mentioned in this chapter.

Netcraft Server Survey
http://www.netcraft.com/Survey/

A very nicely done monthly survey and report of server statistics with lots of information on which server solutions are hot and which aren't. A great place to go to find out what everyone else is using.

Books

Building a Linux Internet Server by George Eckel and Chris Hare (published by New Riders, 1996, ISBN 1-56205-525-9)

Building a Unix Internet Server by George Eckel (published by New Riders, 1995, ISBN 1-56205-494-5)

Building a Windows NT Internet Server by Eric Harper (published by New Riders, 1996, ISBN 1-56205-484-8)

Building a Windows NT Web Server by Ed Tittel (published by IDG Books, 1996, ISBN 0-76458-004-3)

Building and Maintaining an NT Web Server by Jeff Bankston (published by Coriolis Group Books, 1996, ISBN 1-88357-790-X)

Configuring and Troubleshooting Your Web Server Unix Edition by Mary Bennion and Geoff Galitz (published by Prentice Hall, 1996, ISBN 0-13459-405-3)

Internet Server Construction Kit for Windows by Greg Bean (published by Wiley, 1995, ISBN 0-47112-696-9)

The Mac Web Server Book: Tools & Techniques for Building Your Internet Site by Mark Bell (published by Ventana, 1996, ISBN 1-56604-341-7)

Mastering Windows NT Web Servers by Peter Dyson (published by Sybex, 1996, ISBN 0-78211-899-2)

Microsoft Windows NT Server One Step at a Time by Brian L. Brandt and Mike Nash (published by Microsoft Press, 1996, ISBN 1-57231-246-7)

Official Netscape Fasttrack Book: Set Up Your Windows Web Server the Easy Way by Phil James (published by Ventana, 1996, ISBN 1-56604-483-9)

Programming Web Server Applications by Eric C. Richardson (published by Hayden Books, 1996, ISBN 1-568-30271-1)

Serving the Web by Robert Jon Mudry (published by Coriolis Group Books, 1995, ISBN 1-883577-30-6)

Sybase SQL Server on the World Wide Web by Ed Ashley (published Intl Thomson Computer Press, 1996, ISBN 1-85032-815-3)

The Unix Web Server Book by Jonathan Magid (published by Ventana, 1996, ISBN 1-56604-480-4)

The Web Server Book by Jonathan Magid (published by Ventana, 1996, ISBN 1-56604-234-8)

Web Server Construction Kit for the Macintosh by Stewart Buskirk (published by Hayden Books, 1996, ISBN 1-56830-271-1)

Web Server Handbook by Cynthia Chin-Lee and Comet (published by Oracle Press, 1996, ISBN 0-07882-215-7)

Web Server Handbook by Pete Palmer, Adam Schneider, and Anne Cherette (published by Prentice Hall, 1996, ISBN 0-13239-930-X)

The Windows NT Web Server Book by Larry Budnick, Jonathan Magid, R. Douglas Matthews, and Paul Jones (published by Ventana, 1996, ISBN 1-56604-342-5)

The Windows NT Web Server Handbook by Tom Sheldon (published by McGraw-Hill, 1996, ISBN 0-07882-221-1)

CHAPTER 17

People will access the Web in different ways than you might think. Be prepared now.

A Closer Look at Clients

What Is a Web Client?

The question seems simple enough. Is a Web client a personal computer that runs one of the leading Web browsers? A personal computer that uses PointCast to access the latest news and weather? Or is it your TV set, VCR, and phone? How about your new car?! You may think I've gone off the deep end, but I'm deadly serious—and I've got company, too. The founders of Netscape—Jim Clark, James Barksdale, and others—have formed a company (Navio, which I'll talk a little more about later) that intends to develop Web access software to run on a multitude of products, including cars. In fact, in the firm's vision statement they note that there are more than 600 computer chips in today's latest cars. One of the top things ripped off now from leading cars aren't the hub caps but the Pentium chip that helps run the car!

The fact is that as the world expands digitally—and as the Web grows exponentially—the products we use to access Web content won't necessarily look like computers at all. And our computers themselves will have all sorts of Web-accessing software that won't necessarily look like traditional browsers.

Web developers need to know as much as possible about Web client innovations because of how they'll change the way developers work and the new opportunities they will provide. That's why I personally think this is one of the most important chapters in the book.

The Major Browser Technologies

There are two big-time browser technologies and several smaller ones that developers should be aware of.

Netscape Navigator

Netscape Communications
501 E. Middlefield Road
Mountain View, CA 94043
Phone: 415-254-1900
Fax: 415-528-4125
WWW: http://www.netscape.com

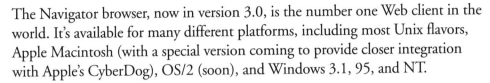

The Navigator browser, now in version 3.0, is the number one Web client in the world. It's available for many different platforms, including most Unix flavors, Apple Macintosh (with a special version coming to provide closer integration with Apple's CyberDog), OS/2 (soon), and Windows 3.1, 95, and NT.

Navigator is available in plain browser form and as Navigator Gold, which includes built-in editing capabilities.

Microsoft Internet Explorer

Microsoft Corporation
One Microsoft Way
Redmond, WA 98052-6399
Phone: 206-882-8080
Fax: 206-883-8101
WWW: http://www.microsoft.com

Microsoft certainly wowed many people in the summer of 1996 with the Internet Explorer 3.0 browser, which established itself as perhaps the only legitimate challenger to Netscape Navigator. Even as the finishing touches were being put on that product, however, Microsoft was showing many people its version 4.0 browser (code-named Nashville), which merges the Windows interface and OS with a Web browser. The browsing window is actually an OCX control, which means any decent (or even beginning) Windows programmer can use the MSIE browser engine to build his or her own custom Web applications. This integration of capabilities will only increase with the release of Nashville and future versions of Windows.

CyberDog

Apple Computer
One Infinite Loop
Cupertino, CA 95014
Phone: 408-996-1010
Fax: 408-974-2113
WWW: http://cyberdog.apple.com

CyberDog is the core Web browser engine Apple has developed for the Macintosh. CyberDog is significant, not only because a lot of Mac owners use it, but for its support and integration of Apple's OpenDoc technology with the Web. (OpenDoc is Apple's answer to Microsoft's OLE.) With OpenDoc

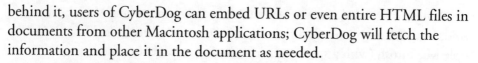

behind it, users of CyberDog can embed URLs or even entire HTML files in documents from other Macintosh applications; CyberDog will fetch the information and place it in the document as needed.

Recently, Apple announced that Netscape will support the CyberDog engine with the next release of its Apple Navigator browser. By agreeing to this, Netscape has essentially committed itself to supporting the OpenDoc technology.

HotJava

Sun Microsystems
2550 Garcia Avenue
Mountain View, CA 94043-1100
Phone: 415-960-1300
Fax: 415-969-9131
WWW: http://www.sun.com

Originally a browser that Sun developed to showcase its Java technology, HotJava is now a technology unto itself and a major part of Sun's Java plans. Companies can license and download the source code (written in Java) to create their own browsers that can run on any Java virtual machine.

The HotJava browser is only one example of an Internet-aware application that you can build out of a class of Java libraries available from Sun. The HotJava browser executable program for SPARC/Solaris and Microsoft Windows NT/95 is available for free personal noncommercial use.

You can read more about HotJava at **http://java.sun.com/HotJava/index.html**.

Spyglass Browser

Spyglass
Naperville Corporate Center
1230 E. Diehl Road, Suite 304
Naperville, IL 60563
Phone: 708-505-1010
Fax: 708-505-4944
WWW: http://www.spyglass.com

Formed as the official licensee of the original NCSA Mosaic browser (after Netscape had recruited many of the programmers who helped create it at the University of Illinois), Spyglass has developed the browser and licensed code from it to other companies like Microsoft, a key partner. For the most part,

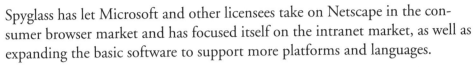

Spyglass has let Microsoft and other licensees take on Netscape in the consumer browser market and has focused itself on the intranet market, as well as expanding the basic software to support more platforms and languages.

The Spyglass browser technology can easily be added into existing products or customized for corporations using its client SDK product. For companies building Web access directly into their products (such as for help files), incorporating this technology ensures that all users accessing the site will have the same browser capabilities. One high-end CAD software company is doing just that, and Microware—the set-top box software company—has licensed Spyglass technology to use as its browser for its Internet-capable WebTV products.

Oracle PowerBrowser

500 Oracle Parkway
Redwood City, CA 94065
Phone: 415-506-7000
Fax: 415-506-7200
WWW: http://www.oracle.com

When Oracle needed to develop its own browser for its network computer, it licensed technology from Spyglass and built the Oracle PowerBrowser. The product is available for Windows 3.1, 95, and NT, with Unix and Mac versions coming soon.

In addition to the browser itself, PowerBrowser includes a Web server, an integrated Basic scripting environment, Java support, and support for third-party applications (which Oracle calls Network Loadable Objects). There is also a database wizard—Oracle is, above all, a database company—that allows you to quickly set up database-enabled Web applications.

The browser currently supports up through version 2.0 of HTML, 3.0 tables, animated GIFs, and frames. The personal server allows you to serve documents over the Web, and it comes with an authoring wizard too. Oracle's Basic scripting language lets you write Web scripts with the Oracle Basic programming language; you can also use it to program scripts for the personal server in order to avoid CGI scripting.

The Network Loadable Objects work like plug-ins—and, in fact, are compatible with Netscape 2.0 plug-ins. This product may be a very good solution; especially for companies that already rely on Oracle database tools.

Tango

Alis Technologies
100 Alexis Nihon Boulevard, Suite 600
Montreal, Quebec, Canada H4M 2P2
Phone: 514-747-2547
Fax: 514-747-2561
WWW: http://www.alis.com

Tango is the perfect browser for the multilingual, multinational, or international company. The product is a multilingual browser created in partnership with Spyglass. The browser includes interfaces in English, French, Italian, German, Russian, Spanish, Dutch, Norwegian, Danish, Finnish, Swedish, Arabic, Chinese, Japanese, and Malay. Users can set the language option to query servers for different languages and continue doing so until they get a match; so someone who speaks English, French, and Spanish might set English as first preference, French second, and so on.

The product is made by Alis Technologies, which has specialized in language-based software applications for many years. The browser technology is based on the latest version of Spyglass' Mosaic, and Alis has added support for over 85 languages, including all the special character sets. If the Web is truly going to be world-wide, then it will be products like Tango that make it so.

 Right now a lot of developers on the Web are somewhat concerned about AOL customers who use AOL's custom browser when they access the Web. The browser, which has been improved, is still not half as good as MSIE or Navigator. This will all change within about a year, though, since AOL is going to use MSIE as its default browser.

Here Come SWATs

What is a SWAT, you ask? Well, it's an acronym—for Specialized Web Application Technology, or Specialized Web Access Tool—I made up for a newsletter article in the summer of 1996. I use it to describe any product that is built to access Web content outside of your standard browser. A perfect example would be PointCast, a product that works with many of the same standards as a browser, but isn't one. Other examples would be FreeLoader (which works in conjunction with your browser to download certain pages automatically while

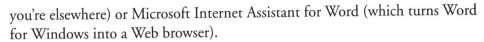

you're elsewhere) or Microsoft Internet Assistant for Word (which turns Word for Windows into a Web browser).

As more browser features become embedded directly in the OS, expect to see more SWATs focused on key tasks—and, because they're focused, expect them to do those jobs better and more easily than a plain browser might. All the while, though, these applications will be working with common Web technologies like Java, HTML, ActiveX, JavaScript, and VBScript.

Here is a roundup of some of the more common SWATs on the Web right now—but remember, they're just an indication of things to come.

FreeLoader

FreeLoader, Inc.
3299 K Street NW, Suite 300
Washington, DC 20007
Phone: 202-686-0660
Fax: 202-686-0685
WWW: http://www.freeloader.com

FreeLoader works in conjunction with Netscape to call up sites, download the pages, and store them for later reading—without the user being at the machine. Many users program FreeLoader (and its competitors, WebWhacker and RoundTable) to surf overnight, having the content ready in the morning. The idea is that browsing offline is less expensive and time-consuming than traditional methods.

PointCast

10101 N. De Anza Boulevard
Cupertino, CA 95014
Phone: 408-253-0894
WWW: http://www.pointcast.com

PointCast is probably the most famous SWAT created thus far. The product essentially acts just like a newswire machine—it pulls the latest news off the Web and displays it in a neat package on your desktop, and as a screensaver as well. Users can fill out profiles indicating the type and frequency of news they want to retrieve. PointCast saves news stories as HTML files and uses links in those files to fire up the PointCast (or user-defined) browser and link to the referenced site. In the meantime the user is exposed to a constant barrage of ads

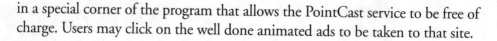

in a special corner of the program that allows the PointCast service to be free of charge. Users may click on the well done animated ads to be taken to that site.

TheDJ

Terraflex
172 Coronado Avenue
San Carlos, CA 94070
Phone: 415-595-1340
Fax: 415-596-8715
WWW: http://www.thedj.com

TheDJ is a SWAT with a very radio-like front end that uses the RealAudio SDK to simplify the entire process of listening to RealAudio music via the Web.

Create Your Own SWAT

Creating your own SWAT is much easier than it used to be. Lots of companies are creating the necessary tools—like OCXs, C libraries, embeddable browsers, and more—to enable programmers to create specialized Web access products. One thing to consider as a programmer is how you can create SWATS as components to software you already have. Such an application could have a custom Web browser portion to enable help files, or help visually impaired users dial up RealAudio files that read instructions out loud. I'll cover some of the specifics about designing your own SWATs later in this book.

The Internet Appliance Race

In Chapter 4 I wrote about how the Web would power appliances with digital information, much like electric lines provide them with energy. Well, the day when your coffee maker and TV set plug into the Web and the wall at the same time is a lot closer than you think. For Web developers, these new systems for accessing the Web will provide unique opportunities. Here's a quick rundown on the major new players.

Diba, Inc.

3355 Edison Way
Menlo Park, CA 94025
Phone: 415-482-3300
Fax: 415-482-3400
WWW: http://www.diba.com

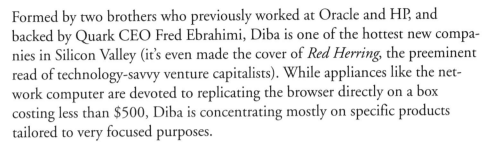

Formed by two brothers who previously worked at Oracle and HP, and backed by Quark CEO Fred Ebrahimi, Diba is one of the hottest new companies in Silicon Valley (it's even made the cover of *Red Herring*, the preeminent read of technology-savvy venture capitalists). While appliances like the network computer are devoted to replicating the browser directly on a box costing less than $500, Diba is concentrating mostly on specific products tailored to very focused purposes.

The idea is that consumer electronics companies and appliance manufacturers will work with Diba software to create smart devices which use the Web to retrieve and work with various information forms. One device Diba is working on would help the elderly keep in touch with their doctors; it might include access to medical records, prescription ordering, and direct links to emergency services. Its Diba Kitchen device plays audio CDs and has the ability to connect to various information, like recipes. Diba is also working with Zenith on a Web TV box called NetVision.

Diba has a developer program called the Diba Innovator's Alliance (DIA). The program includes a software development environment with an API simulator, Diba debugging tools, run-time tools, phone support, and other developer help through email, conferences, and newsletters. Once a device is developed, Diba has a developed a licensing structure for products that starts around $10 a unit down to $3, depending on the number of products you sell. (Of course, all products developed with Diba technology are subject to certification and must also brand themselves with Diba logos in addition to their own.) Because of its Quark backing, Diba is porting the QuarkImmedia viewer to its environment, which means that QuarkImmedia will be a major component of the authoring tools used to create Diba appliance content.

Diba is one of the two companies leading the overall Internet appliance movement (Navio from Netscape is the other). Certainly it can expect more focused competition from the likes of Microsoft and Apple in the near future, but right now Diba is making significant progress toward turning your favorite appliance into a Web client. Toast may never be the same.

Navio Communications, Inc.

477 Potrero Avenue
Sunnyvale, CA 94086
Phone: 408-328-0630

Fax: 408-328-0631
WWW: http://www.navio.com

Navio, a new sister company to Netscape, is working much like Diba is—developing a common architecture for consumer electronics companies to run Netscape-based browser products.

As I said earlier, Netscape is looking into making its software compatible with nontraditional platforms, including Nintendo Ultra-64 and other consoles, set-top boxes, PDAs, and Web appliances. Navio is now the company in charge of this effort, while Netscape concentrates on servers, PC-based software, and overall technology.

Marc Andreessen, Netscape's technology director, is currently leading an effort to break the entire browser product into compact parts. The components—display, security, networking, email, and so on—are being rewritten for as many different systems as possible, even using assembly to make each component smaller (an especially important need for noncomputer devices). As new platforms emerge, the plan would be to build a software package from the pieces needed for that given device.

Expect Navio to lead the charge with browsers for the various console devices, like Nintendo's Ultra-64, Sony's PlayStation, and Sega Saturn. Then expect it to start licensing software and developing devices much like those Diba is working on, except with Netscape technology at the core.

Geoworks

960 Atlantic Ave.
Alameda, CA 94501
Phone: 510-814-1660
Fax: 510-814-4250
WWW: http://www.geoworks.com

Geoworks has been around for a long time developing GUI OS environments; in fact, it got its start developing a Macintosh-like user environment for the Commodore 64 and Apple II. This experience transferred beautifully to the company's current work developing OS products for smart phones, PDAs, and other consumer digital devices (CDDs).

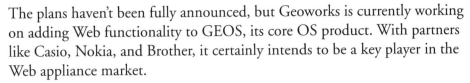

The plans haven't been fully announced, but Geoworks is currently working on adding Web functionality to GEOS, its core OS product. With partners like Casio, Nokia, and Brother, it certainly intends to be a key player in the Web appliance market.

The Geoworks Web site contains details on the GEOS development environment, the various products the company has under development with its partners, and how to support them.

Microsoft

One Microsoft Way
Redmond, WA 98052
Phone: 206-882-8080
Fax: 206-883-8101
WWW: http://www.microsoft.com

Microsoft may have been formed around the vision of a computer on every desk, but Bill Gates and his colleagues have broadened the concept of a computer to include numerous devices like wallet PCs and PDAs. Microsoft's effort in appliances is operating under the code name of Pegasus, and early reports suggest that it's mostly aimed at moving Windows OS technology into a form for smaller, less robust devices. The Web tie-ins may be limited at first, but you can bet that the ultimate plan is to compete heavily with Navio and Diba to build the software framework for any number of Web appliances.

Microsoft is retooling the Windows OS in much the same way as Netscape is reprogramming its Navigator browser—stripping the entire product down to essential components that will be pieced together depending on the device's requirements. The well-known Windows API model, though, guarantees that an ample supply of programming talent will be able to work with the products based on this platform.

The problem (or challenge, as Microsoft sees it) is that that Windows OS is a very big program, with a larger legacy than Netscape's to keep pace with. Though presumably this version won't need the same backward compatibility as the PC-based system, hardware companies may still be tempted to look at fresher systems like GEOS and Diba. Rest assured, though, that Microsoft will find a way to play in this market.

The Network Computer

There are two areas in the Web appliance movement that deserve special attention: the network computer and the Web TV. Their purpose is similar—to give people a Web-specific machine in place of a more expensive PC—but the two are somewhat different in terms of strategy, cost, and the major players.

The network computer, which became a hot concept in early 1996, is geared more toward corporate intranet environments. The idea is that instead of placing an expensive PC on the desk of every worker, companies would use network computers. (The Web TV industry is doing a better job of adjusting this same concept to work with the lower-resolution TV screen and existing home audiovisual equipment, not to mention providing the customer support and online services to complement the home market.)

The main proponents behind the network computer are Sun and Oracle. Both (especially Oracle) think corporations will use NCs to access huge databases of content and Java applets stored on servers. Instead of employees having Microsoft Excel on a powerful desktop CPU to calculate loan proposals, they could use a specific Java applet running on an intranet that would be accessed, used, and then discarded back to the server. Since Sun and Oracle are both huge network computing and database companies, it's no wonder they want to bring this particular future about.

Sun and Oracle, though, overreached when they started saying consumers would drop their PCs for these devices, and that eventually everyone would be using NCs. While the latter will certainly have a very big role, in many homes and companies a full-fledged PC is needed. Like videogame consoles do now, NCs will serve specialized markets, complement existing computer bases, and generally open the world up a little more to digital technology.

The following is a rundown on the key companies working specifically in this market.

Oracle

500 Oracle Parkway
Redwood City, CA 94065
Phone: 415-506-7000
Fax: 415-506-7200
WWW: http://www.oracle.com

Oracle CEO Larry Ellison is probably the biggest booster for the network-computer concept. Oracle is working directly to build the hardware model for NCs, in partnership with England-based Advanced RISC Machines (ARM).

The plan for Oracle is to design a reference specification that it will then license to other hardware manufacturers. The operating system being proposed for the Oracle NC spec is called Oracle NCOS. It's a small-footprint operating system with multimedia capabilities and support for Java, Adobe's Bravo technology, and Macromedia Shockwave.

The Oracle spec calls for an NC with at least 4 MB of RAM, a network interface, I/O interfaces, and an ARM 7500 processor. What's most striking about the NC is what it *doesn't* have: no hard drive, no 32 MB of RAM, no full-blast operating system, and no disk drives or expansion slots.

The NC reference profile also has detailed specifications for NCTVs (Web TVs) and a telephone NC.

Sun Microsystems

Sun Microsystems
2550 Garcia Avenue
Mountain View, CA 94043-1100
Phone: 415-960-1300
Fax: 415-969-9131
WWW: http://www.sun.com

Sun Microsystems has been considering several NC ideas for a while—in fact, it almost bought Apple Computer in 1995 in a bold move to develop the NC concept using Apple technology like Pippin. For now, though, Sun has aligned itself alongside Oracle in the NC movement and has built several prototypes of NC computers.

Sun sees the NC as an important device, because its Java technology is so important to the entire idea of the NC. If network computing becomes a major market, Sun will be at the heart of it due to Java alone.

NC Inc.

WWW: http://www.nc.com

Oracle has set up this full subsidiary to move the NC spec forward; it is meant to be the point of contact for companies building machines that comply with

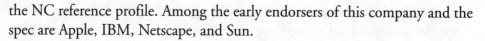

the NC reference profile. Among the early endorsers of this company and the spec are Apple, IBM, Netscape, and Sun.

Visiting this site will lead you to the documents that detail the NC reference profile and the backers of the product.

Acorn Computer Group PLC

Acorn House
645 Newmarket Road
Cambridge, England CB5 8PB
Phone: 44-12-23-725000
Fax: 44-12-23-725100
http://www.acorn.co.uk

This major computer company's new division, Acorn Network Computing, was set up to produce designs for NC devices. It works under contract for Oracle and has strong links with their sales, marketing, and technical teams. So Oracle is doing the spec, Acorn is making the machines, and ARM is producing the chip.

Acorn won the contract with Oracle against worldwide competition and will be producing a range of reference designs. Acorn Network Computing is also the source of products available through Acorn Online Media, Xemplar Education Ltd., and NChannel International Ltd.

Advanced RISC Machines Ltd.

90 Fulbourn Road
Cherry Hinton
Cambridge, England CB1 4JN
Phone: 44-12-23-400400
Fax: 44-12-23-400410
WWW: http://www.armltd.co.uk

Advanced RISC Machines (ARM) is helping many companies build NCs. It's the main partner with Oracle behind such systems, and its CPUs are at the heart of them. ARM is also a major player in smart phones.

Web TV

One of the largest aspects of the entire Web appliance movement is the combination of television and Web browsing. While some research has shown significant consumer interest for an Internet TV appliance, there are skeptics with their own research to back them up. Based on the deals that I know are taking place, however, I foresee considerable demand and numerous developments in the near future.

Why is WebTV important to developers? First of all, it promises to bring the Web to millions of customers who might not otherwise buy a computer. Second, many of these systems do not necessarily have browser interfaces or capabilities that developers have come to expect from their clients—if WebTV browsers take over, developers will need to adjust their plans to accommodate these systems. So here's a quick review of some of the more prominent deals.

Mitsubishi

5665 Plaza Drive
Cypress, CA 90630
Phone: 714-220-2500
WWW: http://www.mitsubishi.com

This Japanese electronics giant is planning on offering an Internet-capable TV in 1997. DiamondWeb would only have Internet service with a single remote, using Motorola's PowerPC microprocessor and Microware's DAVID software operating system.

Sony

550 Madison Avenue, 33rd Floor
New York, NY 10022
Phone: 212-833-6800
Fax: 212-833-6938
WWW: http://www.sony.com

Sony made a big splash when it said it would begin selling an Internet box for TVs in September 1996, making it the first major company to be "out of the box" with a box. The Sony WebTV Internet Terminal sells for $349 and hooks up to a regular TV set; a remote control device and optional keyboard will also work with the product. Access will be provided through WebTV Networks of Palo Alto, California, who developed the original technology and licensed it to Sony and Philips for production. Sony is also putting out a printer adapter that will allow the device to hook up to popular PC printers.

Microware

1900 North West 114th Street
Des Moines, IA 50325
Phone: 515-223-8000
Fax: 515-224-1352
WWW: http://www.microware.com

Iowa may not strike you as a hotbed for Web TV development, but it's the home of this key player in the Web TV world, whose DAVID operating system is used in many set-top boxes. Microware says it will target Internet TV as a key component for its OS-9 DAVID system software, and (as I noted earlier) Mitsubishi is signing on. Microware has already licensed Java and the HotJava Web browser from Sun to port to its OS. It has also licensed the Spyglass client SDK to build a customized browser.

Expect many more licensees if Microware's browser is strong enough to keep pace with PC-based systems and if the Mitsubishi or Sony products take off.

Gateway 2000

610 Gateway Drive
North Sioux City, SD 57049-2000
Phone: 605-232-2000
Fax: 605-232-2023
WWW: http://www.gw2k.com

Sony may be ready to debut the first major set-top box solution, but Gateway 2000 could be considered the first major player to put the TV, computer, and Web all in one unit; its Destination PC product combines a 31-inch TV set with a regular Pentium-based PC in an integrated package. According to a Gateway press release, "The Destination system was developed following extensive research to determine what consumers want from technology. The research showed that consumers want technology that allows people to share the experience."

Destination is expensive ($3,999 or more, depending on configuration), so this system is not in the same market as Web TVs. Unlike Sony's $349 box, though, the consumer is getting a full-fledged Windows 95 PC that can do far more than surf the Web—even if that and gaming are the obvious centerpiece reasons to own this system.

Gateway normally sells its products exclusively through its own direct mail system, but recently it announced deals with CompUSA and East Coast–based Nobody Beats the Wiz to market Destination through retail stores.

Bertelsmann and British Sky Television

Carl-Bertelsmann-Strasse 270
D-33311 Gutersloh, Germany
Phone: 49-(0)52-41-80-0
Fax: 49-(0)52-41-7-51
WWW: http://www.bertelsmann.de

German publishing giant Bertelsmann has announced that it will start selling Mediabox, a digital TV decoder that brings the Web to TV. Mediabox will come equipped with a modem to allow access to the Internet and is to be developed jointly by Bertelsmann and Canal Plus of France. Bertelsmann is also teaming with Bavaria-based Kirch, which has a similar device, to make their decoders compatible with each other and eventually develop a single solution.

British Sky Television, the pay-television unit of Rupert Murdoch's News Corporation, announced on the same day as Bertelsmann that it would begin marketing a set-top box system as well. While details are still sketchy, the company apparently plans a system just like that of Bertelsmann, and it is also in a TV network alliance with Kirch.

Apple Pippin

One Infinite Loop
Cupertino, CA 95014
Phone: 408-996-1010
Fax: 408-974-2113
WWW: http://www.pippin.apple.com

Apple began work on the Pippin technology in late 1994. The original idea was to use the Macintosh technology to create a new type of game console device. Well, something strange happened on the way to the marketplace— the Web exploded into public awareness, and Pippin became the closest thing to a network computer or set-top Internet box.

Pippin is essentially the Mac crammed into a computer box with a CD-ROM, a mouse, technology for solid TV display, 4 MB of RAM, and a stripped-down version of the Mac OS. The key to this product is having the existing Mac library of software and community of developers behind it. At the Electronic Entertainment Expo in Los Angeles in the spring of 1996, the Pippin booth was full of systems with keyboards surfing the Web with Netscape Navigator.

Apple has been somewhat coy about the final plans for Pippin, and many think the company's waiting to reposition it fully as a Web access product. Unfortunately, Pippin isn't a very good game system, and in many ways it's ahead of its time as a Web TV device (it's still a little expensive, too). Apple has had a terrible history of being far ahead of the curve; both the Macintosh itself and the Newton PDA suffered from being too cool too soon. I hope Pippin won't suffer the same fate, because as far as I'm concerned it's the best Web appliance on the market today.

WebTV Networks

305 Lytton Avenue
Palo Alto, CA 94301
Phone: 415-326-3240
Fax: 415-326-5277
WWW: http://webtv.net

This company specializes in developing set-top box products for use as Web terminals when hooked up to TV sets; it has designed a product and access service called WebTV and is licensing the technology to Sony and Philips. The two components of WebTV are the WebTV Reference Design and the WebTV Network.

The Reference Design is a set of standards that consumer electronics companies can license like Sony and Philips have done, and the WebTV Network will be a subscription-based online service. WebTV Networks says it has developed "advanced caching and transcoding features that improve the performance of the Internet, making the WebTV Internet browsing experience faster and more reliable than current browsing on an IBM-compatible or Macintosh personal computer."

Sony is already shipping its first product based on this technology, the Sony WebTV Internet Terminal.

ViewCall Europe PLC

Chesham House
150 Regent Street
London, England W1R 5FA
Phone: 44-(0)171-439-3187
Fax: 44-(0)171-734-4166
WWW: http://www.viewcall.com

This British company sells a product called WEBSter, which is a set-top box for enabling Web access from TVs. When WEBSter is turned on, it dials the closest ViewCall access number; after some startup screens with local services are displayed, you can surf the Web.

The system is based on an ARM processor and is using much of the technology based on ARM/Oracle's NC work. It uses a Netscape-compatible built-in browser and works with the basic SLIP, TCP/IP, and HTTP protocols.

IBM Network Station

Network Computing Devices, Inc.
350 North Bernardo Avenue
Mountain View, CA 94043
Phone: 415-694-0650
Fax: 415-961-7711
WWW: http://www.ncd.com

The IBM Network Station is a $700 PowerPC-built system using Navio-based Netscape software. It will be built by IBM and Network Computing Devices (a major leader in network terminals). IBM intends to aim the Network Station at corporate customers building wide-scale intranets.

What Is a Web Developer?

I started this chapter off by asking, "What Is a Web Client?" By now, your answer is probably different than what you thought it might be when you started reading.

So now comes a more complex question—what is a Web developer? After all, if the world of Web clients is about to take on many different forms, then so too will Web development. The core, I think, is this: Web developers will be people *who fundamentally know how to collect, package, and present information and services in a scaleable system through entirely digital means.*

The word scaleable is important because it implies that the developers know how to format the service to deliver it to many different types of Web devices, from those with huge color screens to those with just 5 LCD lines of text. For example, a phone book service would be developed in such a way that if a user accessed it from a personal computer using a Web browser it might display a picture and home page links, offer an Internet phone link, include a map to their house, and more. That same exact site accessed by a Web-capable phone with a simple LCD display would display a simple name, text address, and phone number, perhaps using a Java applet to scroll through the LCD screen to display more information. The site on the Web would be able to sense which device was attached to it and adjust its delivery to accommodate the specific client. All of this is doable today to some degree.

Clients will change, and developers will adjust. But the core role of developers—the people who figure out how to apply all this technology to change the way the world works—will remain the same.

CHAPTER 18

HTML, JavaScript, and VBScript are at the heart of a Web page's overall structure. Here are the tools and information you need to master them.

Resources for HTML, JavaScript, and VBScript

At the heart of the World Wide Web is a simple markup language called HTML. But is it so simple? The latest widely accepted spec, HTML 3.2, is far more powerful and complex than HTML ever used to be. It includes support for style sheets, tables, and frames; down the line are additions for math, precision layout, and more. In short, HTML is morphing from a simple markup language into an entire publishing system. Thankfully, there are several things you can do to stay at the top of the HTML game—I'll try to clue you in to some of them here.

HTML Editors

The centerpiece tools any Web developer needs are an HTML WYSIWYG editor and an HTML text editor. While a WYSIWYG editor helps you to get the basic layout down, most experienced developers also turn to an HTML text editor to handle things like JavaScript/VBScript editing, tightening up HTML code, and embedding other applets. Since I've yet to come across a package that truly did both jobs well, my advice is to get two top-notch applications instead of a mediocre one that tries to do everything. Many WYSIWYG editors let you set the text-editing option to the program of your choice.

At this point I could list pages of resources just for HTML editors, but there are only a few major contenders (and even then I haven't listed them all). I've settled for describing the most important HTML WYSIWYG and text editors, plus some sites that can provide further background on these products, as well as those I've had to leave out.

WYSIWYG Editors

PageMill & SiteMill (Mac & Windows)

Adobe Systems, Inc.
1585 Charleston Road
Mountain View, CA 94043-1225
Phone: 415-961-4400
Fax: 415-961-3769
WWW: http://www.adobe.com

PageMill, now available in version 2.0, is Adobe's frontline WYSIWYG Web editor. It's quite good, covering everything HTML can throw at you, as well as special support for Adobe Acrobat files, Shockwave and Java applets, and much more.

SiteMill, which is a Mac-only product (a temporary limitation, I hope) is PageMill plus a ton of features that help with overall site construction efforts. SiteMill helps you automatically rename, repair, and create links; it gives you full views of your site, listing all the pages and objects; and it can find errors like linking inconsistencies within your site and help you fix them.

Backstage (Mac & Windows)

Macromedia
600 Townsend Street
San Francisco, CA 94103-4945
Phone: 415-252-2000
Fax: 415-626-0554
WWW: http://www.macromedia.com

Marcomedia's Backstage is a fully integrated Web design system. The overall product is actually sold in four different flavors:

- *Backstage Designer*—The basic WYSIWYG HTML editor.

- *Backstage Designer Plus*—Adds Macromedia PowerApplets (a collection of customizable Shockwave and Java applications) and Macromedia xRes SE (an image editor).

- *Backstage Desktop Studio*—Added features include Backstage Manager (which gives you project management for your Web page development), Backstage Object Server (a system for creating custom Web pages generated on run-time information), and Backstage Objects-16 (which gives you database connectivity).

- *Backstage Enterprise Studio*—Combines all of the above with OBDC database connectivity.

FrontPage (Windows)

Microsoft
One Microsoft Way
Redmond, WA 98052-6399
Phone: 206-882-8080
Fax: 206-883-8101
WWW: http://www.microsoft.com/frontpage/

Microsoft purchased this product from a company called Vermeer for a ton of money. The product, renamed FrontPage and included as a standard element

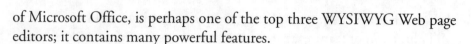

of Microsoft Office, is perhaps one of the top three WYSIWYG Web page editors; it contains many powerful features.

FrontPage includes an entire suite of site management tools, a strong database publishing system, and a built-in server system that can be used to set up a simple personal server.

NetObjects Fusion (Windows)

NetObjects, Inc.
2055 Woodside Road
Redwood City, CA 94061
Phone: 415-482-3200
Fax: 415-562-0288
WWW: http://www.netobjects.com

NetObjects Fusion, the newest kid on the Web editor block, is a great new entry. The product is very simple to use but extremely powerful. One aspect I like a lot about it is the excellent synergy it has between page design and locations and content you place on a page.

The entire system is WYSIWYG, and the layout system makes it almost ridiculously easy to place graphics, Shockwave and Java applets, sounds, and any type of content. Text can be placed in containers that can be rapidly moved around for quick layout decisions.

Fusion manages the design using a simple site-hierarchy interface or an outline view. Another neat feature is built-in graphics and styles for typical Web page items like banners, links, bullet points, and rules. The program allows you to determine the look and feel of your pages quickly by defining these items and customizing them from an extensive library of graphics.

Although most of the Web editors here excel in one way or another, NetObjects Fusion is certainly one of the top three I've used.

Navigator Gold (Windows)

Netscape Communications
501 E. Middlefield Road
Mountain View, CA 94043
Phone: 415-254-1900
Fax: 415-528-4125
WWW: http://home.netscape.com

Navigator Gold is a special edition of Netscape Navigator with a built-in WYSIWYG HTML editor. The basic editing package is very straightforward and easy to use, but not very powerful. I'm most likely to use it to hack out something simple, almost like a word processor. Aimed primarily at small business or intranet users, Navigator Gold is a solid solution for people who aren't creating Web pages every waking moment.

Home Page (Mac & Windows)

Claris Corporation
5201 Patrick Henry Drive
P.O. Box 58168
Santa Clara, CA 95052
Phone: 408-727-8227
WWW: http://www.claris.com

Claris Home Page is my favorite simple WYSIWYG editor. It works a lot like Navigator Gold, but it has a little more power—table editing, for instance, offers a few more options—and the overall package has a slightly better interface. While most major Web developers will use something else, Claris Home Page is one of the best low-end solution for either Macintosh or Windows.

Text Editors

HotDog Professional (Windows)

Sausage Software
660 Doncaster Road, Suite 1
Doncaster, VIC 3108
Australia
Phone: 613-9855-9800
WWW: http://www.sausage.com

HotDog is one of the best HTML code editors for Windows. It supports all of the major tags and has a super interface.

WebEdit 2.0 (Windows)

Nesbitt Software
c/o Link sandiego.com, Inc.
2251 San Diego Avenue, Suite A-141

San Diego, CA 92110
Phone: 619-220-8601
Fax: 619-220-8324
WWW: http://www.nesbitt.com

I only planned to mention one Windows-based HTML text editor, but I had such a hard time deciding whether HotDog or WebEdit was better that I decided to list them both. Ken Nesbitt's WebEdit 2.0 is a dynamite HTML text editor that is well worth the cost.

BBEdit (Macintosh)

Bare Bones Software, Inc.
P.O. Box 1048
Bedford, MA 01730
Phone: 508-651-3561
Fax: 508-651-7584
WWW: http://www.barebones.com

BBEdit is the premiere HTML text editor for the Macintosh. It's a very powerful package that will complement any WYSIWYG editor you get—in fact, if you already own one of the more popular WYSIWYG editors, you may qualify for a discount on BBEdit (check the company's Web site for details).

For a far more complete list of HTML editors, including those platforms other than Mac or Windows (which I've concentrated on here), check out these two Web sites:

W3C's List of World Wide Web and HTML Tools
http://www.w3.org/pub/WWW/Tools/

Mag's Big List of HTML Editors
http://union.ncsa.uiuc.edu/HyperNews/get/www/html/editors.html

This site also includes a bulletin-board discussion of various HTML editors.

HTML Converters and Assistants

Lots of companies have created add-ons or standalone utilities that let you convert existing documents and application content into HTML form for quick publishing on the Web.

Internet Assistants

Microsoft
One Microsoft Way
Redmond, WA 98052-6399
Phone: 206-882-8080
Fax: 206-883-8101
WWW: http://www.microsoft.com

At its Web site, Microsoft offers—for free—four excellent products for converting content from the popular programs that make up Microsoft Office to HTML:

- Word Internet Assistant—http://www.microsoft.com/msword/fs_wd.htm

- Excel Internet Assistant—http://www.microsoft.com/msexcel/fs_xl.htm

- PowerPoint Internet Assistant—http://www.microsoft.com/
  mspowerpoint/fs_ppt.htm

- Schedule+ Internet Assistant—http://www.microsoft.com/
  msscheduleplus/fs_sch.htm

Adobe File Utilities

Adobe Systems, Inc.
1585 Charleston Rd.
Mountain View, CA 94043-1225
Phone: 415-961-4400
Fax: 415-961-3769
WWW: http://www.adobe.com

This commercial package converts documents easily from many different formats—including most popular word processing, spreadsheet, database, and graphics formats—to each other and to HTML, while preserving the formatting and layout of the original documents. It's available for multiple platforms, including Mac, Windows, and Unix variants.

WWW Consortium HTML Converter Page
http://www.w3.org/pub/WWW/Tools/Filters.html

The WWW Consortium is run by Dr. Tim Berners-Lee, who invented HTML and HTTP—and thus the World Wide Web. The consortium helps to develop and determine the standards upon which the Web is based; one of those standards, of course, is HTML.

This page will lead you to a number of sites and pages that can help you locate or find out about converters, filters, and utilities to create HTML from existing content. This page has links to converters for many programs, so never assume there isn't a filter or converter before you've checked here.

General HTML Resources

WWW Consortium HTML Reference Page
http://www.w3.org/pub/WWW/MarkUp/MarkUp.html

This page helps you access everything about HTML that the W3C (which is shorthand for the World Wide Web Consortium) is up to, including a good reference manual. Every Web developer should bookmark this page, because it is the first to have solid information on new HTML additions and standards.

HTML Working Group
http://www.ics.uci.edu/pub/ietf/html/

This is the page for information about the HTML Working Group of the Internet Engineering Task Force, a large group of engineers and developers who work on the overall development of the Internet. While the W3C only concerns itself with the Web and is the working arm of a number of key Web creators, the IETF plays a part as well. This group works on issues concerning HTML, and you can find their work and discussions about it here.

Web-AID
http://www.webaid.com

This HTML site to end all HTML sites contains an excellent and complete HTML reference guide, a discussion forum, and lots of links and tools. It's sure to please even the most hardcore HTML nut.

Web/HTML Documentation and Developers' Resource
`http://www.utoronto.ca/webdocs/webinfo.html`

Ian Graham is the author of *The HTML Sourcebook*, one of the best-selling HTML guides around. Needless to say, this site has a lot of great information about HTML.

HTML Validation Tools
`http://www.khoral.com/staff/neilb/weblint/validation.html`

This nicely done page gives you summaries of and pointers to some of the best HTML checkers and lint tools.

Microsoft's HTML Reference Guide
`http://www.microsoft.com/workshop/author/newhtml/htmlr018.htm`

I chose to list this HTML reference guide because of its excellent formatting, and because there is a Word file version available for downloading.

HTML Style Sheets

The hottest new development in HTML is the advent of style sheets, which allow you to organize your site's pages along general guidelines, and then change these guidelines across hundreds of pages with just a simple correction to the style sheet.

Style sheets let you define what colors, fonts, sizes, and other attributes common HTML tags should have. When you assign a style sheet to your Web page, all of the defined tags—<H1>, for example—will contain all of this information automatically. And if you want to change the color of the 200 <H1> headings in your site from blue to green, for instance, all you'd have to do is change the definition in the style sheet instead of typing it into each individual tag. Obviously, this saves a lot of work.

I've really just touched on the surface of the power of style sheets. For more information, check out these two excellent Web pages.

A User's Guide to Style Sheets
`http://www.microsoft.com/workshop/author/howto/css-f.htm`

This explanation of HTML style sheets from the Microsoft Developer Network is well worth reading.

W3C's Cascading Style Sheets, Level 1 Specification
http://www.w3.org/pub/WWW/TR/WD-css1.html

This is the official HTML style sheet specification as developed by the World Wide Web Consortium.

JavaScript

JavaScript was first known as LiveScript to denote its connection to Netscape's LiveWire publishing platform, but Sun and Netscape eventually decided to call it JavaScript to build on the success of Java itself. JavaScript is also supposed to work directly to tie together HTML and Java applets using Netscape's LiveConnect technology.

Tutorials

JavaScript is not an easy language to learn; I pulled my hair out trying to learn this language for a chapter I wrote in another Coriolis book. The biggest problem is that JavaScript is hard to debug, and there wasn't a ton of information available at the time I was writing. Fortunately, now there are a few decent tutorials (and books, which I'll list later) that can help you.

Netscape's Java Tutorial
http://home.netscape.com/comprod/products/navigator/version_2.0/script/script_info/tutorial/main.htm

Introduction to JavaScript
http://www.webconn.com/java/javascript/intro/

Gordon McComb's JavaScript Column for JavaWorld
http://www.javaworld.com

webreference.com's JavaScript Tip of the Week
http://www.webreference.com/javascript/

This page delivers just what it promises: one handy JavaScript tip every week.

Resource Sites

JavaScript 411
http://www.freqgrafx.com/411/index.html

This is probably one of the top sites on JavaScript (and home to the JavaScript FAQ, which is listed next). Anyone working with JavaScript should check it out.

The JavaScript FAQ

`http://www.freqgrafx.com/411/jsfaq.html`

Even for those of you who are pretty fluent in JavaScript, this FAQ is an excellent read.

Official JavaScript Documentation

`http://home.netscape.com/eng/mozilla/2.0/handbook/javascript/index.html`

Download the official JavaScript documentation for your files here.

JavaScript Index

`http://www.c2.org/~andreww/javascript/`

A solid index of sites, example code, and other resources pertaining to JavaScript.

Netscape's JavaScript Resources Page

`http://home.netscape.com/comprod/products/navigator/version_2.0/script/script_info/index.html`

Netscape's JavaScript resource page could be better, but the quick links to their JavaScript examples are useful.

Gamelan's JavaScript Site

`http://www.gamelan.com/pages/Gamelan.javascript.html`

Gamelan is the number one resource site for Java, but it also has a first-rate set of links to JavaScript examples on the Web.

Live Software's JavaScript Resource Center

`http://jrc.livesoftware.com`

Books

Wherever possible, I've listed the Web page that supports the book (and usually has example code ready for demonstration).

The Complete Idiot's Guide to JavaScript by Aaron Weiss and Scott J. Walter (published by Que, 1996, ISBN 0-7897-0798-5), **http://www.mcp.com/que/new_users/cig-jscript/!start_here.html**

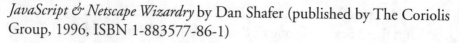

JavaScript & Netscape Wizardry by Dan Shafer (published by The Coriolis Group, 1996, ISBN 1-883577-86-1)

JavaScript by Example by Stephen Feather (published by Que, 1996, ISBN 0-7897-0813-2)

The JavaScript Handbook by Danny Goodman (published by IDG Books, 1996, ISBN 0-7645-3003-8), **http://www.dannyg.com/ recentwriting.html#Danny Goodman's JavaScript Handbook**

JavaScript How-To by George Pickering (published by Waite Group Press, 1996, ISBN 1-57169-047-6)

The JavaScript Sourcebook by Gordon McComb (published by Wiley Computer Publishing, 1996, ISBN 0-471-16185-3), **http://gmccomb.com/javascript/**

Plug-N-Play JavaScript by Kevin Ready, Paul Vachier, and Benoit Marsot (published by New Riders, 1996, ISBN 1-56205-674-3)

Special Edition Using JavaScript by Mark Reynolds and Andrew Wooldridge (published by Que, 1996, ISBN 0-7897-0789-6), **http://www.mcp.com/que/ et/se_javascript/**

JScript

JScript is an open implementation of JavaScript written by Microsoft, and it is also a version of JavaScript compatible with Microsoft's ActiveX scripting procedures. The JScript engine is available for Windows 3.1/95/NT and for PowerMac, as well as Windows NT for PowerPC and DEC Alpha chips.

As a software developer, you may want to license JScript from Microsoft to use as the scripting language in your own Web applications. The JScript engine is available from Microsoft in two forms: as a ready-to-run (compiled) binary for several platforms, or as source code.

Which one should you license? The choice depends on what you intend to do. To learn more, check out Microsoft's JScript home page at **http:// www.microsoft.com/JScript/**.

JScript FAQ

http://www.microsoft.com/JScript/us/JSmain/JSfaq.htm

If you're still confused about JScript and exactly what it is, then this FAQ on Microsoft's site should help clear things up.

VBScript

The thing to understand about VBScript is that while its syntax borrows a lot from Microsoft's Visual Basic programming language, it is not Visual Basic. Microsoft, though, has drawn from its deep experience with that very successful language to make VBScript both easy to use and quite powerful.

Microsoft announced VBScript shortly after Netscape debuted its LiveScript (later to become JavaScript) scripting language for Netscape Navigator. So VBScript wouldn't be labeled as a closed standard, Microsoft announced it would license the run-time or source code for the engine to any and all interested parties. Microsoft also has used VBScript to integrate HTML pages with its ActiveX technology; programmers can use VBScript to pass values and other information to ActiveX controls.

All in all, VBScript is an exciting product for Web developers to use. Not only are there many programmers who can quickly pick it up from their experience with Visual Basic, but it is the best way to work with ActiveX controls. In my opinion, it's also more powerful than JavaScript.

Microsoft's Official VBScript Home Page
http://www.microsoft.com/vbscript/

Microsoft's Official VBScript Documentation
http://www.microsoft.com/vbscript/us/vbsmain/vbsdocs.htm

Scribe
http://www.km-cd.com/scribe/

Scribe is one of the best sites so far—other than Microsoft's own site—for finding out about VBScript. It contains lots of information and links to sites using VBScript. (You can add your site to their growing list.)

inquiry.com's Visual Basic Script Central
http://www.inquiry.com/vbscentral/

inquiry.com is the leading site for information of concern to computer power users and professionals. Although the pickings at the VBSCentral area were spare when I visited it, expect this page to grow tremendously to match the rest of the site's high standards.

Books

Building Web Applications Using VBScript by Joe Galloway (published by New Riders, 1996, ISBN 1-56205-666-2)

The Comprehensive Guide to VBScript: Building Live, Interactive Pages on the Web by Richard Mansfield (published by Ventana, 1996, ISBN 1-56604-470-7)

Inside VBScript and ActiveX by Chris Goddard and Steve Waterhouse (published by New Riders, 1996, ISBN 1-56205-651-4)

Mastering VBScript by Chris Goddard and Mark White (published by Prima Publishing, 1996, ISBN 0-76150-769-8)

Teach Yourself VBScript in 21 Days by Keith Brophy and Timothy Koets (published by Sams, 1996, ISBN 1-57521-120-3)

VBScript by Bill Orvis (published by Prima Publishing, 1996, ISBN 0-76150-684-5)

Web Page Scripting Techniques: JavaScript, VBScript and Advanced HTML by Hayden Development (published by Hayden Books, 1996, ISBN 1-56830-307-6)

Web Scripting with Visual Basic by Scott Holzner (published by M & T Books, 1996, ISBN 1-55851-488-0)

CHAPTER 19

Despite other solutions, CGI is still the life force behind most Web sites.

CGI Scripting Resources

What Is CGI?

CGI stands for Common Gateway Interface, and it's a way to create programs that let the user and the server interact. The most common examples are HTML forms where the user enters and submits information that the server either catalogs or uses to respond with a customized Web page.

The key word, of course, is *common*. Because the CGI spec defines how information should be passed back to servers, CGI scripts are a universal open Web standard that all compliant servers understand. Scripts can be readily reused over and over.

A CGI script can be thought of as nothing more than any program that is run on the server when a user completes a triggering action. CGI scripts can be written in C/C++, Pascal, Delphi, or Visual Basic, but most of the examples you'll see on the Web are written in Perl, a language many people may not be familiar with.

Perl stands for Practical Extraction and Report Language, and it's a long-established Unix scripting language. Since the largest portion of the Web's servers are Unix based, it's no wonder that Perl quickly became the major language for CGI. Indeed, it is so prevalent that I'm sure some people believe you can't write CGI with anything but Perl.

CGI Vs. Server APIs

At first, CGI was the only way to work dynamically with a Web server. As newer, more commercially designed servers have come about, though, server-specific APIs like Netscape's API (NSAPI) and Microsoft's Internet Information Server API (IISAPI) and other alternatives have been published to increase the speed and security of backend server programs.

A CGI program can be quite slow relative to a flashier C++ program that is directly plugged into a custom server API. Those custom APIs, however, represent more proprietary systems than CGI; there's a reason that none of those API names begin with the word *common*. While the two major examples, NSAPI and IISAPI, are trying to get broader acceptance, CGI is still the most universally workable solution.

The makers of the server systems generally offer Web pages comparing their company's API to CGI scripts, although while reading them you should always keep in mind that these companies are trying to sell you on their API. The following are some of the best comparison pages to look at.

Robert Denny's Overview of CGI, SSI, and APIs
http://solo.dc3.com/wsdocs/extending.html

This part of O'Reilly WebSite developer Robert Denny's home page has a nice overview of the APIs versus CGI scripts.

The NSAPI Vs. the CGI Interface
http://home.netscape.com/newsref/std/nsapi_vs_cgi.html

Netscape's answer to this question is available here.

Microsoft IISAPI Vs. the CGI Interface
http://www.microsoft.com/infoserv/docs/iisperf.htm#application

This document is actually the Microsoft IISAPI versus the world (what did you expect?), but I've referenced you directly to the portion of the document concerning CGI.

General CGI Resources

There are some very good general references and tutorials about CGI, and I've rounded up the best for you right here.

The NCSA Guide to the Common Gateway Interface
http://hoohoo.ncsa.uiuc.edu/cgi/

This is the NCSA site that defines and references the CGI interface. On its FTP server at **ftp://ftp.ncsa.uiuc.edu/Web/httpd/Unix/ncsa_httpd/cgi/** there is a large collection of useful CGI scripts.

The WWW Common Gateway Interface Version 1.1
http://www.ast.cam.ac.uk/~drtr/cgi-spec.html

This page, another definition and reference to the CGI interface, helps you understand the specification for CGI 1.1.

The Web Developer's Virtual Library: CGI
http://www.stars.com/Vlib/Providers/CGI.html

An immense amount of CGI resources. From pointers to FAQs, tutorials, archives of scripts, and scripting tools, this site is a masterful resource for CGI programmers.

Sanford Morton's CGI Resources

http://www.halcyon.com/sanford/cgi/index.html

Perhaps one of the best all-around CGI resources I've found, this site is well written and contains excellent tutorial help. It also offers lots of links to example scripts and other tutorial help, and a Perl workshop as well.

CGI Programming 101

http://www59.metronet.com/dev/class/

A growing online site that offers a tutorial on CGI programming.

CGI Tutorial

http://agora.leeds.ac.uk/nik/Cgi/start.html

A well-done primer with exercises on CGI scripting.

A CGI Programmer's Reference

http://www.best.com/~hedlund/cgi-faq/

A very informative primer and FAQ on CGI; this is a good solid introduction to the complexities of CGI programming.

W3C's CGI: Common Gateway Interface

http://www.w3.org/pub/WWW/CGI/

The World Wide Web Consortium's CGI reference page.

Information About CGI Security

Because CGI programs are being run on your server, the CGI system is a very tempting target for nonvirtuous individuals seeking to cause trouble with your site. There is a lot you can do to protect yourself, though, as you'll learn by checking out these resources.

Paul Phillips' CGI Security Links

http://www.cerf.net/~paulp/cgi-security/

Paul Phillips of CERFNet has put together a small but potent reading list of CGI security information on the WWW.

The World Wide Web Security FAQ/CGI Security FAQ

http://www-genome.wi.mit.edu/WWW/faqs/www-security-faq.html

The security issues raised by CGI scripts are extremely important. Many holes in server security are a result of CGI security problems. This FAQ will help you understand and plug those security holes.

Archives of Plug-and-Play Script Examples

Web Engineer's Toolbox
`http://www59.metronet.com/cgi/`

A collection of ready-to-run Unix Perl CGI scripts, plus links to other Perl/CGI resources.

Matt's Script Archive
`http://worldwidemart.com/scripts/`

Matt's Script Archive contains many *free* Perl and CGI scripts to spice up your pages. Each script link leads to a page where you can download the script, look at demonstrations and working examples of that program, and check out the FAQ for that script. Who says you can't get something for nothing anymore?

Windows-Specific CGI Resources

Because there are so many different programming languages available for Windows, there are a lot of solid options for doing CGI programming on that platform. I've tried to find complementary resources for programming CGI scripts in most of the major Windows-based languages.

Robert B. Denny's Home Page
`http://solo.dc3.com`

Robert B. Denny is the author of O'Reilly's WebSite server product—a product that is built to the core for Windows programmers and allows for extensive CGI scripting with Visual Basic, a tool lots of Windows programmers love. On his home page you'll find lots of information about using VB for server scripting with WebSite and more.

Welcome to Delphi, CGI, and WebSite 101
`http://www.2solve.com/cgi101.htm`

A tutorial site for programmers who would like to create CGI scripts with Delphi.

Delphi CGI Component Package (Version 1.0)
`http://www.programmers.net/mirrors/DSP/free7.html`

On this page you can download a free components package for Delphi CGI programming that works with several Windows-based servers like O'Reilly's WebSite.

CGI Scripting Resources for Windows NT
`http://www.primenet.com/~buyensj/ntwebsrv.html`

This site not only has a lot of Windows NT resources for CGI buffs, but is an all-around major site for anything concerning NT and Web servers. A must bookmark!

AppleScript CGI Resources

CGI programmers who are using Macintosh servers and want to use Apple's AppleScript language to create CGI programs can find help and resources at the following places.

Felipe's AppleScript CGI Examples
`http://edb518ea.edb.utexas.edu/scripts/cgix/cgix.html`

A really good archive of AppleScript CGI programs, plus links to other AppleScript and CGI pages.

Extending WebSTAR with AppleScript
`http://www.comvista.com/net/www/lessons/START_HERE.html`

WebSTAR is a commercially available Mac server from Quarterdeck; this tutorial shows you how to create CGI programs for it using AppleScript.

Perl Resources

As I said earlier, Perl is the major language used to write CGI programs. I've rounded up some general resources where you can find out more about a language most non–Web-savvy developers might not even have heard of.

PERL.COM
`http://www.perl.com/perl/index.html`

A very good resource on the world of Perl.

The Perl FAQ
http://www.cis.ohio-state.edu/hypertext/faq/usenet/perl-faq/top.html

Perl has been around the Unix world for some time, but most Web designers aren't very familiar with it. Thus, this Perl FAQ could be very useful to the beginning CGI programmer.

Index of Perl/HTML Archives
http://www.seas.upenn.edu/~mengwong/perlhtml.html

This excellent index will lead you to many resources on Perl.

Freeware CGI Tools

The majority of freeware associated with CGI consists of sample scripts, but the following site has links to other equally useful free CGI-related tools.

Homeworld's Free CGI Tools
http://www.homeworlds.com/freesoft/cgitools.htm

This awesome resource includes lots of links to downloadable implementations of Perl for various platforms, Perl scripts, C++ CGI libraries, and database CGI tools.

Commercial Products

The majority of CGI resources are freeware or shareware products. There are several major commercial-oriented CGI resources, however, that I found for people who want to attach a company to their CGI scripting development.

Perl for Windows
hip communications, inc.
#350-1122 Mainland
Vancouver, BC V6B 5L1
Canada
Phone: 604-606-4600
Fax: 604-654-9881
WWW: http://www.perl.hip.com

Hip Communications maintains a port of Perl 5 for Windows 32 (including binaries for other hardware platforms that support Windows NT). The entire

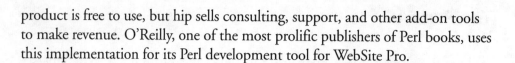

product is free to use, but hip sells consulting, support, and other add-on tools to make revenue. O'Reilly, one of the most prolific publishers of Perl books, uses this implementation for its Perl development tool for WebSite Pro.

FastCGI

Open Market
245 First Street
Cambridge, MA 02142
Phone: 617-621-9500
Fax: 617-621-1703
WWW: http://www.fastcgi.com

FastCGI is a new version of the CGI specification that was developed by Open Market, a server software company. The idea is to bring CGI closer to the level of faster custom server API programs while maintaining the open, language-independent system that makes CGI so useful.

It's being proposed as an open extension to CGI, and server software companies can license the engine for free for their own software—Open Market and the NCSA server team have already incorporated it, and there is an Apache version as well. The World Wide Web Consortium is looking over the FastCGI proposal for adoption as a fully endorsed element of its next-generation CGI specification.

You can find out everything there is to know about FastCGI here, including white papers, language reference, sample scripts, and more.

WebBatch

Wilson WindowWare
2701 California Avenue SW, Suite 212
Seattle, WA 98116
Phone: 206-938-1740
Fax: 206-935-7129
WWW: http://webbatch.windowware.com

Wilson WindowWare's WebBatch is an easy-to-learn CGI scripting language for NT Web servers that is as easy as programming DOS batch files or in Basic. If Perl isn't your cup of tea and C/VB or Delphi are just too much, then WebBatch may be a good solution. Check out the Web page for demos and information.

CGI*Star

WebGenie Software Pty Ltd.
P.O. Box 149, Rundle Mall
SA 5000
Australia
Phone: 61-8-8303-5020
Fax: 61-8-8303-4355
WWW: http://www.webgenie.com

CGI*Star helps you automatically create CGI scripts without having to know any programming language. The program creates the scripts in Perl, so Perl programmers can use it to rapidly put together a framework before jumping in on their own.

CGI*Star is available in Windows 3.1/95 and Windows NT versions, and the scripts it generates can be used on either Unix or Windows NT servers.

PolyForm

O'Reilly Software
101 Morris Street
Sebastopol, CA 95472
Phone: 800-998-9938
Fax: 707-829-0104
WWW: http://software.ora.com

PolyForm is a GUI software tool that helps Windows users easily create Web forms. Each form can be set up to do all sorts of transactional operations, like customer feedback, surveys, and order forms. The product is a good complement to your CGI programming. It works with any Win-CGI 1.1 or IISAPI-compliant server (such as O'Reilly's own WebSite package).

Clickable Software

P.O. Box 10233
San Rafael, CA 94912
Phone: 415-456-5582
Fax: 415-456-4018
WWW: http://www.clickables.com

Clickable, a startup geared toward becoming a one-stop shop for CGI scripts, makes plug-and-play CGI software. It builds custom scripts as well as a large pool of scripts for cut-and-paste development. All of the scripts are designed to be as generic as possible, but in such a way as to be rapidly customized to your specific needs. All of the Clickables scripts come with sample HTML code and templates for you to build customized forms to work with them. The company will even install them directly on your server for you.

Books

Wherever possible, I've listed Web pages associated with the books.

About CGI

60 Minute Guide to CGI Programming With Perl 5 by Robert Farrell (published by IDG Books, 1996, ISBN 1-56884-780-7)

Advanced HTML & CGI Writer's Companion by Keith Schengili-Roberts (published by AP Professional, 1996, ISBN 0-12623-540-6)

The CGI Book by William E. Weinman (published by New Riders, 1996, ISBN 1-56205-571-2), **http://www.cgibook.com**

CGI by Example by Jeffrey Dwight (published by Que, 1996, ISBN 0-78970-877-9)

CGI Developer's Guide by Eugene Eric Kim (published by Macmillan Computer Publishing, 1996, ISBN 1-57521-087-8)

CGI How-To by Stephen Asbury (published by Waite Group Press, 1996, ISBN 1-57169-028-X)

CGI Manual of Style by Robert McDaniel (published by Ziff-Davis Press, 1996, ISBN 1-56276-397-0)

CGI Primer Plus for Windows by Mike Heins and Nathan Vijay Patwardhan (published by Waite Group Press, 1996, ISBN 1-57169-025-5)

CGI Programming in C & Perl by Thomas Boutell (published by Addison-Wesley, 1996, ISBN 0-20142-219-0)

CGI Programming on the World Wide Web by Shishir Gundavaram (published by O'Reilly & Associates, 1996, ISBN 1-56592-168-2)

CGI Programming Unleashed by Daniel Berlin (published by Sams, 1996, ISBN 1-57521-151-3)

Developing CGI Applications with Perl by John Deep and Peter Holfelder (published by John Wiley & Sons, 1996, ISBN 0-47114-158-5)

Foundations of World Wide Web Programming with HTML & CGI by Ed Tittel, Mark Gaither, Sebastian Hassinger, and Mike Erwin (book and CD-ROM published by IDG Books Worldwide, 1995, ISBN 1-56884-703-3)

HTML 3.2 & CGI Unleashed by John December and Mark Ginsburg (published by Sams, 1996, ISBN 1-57521-177-7), **http://www.december.com/works/wdg.html**

Introduction to CGI/Perl: Getting Started with Web Scripts by Steven E. Brenner and Edwin Aoki (published by M & T Books, 1996, ISBN 1-55851-478-3)

Using CGI by Jeffrey Dwight, Michael Erwin, Tobin Anthony, and Danny Brands (published by Que, 1996, ISBN 0-78970-740-3)

Web Programming Secrets with HTML, CGI, and Perl by Ed Tittel (published by IDG Books, 1996, ISBN 1-56884-848-X)

Webmaster's Building Internet Database Servers with CGI by Jeff Rowe (published by New Riders, 1996, ISBN 1-56205-573-9)

About Perl

Learning Perl by Randal L. Schwartz, with foreword by Larry Wall (published by O'Reilly & Associates, 1995, ISBN 1-56592-042-2)

Perl 5 Desktop Reference by Johan Vromans (published by O'Reilly & Associates, 1996, ISBN 1-56592-187-9)

Perl 5 How-To by Mike Glover, Aidan Humphreys, and Ed Weiss (published by Waite Group Press, 1996, ISBN 1-57169-058-1)

Perl by Example by Ellie Quigley (published by Prentice Hall, 1994, ISBN 0-13122-839-0)

Programming Perl by Larry Wall and Randall L. Schwartz (published by O'Reilly & Associates, 1991, ISBN 0-937175-64-1)

Teach Yourself Perl in 21 Days by Dave Till (published by Sams, 1994, ISBN 0-67230-586-0)

CHAPTER 20

*Dynamic Internet-
based applets are at
the heart of powerful
Web development.*

Java and ActiveX
Resources

What Is Java?

Java is a specialized language used to create programs that can be downloaded and run directly from the World Wide Web. Because these programs run within applications (such as Web browsers) on any number of platforms, Java itself is hardware-independent. The language was originally created in the 1980s by Sun Microsystems as a development language (code-named Oak) for interactive television systems, which were all the rage at the time. As interactive TV systems failed and the Internet took off instead, the Oak development team turned its attention toward reapplying its system to the Web, and thus Java was born.

Instead of being tailored to a specific platform, compiled Java code runs on an imaginary "virtual machine." Multiple-platform applications that support the Java Virtual Machine code therefore can read and execute Java "applets" on many different type of computers. (Note that the Java Virtual Machine code has to be ported specifically to each platform by the application.)

So Java is really a software technology broken into two parts: Java code, and the Java Virtual Machine program. This combination creates a write-once, read-many situation that operates to the platform-independent principles behind the Web itself.

What Is ActiveX?

Like Java, ActiveX is used to create downloadable applets, but it uses a very different route to achieve this same result. The most important difference is that ActiveX is an object technology, not a language. As an object technology, it defines how programmers can create applications in any language that can work like Java applets do.

ActiveX controls are derived from Object Linking and Embedding (OLE) controls, a technology that Microsoft developed to create programmable objects that would run within more than one application in the Windows operating system. For example, an OLE control that creates charts from data could be used with Word, Excel, PageMaker, or whatever other program could provide the proper framework and data.

Microsoft has since repositioned OLE controls for the Web and renamed the technology ActiveX. The appealing thing about ActiveX controls, as Microsoft points out, is that you can write them as you would any other programming language, without learning the ins and outs of a whole new language, which Java requires. The downside is that ActiveX controls are not as universally supported in playback as Java applets are—though Microsoft is trying to do the necessary ports to other platforms to change that.

The Java API

The Java API, as Sun is developing it, consists of many components. Up until recently, most people were working only with the Java Core API, but Sun is bringing out a whole suite of APIs that give Java incredible new capabilities.

One of these new APIs is Java Beans, which lets programmers create applets that can work like objects and communicate with one another. The Java Media API will add advanced 2D, 3D, telephony, animation, and collaborative technologies to Java. A Java Server API helps in creating back-end server programs; Java Wallet adds an API for secure transactions and commerce; and the Java Security API and Enterprise API give developers Java-level tools for working with databases.

Some of these APIs are not finished yet, and they will still have to be ported to the different platforms once they are done. As soon as they are complete, however, Java will be even more powerful than it is now, so keep your eyes peeled for news about the progress of Java APIs.

Java Beans

Because Java applets exist in a world of objects, they need to be able to work together with other objects—but, until now, they really couldn't. Java Beans is the technology that will allow non-Java object systems to interact with Java. It also enhances programmers' ability to port their Java code to other projects for other uses (something that is still very much a chore in C, even with well-written pieces of code).

Similarly, ActiveX is actually based on Microsoft's component object model (COM) for Windows. A COM tells programmers how to create applications for a certain environment that can interact with other applications (and other COMs) without having the underlying code reprogrammed. In the ideal future of COMs, if we wanted a word processor that had cut-and-paste, spell checking, printing, and HTML editing functions—but not, say, a thesaurus or indexing—we'd just glue together the appropriate objects to create exactly what we wanted. And because the components would all know how to talk to one another and work together, we wouldn't have to reprogram the whole application just to add a new function or two; instead, we'd just add new objects.

Remember, this is how the Web itself works: as a framework for delivering multiple objects that work in unison, regardless of their origins. This can only happen, though, if there is a standard way of defining how objects can interact with each other. The Java Beans technology is Sun's attempt to create such a standard for Java.

Objects created using Java Beans—known as "beans," of course—can vary greatly in size and complexity, from simple animations to entire word processors. No matter how large or small they are, however, they can be combined together to create whole new programs.

The Battle for the Market

Although Microsoft is pushing ActiveX hard, with the help of hundreds of small developers and companies that are providing a huge library of ActiveX controls, so far Netscape and Sun have been very worried and resistant to the technology. In addition, many Web developers are staying away, afraid that ActiveX will remain a closed system. Recognizing that keeping a tight grip on the technology could jeopardize its existence, Microsoft has said it will turn control of ActiveX over to a public consortium. One step toward easing the fears would occur if Microsoft ever does provide support for ActiveX to non-Windows platforms.

Because they see so much of their individual futures riding on who controls Internet technologies, the major Web companies are not cooperating to provide clear direction to programmers and the public. Sun is promoting Java Beans, while Microsoft has put its weight behind ActiveX, and Apple is pushing OpenDoc, a similar object technology. Netscape likes Java Beans, but it's also offering its LiveConnect technology. In short, the whole situation is a mess.

For now, this means a fight for customers and supporters until the scales are tipped clearly in favor of one solution—probably ActiveX or Java only, or a symbiotic combination. If Microsoft is successful with ActiveX, I expect that at some point we'll see a fully supported Java/ActiveX combination system for the Internet. But since I think Java Beans will survive, too, why couldn't various Java Beans build up an ActiveX-compliant control? Both have so much to offer that it seems to be the most useful outcome.

 Microsoft has prepared a nice explanation of exactly how it sees Java and ActiveX working together. You can find it at **http:// www.microsoft.com/activex/actx-gen/ajava-f.htm**.

HotJava

HotJava is a browser, written entirely in Java, that also runs Java applets. And because it is written in Java, of course, the browser can run on any Java virtual machine. You can read more about it at **http://java.sun.com/HotJava/index.html**.

Making Java Faster

There are two inherent problems with Java. First, Java applets are relatively slow in terms of their downloading time. Second, it's not the world's fastest language in terms of execution either, because the compiled code is not native to the system it actually executes on. Fortunately, a new type of Virtual Machine technology contains elements designed specifically to speed up these two aspects of Java.

First, the downloading is sped up by allowing programmers to send through Java class libraries as if they are one gigantic file rather than dozens of smaller files. (Even when they are zipped, downloading 30 separate class libraries isn't as fast as downloading them in a group.)

The second and more important aspect improves Java's execution speed significantly through "just-in-time" (JIT) compiling. As a language, Java is designed so well that it's easy to compile the code into a form that can run directly on the processor downloading the application. Once the application has been downloaded and compiled to a more native form, execution time drops dramatically. Several companies are already working on JIT technology, led by Borland with its Latté engine (which is being licensed to Netscape) and Microsoft with its Jiffy engine (for Internet Explorer).

What If I'm Not a Programmer?

Although good programming knowledge is almost required if you're going to create your own ActiveX controls or Java applets, you don't have to be a

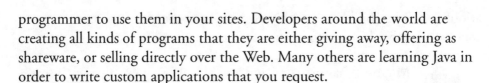

programmer to use them in your sites. Developers around the world are creating all kinds of programs that they are either giving away, offering as shareware, or selling directly over the Web. Many others are learning Java in order to write custom applications that you request.

Once the programming is done, placing an ActiveX control or Java applet on a site isn't very hard, and even then there are tools to help. Although many Java applets and ActiveX controls don't need scripts at all, they may be important in some cases, so you probably should learn a little bit about the two major scripting languages, VBScript and JavaScript. Most applets and controls will come with some sample scripting code to help you figure out how to create scripts if they're needed for a control. There are also a host of products coming out that help entry-level programmers and non-programmers create their own Java applications.

As more and more software developers learn Java, in fact, expect the majority of Web site builders to be experts only about the applets themselves rather than the Java language. There will be thousands of applets and controls to choose from to work into your site. Already, because ActiveX is really the Microsoft OLE repackaged, there are hundreds of vendors selling ActiveX controls for your use.

How Do I Write Java Applets or ActiveX Controls?

There are two primary routes for writing your own Java applets or ActiveX controls. The first is to use what I call a programming environment—that is, one of the basic programming language systems. I know of five major authoring environments that allow you to create compiled Java applets; for ActiveX controls, you can use any language as long as the program works according to the ActiveX specification.

The second type of development environment is what I call an authoring system. These systems try to hide the programming side of application development, often by using a totally visual system to create programs. (Some may have programming involved in order to let users go beyond the power of the non-programming capabilities of the product.) While ActiveX doesn't lend itself well to pure authoring system development, Java does, and there are several authoring systems available for the latter.

Java Programming Environments

Here are summaries of the five major Java programming environments I've come across.

The Java Development Kit (JDK)

Sun Microsystems
2550 Garcia Avenue
Mountain View, CA 94043-1100
Phone: 415-960-1300
Fax: 415-969-9131
WWW: http://www.sun.com

The original Java development environment created by Sun, the JDK is now developed and distributed by Sun's JavaSoft subsidiary. It's available for SPARC Solaris, Windows NT/95, and Macintosh, and also from the Open Group for AIX, HP-UX, Digital Unix, NCR SysV, and Sony NEWS, making it the most widespread development system in a platform sense.

You can download the JDK from JavaSoft's Web site (**http://www.javasoft .com**), as well as a host of documentation in a variety of formats.

Visual J++ (Jakarta)

Microsoft Corporation
One Microsoft Way
Redmond, WA 98052
Phone: 206-882-8080
Fax: 206-883-8101
WWW: http://www.microsoft.com

At first glance, it appears that ActiveX and Java are unrelated—one is a programming language, and the other is an OS technology specification. As Microsoft has demonstrated, however, Java is also a perfect language for creating and using ActiveX controls themselves. Microsoft has facilitated this hybrid form with the debut of its Java programming environment, Visual J++ (regrettably abandoning the product's cool code name, Jakarta, along the way).

J++ has been modeled after Microsoft's Visual C++ programming system, and it's an awesome Java development environment in its own right, as well as the first one to support ActiveX programming with Java. Read more about it and download betas and patches from **http://www.microsoft.com/java/**.

Latté

Borland
100 Borland Way
Scotts Valley, CA 95066
Phone: 408-431-1000
Fax: 408-431-3249
WWW: http://www.borland.com

While Borland's Java development environment isn't yet available as I write this, it's important enough for me to tell you what I know about it. Latté incorporates a visual design environment, a very fast Borland quality compiler, Java Database Connectivity (JDBC), and much more. As a result, it's become a very highly anticipated programming system for Java.

The Latté visual development system is modeled after Borland's Delphi programming system, which was widely praised for its visual environment. You can even build Java applets by visually dropping software components onto a form, then tying them together with small pieces of Java code.

Drawing on its extensive history of database application development, Borland has loaded Latté with support for databases. One cool feature is that all of the database library code is written in Java itself, which makes integration much easier.

Visual Café

Symantec
10201 Torre Avenue
Cupertino, CA 95014
Phone: 408-253-9600
Fax: 408-253-3968
WWW: http://www.symantec.com

Symantec's Visual Café combines Java with an interactive design environment that integrates text-based and graphical tools, letting either one take the lead. Edit a value in a source code file, and see the size or location of a graphical control change as soon as that file is saved. Or use your mouse to stretch or move the control, and see the number in your source code change to match it.

Metrowerks CodeWarrior

Metrowerks, Inc.
2201 Donley Drive, Suite 310
Austin, TX 78758
Phone: 800-377-5416
Fax: 512-873-4900
WWW: http://www.metrowerks.com

Metrowerks is the leading programming tool vendor for Macintosh and PowerPC-based systems. Its CodeWarrior development environment has been praised by developers, and it has created CodeWarrior tools for a variety of languages and platforms (though the company is best known for its Mac tools). Now Metrowerks has brought CodeWarrior to bear on Java, giving Mac Java programmers an alternative to Symantec's Café.

Metrowerks' Java includes an electronic version of *Learn Java on the Macintosh* by Barry Boone, as well as a full suite of electronic tutorials.

Applet Designer for Visual Basic 4.0

TVObjects
29 Emmons Drive
Princeton, NJ 08540
Phone: 609-514-1444
Fax: 609-514-1004
WWW: http://www.tvobjects.com

Applet Designer is a VB4 add-in that allows Visual Basic developers to convert their code directly to Java. If you're a VB programmer interested in becoming a Java programmer literally overnight, you've got to check out this product.

Java Authoring

A slew of products have come out to make creating your own applets in Java much easier than learning to code Java. While programming is required to build the most robust applets, a lot of what people want to do with Java can be done without direct programming. Here are the major packages that are being used for Java authoring.

Liquid Motion (Win95/NT, Mac, and Solaris)

Dimension X, Inc.
181 Fremont Street, Suite 120
San Francisco, CA 94105
Phone: 415-243-0900
Fax: 415-243-0997
WWW: http://www.dimensionx.com

In 1995 Dimension X developed a product called JAM, which allowed people to create simple animations in Java. That product has been refined and extended into Liquid Motion, an excellent non-programming tool for creating Java applets geared toward animations and other simple multimedia productions.

The system is easy to use, with a simple scene-based editing scheme. Users add images, text, audio, and behaviors to create animations; path-based tools allow you to tell a simple graphic to move from one end of the screen to the other with just a few clicks. Once you're done, Liquid Motion will create all the HTML code and compile the applet for insertion on your page.

Liquid Motion also offers an API that Java programmers can use to create new features.

Jamba (Windows)

AimTech
20 Trafalgar Square
Nashua, NH 03063
Phone: 603-883-0220
Fax: 603-883-5582
WWW: http://www.aimtech.com

AimTech is best known as the producer of the popular multimedia package IconAuthor. Now it has applied its development skills to create Jamba, a visual Java authoring environment that requires no programming or scripting. Jamba is highly visual indeed; it works a lot like a well-done multimedia presentation package.

Jamba supports ActiveX as its object model, and it will support Microsoft's effort to produce ActiveX controls with Java code. Of course, Jamba supports plugging in native Java code as well, and future versions will support ActiveX objects and Java classes inside applications. Jamba also supports CGI and

JDBC for database connectivity and FLC/FLI animation files (a popular animation format on PCs, used by programs such as Autodesk Animator).

Hyperwire (Windows)

Kinetix Corporation
642 Harrison Street
San Francisco, CA 94107
Phone: 415-547-2000
Fax: 415-547-2222
WWW: http://www.ktx.com

Hyperwire, by Autodesk subsidiary Kinetix, is a fully graphical Java authoring environment. No programming experience is necessary to create very cool Java programs with Hyperwire; the latest version even incorporates VRML authoring into the product, making it an unusually powerful Web development tool.

Hyperwire uses a simple icon-based authoring environment, and users can create visual scenes that include hotspots for things like sounds, animations, and other event-based actions. Authors can lay out graphics, sounds, timer events, and much more, then choose behaviors for those objects. Hyperwire is also extensible—developers can add their own modules using the Module Development Kit (MDK) to extend the functionality of the entire product. There is support for databases via JDBC as well.

Texture

FutureTense, Inc.
33 Nagog Park
Acton, MA 01720
Phone: 508-263-5480
Fax: 508-263-1769
WWW: http://www.futuretense.com

Texture is a really unique Java product and one that holds immense promise. Essentially, it's a Java-based layout system for Web pages. Instead of using the limited layout capabilities of HTML, Texture lets you design and lay out pages, and then distribute those pages as full-fledged Java applets. Pages can be interactive and include other programs as well. The real impact of Texture will be for Java devices, where it will be a major authoring environment in place of

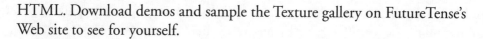

HTML. Download demos and sample the Texture gallery on FutureTense's Web site to see for yourself.

Egor (Windows)

Sausage Software
Suite 1, 600 Doncaster Road
Doncaster, VIC 3108
Australia
Phone: 613-955-9800
WWW: http://www.sausage.com

Egor, now in version 3.0, lets you create simple Java applications for animated banners, GIFs, and much more without a single line of Java programming experience. The latest version is shipped with a number of sample animations and sound effects (created by Sausage Software) that you can put into a Web page to spruce it up instantly.

A trial version and demo page exist on the Sausage Software Web site.

ActiveX Programming Info

Programming ActiveX components, as I noted earlier, relies on your favorite programming environment, and perhaps some good technical information and tools to help the process along. Most ActiveX controls are being written in C++, but you can use Visual Basic, Delphi, and even Java to program ActiveX controls. Many of the Java programming environments listed earlier will be adding support to build ActiveX controls with Java (as Microsoft already has with J++).

There is an excellent article by Neil J. Rubenking that explains the basics of ActiveX programming. It's located in ZD Net's ActiveXfiles at **http://www.pcmag.com/issues/1516/ pcmg0142.htm.**

Chances are that if you're considering ActiveX development, you've already settled on a favorite development tool and don't need me to point out all of the potential choices to investigate. Here, though, is a key resource to check out.

Microsoft ActiveX SDK

Microsoft Corporation
One Microsoft Way
Redmond, WA 98052
Phone: 206-882-8080
Fax: 206-883-8101
WWW: http://www.microsoft.com

The ActiveX SDK is a suite of tools and technologies to help developers create ActiveX controls. It is available in download form now and will be part of a line of Microsoft Developer Network (MSDN) CD-ROMs, which you can learn more about at **http://www.microsoft.com/msdn/**.

Integrating Applications into Your Site

Finished programming a Java applet or ActiveX control for your site? The work doesn't stop there. Now you have to place it on the page and write the supporting HTML and/or VBScript or JavaScript. I've covered scripting language resources already, but there are some additional items out there to help you with your Java/ActiveX developing.

AppletAce

Macromedia
600 Townsend Street
San Francisco, CA 94103-4945
Phone: 415-252-2000
Fax: 415-626-0554
WWW: http://www.macromedia.com

Macromedia developed AppletAce to help non-Java programmers embed Java and Shockwave applets on their sites; the product comes with a slew of useful Java applets, too. AppletAce makes it easy for developers to customize the applet and generate the proper **<PARAM>** tags and HTML framework to place it on the site. A new version that Macromedia is building lets you use AppletAce as the front end for your own applets, making it just as easy for you to build and embed them during Web development.

ActiveX Control Pad

Microsoft Corporation
One Microsoft Way
Redmond, WA 98052
Phone: 206-882-8080
Fax: 206-883-8101
WWW: http://www.microsoft.com

This is a free product from Microsoft (available on its Web site) that helps you work with the thousands of available ActiveX controls by positioning controls on a Web page and setting all of the variables for them. The Control Pad helps you generate various VBScripts for the controls as well; once you're done, you can cut and paste the generated HTML source code right into your favorite editor.

The FAQ for the ActiveX Control Pad is located at **http://www.microsoft. com/workshop/author/layout/**.

Java Web Sites

For proof that the world has gone Java, look no further than the immense number of Java sites on the Web. Not only are there lots of sites using Java, there are a lot more about Java or selling Java products and services—so many, in fact, that I couldn't possibly list them all. I've settled for listing a few key sites, including Gamelan, the major Java Web site you should be aware of.

Gamelan
http://www.gamelan.com

The number one independent Java resource on the Web, Gamelan is a huge directory to all of the sites with quality Java applets that are available either for sale, as shareware, or just to utilize on Web pages. (I love exploring new Java games, and this is the site I use to find them.) Gamelan also has extensive listings for Java tutorial sites, programming in Java sites, and much more. All in all, this is probably one of the top five Java-related sites on the Web.

Note: Gamelan is also building links to lots of ActiveX controls and resources now, too.

How to License Java
http://java.sun.com/java.sun.com/licensing-FAQ.html

This is the URL for JavaSoft's FAQ on how to license the Java Virtual Machine code for your own purposes. While Java developers don't have to license Java to make applets, you'll need to obtain a license for the Java VM if you're going to make a special custom application or machine that runs Java applets.

Java Tools: IDEs at a Glance

http://www.cybercom.net/~frog/javaide.html

A super-site similar to BrowserWatch, this site tracks the releases of all the major Java development tools, including more than 40 Java development environments (I listed the top ones earlier). If you want to know about every last development option available, surf over to this page.

Java Mailing Lists and Newsgroups

http://www.javasoft.com/mail.html

On this page, you'll find a complete listing of various Internet mailing lists and Usenet newsgroups related to Java.

TeamJava's Links Page

http://www.teamjava.com/links/

This site is a well-organized and very substantial set of links to dozens of Java sites and resources.

IDG Books Java Resource Center

http://www.idgbooks.com/java/index.html

Get updates on IDG's Java books, read articles from its magazines about Java, and more, all here at this very informative Java site.

Black Coffee

http://www.km-cd.com/black_coffee/

Black Coffee provides lots of links to Java applets, programming tools, resources, and other devotee sites. One special thing it offers (for $24.95) is the Black Coffee CD-ROM, which is packed with all kinds of useful Java stuff. The CD is constantly being republished with new and more stuff, and is a very good resource.

The Java Applet Rating Service
http://www.jars.com

JARS reviews and rates Java applets available on the Web. It has a panel of certified Java judges who rate applets and place them in various categories, including Top 1% Web Applets, Top 5% Web Applets, Top 25% Web Applets, monthly Top 10 Web Applets, and a monthly Top 100 Web Applets.

Applets that have accompanying source code are also noted, and links to all of them can be found here. You can submit your applet for review and even offer to be a judge. JARS also provides a bulletin board to discuss Java programming.

The Java Performance Report
http://www.webfayre.com/pendragon/jpr/

Are all implementations of Java equal? Apparently not, as the Java Performance Report will show you; various Java Virtual Machines and JIT compilers run Java programs faster than others. The JPR shows you exactly what sort of speeds various Java VMs are getting.

The Java User Resource Network
http://www.nebulex.com/URN

Instead of writing their own Java applets, a lot of people will turn to other developers by either buying one of the many ready-made applets available on the Web or hiring their own programmer to write custom applets. For those people looking for experienced Java programming help, this site has listings of consultants, developers, and Java sites and applets.

The Java Message Exchange
http://porthos.phoenixat.com/~warreng/WWWBoard/wwwboard.html

A large bulletin board to exchange Java programming information.

ActiveX Web Sites

ZD Net's ActiveXfiles
http://www.zdnet.com/activexfiles/

While you won't find Agent Scully or Agent Mulder here trying to prove that Bill Gates is an alien conspiracy, you will find one of the best sites around about ActiveX controls, programming, and technology. A good links directory to all sorts of ActiveX controls is provided as well.

ActiveX.Com
http://www.active-x.com/ie.htm

A growing site filled with resources about ActiveX.

ActiveXtra
http://www.activextra.com

This site calls itself "The Ultimate Web Site for the ActiveX Community," and it very well could be. Produced by CMP (the country's large computer magazine publisher), the site is a very comprehensive resource with a large database of ActiveX controls and vendors.

Java Libraries and Toolkits

The great thing about Java's hot status is that so many developers are creating tools and products to help you do more things with Java. These range from full-fledged applets you can run or modify to code libraries that help you write specific types of Java programs. I could spend pages listing them all here, but I don't have to because many of the sites I've mentioned—especially Gamelan—list them already. I do, however, want to highlight a few multimedia Java libraries that I think might be of special interest, because most Web developers want to use Java for such work.

Check with Gamelan for much more information on these and other libraries. Also, bone up on the latest Java news there and at *JavaWorld* magazine, because the rate at which new Java programming tools are appearing makes it necessary to keep up regularly.

Intel Multimedia Java API
http://www.intel.com/ial/jmedia/

Intel, JavaSoft, and many other companies have been working on a multimedia API for Java. On this page you can learn all about Intel's implementation of the Media API for audio, video, and animation for Intel-based PCs running Windows 95 and Windows NT.

Gamelet Toolkit
`http://www.next.com/~mtacchi/Java/GameletToolkit/README.html`

Written by some programmers at NEXT, the Gamelet Toolkit (available for free at this URL) is a set of Java classes and interfaces to help develop arcade games in Java. It has classes for animation, scoring, events, and more. Sample code helps you learn the library.

Fireworks
Macromedia
600 Townsend Street
San Francisco, CA 94103-4945
Phone: 415-252-2000
Fax: 415-626-0554
WWW: http://www.macromedia.com

Macromedia Fireworks is a new Java API for Windows, Macintosh, and Unix that was still in development as I was finishing this book. Essentially a multimedia API that integrates Shockwave with Java, Fireworks will allow Director programmers to compile their Director movies into Java applets. Java programmers will also gain access to a powerful API for multimedia effects like animation, imaging, streaming sound, and more.

Java Magazines
In the future there will probably be more than just a couple of Java magazines. For now, though, the monthly Java reading list is comprised of the following.

JavaWorld
Web Publishing Inc.
501 Second Street
San Francisco, CA 94107
Phone: 415-243-4188
Fax: 415-267-1732
WWW: http://www.javaworld.com

JavaWorld is an electronic-only magazine published by IDG's new Web publishing division. It publishes monthly on the Web, but still has a very magazine feel with regular columns, new product snippets, and features.

Java Developer's Journal

SYS-CON Publications
46 Holly Street
Jersey City, NJ 07305
Phone: 914-735-1900
Fax: 201-333-7361
WWW: http://www.javadevelopersjournal.com/java/
Subscription: $59.95
Newsstand: n/a
Publishes: Monthly
Pages: n/a

JDJ is the only full-print Java developers' magazine I found. Its first issue was still under development at the time I was writing this.

Digital Espresso

`http://www.io.org/~mentor/jnIndex.html`

With its keen insights and straightforward news, bug reports, and views, *Digital Espresso* is a well-done online zine with lots of Java news and information.

Books about Java and ActiveX

Sometimes I think there are more books on Java than there are Java programmers; it's just one more indication of how hot Java is. I've tried to put together a good list of the books most worth having for the serious Java programmer, plus a couple of ActiveX books to check out.

Java API Reference Guides

Java API Reference by Colin Frazier and Jill Bond (published by New Riders, 1996, ISBN 1-562055-98-4)

The Java Application Programming Interface (The Java Series), Volume 1 by James Gosling and Frank Yellin (published by Longman Publishing Group, 1996, ISBN 0-201634-53-8)

Java Language API Superbible: The Comprehensive Reference to the Java Programming Language by Daniel Groner, Todd Sundsted, Casey Hopson, and Harish Prabanham (published by Waite Group Press, 1996, ISBN 1-571690-38-7)

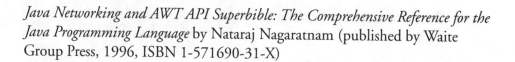

Java Networking and AWT API Superbible: The Comprehensive Reference for the Java Programming Language by Nataraj Nagaratnam (published by Waite Group Press, 1996, ISBN 1-571690-31-X)

Tutorials/How-Tos

60 Minute Guide to Java by Ed Tittel and Mark Gaither (published by IDG Books, 1995, ISBN 1-568847-11-4)

Core Java by Gary Cornell and Cay S. Horstmann (published by Prentice Hall Computer Books, 1996, ISBN 0-135657-55-5)

Creating Web Applets with Java by David Gulbransen and Kenrick Rawlings (published by Sams, 1996, ISBN 1-575210-70-3)

Essential Java: Developing Interactive Applications for the World-Wide Web by Jason J. Manger (published by McGraw Hill, 1996, ISBN 0-077092-92-9)

Exploring Java by Patrick Niemeyer and Joshua Peck (published by O'Reilly & Associates, 1996, ISBN 1-565921-84-4)

Hooked on Java: Creating Hot Web Sites with Java Applets by Arthur Van Hoff (published by Addison-Wesley, 1996, ISBN 0-201488-37-X)

Instant Java by John A. Pew (published by Prentice Hall Computer Books, 1996, ISBN 0-132722-87-9)

Java by Example by Jerry R. Jackson and Alan McClellan (published by Prentice Hall Computer Books, 1996, ISBN 0-132722-95-X)

Java Developer's Resource: A Tutorial and On-Line Supplement by Elliotte Rusty Harold (published by Prentice Hall Computer Books, 1996, ISBN 0-135707-89-7)

Java How-To by Madhu Siddalingaiah (published by Waite Group Press, 1996, ISBN 1-571690-35-2)

Java in a Nutshell: A Desktop Quick Reference for Java Programmers by David Flanagan (published by O'Reilly & Associates, 1996, ISBN 1-565921-83-6)

Java Primer Plus: Supercharging Web Applications with the Java Programming Language by Paul Tyma (published by Waite Group Press, 1996, ISBN 1-571690-62-X)

The Java Programming EXplorer by Neil Bartlett, Alex Leslie, and Steve Simkin (published by The Coriolis Group, 1996, ISBN 1-883577-81-0)

Java Workshop Programming by Steven Holzner (published by M & T Books, 1996, ISBN 1-558514-91-0)

Just Java by Peter Van Der Linden and Peter Van Der Linden (published by Prentice Hall Computer Books, 1996, ISBN 0-135658-39-X)

KickAss Java Programming by Tonny Espeset (published by The Coriolis Group, 1996, ISBN 1-883577-99-3)

Learn Java Now by Stephen R. Davis (published by Microsoft Press, 1996, ISBN 1-572314-28-1)

On to Java by Winston Patrick Henry and Sundar Narasimhan (published by Addison-Wesley Publishing, 1996, ISBN 0-201498-26-X)

Presenting Java by John December (published by Sams, 1995, ISBN 1-575210-39-8)

Talk Java to Me: The Interactive Click, Listen and Learn Guide to Java Programming by Harry McIntosh (published by Waite Group Press, 1996, ISBN 1-571690-44-1)

Web Site Programming with Java by David Harms (published by McGraw-Hill, 1996, ISBN 0-079129-86-2)

On Café

Café Programming FrontRunner by David H. Friedel Jr., Joshua Kerievsky, Anthony Potts, and John Rodley (published by The Coriolis Group, 1996, ISBN 1-576100-03-0)

Java Programming with Symantec Café by Gary Cornell and Cay Horstmann (published by Prentice Hall Computer Books, 1996, ISBN 0-13270-45-5)

On J++

Java Programming with Visual J++ by Martin Rinehart (published by M & T Books, 1996, ISBN 1-558515-06-2)

Visual J++ Programming FrontRunner by Peter Aiken, David H. Friedel, Jr., and Anthony Potts (published by The Coriolis Group, 1996, 1-57610-064-2)

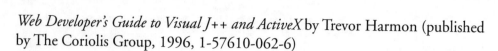

Web Developer's Guide to Visual J++ and ActiveX by Trevor Harmon (published by The Coriolis Group, 1996, 1-57610-062-6)

Web Programming with Visual J++ by Sams Development (published by Sams, 1996, ISBN 1-575211-74-2)

On Latté

Latté Programming EXplorer: The Best Way to Master Java Programming with Latté by Jeff Duntemann and Don Taylor (published by The Coriolis Group, 1997, ISBN 1-57610-005-7)

Latté Programming FrontRunner: The Hands-On Guide to Mastering Java Development With Latté by Joshua Kerievsky, Terence Goggin, Matt Telles, and Steven Fraser (published by The Coriolis Group, 1997, ISBN 1-57610-04-9)

ActiveX

The ActiveX Sourcebook: Build an ActiveX-Based Web Site by Ted Coombs, Jason Coombs, Don Brewer, and Donald Brewer (published by John Wiley & Sons, 1996, ISBN 0-471167-14-2)

Exploring ActiveX by Shannon R. Turlington (published by Ventana, 1996, ISBN 1-566045-26-6)

Visual J++ With ActiveX Controls by John Fisher (published by Prima Publishing, 1996, ISBN 0-761509-14-3)

Web Programming with ActiveX by John Mueller (published by Sams, 1996, ISBN 1-575211-60-2)

ActiveX from the Ground Up by John Mueller (published by Osborne McGraw-Hill, 1996, ISBN 0-078822-64-5)

Interesting Topics

Black Art of Java Game Programming: Creating Dynamic Games and Interactive Graphical Environments Using Java by Joel Fan, Eric Ries, and Calin Tenitchi (published by Waite Group Press, 1996, ISBN 1-571690-43-3)

Cutting-Edge Java Game Programming: Everything You Need to Create Interactive Internet Games with Java by Neil Bartlett, Alex Leslie, and Steve Simkin (published by The Coriolis Group, 1996, ISBN 1-883577-98-5)

Java for C/C++ Programmers by Michael C. Daconta and Mike Daconta (published by John Wiley & Sons, 1996, ISBN 0-471153-24-9)

Java Database Programming with JDBC: Discover the Essentials for Developing Databases for Internet or Intranet Applications by Pratik Patel (published by The Coriolis Group, 1996, ISBN 1-57610-056-1)

Java Essentials for C and C++ Programmers by Barry Boone (published by Addison-Wesley Publishing, 1996, ISBN 0-201479-46-X)

Java Programming Basics by Edith Au (published by MIS Press, 1996, ISBN 1-558284-69-9)

Java Programming for the Internet: A Guide to Creating Dynamic, Interactive Internet Applications by Michael D. Thomas, Pratik R. Patel, Alan D. Hudson, and Don Ball (published by Ventana, 1996, ISBN 1-566043-55-7)

The Java Sourcebook by Ed Anuff (published by John Wiley & Sons, 1996, ISBN 0-471148-59-8)

Java with Borland C++ by Chris H. Pappas and William H. Murray (published by AP Professional, 1996, ISBN 0-125119-60-7)

Learn Java on the Mac by Barry Boone and Dave Mark (published by Addison-Wesley Publishing, 1996, ISBN 0-201191-57-1)

CHAPTER 21

*Put your site a notch
up on the Richter
Scale with
Shockwave*

Macromedia's
Shockwave
Resources

When Macromedia first created Director, little did it know that eventually the Internet would propel the company into the stratosphere. By the time the World Wide Web burst into prominence, Macromedia had spent years perfecting runtime modules for a number of platforms, including Windows, Macintosh, SGI, and some of the videogame consoles. This cross-platform strategy and core "player" technology made Director a natural product to create Web-based programs. Melding this well-tested, seasoned product to the Web in a very integrated manner made Shockwave one of the most important online technologies around almost overnight.

Shockwave is not so much a product as it is a catch-all brand name for Macromedia's complete line of Web multimedia formats. The basic technology revolves around a compression scheme (using Macromedia's Afterburner program) that makes it possible to transmit Director files quickly over the Web, as well as a set of extensions to make Director's scripting language, Lingo, more Web savvy. The Shockwave technology also incorporates several other components, such as a newly announced streaming audio technology, a compatible FreeHand plug-in, and more.

Macromedia is hardly resting on its laurels. It's trying to add streaming capabilities to the entire Shockwave system, and it's working with America Online to bring Shockwave to native AOL service as well. Despite Macromedia's edge, though, other Web multimedia systems will soon come into play. Already mFactory's mTropolis, a major competitor to Director elsewhere in the multimedia world, is breaking onto the Web, and AimTech (which makes IconAuthor, a more corporate multimedia system) has also debuted a plug-in. Nevertheless, Shockwave's established base of 400,000 developers make it enough of a force to warrant special attention in this book.

Macromedia Resources

The first way to learn what Director and Shockwave are, and how to develop with the system, is to see what resources Macromedia itself offers. Aside from the main Director package and Shockwave plug-in, it provides a number of useful aids for their developers, from technical help to conferences. This excellent support is another reason Shockwave has been so successful.

Director

600 Townsend Street
San Francisco, CA 94103-4945
Phone: 415-252-2000
Fax: 415-626-0554
WWW: http://www.macromedia.com

The main component of Macromedia's resources is the Director authoring environment, which is available for Windows 95/NT and the Macintosh. It's sold either separately or in a bundled form, known as Director Multimedia Studio. The latter is probably the best way to purchase Director, because for a little more money you also get either SoundEdit 16 version 2 plus Deck II 2.5 (Macintosh) or Sound Forge XP (Windows) for sound, Extreme 3D 1.0 for three-dimensional graphics, and xRes 2.0 for imaging.

As I noted earlier, in order to compile Director files for use as Shockwave applications you'll need the Afterburner program, which is located at **http://www.macromedia.com/shockwave/devtools.html**.

Director Xtras

Macromedia Xtras (the name for Director extensions) are third-party Director plug-ins that give you access to new program features that enhance your Director applications. For example, the new streaming audio functionality that Macromedia announced for Shockwave is a Director Xtra. A large list of available Xtras can be found at **http://www.macromedia.com/software/xtras/director/index.html**, as well as on another list kept by Firmware, an Australian company, at **http://www.firmware.com.au/support/xtra.htm**.

Developing Your Own Xtras

Some developers may want to develop their own Xtras. You can do this by downloading the appropriate version (Macintosh or PC) of the Director XDK, which allows you to create Xtras in C. You can find all the help you need at **http://www.macromedia.com/software/xtras/xdc.html#director**.

Streaming Director Files and the Future of Shockwave

The biggest problem for Director right now is that Shockwave itself is not yet a streaming technology. Thankfully, there is a product called Enliven that works to stream Director files with a backend server system. As I explained in Chapter 14, the complete Enliven package consists of Enliven Producer, Enliven Server, and the Enliven Viewer, a plug-in/helper application for users to download. The system's proprietary technology allows Narrative to manage the simultaneous delivery of large volumes of content to lots of users, especially the mixed content types found in multimedia files. Macromedia is also working on adding more streaming capabilities to future versions of Shockwave.

For its part, Macromedia is moving forward on two major fronts: the release of Director 5.0, and the progression of Macromedia's Open Architecture (MOA), the Macromedia Information Exhange, and the Macromedia Common Scripting Language. The idea with these technologies is to integrate all of Macromedia's products—xres, Director, Extreme 3D, SoundEdit, FreeHand, and Authorware—into a framework that shares a common scripting language (which is essentially an energized version of Lingo) and can accept a variety of dynamic extensions via the MOA technology (for more information, go to **http://www.macromedia.com/support/moa/index.html**). Macromedia has also announced The Fireworks API, which is a Java-based technology that seeks to merge Shockwave with Java. Details are still being announced, but at the 1996 Macromedia International User Conference this announcement was creating a major buzz.

In short, Macromedia is working to give multimedia developers a very tightly integrated set of tools to create awesome Web-based multimedia. In addition, the MOA architecture and new Fireworks Java technology are going to help the company integrate its Shockwave technology more closely with Java. As these steps and the Shockwave system itself demonstrate, Macromedia really understands the Web. As a result, the future for Shockwave looks great.

Director Conferences
Here are a couple of conferences that Shockwave developers and other interested parties should know about.

Macromedia International User Conference
http://www.macromedia.com/macromedia/ucon/

This event is the largest Macromedia conference around. It's held annually in the fall by Macromedia, usually at San Francisco's Moscone Convention Center. Contact Macromedia for more information.

g/Matter Inc. Worldwide Training Seminars

300 Brannan Street, Suite 210
San Francisco, CA 94107
Phone: 415-243-0394
Fax: 415-243-0396
WWW: http://www.gmatter.com

g/Matter Inc. is a large multimedia software reseller and training company that hosts a series of training conferences on Macromedia Director around the world. Check out the company's Web site for scheduled times and places.

Director/Shockwave Web Sites

While there are dozens of sites that use Shockwave, only a handful of sites are meaningful resources for Director/Shockwave developers.

Alan Levine's Maricopa Site

`http://www.mcli.dist.maricopa.edu/director/index.html`

This incredibly comprehensive site is probably the number one reason that there are so few major Director-oriented sites. It has links to hundreds of Shockwaved sites, information on Director, tips, tricks, news, and much more. This is a must link for even casual Shockwave developers.

The Director FAQ

`http://hakatai.mcli.dist.maricopa.edu/director/faq/index.html`

This is a home page for the official Director-Lingo FAQ.

Dr. Diego's FAQ about Macromedia Director and Lingo

`http://www.xtramedia.com/lingoTips.html`

Not only a FAQ, but tips and tricks for Director programmers from XtraMedia's Dr. Diego.

Update Stage

`http://www.updatestage.com/buglist.html`

Maintained by Gretchen Macdowall, this online biweekly newsletter contains invaluable information about Director. Complete with a long list of helpful Director add-on products, a bug-reporting column called Quirks, and a full helping of useful tips and tricks, it should be immediately bookmarked by Director/Shockwave aficionados.

Marvyn's Little Cubbyhole
`http://sharedcast.hccs.cc.tx.us`

This FTP site is full of example code.

Dave Yang's/QuantumWave Interactive Director Links Page
`http://www.magic.ca/~qwi/Director.html`

An impressive links page for Director/Shockwave resources.

Shockwave Developers Forum
`http://www.cybersurf.co.uk/cgi-bin/cyberia/developb.pl`

A simple chat board on the Web devoted to discussions of Shockwave.

g/Matter, Inc.
`http://www.gmatter.com`

As I noted earlier, g/Matter is a leading reseller of products for Director-oriented developers, and so its site is an excellent resource. Here you'll find information about products, lots of commercial Xtras to order, and information about training the company also offers.

Shockwave Penny Arcade
`http://www.utw.com/~ressh/HowToPenny.html`

One of the key uses of Shockwave is creating games for your Web sites. This site has a rather large list of Shockwave-powered games that can be good examples.

Director/Shockwave Magazines

So far, Macromedia hasn't brought out its own magazine, but rumors say that such a product will debut soon. Until that time, these two specialized journals covering the Director/Macromedia scene are the best regular sources of information and help.

Lingo User's Journal

P.O. Box 531
Holderness, NH 03245
Phone: 603-968-3341
Fax: 603-968-3361
WWW: http://www.penworks.com
Subscriptions: $42
Newsstand: n/a
Published: Monthly
Pages: 16

This journal, from longtime Director developers Penworks, has no advertising and is packed with articles that focus entirely on Lingo and XObj/Xtra programming. Sample code is made available online when appropriate. Back issues are available for $7 per issue. If you're contemplating a subscription, they'll mail the first issue with no obligation.

Macromedia User Journal

HyperMedia Communications Inc.
901 Mariner's Island Boulevard, Suite 365
San Mateo, CA 94404
Phone: 415-573-5170
Fax: 415-573-5131
WWW: http://www.hyperstand.com/MUJ/muj.html
Subscription: $175
Newsstand: n/a
Published: 24 times/year
Pages: 16

This is a special magazine/newsletter put together by the same folks who bring you NewMedia Magazine. It's packed with information about all Macromedia products, which of course includes Director/Shockwave. There is also a large online component open to subscribers; on the Web site, you can request a free trial subscription and download a sample issue.

Director/Shockwave Books

60 Minute Guide to Shockwave by William W. Hurley, T. Preston Gregg, and Sebastian Hassinger (published by IDG Books, 1996, ISBN 0-76458-002-7)

The Comprehensive Guide to Lingo by Gary Rosenzweig (published by Ventana Books, 1996, ISBN 1-56604-463-4), huge online companion at **http://www2.csn.net/~rosenz/Book/contents.html** and at **http://clevermedia.com/lingo.html**

Creating Interactive Applications with Macromedia Director by Gary Rosenzweig (published by Ventana Books, 1996, ISBN 1-56604-463-4), online companion at **http://www.vmedia.com/director.html**

Director 5 Wizardry by Christopher Coppola and Shane Edmonds (published by Coriolis Group Books, 1996, ISBN 1-57610-048-0)

Inside Macromedia Director 5 With Lingo for Macintosh by Lee Allis, Robert Connolly, Matt Davis, and Scott Kildall (published by New Riders, 1996, ISBN 1-56205-567-4)

Lingo Sorcery: The Magic of Lists, Objects and Intelligent Agents by Peter Small (published by John Wiley & Sons, 1996, ISBN 0-471-96302-X)

Macromedia Director 5 Power Toolkit by Deborah M. Miller and Michael D. Miller (published by Ventana, 1996, ISBN 1-56604-289-5)

Macromedia Shockwave fo r Director: User's Guide by Sasha Magee and Noel Rabinowitz (published by New Riders, 1996, ISBN 1-562-05595-X)

Shockwave Power Solutions by Noel Rabinowitz and Sasha Magee (published by New Riders, 1996, ISBN 1-56205-646-8)

Shockwave! Breathe New Life into Your Web Pages: For Windows & Macintosh by Darrel Plant (published by Ventana, 1996, ISBN 1-56604-441-3)

22

To find out how you can get work in this industry, you need to understand how the industry works.

Overview of the Web Business

What's This Business All About?

In my first book, *The Ultimate Game Developer's Sourcebook,* I wrote a chapter much like this one concerning the games industry. But describing the ins and outs of the games business was fairly easy. The World Wide Web is a far more wide-ranging enterprise; indeed, games themselves are but one large section of the Web industry. Also, the Web is so new that many still-unknown pieces will have to be put into place before anyone can figure out the overall structure of the industry.

Examining the business structure of the Web thus becomes an exercise in identifying major players, describing the major business models, and taking a peek or two into a crystal ball. Then comes the biggest question all developers need to face: "Where and how do I fit in?"

The Structure of the Web Industry

I've arranged my structure of the industry around the key players as I see them now. The idea of the chart shown in Figure 22.1 is to show the basic flow of turning capital and ideas into sites that are published and used on the Web.

Believe it or not, this was the simplest chart I could create—and it still has some slight flaws because I tried not to create any crossed lines (which would be really confusing). One flaw is that there should be direct lines extending from advertisers to the "Specific Sites on the Web" and "Search Engines and Special Interest Hubs" boxes (to indicate the direct purchasing of ads on sites). Another inaccuracy is that the chart reduces the role of hardware companies to merely providing equipment to ISPs and building the overall Internet infrastructure. Nevertheless, the chart does explain the overall relationships, positioning, and ebb and flow within the World Wide Web industry. The chart's major elements are described in the following sections.

The Capital Gang

Killer sites can require hundreds of thousands, even millions, of dollars to develop and maintain. That means someone, somewhere has to be willing to risk a lot of cash to see a particular site get built. While some developers got their start with limited or out-of-pocket funding, the majority of tomorrow's sites (and even today's, to be honest) will take more than a few weeks with an HTML editor and some pizza money to get started. So let's follow the money trail and see who's in "the capital gang."

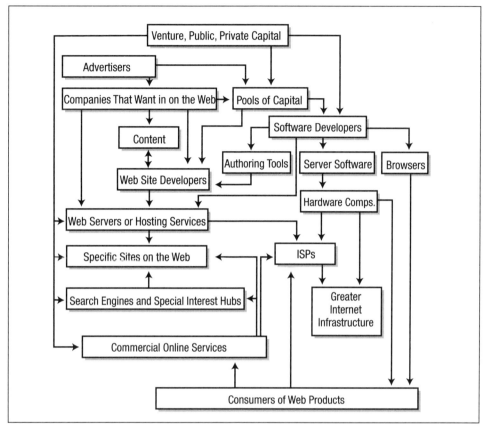

Figure 22.1   My organizational chart shows the interaction between the various parts of the Web industry.

Venture, Public, Private Capital

Companies that provide access to large pools of capital are the biggest source of independent development money, whether for sites already on the Web or to back business plans for new site ideas. These companies tend to offer venture capital, arrange initial public offerings of stock (usually not for startups, but often at crucial expansion stages for successful sites), or serve as private investors. Some of these companies make direct investments, while others invest in large managed pools of capital controlled by other entities, like investment banks or mutual funds.

On the Chart: I drew lines connecting this group to the various areas where their money tends to go. Right now these groups are investing directly in specific sites (as Reuters has done with the Yahoo site) or specific software developers (for example, by buying stock in Microsoft and Netscape). An additional line toward the "Pools of Capital" area represents investments in joint ventures with developers, advertisers, or companies launching their own Web services.

Advertisers

Advertisers are a small but growing source of initial capital for new sites. If a site plan looks good, a developer might be able to obtain funds based on the promise of advertisers paying off at the launch of a site. Other advertisers might even offer to fund the creation of a site in exchange for exclusive rights—just as Procter & Gamble did when it pioneered the television soap opera. As the chart shows, advertisers might make direct investments in sites via assistance to developers (usually to carry out a specific site idea the advertiser likes or wants) or as sponsors through various other companies' ideas (such as a sponsor for a magazine Web site). In either case, advertisers have literally billions of dollars to spend. As more of that is directly spent on the Web, advertisers will evolve into a major source of investment capital.

On the Chart: I positioned advertisers as entities that provide investment capital to various developers. Some pick and choose specific sites to invest in, while others team up with developers on a long-term basis.

Companies That Want in on the Web

It seems everyone wants to be part of the Web revolution, from big media conglomerates to small individual publishers. These companies have two paths they can take—some take only one, while others mix and match. They can build an in-house studio (much like Time-Warner, Disney, and others are doing), or they can approach outside developers either as a client commissioning a site or as a licenser of content to one or more other sites. It's in their role as outsourcing clients that many companies will be major players in the capital investment arena.

On the Chart: One of the lines into the "Pools of Capital" box represents firms investing in companies with major Web sites or products.

The Developer Groups

Who turns Web wishes into http://www.reality.com? Well, developers, of course. The chart shows several key developer types at play in the land of the Web.

In-House Site Creators

As I just noted, companies launching their own Web offerings are a major group of developers. Especially among major software developers and media outlets (such as magazines and newspapers, as well as giants like Disney and Time-Warner), many companies are building extensive in-house development operations to create major sites on the Web. Other companies rushing to the Web for new opportunities include corporate entities like FedEx and GE.

On the Chart: I detached "Content" as a separate component to represent companies moving their content to the Web either directly (as denoted by the arrow going from "Content" to "Specific Sites on the Web" through "Web Servers or Hosting Services) or in conjunction with independent Web developers. The double arrow in the latter case represents the fact that in some cases developers approach companies for content, while in other cases the companies approach developers to contract for site making.

Software Developers

While many in this group of companies actually construct and manage Web sites, their main role is to develop the actual computer software that helps others create and maintain sites. Perhaps the biggest development push in the Web industry involves building the infrastructure for major sites. Lots of Web-savvy developers will find more success making authoring tools, browser plug-ins, Java libraries, and ActiveX controls than they will in creating sites. Examples of such software developers, of course, are Netscape, Microsoft, Spyglass, Javasoft, and Adobe.

On the Chart: Software developers are shown in terms of building the three biggest components of Web software: the browsing/access software, the back-end systems and servers, and the development tools and editors used to create the content.

Web Site Developers

The Web developer is part graphic designer, part multimedia/interactive developer, part programmer, part writer, and part networking manager. A Web site developer, in other words, isn't just someone who knows HTML, but is an experienced master of the entire site creation process (which involves products like RealAudio, database back-ends, animated graphics, and more). Examples of this type of developer—the newest type in the computer world—would be iVillage, Studio Archetype, and Digital Planet.

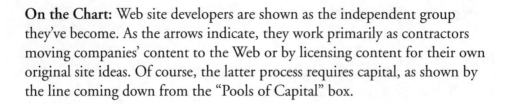

On the Chart: Web site developers are shown as the independent group they've become. As the arrows indicate, they work primarily as contractors moving companies' content to the Web or by licensing content for their own original site ideas. Of course, the latter process requires capital, as shown by the line coming down from the "Pools of Capital" box.

The Infrastructure Crowd

A Web site isn't much good unless someone pipes it onto the Web and connects it to the millions of Internet users who might want to surf over to it. And so I turn to the amalgamation of hardware and software companies that build, maintain, and provide access to the millions of miles of wiring, hubs, routers, and fiber optics that carry information from one part of the Internet to the other.

Software Developers

Software developers participate in the infrastructure mostly through their construction of server, networking, and security software and such back-end systems as Internet-savvy relational databases. Examples of companies in this area would be Microsoft and Netscape (with their server software) and RSA (with its security software).

On the Chart: A line connects "Software Developers" via "Server Software" to the "Hardware Companies" and "ISPs", who use this software to build and manage the overall Internet infrastructure. In some cases the lines can get very blurred, as hardware makers such as SGI and Sun Microsystems seek to create server software as well.

Hardware Companies

Much of the infrastructure of the Internet is made up of networking hardware, routers, hubs, cable, and even satellite systems that are built and connected to the Internet. Players in this area include network hardware makers such as 3Com and Cisco Systems; workstation makers like Sun Microsystems, Digital, and Hewlett-Packard; and major phone equipment companies like Lucent Technologies (AT&T) and Siemens.

On the Chart: I give these hardware companies short shrift, mainly organizing them as a back-end infrastructure builders. In that regard they do a lot to construct the various components that allow ISPs to hook up people and companies to the overall infrastructure (which hardware companies also build). I also show the important role hardware companies play in supplying people with the modems and computers used to hook up to the Internet, as well as the major multimedia-type computers that let designers make the Web come alive with features like VRML and Shockwave.

ISPs

At one time, the companies that actually set up and maintained connections to the Internet were known collectively as Internet Service Providers (ISPs). Now, following various mergers and the growth of the Internet, the ISPs are being joined or purchased by major telecommunications companies like AT&T and Bell Atlantic. Major players in this area of the Web industry include PSInet, MFS Communications/UUnet, and hundreds of smaller mom-and-pop ISPs (such as Maine's Biddeford Internet).

On the Chart: ISPs serve a dual role in the Web industry, as shown by the lines from "Consumers of Web Products" to "ISPs" (representing the latter's role in hooking consumers up to the Internet), and from "Web Servers or Hosting Services" to "ISPs" (representing the latter's role in connecting servers to the Internet, as well as some that also rent space on their own servers). The line from "Commercial Online Services" to "ISPs" represents combined ventures in which the online services are also ISPs (for example, Netcom, CompuServe, and America Online) or hook up via a joint venture with a major ISP (for example, Microsoft uses UUnet, and mPATH uses PSInet).

Greater Internet Infrastructure

This box on the chart helps to show how ISPs have positioned themselves between servers and users, acting as the gateway to the overall infrastructure of the Internet. The line to "Hardware Comps." symbolizes the latter's role in building the bricks and mortar of the physical Internet.

The Consumer Masses

At the bottom of the chart is the real reason for the Internet's existence—the people who actually connect to and use the various sites that are available on the World Wide Web. As shown, they access it via either a commercial online service (such as CompuServe, MSN, or America Online) or a traditional ISP. Consumers also deal directly with software and hardware developers, who they depend on for the actual equipment and software they use to interact with the Web.

Forming the Team

All in all, the lines are becoming quite clear in the Web world. What's great is that as companies realize their role in relation to the Internet, they get better at executing that role. Lots of ISPs originally thought of becoming major online services, focusing on the mass consumer market; now they leave it to the existing services, who have proven extremely successful at serving the masses. In other areas, lots of companies are learning to deal with larger, more focused Web site development houses rather than do the same work internally. As with any a good team, each element has begun to focus on what it does best—and as these lines become clear, the result will be a team that plays well together.

What Developer Model Will You Use?

Now let's delve a little more into the specific structures of entities that actually make Web sites and products. I call these the *developer models*.

Site Originator and Owner

A number of top Web developers are creating sites by and for themselves. One example is iVillage, a New York-based producer of Web sites like its Parent Soup (**http://www.parentsoup.com**). iVillage creates sites to which it hopes to attract people for the purpose of selling them items or perhaps subscriptions for access (or attracting advertisers).

Site Designer and/or Constructor

In contrast to the site owners, many developers simply develop sites for others. For instance, a store may decide to launch its business on the Web, then contract out the design, development, and even management of the site to a developer. These developers tend to operate like traditional advertising agencies: A company approaches them with an idea, a product, or just a general concept (such as for a corporate site), asks them for assistance in fleshing out the details, and then has them see it through to completion.

The Web Tools/Content Developer

Some major Web developers don't build sites at all (well, perhaps a site for their own products), but are nevertheless important because they create the tools, content, art, music, and so on for other developers. In fact, the Web tools and content market—including new server products, new Web editors, specialized databases for the Web, and security tools—is the biggest new software market in years.

Among these developers are Microsoft and Netscape, two prolific tools manufacturers. They also include content developers such as Reuters, which is licensing headline news systems to various sites (much as it has done for Yahoo). Another company is developing specialized games for sites to incorporate. Eventually companies like Sony and Warner Music might license music for sites, much as they already do with television and movie soundtracks.

Just for the Fun of It: Not-for-Profit Developers

No one said the Web had to be a business-only medium, and some Web developers are not interested in making money. They love the Web for its artistic possibilities, or for the chance to put up sites dedicated to their favorite baseball player or movie star. For some, the World Wide Web is a hobbyist medium, a place where anyone can create and participate. In fact, the "amateur" Web developer is the most common type of developer.

Multipurpose Developers

While some companies are just plain shops for hire and others are merely building Web sites into their own businesses, some firms opt to do both. For example, Starwave created the Mr. Showbiz site (**http://www.mrshowbiz. com**) for itself, yet it also produced the NBA.com site for the National Basketball Association.

Other multipurpose developers create software (like browser plug-ins, games, or authoring products) but also use their superior software development skills as Web-site producers. Many game companies fit this description because their experience with graphics, design, sound, and programming gives them the full stable of talent needed to design killer Web sites.

A Look at Business Justification Models

I've outlined the geography of the Web industry—the positioning of the major components and the relationships they have with one another. Now I want to discuss the types of business models companies are using to justify their work on the Web.

Before any of the changes that make up the long-promised cyberspace revolution can happen, people will have to figure out what sort of business models will work on the Web. Will advertising work? How about retailing? How do you cost-justify the investment in a Web site? These are the types of things a basic business model can help address, and a look at the fundamental models in use on the Web today can help shed light on the industry itself.

There are three distinct categories of business models on the Web: firms that try to *pull in revenue directly* via the Web site, those that *derive revenue from other sources* but are supported by a Web site, and those whose sites *help save the business money* and thus enhance profits without increasing revenues.

Why Are These Models Important?

Well, that's simple—the way in which companies see value in the Web molds their positioning in the industry.

Companies that see the Web as a great source of direct revenue are more aggressive in their involvement. This attitude is easy to see in the number of software companies that are already gaining heavily from the Web explosion, or in Disney, which sees an awesome potential to sell new software and items via its Web site.

Companies that see the Web as a place to derive revenue from will most likely be active but cautious developers. This description would cover most advertising companies, whose go-slow attitude toward the Web has been well documented.

Companies that see the Web mainly as a source of business savings will tend to be very large firms who don't necessarily have content to provide or items they want to sell online; instead, they will use the Internet to supplement and reduce the cost of existing services.

Direct Revenue Models

The direct revenue business model means your Web site is actually the source of the revenue. Money is either accepted directly through electronic transfers over the site, or paid through other means for services rendered directly from the site.

Advertising Model

The most popular Web business model today envisions sites that gain advertising revenue because they attract consumers who an advertiser wishes to reach. While the advertising model is severely oversubscribed right now (way too many sites, not enough advertisers), this imbalance is expected to end over the next few years as annual billings for ads on the Web grow into the billions of dollars.

Advertising-supported sites can vary greatly in their content and services, but to succeed all must offer some reason for a distinct (or very large) group of consumers to show up on a regular basis and thus be exposed to some form of advertising. Many of these sites tend to be broad-based fare such as Web-based magazines, game and entertainment sites, or search engines. As more people begin flocking to the Web, advertising-supported sites should branch out to resemble the vast range of niche media (including magazines, TV and radio shows, and newspapers) that use ads to earn their keep.

On the surface, the advertising model on the Web works much as it does for traditional media: Advertisers pay rates based on some form of the common cost-per-thousand-impressions (CPM) formula. The CPM rate can rise or fall based on the quality of the demographic market for advertisers. For example, a site that appeals to corporate CEOs might only get a thousand visits a week, but charge advertisers a $500 CPM because the consumers' income level is so high, while a site that reaches a much less upscale market might have a CPM of $50. The former site can make money based on the quality of its audience, while the latter might have to strive for quantity to survive.

What makes the Web advertising model so potentially exciting is that it may soon provide advertisers with a far more advanced way to target ads to precise groups of customers. Not only might the Web be able to bring such targeting right down to the level of individual consumers, it might also aid advertisers by determining who actually accessed ad information and for how long they viewed it.

Pay-to-Access Model

More and more people in the Web industry are questioning whether advertising alone can support a site. In part, this is because other Web-based services don't need advertising; people are willing to pay directly for them. Thus, a growing number of sites are counting on user fees for revenue. This can take

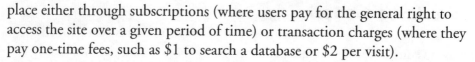

place either through subscriptions (where users pay for the general right to access the site over a given period of time) or transaction charges (where they pay one-time fees, such as $1 to search a database or $2 per visit).

Right now the number of sites that use this model is limited by the lack of an easy-to-use, widespread Web-based commerce system. This situation is quickly changing, however, and as Web users become familiar with such commerce systems, pay-to-access models will certainly become far more common.

The key to the pay-to-access model is simple: You need to have a product people are willing to pay for above and beyond their Web access costs. This seems like quite an obstacle right now, considering the amount of free content on the Web. However, many pay-to-access services already exist. Pathfinder is charging, as are online services (such as MSN, CompuServe, and AOL) and Starwave/ESPN's SportsZone. Microsoft's Slate plans to start charging in Fall 1996.

Retailing Products

Another major business model that you will certainly see more of consists of sites selling products via the Web. Some of these products can be delivered over the Web, while others have to be delivered via different means.

Of course, the most exciting of these two options is the retailing of products that can be delivered directly via the Web. Many products have the potential to be delivered this way, although much will depend on the spread of higher-speed access lines and other technology that has yet to be put in place. In the future, however, it is possible that music, videos, software, printed publications, and even books will be purchased and arrive at our homes through entirely electronic means.

Derived Revenue Models

The derived revenue model means a site contributes to the growth of the company's revenues, but not because people are paying for the site's content or because they are ordering products online.

Online Advertising and Promotion

Any well-organized form of Web-based advertising and promotion can lead to revenue, and lots of companies have used this model to justify their Web efforts. Many high-tech companies post product information on the Web,

game companies make demo versions of their latest efforts available at their sites, and other companies simply entertain and inform Web consumers as a way of introducing themselves. Following are some of the major areas companies can work in that can lead to derived revenue:

- Web-based advertising

- Web-based brochures and catalogs

- Generating leads from gathered demographic information

- Interactive product demonstrations

- Customer service operations

The biggest problem with pursuing a derived revenue economic model is trying to figure out how much actual revenue is derived via the Web. If the site is part of an overall advertising and promotion plan, what portion of the credit should go to the Web part of that effort? Some companies have worked hard to track the results of their sites by collecting names and demographics of visitors, asking people where they got a sales lead from, and so on.

So if you plan on going the derived revenue route to cost-justify your site development efforts, spend a lot of time trying to calculate exactly how much revenue is either saved or earned as a direct result of the Web site. That means asking customers where they got their information about a purchase, calculating visits to the site, looking at the difference between Web-using customers and non Web-using customers, and so on.

Cost Savings Models

Many companies are finding out that they can afford to spend millions of dollars on their Web sites without generating either direct or derived revenue from them, because the sites save money the company spent delivering services via other means.

Service Replacement Model

Is there some service that a company can implement on the World Wide Web to replace something it does through more expensive means? You bet! And a lot of companies are pursuing this type of development strategy with the Web. For example, Federal Express and UPS offer package tracking services via their Web sites that cut employee and phone costs tremendously. Lots of computer

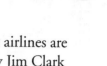

companies offer technical support via the Web, and hotels and airlines are taking bookings online. Healtheon, a new company formed by Jim Clark (who founded Netscape), is planning on helping HMOs use the Web to accept insurance forms and interact with their customers. All of these schemes are aimed at replacing more expensive traditional service methods.

Materials Reduction Model

In most service replacement models, the major goal is to cut labor costs. But the Web also can be used to reduce the cost of materials. For example, Kodak uses its Web site to disseminate lots of product literature, saving millions of dollars in mailing and printing costs alone. Lots of companies have documents they distribute around the world. While fax machines are somewhat useful for this, a Web site is even better—the color and multimedia options make a big difference all by themselves.

Productivity Increase Model

Is there some service that can't be replaced but can be improved with a Web site? Think back to the General Electric site I mentioned in Chapter 8, which included a lot of information to help people work more easily with GE. Vendors could find out how to participate in GE programs, graphic designers had help with corporate identity information, and so on. In these cases the company isn't so much replacing existing services as it is improving the efficiency with which it interacts with people.

While productivity-improving sites will mostly be made for corporate intranets, there are certainly aspects of this goal involving the outside world (help-wanted ads come to mind) that only the Web can offer.

One Size Doesn't Fit All

The best business plans on the Web tend to combine the models listed above. While a site may use one model in a dominant fashion, it also may include parts of the other models. In real-world situations it's more important to look at what each piece of your site actually accomplishes than it is to force all of the parts into a single theory.

Where and How Do I Fit In?

This is the $64,000 question for many people looking at doing business on the Web. Most people will fall under the "Companies That Want in on the

Web" or in the "Software Developers"/"Web Site Developers" categories. However, as we've seen, there are many options to pursue under these broad classifications. Only when you sift through all the information and look at your own situation will you pursue the one that makes the most sense. Of course, the most important part of planning is that you pick a plan and stick to it. The Web is filled with companies that are constantly jumping around from one economic model to the other in the hopes that something will stick and they'll start making money. Don't be one of them.

No matter what, you need to think about what sort of developer you are (an owner, a client, or a production house, for instance) and what sort of business model—or combination of models—will justify your investment into Web development.

CHAPTER 23

The Web industry requires more than just talent; it needs Web-savvy talent.

Jobs and Hiring in the Web Industry

Talent Vs. Web-Savvy Talent

The Web is going to create an incredible number of new jobs. Some will be at the expense of other job lines, but for the most part I think the Web is going to usher in a lot of entirely new work. The real problem may be that the initial rise of the Web relied on technologies and practices that many people had experience with. As the Web rapidly matures and moves from being a publishing-like medium to something that more closely resembles software development, though, the need for more people with heavy high-tech experience is growing. Increased competition makes it all the more important to hire people who "get it"—that is, who understand interactivity, Web culture, and the real differences between the Web and traditional mediums.

This isn't to say people who are inexperienced about the Web are bad hires; some of them could potentially provide the best talent. But because a premium will be placed on Web savvy and experience, a listing of exactly what a person needs to know to take on a particular type of job can be a valuable resource.

In this chapter I've tried to mix together two questions to get one answer. The person who wants to hire and the person who wants to be hired have somewhat different needs, but the qualifications that must be met are the same. I've tried to outline each type of position available out there, then explain the characteristics and specific skills that someone filling that position should possess. At the end I've done some leg work for you and listed the major sites for placing want ads and looking for work in the Web development industry.

The Basic Skills Many People Look For

Before we look at specific positions and skills sets, it make sense to cover some of the more fundamental abilities Web industry types expect (or at least hope for) in potential employees.

Understanding Web Basics

A question many employers ask early in job interviews is surprisingly simple: "Have you ever surfed the Web?" It's still not surprising to hear "no" as the answer. When something as hyped as the Web comes along, people want in on it—and some will think their present-day skills as graphic artists, musicians, writers, or even programmers are transferable to the Web at the sign of a paycheck.

The moral here is that in this area, the Web is like any other business; you will be quizzed as to your knowledge and passion for the industry in general. Do you know what Yahoo is? Can you tell me what an HTML tag is? What are frames? What does URL stand for? Who made Java, and what does it do? What is a browser? A plug-in? If you can't be at least this broadly familiar with every concept presented in this book, start playing catch-up *now*.

Platform Familiarity

Depending on the company, there may also be some requirements about which computer platforms you're familiar with. Many Web servers are run on Unix-based machines such as Sun, SGI, and Hewlett-Packard workstations; there are also servers available for Macs and Windows NT that are quite popular. And regardless of the server system they're running, many developers use different systems for creating their content, and they may mix and match platforms.

As a result, it's easy to find shops that have a Unix server but do all their artwork on Macs and do their Java/ActiveX development on Windows machines. Make sure you know the platforms that a position will require knowledge of. It would be a waste to hire a top NT Webmaster to work with a Unix server if an equally good Unix Webmaster is available.

Even though products like JavaScript, Java, and Shockwave are meant to be platform-independent on playback, the development environments can be different on each platform (for example Microsoft's J++ Java development system is different from Sun's Java creation tools). In addition, there can be back-end differences in programming for the server systems. For example, you may know O'Reilly's excellent server package WebSite inside and out, programming its scripts in Visual Basic with Microsoft Access databases...but try transferring that knowledge to a Netscape Server running on Unix.

Position Categories

Let's start by outlining the major types of workers in the Web industry. I've broken them down like this:

- Programming Positions
- Site Technology and Support Positions
- Content Creation Positions

- Site Development-Specific Positions

- Marketing/Business Positions

I'll run through each category and explain the specific job types you will encounter, but first let me make a few disclaimers. I've only outlined *some* of the major positions that you most often see and hear associated with Web development. There are many variations in these positions; these are meant to give a basic idea of the types and personalities that are involved in developing for the Web. For example, I list three programmer types—Web-based languages, traditional languages, and Web databases—but many companies will have junior and senior levels for each of these, much as they do in other types of software development. The same logic goes for almost all the positions mentioned here.

For the most part I skip over the subject of educational backgrounds, but rest assured that degree requirements are very much a part of the game. Don't expect to get a programmer position without a computer science degree, and don't think that art staff job you want isn't being pursued by graphic designers with four-year college degrees. Yes, the Internet and the Web industry are full of college-dropout successes (Bill Gates, for instance, and that kid down the block from you who makes $40 an hour doing HTML editing), but these are the exceptions—and many of them are *not* employed full time at companies; they're freelancers or entrepreneurs. If you're reading this book and thinking that the World Wide Web is some sort of degreeless industry, guess again: The stakes are high, and lots of very smart degree-holding people want in.

Also, take my salary figures with a grain of salt. You're not going to get $100,000 as a programmer for a Web development shop if you're not *worth* $100,000. Not only that, but salaries are affected by such things as benefits, the cost of living in a particular area, and the specific company itself. Most people who are earning oodles of money in this industry are longtime designers and/or developers who were doing lots of cool computer or publishing stuff before they hit the Web; their talents give them the ability to command high salaries. In fact, the few friends I have working for Web development shops are making small change, because most of their companies are shoestring-financed startups competing ferociously for a payday that is well down the line. In almost every case, people getting rich in the Web field would be worth a lot of money no matter what industry they were in.

Programmer Positions

Salary: $30,000–$100,000+ (the low end would be script language experts, while the high end would be multilanguage programmers with lots of past experience)

Software developers associated with the Web industry work in essentially three categories: Web-centered languages such as Java, JavaScript, and Shockwave; more traditional languages such as C/C++ or Delphi; and Web-related database programs with Web experience. While there are many programmers who can move easily among these areas, there are certainly specialists as well.

The Web Language Programmer

To be a Web language programmer, you need to have lots of programming experience in general, as well as recent experience with Web-based programming. This means strong Java, JavaScript, Visual Basic Script, and ActiveX programming skills. The best jobs will go to those programmers who can easily move and coordinate development among the many different Web-based languages, but as I just noted, there will also be a lot of work for specialists.

Specific Skills Desired

- Solid experience with any number of Web-based languages. (Remember, some of these have only been out less than a year, so it's hard to say, "I've got seven years' experience." Examples count.)

- Many companies will also look for strong C++ skills, because Java is very much like C++ and therefore extensive experience in the latter will be transferable.

- Good communication and team skills. (Web development often results in lots of different non-programmer types trying to work together, making interpersonal skills more important than ever.)

- Internet experience, because knowing a Web language isn't enough; a good programmer also needs to be very aware of program size, access speeds, latencies, and Internet culture.

Specific Product Knowledge Desired

- The main languages looked for are Java, Shockwave (i.e., Director's Lingo language), JavaScript, Perl/CGI, Visual Basic Script, and Telescript.

- Authoring tools, which range from visual Java tools like Hyperwire (from Kinetix) to specialized Java programming tools like Latté (from Borland) and Café (from Symantec).

- Programming various libraries and components, such as Microsoft's ActiveMovie API or Netscape's server API.

Desired Future Skills

Experience—because almost everyone is still green, those who quickly become experienced Web programmers will soon be as in demand as top C++ programmers are today.

The Traditional Language Developer

As I've discussed elsewhere, not all Web programming is done in Java or one of the script languages. For the most part, attractive "traditional" programmers will include those with strong C, Delphi, or Visual Basic skills who understand the Web, plus those whose experience includes applications like Winsock and other Internet programming APIs (such as DirectPlay, Microsoft's multiplayer/Internet API).

Specific Skills Desired

- Strong programming skills with several years of experience, including recent experience with the Internet and TCP/IP.

- Familiarity with programming APIs like socket programs (such as Winsock.DLL), DirectPlay or other Internet gaming APIs, and server APIs.

- Experience with Web-based languages like Java.

- Familiarity with plug-in or ActiveX component programming.

- Familiarity with different platforms, specifically Macintosh, Windows 95 and NT, and Unix (mostly SGI and Sun implementations).

Specific Product Knowledge Desired

- Server systems like Microsoft's Internet Server and BackOffice platform or Netscape's array of server systems.

Desired Future Skills

I'd wager that the biggest change for traditional language developers will be the rise of more robust APIs and, most importantly, the massive integration of Web and Internet technologies directly into computer operating systems (OS). At that point there will be even more developers who combine training in traditional programming languages with Web smarts; they will be called upon to harness this tighter integration between an OS, its applications, and the Web.

The Web Database Programmer

Database programming has changed a lot over the years, and the World Wide Web is changing it once again. More than anything else, the Web is creating a huge demand for database programmers, especially those familiar with Standard Query Language (SQL), Microsoft Visual Basic and Access, Informix, and Oracle.

Specific Skills Desired

- Experience with building front ends to Web databases using HTML forms and CGI scripting.

- Familiarity with advanced Internet database tools like NeXT's Web Objects.

- Knowledge of Web server systems and how to link them with back-end database systems.

Site Technology and Support Positions

Salary: $25,000–$100,000+ (The breadth of the server job is the key issue for higher-paying jobs. Site coordinators will be on the very low end of the pay scale, but will serve as entry positions to those looking to "bump up" to the level of product manager, designer, or even Webmaster.)

Aside from programming, Web sites have one very technological aspect: the entire networking, server, and site upkeep component. While programmers construct the tools and applications, another group of engineers must pull together this software and marry it to the hardware that makes it possible to serve up pages.

Webmaster

The best-known position in this category is that of Webmaster. Although I confine my definition of a Webmaster to the specific set of responsibilities listed below, in some organizations they take on many other aspects of Web development (such as programming, design, and even content creation). For large sites or big companies, though, a Webmaster is most commonly an advanced network engineer who specializes in Web hardware and software.

Specific Skills Desired

- Experience with all types of server setups and hardware.

- Knowledge of network connections and Internet connection hardware.

- Strong programming skills, especially with scripting, Perl, and HTML; other programming experience is certainly a plus.

- Good experience with Web server security systems.

Desired Future Skills

As more Web industry positions become clearly defined, there will be fewer Webmasters of the jack-of-all-trades type and more who are specialized network administrators maintaining the server, its files, and overall issues concerning connections and the server software setup. Instead of being called upon to do things like HTML editing or programming, they will manage or work with programmers to fulfill those functions.

Site Coordinators/Facilitators

This is a position that's just starting to rise in importance, but is in ample evidence on most commercial online services. Like these services, more and more Web sites are building interactive areas where people can chat in real-time or post messages. These areas often require the presence of a moderator or "host," whose responsibilities can range from patrolling for illegal posts (freedom of speech doesn't mean you can't be liable for slanderous allegations) to generating responses by suggesting topics to be discussed.

Specific Skills Desired

- Good interpersonal skills and excellent familiarity with Internet issues and culture.

- Excellent knowledge of the subject being monitored and coordinating.

- Basic knowledge of the hardware and software used on the site, especially bulletin-board messaging software, email, and chat systems.

- Familiarity with Web page editors and HTML command sets.

Content Creation Positions

Salary: $25,000–$75,000+ (Lots of people here will work freelance; those in-house will trade higher potential returns for security. The highest-paying jobs will be reserved for those who serve as production directors managing staffs of content creators.)

While programmers and Webmasters may help get a site up and running, and even provide a bunch of cool applets to support it, all sites need to have content. Someone has to write up the text portions, create the graphics, develop the sounds, fill up the databases, and so on. In the Web industry I see four basic content creation types: artists, music and sound creators, multimedia developers, and writers.

The Web Artist

Good Web artists tend to be quite technically oriented—that is, they understand a great deal about computers and the World Wide Web. It's not enough just to be a good artist; they need to be familiar with such technical items as the various file formats, data transfer rates, and interface design aspects of the Web.

Specific Skills Desired

- Familiarity with JPEG, GIF89A, progressive JPEG, animated GIFs, and various plug-in graphics formats (like Corel's CMX or Macromedia's FreeHand plug-in).

- Familiarity with the role of graphics in interface design, and the ability to create strong "icon-like" imagery that is both artistic and intuitive.

- Strong graphic products skills with leading packages like Adobe Photoshop, Freehand, Illustrator, and Web 3D.

Desired Future Skills

The biggest change in the future skill set for Web artists will be a need for 3D modeling and animation skills. As VRML becomes more of a force and as

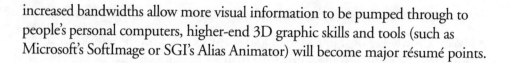

increased bandwidths allow more visual information to be pumped through to people's personal computers, higher-end 3D graphic skills and tools (such as Microsoft's SoftImage or SGI's Alias Animator) will become major résumé points.

The Web Music/Sound Creator

As more developers discover the enormous amount of room for sound and music on their sites, there will be a large push for musicians and sound engineers in the Web industry. Many of them will move over from the multimedia, game development, and MIDI industries. MIDI is small potatoes now, but expect it to become a bigger player on the Internet soon. The biggest block of experienced computer MIDI and interactive musicians work in multimedia and game development, but the Web is much bigger than either of those two industries, and there are lots of other technologies for sound and music playback to think about as well.

In most cases, though, music will tend to be outsourced rather than produced in-house. Lots of musicians in the games and multimedia industries work as freelancers already, and some have banded together into larger music shops (like Rob Wallace Music or the Sega Music Group). These musicians tend not only to be good, MIDI-capable craftsmen, but to understand a lot about computers as well, including the vast array of music formats that have been developed.

The most common positions you see for in-house people are areas such as sound engineers, who work with the various encoding schemes associated with products like Streamworks and RealAudio. Additionally, they might also double up as recording engineers, recording sound effects or sampling music or interviews for downloading.

Specific Skills Desired

- Ability to work with the myriad sound formats found on the World Wide Web.

- Familiarity with the ins and outs of the various systems used to deliver sound through the Web.

- Knowledge of how to optimize sound for delivery over the Web.

Specific Product Knowledge Desired

- Streaming software like Xing StreamWorks, TrueSpeech, and RealAudio.

- MIDI sequencers and plug-ins like Crescendo.

The Web Multimedia Developer

A multimedia developer is a different kind of artist—a person who understands how to create multimedia applications or presentations for a site. While he or she might work with artists and musicians, the multimedia developer brings the extra talent of authoring expertise (most likely with Director, or perhaps Java or C++) that ties these elements and others into a cohesive application.

Specific Skills Desired

- Familiarity with Shockwave/Director is an important skill. There are other systems for delivering multimedia content over the Web (and familiarity with those systems is a plus), but for all practical purposes, Shockwave is the way to go right now when you're looking to put a multimedia application on the Web. Most current multimedia programmers are already very familiar with Director.

- Shockwave has a lot of interesting multimedia-specific capabilities, but Java is also going to be a major player in the multimedia authoring market.

- Familiarity with other new multimedia authoring tools for the Web like Enliven, Top Gun, and others are also important.

Desired Future Skills

Right now, the key skill is the ability to create cool applications that fit in small packages, especially using Shockwave. Java and other ways of delivering multimedia applications are emerging, however, and multimedia programmers with the flexibility to use the best tool for the job will have an advantage.

The Web Writer

Until the world is full of cable modems, low latencies, and hundreds of millions of users, text is likely to remain the most predominant means of communication at Web sites. Thus there will continue to be a heavy demand for writers. Recent arrivals like Salon1999, Word, and Slate are entirely new highbrow publications to which writers can submit work, but lots of sites that aren't magazines require their talents as well.

Specific Skills Desired

- An understanding of the opportunities that Web-specific things like sound bites, links, and multimedia presentations offer writers.

- A visual understanding of their work. While some sites will have full-blast designers, a writer who knows about HTML and Web design can do a lot to be even more communicative. For example, rather than let the designer decide how to display the copy in HTML, the writer can flesh out the copy to make it sound better. In addition, if the writer understands URLs and interactive design, they can take advantage of those abilities as they create new work.

- Good technology skills, since they may have to understand (or help outside writers understand) file transfer applications such as email, FTP, and file compression.

Specific Product Knowledge Desired

- Experience with an Web page editor like FrontPage or Netscape Navigator Gold is a plus.

Desired Future Skills

The future for Web writers is hard to predict, but certainly one can expect a greater need for interactive storytelling like that in the various existing Web soap operas, as well as other interactive fare like adventure games and trivia contests.

Site-Specific Development Positions

Salary: $25,000–$75,000+ (On the lower end of the salary range you'll find page developers who work underneath an overall design director. Beyond the $75,000 level for top in-house talent, you'll find individuals who most likely are heads of their own design firms.)

Development Manager

This person is the lead designer/producer of a site. In some companies he or she will be the overall designer or art director (developing the basics of the site's content and navigation), while in others he or she will be more of a software product manager (facilitating a staff of creative artists, marketing people, and programmers).

Staff Designers

Well, someone has to do the grunt work. Lots of companies need people who can design and produce the pages that make their site look great. While at a very small site that can all be done by one person, at others this is simply impossible. Thus, depending on the company and size of the site(s), there will certainly be junior staff designers working under a manager to produce Web pages. These employees will primarily work with both editing programs and raw HTML code to produce the sites.

Specific Skills Desired

- Designers should know HTML cold (including all the browser-specific tags) and be able to produce "clean" work quickly.

- An understanding of cross-platform issues—that is, how to design sites for multiple browsers.

- A solid history of graphic design and/or Web design experience, or a degree reflecting such experience.

- Understanding of and familiarity with other types of Web design, such as JavaScript, plug-in types, and Java applets.

- Candidates for overall designer or managerial positions will need to have extensive design experience (and perhaps software development experience as well). Beyond management skills, they must demonstrate a good deal of Web-specific knowledge about navigation systems and interface design.

Specific Product Knowledge Desired

- Experience with a Web page editor like FrontPage, Netscape Navigator Gold, and/or Adobe PageMill/SiteMill.

Desired Future Skills

Style sheets are coming, and so are a lot more extensions to HTML. As the browser wars heat up in 1997, expect more special tags, more flexibility in page design, and an ever-greater need for Web-specific experience rather than similar experiences in other mediums.

Marketing and Management Positions

Salary: $25,000–$100,000+ (PR and sales reps will get the entry-level salaries, while the highest pay most likely will go to people who are not only managers, but also principals of development houses or division heads for a company's online ventures.)

The Web industry is a genuine cross between the software development and publishing industries, so most of the basic marketing and management positions will be the same as those found elsewhere in these businesses. I want to highlight a couple of job types, however, because they may not have been seen much before in the software industry.

Editors

Since the Web is a very text-heavy medium and lots of sites are "publishing oriented" (that is, providing large amounts of news and informational material), many sites are utilizing editors. Much like magazine or newspaper editors, these people work to organize, position, and manage the content on the site. They also might determine what stories are listed, where photos go, the editorial slant of the site, and other important issues.

Advertising Positions

Even in the game development business—which is the part of the software business that has had the highest exposure to advertising—there aren't any companies I know of that have a specific person handling only advertising, marketing, and so on. Such people will definitely be required by companies doing work on the Web.

Beyond these two positions there will be basic marketing and managerial types, such as marketing directors, public relations staff, human resources supervisors, and so on. Remember, not everyone who works in the Web industry is going to be a production-oriented expert. At the same time, the key positions here will go to people who understand a lot about the production of Web products, the World Wide Web itself, and the opportunities it presents—even if they never help design a Web page. The young age of the industry may have camouflaged this reality, but you can bet that in two or three more years there will be a lot more ads that say "two to three years' experience within the Web industry required."

Web Industry Job and Hiring Resources

Is it very hard to think of the best place to post or find help-wanted listings for Web development jobs? I'll give you three guesses....

Okay, you only get one guess: the easy answer is the World Wide Web itself. But that doesn't mean that the Web is the only place to go. There are a slew of good places to look, and here's a good rundown on them (including top Web sites).

Books

Not surprisingly, there has been a dramatic increase in recent years in the number of people looking for and placing job openings on the Internet. Several good books have come along that can help you with this effort.

How to Get Your Dream Job Using the Internet by Shannon Bounds and Arthur Karl (published by Coriolis Group Books, 1996, ISBN 1-883-5776-83)

Hook Up, Get Hired: Internet Job Search by Joyce Lain Kennedy (published by John Wiley & Sons, 1995, ISBN 047-1116-3-00)

Finding a Job on the Internet by Alfred and Emily Glossbrenner (published by McGraw-Hill, 1995, ISBN 007-02405-58)

Magazines and Periodicals

I'm not going to do a full listing of each magazine or periodical that has a good listing of want ads, because you'll find Web-oriented ones in the appendix. The other periodicals you can easily find at their sites on the Internet or pick up the actual pulp version at your favorite large bookstore or newsstand.

Magazines

Among magazines, the best places to look for help wanted listings are the trade tabloids like *Interactive Week*, *Inter@ctive*, *InfoWorld*, and *PC Week*. These tend to be where large companies will advertise. I've listed all of these publications in the magazine appendix. You can find many want ads for

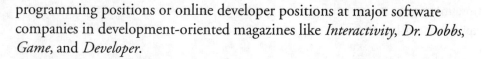

programming positions or online developer positions at major software companies in development-oriented magazines like *Interactivity, Dr. Dobbs, Game*, and *Developer*.

Other Periodicals

An important place to look for job listings are the major newspapers of Web hotspots like Seattle, New York, Boston, and San Francisco. All of the papers (especially the Sunday edition) tend to feature ads from new media/Web-oriented companies. National firms like Microsoft and Netscape will also routinely place ads in these papers when looking for a round of fresh résumés.

Conferences

A great place to hunt for jobs is at the multitude of computer conferences, especially those that center on online/Web development. Many even feature job fairs. Among the more useful would be Software Development/Web Development held in San Francisco every spring, Mecklermedia's huge Internet World conference which is held twice yearly in the U.S. (with many sister shows throughout the world), and smaller specialized conferences like Macromedia's Computer Game Developers conference.

For a complete appendix dedicated to Web-oriented or relevant conferences, look in the back of this book.

Web Sites

Some more general advice here. What are some of the places to look for on your own that can help you find your dream Web development job?

Search Engines & Newsgroups—First and foremost, consider using search engines like Alta Vista, and DejaNews to scan popular newsgroups and the Web itself for job openings. Some of the books mentioned earlier can help you, but I suspect you already are familiar with the ins and outs of most search engines.

Major Web Development Company Home Pages—Another good place to look is on the individual pages of all the major Web developers. Just start surfing to various Web development companies like iVillage and Studio Archetype, or to software developers like Microsoft and Netscape, and you'll find lots of listings—many of which accept résumés online.

Web Development-Relevant Organizations—Another good idea is to check in with the organizations I've listed in an appendix at the end of this book. Lots of major technology-oriented organizations, like the HTML Writers Guild or the International Interactive Communications Society, have good leads and listings.

There are also a host of Web sites that are specifically set up to match job seekers with employers—especially for hi-tech oriented positions. Here are some URLs that can lead you to many different online-based job recruiters and listing services.

Recruiters Online Network

`http://www.ipa.com/`

This is a site devoted to online recruiting and hiring. It's packed with information and can be considered one of the best places to start looking. There are lots of links to other online recruiters and job listings, as well.

Yahoo's Listing of Recruiting and Placement Services

`http://www.yahoo.com/Business_and_Economy/Companies/Employment_Services/`
`Recruiting_and_Placement/`

Recruiting and placement services have gone to the Web in droves, and Yahoo has a very comprehensive listing of them. While not all of them specialize in hi-tech job placement, this list is a good starting place.

CareerPath.com

`http://www.careerpath.com`

CareerPath.com is one of the more popular online job listers. It features over 100,000 ads (of course not all are Web-oriented). It compiles these want ads from participating papers in 19 major U.S. cities.

The Monster Board

`http://www1.monster.com`

The Monster Board not only provides listings for over 55,000 jobs worldwide, it also provides a section targeted for recruiters, where people can post résumés. Another worthwhile site to check out.

CHAPTER 24

Research is the key to success.

Web Market Analysis: Forecasting and Surveys

Question: What used to go down best with a grain of salt added?

Answer: Research about the demographics of the World Wide Web, or about ways to track your site's demographics.

Without a doubt, the earliest studies of the Web were sketchy at best. Today, however, thanks to the help of some good research companies and a growing academic presence to keep them honest, there are some genuinely believable sources of information about who is on the Web, what they are doing, how much they might be spending, and what sort of software (and other paraphernalia) they are using. Their higher-quality findings can be very helpful to developers and the Web industry in general.

In this chapter I'll wade through some of this research, highlight some of what I see as important, and then suggest some of the best places to go to get much more detailed information about the Web and who uses it.

Having good research available to you—for instance, about demographic trends, which sites are the best, and where ad revenues are going—is very important. Not only can it help guide your own Web development ideas, it can help you justify those ideas to potential partners and investors (who may want some sort of quantitative analysis to back up your claims that you can all get rich from a site devoted to women over 65 who live in Australia).

The majority of the research I present here comes in three flavors: free, not free, and preview, which are small abstracts of the research available. While the abstracts are nothing like the full report, they can sometimes offer a few interesting nuggets of information for those who can't afford to buy the reports (which can easily run $2,500 to $10,000).

The Fundamentals of Hardware

While software trends may sometimes seem like the main factor determining the present or future of the World Wide Web, the truth is that hardware is still king. As you'll see below, the way that hardware improves and is distributed among the users of the Web goes a long way toward deciding which people are able to get online, how they do it, and what software they use.

Cost factors are the main reason hardware is so important. Even the most expensive Web software isn't nearly as expensive as top-of-the-line computer hardware. Later in this chapter I'll present some simple data about hardware costs and distribution.

Moore's Law: The Fundamental Hardware Axiom

You might not have heard of Gordon Moore, but you've definitely heard of Intel, the company he helped found. Intel is the largest CPU chip manufacturer in the world, and its Pentium, 486, 386, and 286 chips are the most commonly used chips in personal computers around the world. In the industry, though, Moore is perhaps even better known for a "law" he proposed (which I'll paraphrase here):

Every two years the amount of transistors on a chip will double and the cost for existing computing power will halve.

In layman's terms, this means that the money you pay for a machine today will buy you a machine twice a powerful two years from now, and the machine you buy today will be worth only half the price you just paid. (Aren't you glad the real estate market doesn't work this way?)

When Moore first proposed this idea, many people in the computer industry laughed; they figured that at some point computing power—especially for personal computers—would hit a wall. If anything, however, Moore's Law has proven to be an understatement. Lately, the cycle he describes has seemed to take place in *less* than two years!

Why is Moore's Law important? Because it means that every two years, improved power will lead to the emergence of a new computing platform that can support dramatically wider options for its users. This is great (if sort of expensive) for those of us capable of staying on the cutting edge, but it also explains why you have all kinds of different systems of varying power out there. And all those systems explain why the computer industry has so many narrow and incompatible market segments.

Exposed Interactive Consumers

When I was doing the research for my previous book, *The Ultimate Game Developer's Sourcebook*, I attended a speech by noted game industry analyst Lee Isgur of Jeffries Securities. He talked about a group of people he called "exposed interactive consumers"—people who have never known a world without computer games (or, in our case, the World Wide Web). People who are accustomed to getting the daily paper from the local newsstand, for example, may be reluctant to go online to get the latest news. In contrast, people born into a world where the Web is a familiar source of entertainment and information will be far more likely to make it a central part of their lives.

This powerful concept explains the natural resistance some of us feel toward the Web, simply because of the time we were born into this world. But it also explains how compelling the Web has become—after all, it has found its way into millions of homes, even though no one born into a "Web-active" world has yet reached adolescence. Unlike games, multimedia, and other computer applications, the Web has the chance to bring in many new consumers, in addition to being a de facto choice of anyone born post-1990.

Understanding the Household Demographic Split

When it comes to statistics, I like to keep things simple. With that in mind, here's a very fundamental breakdown of the various categories of potential Web users.

This breakdown will focus on the average household. A *household* is a common unit used in many marketing/survey/polling situations, especially those concerning products that can be purchased and used by an entire family. Table 24.1 shows a household unit breakdown from a survey done by New York–based Alexander & Associates in 1996. While these numbers are always changing, the table does an excellent job of illustrating some basic points.

This survey focused primarily on the computer/video game market, but it applies to the emerging Web market as well because the hardware to view the World Wide Web is the same. In a later section of this chapter I'll discuss the survey's additional tracking of specific households with "Web appliances" or "Web-ready consoles," and you'll see that these numbers translate quite nicely.

The survey defines four distinct types of households:

- *PC-Only Households*—These households are the bread and butter of the home computer industry. They number over 15 million and tend to be middle- to upper-income families.

- *PC and Console Households*—These don't vary much from PC-only households, although they tend to have more children—especially younger ones (which explains the presence of a console system)—and to be less educated. While their overall income is virtually the same as

Table 24.1 Alexander & Associates' survey.

	All HH	PC & VGS	PC Only	VGS Only	None
Millions of Households	92.9	9.6	13.2	17.3	52.9
Mean Household Size	2.73	3.75	2.69	3.46	2.35
Mean Age	45.6	35.9	40.4	33.9	49.9
Mean Household Income	$36,830	$52,803	$54,951	$34,811	$29,207
% Married	55.8	68.3	64.1	59.6	49.8
% Children Present	37.4	68.4	32.6	69.3	21.9
% College Graduate	24.9	36.7	50.3	15.5	19.4
% With PC	24.4	100	100	0	0
% With CD-ROM	7.6	40	32.6	0	0
% With VGS	28.8	100	0	100	0

that of PC-only households, these households tend to have less disposable income simply because they have more kids. The majority of these households are families who buy consoles for their children in addition to the conventional PC they also own. The remainder, for the most part, are hard-core game and computer fanatics who are hooked on interactive entertainment.

• *Console-Only Households*—The console-only crowd has an average income that is dramatically lower than the first two household types we discussed. This explains the lack of PCs in the household; a $150 game system is far more affordable than a $2,000 computer. Average education levels are also significantly lower. The group represents middle- to lower-income families who enjoy games and interactive entertainment, but just don't have the money to buy a full-fledged multimedia-capable computer system.

• *No System*—These households are the poorest and oldest of the bunch. Many consist of senior citizens who have fixed incomes and minimal interest in technology; the rest simply don't want or can't afford to be part of the interactive revolution. This segment will steadily shrink as more and more people who become familiar with the interactive/computer world find they can't do without it. Even so, there will always be those who choose to sit on the sidelines.

Why Is This Breakdown Important?

The survey shows a substantial number of households that want to be part of the Internet but can't afford a top-of-the-line PC system. If these people flock to new, lower-cost devices designed especially to access the Web, developers will need to address the lower capabilities of these systems. The size of this market certainly explains the race to build lower-cost computers and Web access devices, and you can expect to see other ideas (like financing for more robust computers) aimed at giving this large demographic group access to the hardware it needs to surf the Web.

Understanding the Business/Household/ Educational Split

The demographic profile of the Web marketplace is unlike that of the games industry because so many people access the Web outside of the home—either at school or, more often, at the office. A large number of these people may live in non-computer households, while others may access the Web at work with a system that has more memory or higher bandwidth than what they have at home (or vice versa).

People may also have free access at work, but pay an hourly rate at home. (Why do you think college kids are so prevalent on the Web? Does the phrase "free access" mean anything to you?)

There are distinct differences in people's Web access habits depending on whether they are at work, at home, or at school. Also, there is a growing concern among employers about such things as access to Web-based games and other fare that can slow productivity. As employers start to crack down on this problem, you can expect traffic at many areas of the Web to drop off significantly.

Heading Toward a Wired World

Eventually, we won't talk any more about various "have" and "have-not" pools of potential Web consumers, because we will have arrived at a fully wired world. For us to get to this world, however, every demographic group will need the ability to purchase and set up some device that can access the Web, and developers will need to build all the supporting systems required to make those devices work. As you'll see, this isn't a one-size-fits-all endeavor, nor does it include just the process of building the necessary hardware and software.

The Telemedia Index

Alexander & Associates
38 East 29th Street, 10th Floor
New York, NY 10015
Phone: 212-684-2333
Fax: 212-684-0291
Email: info@alexassoc.com
WWW: http://www.alexassoc.com

Several companies are trying to track the emergence of a completely Web-savvy world. One company I work with, Alexander & Associates (along with its partner, Bates USA Advertising), has come up with a neat forecasting idea called the Telemedia Index. It's meant to be a sort of barometer of how close we are to a totally Web-wired world.

The index tracks four major items (each with three to five distinct component factors) that will determine the construction of a worldwide information system. Each component is scored on a scale of 1 to 100; these individual figures are then combined on a weighted basis to come up with a single number that indicates how close we are to a truly wired world.

Transport: The Physical Plant

- Backbone: Trunk Floor

- ISDN and ASDL Services

- Cable Services

- Server Speeds

Customer Equipment Connections

- Personal Computers

- Network Computers/Web Appliances/Consoles

- High-Speed Modems

Content: Topics, Tools, and Techniques

- Publishing Tools

- Security Tools

- Commerce Tools

- Content Providers

- Know-How Pool

Public Policy: The Regulatory Impact

- Legislation

- Regulation

- Government Investment

- Public Issues

What I like most about the Telemedia Index is its simple breakdown of the factors that any Web developer or market watcher should be aware of. Alexander & Associates and Bates USA are continuing to work on this idea, and soon they will be providing the first batch of scores via their newsletter on the Internet.

Breaking Down the Hardware Forecasts

What types of devices do—or will—people use to access the Web? Because people at different income levels and different access sites (home, school, or work) will go for different devices, there are likely to be a wide variety of devices in use. In the following sections, I cover the basic hardware types to watch.

Computers, Web appliances, PDAs, and game consoles are the four major hardware items that need to be discussed concerning the Web. As I mentioned earlier, there is a big split in demographics, with one large market segment using computer-based systems while the rest (shunning PCs as too expensive) opt in favor of gaming consoles.

Computers

The biggest problem in analyzing the overall computer hardware market—especially as it relates to the World Wide Web—is that there are so many different systems and configurations to consider. In terms of machines, there are Pentiums, 486s, Macs, and even a bunch of Unix users out there. For operating systems, you've got the Mac OS, Windows 3.1, Windows 95, and Windows NT, not to mention Linux, Solaris, and a slew of Unix derivatives. Keeping track of them all is enough to make you sick—but then, that's why there are research firms, right?

Essentially, though, there are five ways to look at the computer hardware scene as it concerns the Web:

- You can analyze it by separating the three distinct markets that I discussed earlier: home, business/government, and education.

- You can measure hardware via software—that is, instead of looking at Macs, Unix, and PCs or their various operating systems, just look at the number of machines that support the latest major browser implementation requirements. For the most part, there's no reason to care about a system that isn't capable of using a Netscape 3.0 or Internet Explorer 3.0 browser.

- A third way to look at computer hardware trends is by tracking game software requirements. Why game software? Well, it tends to be the most demanding software around. If most major game packages are being written for Pentium 100 machines with 16 MB of memory, you can bet that a lot of systems with those characteristics will be sold. This method is a great way to track the "power user" market segment, as well as the latest multimedia capabilities showing up in cutting edge PCs.

- Another way is to call up one of the major research firms, like Dataquest or NPD, and get a very detailed report on the systems and components out there.

- Finally, you can look at some of the Web surveys that ask questions about users' platforms. To my knowledge, however, these surveys haven't delved into some of the idiosyncrasies of computer hardware, such as whether users have a sound card, an MPEG card, or a microphone or video capture device. As the Web becomes more of a multimedia environment, information about these extras will be useful to gauge what sort of advanced features your site might offer.

Game Consoles

Don't snicker; I saw a very nicely done HTML 2.0-compliant browser running on a Sega Saturn at the 1996 Electronic Entertainment Expo. The fact is that the 32-bit/64-bit consoles are quite capable of being cheap Web browsers. Sega was the first to show one publicly, but it's widely known that behind closed doors Sony and Nintendo have also been developing Web browsers for their consoles.

It's hard to forecast if these systems will catch on, but remember that a slew of households who can't afford a PC will see this as their only ticket to surf the Web. Game consoles could become popular Web access hardware.

Network Computers/Web Appliances

Right now there is a lot of talk about these devices. As touted by several companies, especially Sun and Oracle, a "network computer" would be a device selling for about $500 that does nothing but surf the Web. The basic idea is to appeal to the many households (discussed earlier) that simply can't afford a $2,000 PC.

The argument against the viability of such machines is twofold. First, there is no way a $500 machine will be as dynamic and Web-capable as a PC is. It may not have to be, of course, but in that case households capable of buying a $2,000 PC will be unlikely to switch. Second, some say that although PC prices have never dropped substantially below $1,000—let alone $500—they will if and when the network computer is introduced.

I would add one other caution. When the first of the current generation of game consoles (such as 3DO) hit the market, they were retailing around $500, if not a little more. They failed miserably at that price point; even early successes like Sony's Playstation and Sega's Saturn both quickly dropped to below $200. The lesson for the network computer is that even if people accept the device as being useful, $500 is still a lot in the consumer electronics business.

Apple's Pippin device and Oracle's network computer will be among the first wave of trial systems in this group. Pippin could prove the most interesting experiment, because it is really a stripped-down Macintosh. For a suggested retail price of $599, this system offers an optional Netscape-compatible attachment for surfing the World Wide Web, which should be a plus.

A couple of companies have done research on the market potential for a network computer. For example, Dataquest and Alexander & Associates published reports on the devices in the early part of 1996—and couldn't have taken more opposite positions. Dataquest didn't see the market being fulfilled, for reasons including the ones I've cited here. Building on their premise of a dichotomy between computer-centered and console-centered households, Alexander & Associates found considerable consumer interest in a "sub-$500 device that surfed the Net" when such a device was described to console-only households.

Personal Digital Assistants

The last segment I want to cover is the personal digital assistant (PDA) market, which has been around for a while but is seeing renewed interest because of the Web. Many people see a significant market for simple pocket-sized wireless devices that can surf the Web, send and receive email, and provide a few other organizational functions, perhaps in conjunction with your PC at home.

Apple is already creating a Web browser for its Newton device, and several other product lines with similar features and Web access are being developed.

Where Will We End Up?

As you can see, there are a lot of hardware factors at play regarding the Web. For the most part, developers will concentrate on keeping track of core PC trends among businesses and households. As I hope I've just made clear, however, a significant number of items will encourage non-PC devices to offer access to the Web. These devices hold a lot of promise for bringing with them millions of consumers still yearning to understand the meaning of all those "http://www.thiscompany.com" things they see in ads.

The Chokehold of Bandwidth

Of course, no market survey of the Web would be complete without a hearty discussion of bandwidth. If anything is holding back the Web's development, it's the cost and widespread availability of increased bandwidth. There are many different takes on the bandwidth situation, so I'll try and clear up some of them as best I can.

Higher Bandwidth Technologies

There are several major bandwidth technologies, each with different capabilities and limitations. Let's look at each one a little more closely.

Standard Modem Speeds

Tracking the progression of standard modem speeds is fairly easy; the Georgia Tech and several other studies (discussed below) routinely ask users about the access speed of the modem they're using. Currently, most people are still using 14.4 Kbps modems, but these should be overtaken by 28.8 modems soon, if not already for more frequent Web users. Already modems with 36.6 speeds are debuting, as are 28.8 modems with higher throughputs via compression schemes. In short, there is still a lot of speed left to be acquired by this consumer base.

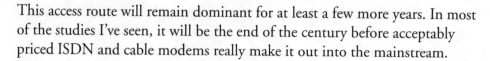

This access route will remain dominant for at least a few more years. In most of the studies I've seen, it will be the end of the century before acceptably priced ISDN and cable modems really make it out into the mainstream.

ISDN

ISDN languished for years until the World Wide Web came along; now, though, it's all the rage. The best thing about it is that the modem manufacturers, "baby Bells," and access providers have gotten serious about expanding its presence and lowering the costs. In a few areas, like the San Francisco Bay Area, it's already becoming fairly common.

Expect ISDN to gain quickly among the power-user set over the next couple of years, especially if hardware manufacturers like Gateway and Dell start offering packages that include ISDN modems. The biggest problem is that most telephone companies seem intent on charging by the minute for ISDN access; only when flat rates are offered will this service take off in many areas.

Developers should also watch for the rise of ASDL, which I'll discuss in just a second. ASDL offers far higher bandwidth and could combine with cable modems to eclipse ISDN just as the latter hits its stride.

Upper Bandwidth Connections

T1 and T3 lines are climbing in popularity, especially among business customers. I even know people who have T1s coming into their house! For the bulk of customers, however, this is not going to be the higher-bandwidth route of choice. Cable modems can actually hit higher rates if designed correctly, and the costs for those are less prohibitive. It does pay to watch the growth of T1 and T3 lines, however, as they will indicate business growth and overall Internet infrastructure growth (as service providers add more lines to handle incoming calls from their modem-equipped customers).

Cable Modems

Cable modems are the "X factor" of bandwidth if there ever was one. They promise the most amazing throughput, no waits—they do everything but end world hunger. Someday they'll actually exist…just when, though, is the question. For all the talk about cable modems, there are still kinks in the system (in fact, @Home, the hyped startup offering cable modem Internet access, has been continually delayed by problems).

Other doubts involve the cable companies that will be providing the bandwidth access. The prices being described for cable modems are not expensive—but then, we've heard this from cable companies before. Also, because cable companies are really networks of tiny fiefdoms, the rollout won't be nearly as uniform as it will be for ISDN and ASDL. Finally, there is the huge customer service problem (and if you're a cable subscriber, I don't even have to discuss this, do I?).

Nevertheless, cable modems offer bandwidth possibilities that will be very hard for many people to pass up. Once the bugs and service plans are worked out, expect sales to rise rapidly. Some studies suggest that cable modems will become the biggest segment of the access market just after 2000. For now, though, the pieces are just coming together.

ASDL

ASDL is a relatively new phone technology that is somewhat like ISDN in that it can work well over existing copper phone lines, but ASDL offers an even more dramatic increase in access speeds. ASDL modems and equipment are just rolling off the drawing boards, but already several research estimates say it—and not ISDN—will be the real successor to POTS (plain old telephone service).

Wireless

Cellular modems have been on the market for a while, but only now are the networks getting both secure and clear enough to offer reliable data transfers. The cost has to drop some more, but as more people jump on the wireless bandwagon, this seems certain to occur.

Other Bandwidth Technologies

The biggest "others" right now are broadcast feeds and satellite feeds. Satellite dishes (like those offered by DirectTV) are becoming a major component of the greater information infrastructure, and some people see a great market in downloading Web pages via these systems. One idea would have the satellite feed system download the top 200 to 500 sites every day right into your computer; these pages would then be very quick to surf.

Another idea involves attaching Web data to TV broadcast feeds. For example, a Web page for a particular show might load automatically while that show is on, or Web pages of statistics would be available during a football game. These

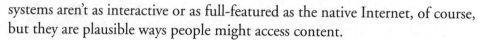

systems aren't as interactive or as full-featured as the native Internet, of course, but they are plausible ways people might access content.

Finally, systems like Iridium and Teledesic (a Bill Gates–backed project) promise a two-way cellular network backed by stationary satellite networks built to support a wide spectrum of data, voice, and video transmissions. Projected to be operational by 2010, these systems could truly cover the world in one giant, ubiquitous data network.

Don't Forget About Access Gatekeepers and Server Speeds

It takes two to tango, and many times three in the Web world. When it comes to watching bandwidth, you've got to pay some attention to the other side of the equation. Access providers (especially online services) don't always have the ability to accept higher-speed setups like ISDN, and connections from individual servers to the greater Internet architecture are not always up to speed. A T1 connection may let you surf to any site on the Web at a dramatically faster rate, but you're not getting the full throughput of a T1 by any means.

Software Wars

Having discussed the hardware and bandwidth questions concerning the Web market, we now come to the top of the fight card! As they say in Vegas:

Let's get ready to ruuuummmmmbbbbbbbbllllleeeee!!!!!

Of course, the key fight I'm referring to is the one taking place among the two major browsers and a slew of technologies that work in conjunction with them to add applets, sound, animation, and other functionality. Let's look at some of the key elements of this battle.

What's the Market Share by Browser?

For all practical purposes, there are only two browsers to watch closely—Microsoft's Internet Explorer and Netscape's Navigator. To watch them closely, you'll need to examine the various deals each company cuts with partners (like online services), peruse the various surveys that are available, and keep a keen eye on where each browser is gaining the technological edge (which can be the key factor in market-share wars.)

BrowserWatch
http://www.browserwatch.com

BrowserWatch, maintained by Dave Graffa, is a great site. It's the definitive tracking place for browser software developments. Not only does it watch the developments of the two browser titans very closely, but it tracks more than 50 other browsers, browser derivatives, and plug-in components. This is a great one-stop shop for browser surveys, rumor mills, reports, press releases, and the like.

Georgia Tech GVU Web Survey
http://www.cc.gatech.edu/gvu/user_surveys/

The GVU Web surveys always ask participants which browsers they are using, and you can find the latest information at the URL shown above. Netscape still dominated as of the last known survey, but the effect of Microsoft's Internet Explorer 3.0 release and its debut with upcoming versions of CompuServe and AOL should show up in the next survey or two.

Netscape/Microsoft Press Releases
http://www.netscape.com
http://www.microsoft.com

There's nothing like the horse's mouth, is there? While you should always take this stuff as the hype it can be, the press releases of Microsoft and Netscape will not only inform you of the deals they're cutting to make their browsers more popular but also cite the latest survey or study that shows them gaining market share. I can't remember how many times I've seen Netscape press releases mention Navigator's 70 to 80 percent market share.

A Note About Specialized Web Application Technologies (SWATs)

Products like PointCast and Freeloader are used to access Web content, but not necessarily in the same manner as your typical browser. For example, I use both Netscape Navigator and Internet Explorer, but I might employ Freeloader overnight to gather some content I look at on a daily basis. As browser technology progresses, these types of applications will play a bigger role. (Until someone calls them something different, I choose to refer to them as "specialized Web application technologies," or SWATs.)

A Note About Embedded OS Browsers

Another change that will affect the war for market share is Microsoft's decision to make its browser an embedded component of its Windows operating system. This means that future versions of Windows will use the Internet Explorer engine to browse the Web. As I show elsewhere in this book, its presence as an object in the OS makes it easier for developers to create integrated Web applications that use the Internet Explorer engine.

So, What's Really Happening?

I've just given you the tools to find out for yourself, but for those who just want to be told, here's a quick summary of what's been going on. Once Netscape was launched, it quickly outpaced the original Mosaic to gain some 80 percent of the browser market. The other 20 percent was held primarily by Quaterdeck's Mosaic, America Online's built-in browser, CompuServe's Spry-Mosaic, and Lynx. Microsoft's Internet Explorer debuted in 1995, but by June 1996 its version 3.0 matched many of the major features available in Netscape 3.0. This dramatic catch-up effort quickly turned the tables on Netscape, which is feverishly trying to push Navigator 4.0 out the door by fall. Microsoft's biggest success came earlier in 1996 when it secured the rights to be the default browser for CompuServe and America Online. While the effect of these deals won't be felt until about September, they will dramatically increase Microsoft's share of the market. Even though Netscape has a similar deal with AT&T WorldNet, which is gaining users, the latter doesn't come close to equaling the 8 million or more customers Microsoft gained access to with its AOL and CompuServe deals.

Once version 3.0 shipped, a few sites I checked were already experiencing a marked runup in Internet Explorer use—in fact, some sites even were seeing IE become the dominant browser. Prior to the 3.0 release, Microsoft had only achieved 8 to 10 percent of the browser market; by the end of 1996 it should have anywhere from 30 to 50 percent, with Netscape holding the other half of the market. A small portion of the market will be left to the usual fringe browsers and SWAT products like PointCast, Lynx, and Freeloader.

Web User Demographic Surveys

In the last two years there have been about a half-dozen or so solid studies or commitments to track the overall Web demographic scene. The studies that have been done haven't gone uncriticized—the most notable example being the Cybercitizen survey by Nielsen and Yankelovich Partners, which was discredited to some degree because of its methodology. While polling is never an exact science, doing it for the Web has been even tougher. Some reports for sale out there, however, are worth looking at…and in the case of the Georgia Tech/University of Michigan studies, you can also find some awesome free data to peruse!

Here is a roundup of interesting demographic surveys about Web users and usages.

O'Reilly & Associates

103A Morris Street
Sebastopol, CA 95472
Phone: 707-929-0515
Email: nuts@ora.com
WWW: http://www.ora.com

O'Reilly & Associates has produced two studies on the Internet. The first was an Internet user survey in 1995; more recently, it has completed an extensive survey on business use and the Internet. Both are available now.

Jupiter Communications

627 Broadway
New York, NY 10012
Phone: 212-780-6060
Email: jupiter@jup.com
WWW: http://www.jup.com

This New York-based firm produces a wide variety of reports and surveys on the Internet and other interactive mediums. Recently it also launched a system (similar to Dataquest) that sells these reports directly over the Internet.

The NPD Group

900 West Shore Road
Port Washington, NY 11050
Phone: 516-625-0700
Fax: 516-625-2347
Email: info@npd.com
WWW: http://www.npd.com

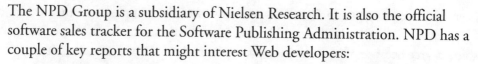

The NPD Group is a subsidiary of Nielsen Research. It is also the official software sales tracker for the Software Publishing Administration. NPD has a couple of key reports that might interest Web developers:

- *PC-Meter*—PC-Meter is a quarterly listing of the top 50 Web sites among U.S. home PC users. It surveys approximately 4,000 people who own computers and have Internet access, and it tracks their site decisions via embedded software.

- *National Survey of Hardware Ownership*—This service surveys around 10,000 people and tracks the types of hardware they own at home; lately it has begun tracking Internet activity as well. This survey contains detailed reports about hardware levels, modem speeds, multimedia capabilities, and Internet demographics.

NPD's Web site also offers a plethora of press releases detailing some of the more important findings contained in the company's research.

Dataquest

251 River Oaks Parkway
San Jose, CA 95134-1913
Phone: 408-468-8000
Fax: 408-954-1780
WWW: http://www.dataquest.com

Dataquest is one of the largest full-service research organizations tracking the high-tech industry. A division of publishing giant IDG, it produces a wide-ranging set of reports on hardware and software trends. While others have been more out front on Web surveys, Dataquest has always been a very good source for information about hardware trends, such as the outlook on cable modems, high-speed ISDN, and so on.

Cybercitizen and Cyber Dialogue

Yankelovich Partners Inc.
101 Merritt 7 Corporate Park
Norwalk, CT 06851
Phone: 203-846-0100
Fax: 203-845-8200
WWW: http://www.yankelovich.com

Yankelovich is one of the most respected market research agencies in the world, so it was very surprising when their first major foray into Web demographics was highly criticized by many academic researchers. The report turned out to be somewhat flawed and has since been seen as indicative of how hard it is to come up with highly accurate numbers concerning Web demographics.

Yankelovich has responded to the criticisms, however, and is improving its online research considerably. It has recently launch Cyber Dialogue (**http://www.cyberdialogue.com**), which it claims is, "the world's first online market research firm—offers a wide range of market research solutions, including online focus groups, email polls, and consumer panels. All participants are drawn from, and research is conducted through, the Internet."

While Cyber Dialogue is going to do lots of different market research on the Internet, it will specifically focus on research about the online interactive world. Cyber Dialogue has a number of special products, including online focus groups, email polling, and other cool stuff that is very affordable, because of the low cost of polling over the Internet. They also produce a newsletter worth checking out called the *Cyber Insider Newsletter*—don't miss the articles about some of their findings, which are located at **http://www.cyberdialogue.com/docs/interc.html**.

Yankelovich may have gotten off on the wrong foot with its initial Cybercitizen report, but it seems that the experience only made them more determined to become a prominent and respected researcher about the online world.

AOL/Nielsen Project

Recently, America Online—the largest online service, with more than 5 million members—hired Nielsen Media Research to help it compile online statistics and ratings for the AOL content areas. Despite its AOL-specific nature, the results of this work will certainly give insights into the Web world as well.

I don't expect AOL or Nielsen to make the core portions of their research available publicly, but various press releases from this work undoubtedly will provide some useful tidbits of information. For example, it was widely quoted at one conference I attended that AOL makes some 70 to 80 percent of its money from its chat rooms! This statistic is often cited by Web developers looking to build sites that feature large chat areas.

Georgia Tech/University of Michigan Business School

`http://www.cc.gatech.edu/gvu/user_surveys/`

Every developer should be at least vaguely familiar with the work being done by the folks at Georgia Tech and the University of Michigan Business School. At the time of this writing, they had conducted five complete surveys of the World Wide Web community. Each survey has obtained far more precise results than the one before it, and added more advanced questioning systems that can explore far more territory.

The results of these surveys are among the most comprehensive available. And best of all, the findings are free to the public to pore over—all the way down to the raw data sets! They can be useful for anyone putting together a Web business plan or just trying to stay informed as they make day-to-day decisions.

I could write an entire book about these studies, but I've got other stuff to cover. Surf over and see for yourself—the information is available in many forms, from executive summaries to graphs to Adobe Acrobat–formatted reports.

What About Your Own Site?

In this book's Chapter 15, you'll find a small sidebar about statistic package resources. There are several programs that can help you compile good statistics about which browsers are logging in on your site. You can also utilize such technologies as sign-ins, "cookies," and I/Pro to gather far more compelling demographic information.

As you develop your own internal demographic reports, though, use the survey resources mentioned here to provide a frame of reference to your site. You're only getting half the story if you're not comparing your internal statistics to data for the greater Web world.

A Poor Developer's Guide to Market Forecasting

If your budget isn't big enough for you to spend $2,500 to $10,000 on a series of reports, but you crave even more information than is available in the Georgia Tech surveys, a few additional resources exist to help you track trends and statistics about the Web industry. One is BrowserWatch, which I've already discussed; here's another.

Seidman's Online Insider

`http://www.clark.net/pub/robert`

Somebody give Robert Seidman a medal (and a new, shock-resistant ThinkPad)! Now a columnist/editor for NetGuide, he produces this free newsletter, which is perhaps the best source for keeping up with the ins and outs of the Web and online industry. Seidman's knowledge of the industry is very deep, and he gives good coverage to the constant numbers game that is being played regarding demographics in this industry. If you're not reading this newsletter on a regular basis, you should have your head examined.

Keep Your Eye on the Top-Tier Players

Want to know when ISDN or cable modems hit it big? One way to do this is to keep good track of what the big site players, software publishers, and access providers are doing. After all, these are the folks who can afford those $10,000 surveys—and then use this research to meticulously decide when it's safe to enter to the water. By watching them closely, you can piggyback onto their management decisions. Just keep informed, watch for trends in announcements and site developments, and you can't miss.

Read the Trade Magazines

I'm assuming that you're reading the requisite trade publications: *Inter@ctive*, *WebWeek*, *PC Week*, and *InfoWorld*. The majority of these are free and provide very good information. If you're *not* reading these publications, flip to the magazine appendix of this book and make sure you're getting all the readily available reading material out there.

CHAPTER 25

Resources for creating real Web advertising strategies.

Advertising and Promotion on the Web

Keeping the Hype in Check

You don't have to be a rocket scientist to see the potential of online/Internet advertising and promotion. But you also don't have to be a genius to figure out that it would take the Golden Gate Bridge to span the gulf between this potential—especially with the hype added in—and the practical reality that exists today. Still, Web developers of all shapes and sizes are scrambling to become experts in Web advertising, simply because the potential is there (and, well, we need to get paid somehow!).

You can read all of the studies and thoroughly unscientific online demographic surveys until the cows come home, though, and still not know the current state or near-term future of online/Internet advertising. There are two reasons for this: First, the hype has actually distracted people's attention away from the really cool stuff that is happening, and second, a lot of work remains to be done before the Web becomes a premier advertising medium. In this chapter I'll try to bring you up to speed on the realities of Web advertising.

Which Side Are You On?

The first thing to think about is: Which side of the Web advertising equation do you intend to work on? Do you intend to be an advertiser, to build sites for advertisers, or both? Many of the resources and interests are the same for both sides of the equation: How much should a Web ad cost? What makes a good Web ad? How do I target this particular group?

If you're a developer of a site, however, you add the extra burden of trying to build a site where advertisers actually want to place their ads. Also, ad sales don't come rolling in just because you placed a site on the Web and then snapped your fingers. Buying is always easier then selling, and the Web ad business is no exception.

What's Wrong with Web Advertising

So, hype begone! What exactly *is*, or soon will be, going on with Web advertising? In the distant past of 1995, many writers (including this one) laughed at the notion that advertising could be the major revenue source for Web developers. But then a few things changed, and some skeptics (including this one) began to change their tune. No one, however, believes that most Web developers will get rich off of ads alone.

How, then, did advertising become the basic revenue model behind many Web sites? The premise was that the World Wide Web is a broadcasting medium like newspapers, radio, or television; since the model for revenue in those media is to advertise time or space, Web sites should sell space on their pages. This belief is especially attractive because the demographics of the Web skew heavily toward white males with high incomes, the crown jewel for lots of big ad spenders. It can also be a simplistic trap, though—albeit one that a lot of people have used as an excuse to create field-of-dreams Web sites, thinking, "Build it and they [consumers and advertisers] will come."

In some cases they'll be right, but many other developers will wait a long time for the return on their investment. Why? Because advertising is based on the confidence of an advertiser that its purchase of time or space will influence a large number of people in a meaningful way. So far, that confidence is missing—and as a result, advertising hasn't exactly been a booming business on the Web.

Most of the Web advertising you see is companies promoting their own products and services—Time-Warner pushing its CD-ROMs on its own site, for instance. Among the rest, a large part (over $100 million worth in a recent survey) consists of sites hoping to lure audiences to "pass them along" to their advertisers. For example, Netscape is one of the biggest advertisers on the search engine pages, which themselves pay Netscape for space on its pages. The true test will be the rise in ads that don't exist for these self-promotion or piggyback purposes. This market hasn't been growing nearly as fast as the overall Web advertising numbers suggest, nor will it for quite some time (in my opinion, at least).

Moreover, if anyone can set up a Web site, why advertise at all? An advertiser like Ford buys time on television shows primarily because it can't afford to start a competitive all-Ford-all-the-time channel. Online, however, it does have that opportunity. While TV struggles to give us 500 channels, the Web has more than 100,000—each as easily accessible as the next. As this form of what I call "adversitements" grows, perhaps some cash will be spent on ads to draw people into specific sites, but one can already argue that more money is going to advertise these sites on other media. I'd bet Ford spends more advertising its Web site in print ads than it does for promotions on the Web itself.

Another problem with the advertising or space-oriented model is that most of the costs are related to time. The more time a consumer spends online, the more likely he or she is to be exposed to more ads—but the primary goal of many consumers is to find what they want while spending as little time as possible doing so. They aren't exactly looking to budget time to experience advertising material. In contrast, consumers in other media find it far harder to compress the time they use to receive information and thus reduce the number of ads they see. So while advertising holds some promise of generating revenues for Web-oriented content providers, it doesn't inherently or perfectly match the consumer's process of being online.

The rule of thumb I use to describe the downside of Web advertising is that time and space don't sell. You can't sell space on the Web because there is an infinite amount of space to sell, and you can't sell time because you can't control when or for how long a person is online.

What's Right with Web Advertising

As you'll see later, though, some companies have learned to exploit this gap in the traditional Web advertising model with awesome success—and the amount of money spent on Web advertising *is* growing. Indeed, as the Web's content and sophistication expand, there will be a direct correlation with the potential for Web ad growth.

Ironically, despite the problems and the inconsistent returns on investment, the time to get in is now for anyone interested in Web advertising—especially developers looking to build revenue-generating sites through advertising. The people who figure out the solutions to today's problems with Web advertising will be in a commanding position when ad revenue finally grows to profitable proportions.

In an attempt to get you up to speed, in the next few sections I'll take a quick look at what's working—and a few resources that might help you.

Banners

Banners are one of the biggest components of online advertising right now, and they're likely to remain that way for some time. Originally used to describe static graphical images (linked to a site) that spanned across a section of a Web page, *banners* is now morphing into a catchall term for any sort of paid link to another section of the Web, primarily the home page of a company or a site devoted solely to a specific product promotion.

The following are some of the recent improvements that have made online banners so popular:

- *Animated Banners*—Thanks to the animated GIF graphics format, many site banners are more attractive and are able to show more information—features that generate more "hits." Expect sound effects and music to join animated GIFs as gimmicks prodding you to click on that banner.

- *Banner Maps*—Instead of mere links to a single home page, some banners now feature image maps (graphic images with multiple clickable areas). The banner-map ad for computer mail-order vendor Insight Direct, for instance, allows users to jump quickly from their current site to any one of more than 20 different product categories to place orders. Expanding the array of choices in a single ad increases your chances of offering something of interest to people viewing it.

- *Greater Placement Options*—Older banners spanned the width of a screen, but the advent of frames and better design techniques are allowing banners to go vertical, and to stay on the screen at all times while other content changes. These improved location choices result in better impressions.

- *Java or Shockwave Enhancements*—By using Java or Shockwave in tiny applets, advertisers can create entire "Webspots" that better entice users to their site. In fact, some can be so skillfully created that they make their case right then and there—without having to lead viewers to another site.

- *Intelligent Placement*—Sophisticated placement systems are giving site administrators fantastic tools to serve up banners tailored to specific viewers. Examples include banners placed according to the content called up on search engines, correlated to reader surveys filled out on the site, or that change depending on the time of day or some other type of targeting method. No other medium offers this possibility of maximizing the connection between the banner content and the user's interests, and the advantages are available now.

Best of all, banner ads are being accepted by users. Click rates have certainly been improving, and they will likely go higher as the banners themselves become more sophisticated in placement and design (and, as I noted, in some cases click-throughs won't even be needed). Additionally, users are learning that banners offer a great navigational tool. The Web has become so big that it's often hard to find things even with the best search engines, and many successful advertising banners are playing a key role in helping people become aware of sites they might want to visit.

In short, if time and space don't sell in the world of Web advertising, a good first impression does. This phrase has a double meaning, of course. First, it means advertising that cuts through the clutter of the Web to grab the desired users right away. Second, it refers to the value consumers see in the ad or site after it catches their attention, causing them to return often and building confidence in that source or advertiser.

Adversitements

The increasing sophistication of the Internet has brought many new technologies to site design, and deep-pocketed companies and advertisers are using those technologies to create sites that are compelling enough to visit as entertainment fare, thus exposing users to a bevy of advertising information. These adver*site*ments are not just sites with advertising banners; they're entire Web sites devoted to promoting a specific brand or product.

The real draw of these sites are such standard ideas as online games, contest promotions, and giveaways. Technology like Macromedia's Shockwave, Sun's Java, and more advanced server and browser systems, however, allow these ideas to be packaged in ways that are actually attractive, intuitive, and entertaining. The result is a compelling mix of information, entertainment, and pure advertising—not to mention some of the best sites on the Web. Among some of the more cutting-edge example sites are Apple's *Mission Impossible* film site (**http://www.apple.mission.com**), Nissan Motors (**http://www.nissan.com**), and Ragu Spaghetti Sauce (**http://www.ragu.com**).

The Internet, with the exception of banners and "Webspots," is a request-attention medium; you have to offer users something they want in order to earn their notice. As advertisers learn how to "give to get" on the Web, their adversitements will become worth the investment. The early successes, though, demonstrate that what users want are cutting-edge sites, with the advertising message built around some advanced form of interactive entertainment or information presentation. Advertisers therefore need to become familiar with interactive entertainment—which, as the failures of many movie studios in the computer-game industry illustrate, is not an easy medium to grasp.

Tracking Technology

The innovation advertisers drool over most when it comes to the Web is tracking technology. The amount of data you can collect on people's habits, purchases, and interests via the Web—through sophisticated database applications, simple statistics on what pages are being accessed most often, or Web cookies—is greater than it is for any other medium. In addition, the ways in which you can use the same technology to tailor content gives advertisers something they covet most: a high-percentage targeting of their advertisements to potentially interested populations.

Zeroing in on people who will be interested in their product, and sifting out those who won't, will be an ever-increasing focus of Web advertisers. Here's a rundown of some products and resources that can help you with this process.

I/PRO

Internet Profiles Corporation
785 Market Street, 13th Floor
San Francisco, CA 94103
Phone: 415-975-5800
Fax: 415-975-5818
WWW: http://www.ipro.com

I/PRO is a leading vendor of Web tools for tracking user information and demographics. Through I/AUDIT, an independent site verification service, I/PRO reports information about visitors to your site—including how many visits per month, the number of pages served, the average length and time of day of visits, and geographic distribution of users. I/CODE is a comprehensive system for sites to register and track users on their sites. Neilsen I/COUNT is a simpler version of I/CODE; it doesn't include the systems for more extensive demographic information tracking, but still provides you with data on favorite files, geographic distribution, how you rank to other sites, and more.

I/PRO is developing a registration system where users register their demographic information once with I/PRO, then receive a password code that can work on all participating I/PRO sites. By making it easier for users to register without re-entering mundane information, this system could benefit sites by providing higher registration rates (and, as a result, the informational benefits of the added demographic data).

DoubleClick

Phone: 888-727-5300
Fax: 212-889-0062
WWW: http://www.doubleclick.net

DoubleClick is one of those services that makes the Web so cool when it comes to advertising. By looking at the .com address of a user viewing your site, DoubleClick's system analyzes the organization's interest, then matches up the best advertisers from a list you provide. For example, a user who happens to be viewing your Web site from a software company might be exposed to an ad for new computer hardware.

NetGravity

1700 South Amphlett Boulevard, Suite 350
San Mateo, CA 94402
Phone: 415-655-4777
Fax: 415-655-4776
WWW: http://www.netgravity.com

NetGravity is the premier developer of specialized server software for facilitating advertising on the Web. AdServer is a database and scheduling package that helps you place, rotate, and track advertising on your Web site. It also generates reports on the advertisements, among many other features.

AdJuggler

Digital Nation
5515 Cherokee Avenue
Alexandria, VA 22312
Phone: 703-642-2800
Fax: 703-642-3747

AdJuggler is another piece of software that helps you manage banner displays on your site. Working through a browser interface, it lets you edit banners, view banner statistics, match pages with banners, and randomize distribution.

Email or Web Caching Programs

No Web developer or advertiser should forget about the power of email when it comes to advertising. I'm not talking about the millions of spam messages that go out every day—as someone who receives a lot of it myself, I am firmly against unsolicited mass email—but about using it as a tool to get your message out to requesting users or provide a means for other people to advertise to your newsletter subscribers. Many sites have email newsletters and/or run mailing lists; by letting users who sign up signal their interest in a given topic, these features can be potent advertising vehicles.

Taking email a bit further, you might also want to investigate the various Web caching programs, which let users receive (or go out and get) various pages from the Web. The advantage of Web caching, of course, is the much richer content that can be delivered to users. Here are some resources that will help you investigate these types of services.

URL-minder
```
http://www.netmind.com/URL-minder/URL-minder.html
```

FreeLoader
```
http://www.freeloader.com
```

Netscape Inbox Direct
```
http://home.netscape.com/comprod/news/marca_inbox.html
```

Ethics, Anyone?

The fast rise of Web advertising, along with the commercialization of the Internet in general, has created a whole new realm of business and advertising ethics. Many Web surfers resent these trends, noting that the Internet was not originally designed as a commercial medium, and they are quick to jump on people who they see as exploiting the Web. The significant clamor raised by this group when it sees practices it objects to, in turn, highlights these practices for the general public.

At the same time, because the Web isn't as regulated as other mediums, unscrupulous companies can skirt ethical reviews that they would have to undergo elsewhere. Again, these practices have sometimes received significant attention in the general public, causing image problems for all Web advertisers. One example of this occurred when marketers used sites that attracted unsuspecting children to collect household data their parents might not have given out.

The potential for Internet advertisers to use technology to learn about and advertise to people on an individual basis is very disturbing to large populations of people who value their privacy. Advertisers and site developers will have to work overtime to assure users that personal data will be used properly. Many sites offer written pledges not to pass on information, and many also have systems that allow users to remove their names from registration lists if desired.

A great deal of advertising is based on trust—consumers need to trust not only the advertiser, but the integrity of the source that is delivering the advertisement. Web developers will need to reinvent for consumers the trust that other advertising mediums already have. This won't be an easy task, but those who succeed will get a sizable edge.

eTRUST
http://www.etrust.org

Started by people from the Electronic Frontier Foundation, this group rates and approves Web sites that take precautions and institute policies to protect the demographic and other personal information of visitors. By operating under these approved conditions and displaying the proper logos, sites can quickly communicate to Web surfers the work they've done to ensure "good housekeeping" of this useful but sensitive information.

The Importance of Being First

Web-based advertising will grow significantly over the short term, but the majority of new investment will come from technology companies shifting what are now huge print advertising budgets to the Internet, where they can target consumers getting the same information they used to obtain from computer and trade magazines. This is the main reason why Softbank, the Japanese software giant, bought Ziff-Davis Publishing and has been merging that operation with major Web enterprises like Yahoo!, inquiry.com, and others.

Why is this important? Because sites whose visitors are attractive customers for Softbank and its ilk—in other words, large consumer electronics, Internet, software, or computer hardware companies—will be the first to establish beachheads on the Internet and master the ins and outs of Web-based advertising. They'll be the experts in banner creation, tracking technology, Web culture, and more. As a result, technology companies such as Softbank, Starwave, Microsoft, Adobe, and Netscape will be positioned to drift easily into other areas of content production as the demographics of the Web increase beyond the current core population of technophiles. Only then, at some point in the next decade, will the larger advertisers come on board—but who will ad buyers like P&G turn to in order to reach that broader market? Traditional advertising companies like BBDO, or technology companies like Starwave or Softbank, who will have been dominating Web advertising for more than 10 years by that time? For obvious reasons, I refer to this as the "right now" theory.

This theory also suggests where current developers can best seek dollars: in technology advertising. The amount of money high-tech companies spend on advertising is increasing rapidly, with most of it representing funds that until recently went to magazines like *PC Magazine* and *Business Week* and newspapers like the *Wall Street Journal* and *USA Today*. As time passes, a larger portion of the billions of dollars budgeted for such advertising will rapidly shift over to the Web. Indeed, the increasing popularity of the Internet will fuel this cycle as more and more people become consumers of high technology. In contrast, products that are sold predominantly through more traditional broadcast mediums (consumer goods, retail store items, political campaigns, and others) won't be switching over nearly as rapidly, and only the top-tier (say, the 1 percent most-visited) sites will see any advertising from these companies for quite some time.

The Lure of Local Advertising

The other major trend visible in the current state of Web advertising is the rush to build extensive sites tailored to specific geographic markets. Microsoft, America Online, Yahoo!, major newspapers from coast to coast, and a host of startup companies have all said they see tremendous business for locally focused sites. These organizations are building what many in the Web world are calling "digital cities": sites that offer everything from "yellow pages" to restaurant guides, movie listings, and much more. The idea is to create a very potent community of users by offering centralized information and thereby attract the millions in advertising dollars currently going toward local TV, radio, weekly and daily newspapers, and magazines.

Being first here is just as important as it is in the technology advertising market on the Web. Print advertising on a local level for things like movies, restaurants and other neighborhood businesses will shift rapidly to the Web as many online consumers learn to use these digital services.

Keeping the Possibilities in Focus

I began this chapter by talking about the hype of Web advertising. It's been promoted as the holy grail of revenue that will propel Web development, and also disparaged as a total bust. This contrast alone should tell you that the answer is somewhere in between. The pragmatic view, to me, is that there are possibilities when it comes to Web advertising—both for site developers trying to attract advertisers, and for advertisers themselves—but they are focused opportunities. The two I discussed, technology-oriented and local-oriented sites, both focus on key advertising pools that will rapidly shift dollars to the Web.

As a Web developer, you'll want to remember this last point most of all. What ad dollars exist are not easy to get; they will require both a cutting-edge site and a clever plan, a combination of product and technology that will attract consumers as well as advertisers. Because the ad dollars aren't as plentiful as some claim, you can be assured that if any part of your advertising plan is out of focus, the results in terms of revenue might be the same. However, if you can deliver on the short-term promise of the Web and concentrate on identi-fied pools of advertising money that will shift to the Web today instead of tomorrow, you may find yourself in the sweet spot as this area of Web growth explodes over time.

Resources

I've only scratched the surface in this chapter, so here are several key resources that can help you learn more about Web advertising.

The Internet Advertising Resource Guide

`http://pilot.msu.edu/unit/adv/internet-advertising-guide.htm`

Maintained by Dr. Hairong Li of Michigan State University, this is a good set of links to other resources and information about advertising, promotion, and the Web.

Who's Marketing Online

`http://www.wmo.com`

From Sayers Publishing comes this excellent resource of advertising, promotion, and marketing information for Web developers and Web advertisers. A must bookmark!

Jupiter's WebTrack

`http://www.webtrack.com`

This service and newsletter seeks to become both an informational source and statistical tracking company with regard to who is advertising on the Web, where, with whom, and for how much.

CyberAtlas

`http://cyberatlas.com/index.html`

A large site dedicated to useful information for those working with Web advertising.

Online Marketing Advisor

`http://intele.net/~johnc/`

Maintained and created by John T. Child, this site is both a promotional site for its author and also the location of articles and general advice and links for those interested in Web advertising.

A1's Searchable Directory of 670 FREE WWW Web Page Promotion Sites!

`http://www.alco.com//index.html`

A large directory that will list your site, with information about it. A good way to build your audience.

Submit It! Inc.

`http://www.submit-it.com`

Via both its software and its site, this company helps you submit your site's information to hundreds of locations around the Web for listing.

SME's WebPost 96

`http://www.2020tech.com/submit.html`

Much like Submit It!, this site is great for transferring a single entry of information to more than 20 search or listing sites.

Internet Advertising Bureau

Phone: 212-704-4446

The IAB was created by a cross-section of advertisers and Web development companies to represent companies that actively sell advertising or advertise on the Internet and online services.

Coalition for Advertising Supported Information and Entertainment

http://www.commercepark.com/AAAA/bc/casie/guide.html

CASIE is a joint venture between the Association of National Advertisers, Inc., and the American Association of Advertising Agencies, with the support of the Advertising Research Foundation. The venture is seeking to help develop rules and principles to guide the entire field of audience measurement for interactive media, including interactive TV, online services, and the Web. It has already authored a very extensive must-read document on the subject, which can be found at the listed URL.

CHAPTER 26

*Discover the
financing options
available for big-time
Web developers*

Financing Alternatives for Internet-Based Companies

By, Dean M. Gloster, Farella Braun & Martel LLP
(415) 954-4472 or glosterd@fbm.com

On the fast-moving frontiers of technology, adequate capital is an essential ingredient for success. This chapter is an overview of financing sources for Web-based and other Internet business companies and entrepreneurs.

Internet Companies

Numerous companies with Internet-oriented businesses have successfully grown until they could finance further expansion through an initial public offering in the stock market. These companies include online services (America Online), Internet access providers (UUNET, Netcom), Web-browser software companies (Netscape, Spyglass), tools companies (Macromedia), and even (departing briefly from the reality that you need a sustainable business model involving revenue somewhere) search engines (Yahoo, Excite, and Lycos). Hundreds of other companies see even more exciting business opportunities arising from the explosive growth of the Internet, particularly with the growing number of people who have access to the graphically-oriented World Wide Web.

The astounding growth of the Web has created new possibilities for reaching millions of consumers directly, with low-cost transmission of information. The result has been an expanding universe of potential businesses for entrepreneurial companies where there is substantial growth potential and low barriers to initial entry. For example, while historically it was extremely expensive to start a magazine (involving expensive mailing lists, four-color printing, large postal costs, and difficulty getting distribution at retail), now anyone with modest resources can put informative and entertaining content on a Web site. Similarly, as little as two years ago, a tax-preparation business like H & R Block was protected by huge barriers to entry: Its trained work force, name recognition, and thousands of storefront locations would be impossible for a competitor to duplicate without a huge investment of resources. Today, a clever entrepreneur with the right software and some marketing savvy could put up a subscription-based Web site with dialog help boxes and a 900 number help line that would assist individuals with simple tax form

---

Dean M. Gloster is a lawyer and a partner in the Internet and Multimedia Group of the San Francisco law firm of Farella Braun & Martel LLP, where he specializes in representing multimedia and online companies

preparation. (They would also have the added opportunity of selling the collected demographic information to mailing lists, and the ability to provide taxpayers with customized ads tied to the information on the return.) Still other entrepreneurs see huge opportunities for technology plays in connection with the expanding use of the Internet, in areas such as Internet telephony, integrated products for the small office/home office market, or a wide variety of technologies aimed at corporate Internet or intranet users.

But even if the cost of creating many new Internet-oriented or Internet-based businesses is less than the start-up cost for some of their nonelectronically-distributed counterparts, the nature of a successful Internet-based business often requires rapid growth. Technology-driven businesses typically require constant innovation to stay ahead of their competitors, and the low barriers to entry for many Internet-based businesses mean that successful ventures must either grow rapidly to achieve dominant mind share and market share (or to become industry standard) or must constantly mutate and take advantage of new opportunities to stay ahead of well-financed competitors. Finally, one characteristic of Internet-based businesses that may add to their capital needs is the astonishing growth rates they may achieve. With the ability to create instant broad access to millions of customers without dealing with an existing retail channel or distribution system, and given existing explosive growth rates of Internet use, many Internet-based businesses have the potential to grow at almost unbelievably steep rates. (Jim Clark's Netscape, for example, reached revenue numbers in a year and a half that took his prior very successful venture, Silicon Graphics Inc., eight years to achieve.) All this, however, means that Internet-based and Internet-oriented businesses need substantial capital to grow successfully.

First Question: Project or Company Financing?

The initial question for an Internet-based or Internet-oriented company is whether to seek *project* financing or long-term *company* financing. There are two different universes of potential funding sources. The first is Web site sponsors, "angel" investors, licensors, and others who might finance specific *projects*. The second universe of funding sources is venture capitalists, private

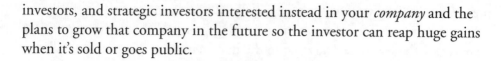

investors, and strategic investors interested instead in your *company* and the plans to grow that company in the future so the investor can reap huge gains when it's sold or goes public.

Project Financing Alternatives

Often, business people or entrepreneurs with an idea (particularly an idea for something on the World Wide Web) are actually seeking project financing, not financing for an entire business. For example, if all you are seeking is funding to complete research and development on an interesting video compression technology designed for Internet use, or developing a new software product like a child-friendly Web browser with built-in smut site lockout features, you may be interested simply in project financing.

There are several different alternatives for project funding. For Web-site–based projects, a current business model is to approach companies or foundations as "sponsors" of the Web site: They underwrite the cost, and the entrepreneur provides the rest. For entrepreneurs creating software products intended to be sold, there is also a standard industry financing source—software publishers. Many software publishers provide small development teams with hundreds of thousands of dollars to create and complete compelling entertainment, education, productivity, or other software titles. For a list of about 100 entertainment, educational, and reference software publishers, with contact information, send me an email (**glosterd@fbm.com**) or look at our Web site (**http://www.fbm.com**).

Some entrepreneurs seeking project-type financing have obtained funding for specific projects from "angel" financiers (individuals who believe in the project or title or believe in its ability to make money). Many films and several multimedia projects have been funded on this model. Some borrow the funds necessary to produce the project (or at least the prototype) from a private investor, and in lieu of interest, give the private investor/lender a share of the royalties/revenue. Where there is a substantial educational, literary, or public policy aspect to the project, some entrepreneurs have obtained grant financing. An excellent guide to grant sources is the *Directory of Computer and High Technology Grants*, Second Edition, by Richard Eckstein (1995, ISBN #0945078072).

Finally, a common approach by entrepreneurs is to bootstrap a project, funding hard costs off limited savings, credit cards, tradeouts for services, and the like, while essentially volunteering their own time on speculation until they get a finished project, or at least the substantial prototype necessary to get further funding.

Company Financing Alternatives

At the initial phase of company financing, entrepreneurs/companies are commonly "bootstrapped" (funded out of the founders' pockets and current operating profits). Keeping a low overhead is crucial. Some companies are creative in doing barter deals, using interns, and giving people online credit in lieu of larger payments. For many companies, however, the bootstrapping model of living off work for hire, service bureau work, founder capital, and cash from operations is far too limiting. It also means giving up too much potential future growth. Venture capitalist Mark Gorenberg of Hummer, Windblad Venture Partners in Emeryville, California, explains that by seeking substantial outside funding, entrepreneurs can often avoid "unnatural acts" to maximize current cash flow. It is dangerous to focus on services or products that generate short-term profits if this diverts energy from maximizing the strategic goals for growing your company. Rapidly growing companies require substantial additional capital to position themselves for anticipated future markets. In order to implement a rapid growth strategy, companies often seek outside funding from venture capitalists, strategic investors, and private investors.

An Overview of the Funding Process and the Business Plan

The search for funding often starts with drafting a business plan that analyzes the market for proposed products and how the company will compete effectively in that market; what differentiates its product from others in the market; and what is particularly exciting about its approach. The critical thinking necessary to create a business plan is important to establishing an overall vision and longer-term focus.

For entrepreneurs looking for outside funding, the business plan also has to be an effective sales document, complete with a concise executive summary. Venture investors see hundreds (or thousands) of business plans a year, and they want a brief executive summary and a limit on gushy adjectives. Business plans are remarkably similar. They start with a short executive summary that describes the company and what is particularly exciting about its business. The business plan goes on to describe the company's business, the key team, competitive advantages like proprietary technology, and the competition. The business plan includes financial projections showing how the investment will be used and the obligatory "hockey stick" projections of future revenue and income, showing explosive growth after the infusion of new capital. How long should a business plan be? If it's used to attract investors, as short as realistically possible, and certainly not over 20 pages. (You can always provide interested investors more information later—in fact, they'll usually insist on it.)

Forget the Business Plan: What Investors Really Care About

You do need to draft (and revise) a business plan to force yourself to do the serious thinking about your strategic focus. Further, interested private investors, venture capitalists, or strategic investors will say "send me a copy of your business plan" when they want to talk with you more. But in truth, to raise capital, you need a much sharper focus than even a well-written 20-page business plan. You need to reduce what is unique, interesting, and worthy of investment about your company to a short spiel that you could practically write on the back of a business card, and could literally tell someone in an elevator going five floors. CEO Steve Blank of Rocket Science Games calls this the "back of the business card or elevator test." Whatever you think of Rocket Science Games, Mr. Blank was successful in raising over $20 million for a startup company in a crowded market. (His initial pitch, I think, was something like, "We'll take the storytelling and character development skills of Hollywood, the production values of Industrial Light and Magic, and bring them to the computer entertainment industry, a bigger market than the feature films business.")

The common complaint venture capitalists and other investors have about most business plans they see is "lack of focus." A related complaint is that the entrepreneur seeking funding for his or her company has never clearly articulated how this company is different from all of the others in the industry (or in the slush pile of unread business plans piling up in someone's reception area).

Common weaknesses of business plans of many Internet-oriented companies include:

1. No clear focus on a realistic revenue source for the business.

2. Failure by the entrepreneur to understand the difficulties in persuading individual consumers to support non-pornographic content provided over the Internet.

3. Failure to address the absence of any meaningful barriers to entry that would protect the new business from future competitors. If it is as easy as you think to create this Internet-based business, how can you prevent your market share from being captured by large, well-financed existing businesses that may choose to compete with you in the future?

Once you have your business plan and, more importantly, your specifically articulated, narrowly focused compelling pitch, you are ready to approach the different categories of potential investors.

Venture Capitalists

Venture capitalists are often the first target source of financing for Internet (and many other) entrepreneurs because:

- they are easy to find

- their avowed purpose is to invest in emerging growth companies

- Internet businesses are currently a hot-money area for VC investors

Traditional venture capitalists serve on the board of directors of the companies where they invest, and often also provide strategic contacts and advice. Venture firms like Kleiner, Perkins, Caulfield & Byers, and New Enterprise Associates, who have more than $800 million to invest, do not often invest sums much smaller than $3 million. Other VC firms (particularly the so-called "seed funds" like Draper Fisher Associates) target much smaller investments, in the $100,000 to $1 million range. Venture capitalists demand a substantial equity stake in return for their investment, and they target companies where they see huge potential gains. How huge? Venture capitalists routinely look for compound annual return rates of 40 percent or more, or four to ten times their money back in a three-to-five year period.

Because many venture capitalist investments end up as write-offs, to meet their own investors' expectations, they need to target "home run" returns, or at least the possibility of gigantic upside success. Successful businesses that merely generate a nice living for the founders ("lifestyle businesses") need not apply. Critical issues for venture capitalists are the idea, the technology, and the strength of a company's team, including management. Venture capitalists also require your company to have an effective exit strategy. They typically expect the companies they invest in to be sold to an acquiror or to go through an initial public offering within three to five years, liquidating their investment. Unless your projections show the necessary growth, and unless you are prepared either to sell or to go public (and to go public, notwithstanding some current examples, you should expect to have substantial and expanding revenues) you are probably *not* a venture capital funding candidate.

Venture capitalists are not in the business of funding *projects*. They fund *companies* they perceive as having exciting potential for dramatic growth over a three-to-five year term. Because venture capitalists are inundated with unsolicited business plans, it is critical to have an introduction, and to concentrate on firms that might fund your kind of company. A list of over 100 venture capital funds that have made Internet company, entertainment software, or multimedia-related investments can be found on the CD-ROM, and is also available through my firm's Web site (**http://www.fbm.com**). Examples of informative Web sites providing an online reference about dealing with venture capitalists include the Web site of Accel Partners (**http://www.accel.com**) and Hummer Winblad Ventures (**http://humwin.com**). You can also find a directory of recent software and information industry investments by VC funds at the Web site for the Price Waterhouse quarterly venture capital survey (**http://www.pw.com:80/vc/**).

There is typically at least one panel at many industry conferences that includes an Internet-friendly venture capitalist, including Intermedia, Multimedia Expo West, E3, Digital Hollywood, and my firm's annual Multimedia/Internet Venture Financing Conference in San Francisco. These panels are an excellent opportunity to introduce yourself, to hand over a business card, and to give them your one-minute elevator investment pitch. Then, you follow up with a polite cover letter and business plan later, starting your letter with a mention that you met recently at the conference.

Although venture capitalists are easy to find, Internet-oriented businesses often do not fit the traditional VC investment criteria. Venture capitalists often prefer companies with proprietary technology and a well-defined market niche with high barriers to entry. They like "dehydrated companies" that will quickly turn into something wonderful with the addition of liquid capital.

Few companies doing business on the Internet today are generating substantial profits. Internet-oriented businesses, especially consumer-oriented ones, are new, and it is hard for venture capitalists (or other people) to predict who will be successful. Nevertheless, many venture capital firms have been extremely active investing in this area.

Strategic Investors

A number of established companies have targeted online businesses for acquisitions, joint ventures, or strategic investments. Sometimes these strategic investors have substantially different agendas than medium-range profit, ranging from gaining expertise, to obtaining access to technology, to locking up a company from dealing with competitors, to leveraging their existing content or services into a new medium.

Private Investors

For companies not far enough along to attract venture capitalists and strategic investors, there is still the alternative of private investors. Private investors are commonly known as "angel" financiers, and they can be an outstanding source of capital—if you can find one. The book *Demystifying Multimedia* defines an angel as someone "who shares the project vision and wants to bring it into existence."

Well, maybe. Typically, what angels share is their money. It is difficult to locate angel financiers unless they have a pre-existing connection with the company principals or advisers, or they have a substantial interest in, or sophistication about, the industry in which they are investing.

Although the venture capital community is far more visible, historically, private investors provide far more capital to startup ventures. There have been extensive studies of the profile of typical private investors in startup business: While a substantial portion have high net worth of over $1 million, the majority of private investors are *not* millionaires, although they do have above-average income. Most of them are business owners or middle managers, who are generally older than the entrepreneurs they finance. Private investors can generally make investment decisions far faster then venture capitalists or strategic investors can, they are particularly willing to invest startups, and they invest much smaller amounts of money. Often the amount of money from any individual private investor will be $50,000 or less.

One source of private investors for startup companies is executives and highly compensated technical people who are leaving much larger companies with golden parachutes, vested stock options, and the like. They often have substantial capital, along with relevant business or technical expertise to help make a startup company successful.

Entrepreneurs often network through professionals they know, such as their attorney, their accountant, and people on their board of advisors, for leads to private investors. Another category of potential investors is highly compensated professionals: Doctors and airline pilots are on the traditional short list of target investors.

In various cities there are also monthly venture capital clubs that are forums for venture investors and intermediaries, and there are even specific networks organized in some areas to put companies together with interested investors. One network is the Silicon Valley Capital Network (for more information, contact Dennis Laudermilch at 408-541-7627). Some intermediaries (finders, business brokers, and perhaps even loan brokers) may help to find private investors, and in return they get a portion of the money they find for you (a 6 percent commission is not unusual, but the number is negotiable). Do get references on any finder or broker, avoid those with stories too good to be true, and be careful (especially at the bottom end of the capital pool) when someone is asking for a substantial fee up front whether or not he or she can deliver investor money.

Internet-oriented companies are in a good position currently for attracting private investment, particularly given media hype and extraordinary (and occasionally silly) Wall Street valuations of "Internet" companies.

Debt Financing Alternatives

A sometimes overlooked funding source is debt, which allows entrepreneurs to grow businesses rapidly, without sacrificing a substantial equity stake. Many small startup companies are funded (at least initially) on the credit cards of the founders. Unfortunately, debt usually requires current interest payments, creating potential cash flow difficulties. Bank loans are also difficult to qualify for. I was amused to read a year ago in the (now-defunct) magazine *Morph's Outpost* an article for multimedia and Internet developers on how to impress your banker. The truth is, the only way most small Internet-oriented entrepreneurs can get money from a traditional bank is with a handgun. For borrowers who do not have a substantial operating history, current cash flow, and assets with a substantial liquidation value, traditional bank financing is impossible.

For companies that *do* have substantial operating history, current cash flow, and substantial assets, several banks are known as particularly aggressive lenders to growing high tech companies. These include Silicon Valley Bank and Imperial Bank.

And for companies with a substantial operating history that still do not qualify for bank loans, even more aggressive lenders, including some commercial finance companies, may offer slightly less conservative working capital loans and other financing, typically at substantially more expensive terms. Many equipment vendors have arrangements with leasing companies to finance the lease of necessary equipment. Receivables financing companies (factors) provide unbelievably expensive financing. Do read the fine print and do the math: In parts of this country people with colorful nicknames are put in jail for charging interest rates not too different from commonly offered factoring terms.

Several banks also have special programs for women-owned and minority-owned companies, and there are special programs in many cities (including San Francisco and Berkeley) for making loans to small businesses, targeted at job creation. Small Business Administration (SBA) loans can also be an excellent financing source for loans of between $25,000 and almost $1 million. Because they are partially guaranteed by the SBA, lenders are more willing to make these loans, even when more risk is involved. Typically, SBA loans must be personally guaranteed, and with certain SBA loans other assets (like a second deed of trust on the business owner's house) must be pledged as collateral. Currently, Citibank is aggressively marketing SBA loans to software developers and other high tech companies.

Going Public on the Internet

The latest hot financing topic for Internet-oriented companies has been the possibility of going public "on the Internet"; perhaps without the assistance (and expense) of traditional underwriters and broker/dealer networks. The 1992 liberalization of certain securities laws to make it easier for smaller issuers to raise capital from the public, coupled with a recent Securities and Exchange Commission release on using electronic media for dissemination of information, now make it possible for companies to do small "Regulation A" offerings (or in California, Section 25102 offerings) to raise $5 million or less, directly over the Internet. Smaller offerings of $1 million or less are even simpler. Spring Street Brewing Company, a New York microbrewery, was the first to go public in a Registration A cyber-offering, raising $1.6 million. Spring Street's president, Andrew Klein, a former securities lawyer, has explained that these cyber-offerings may work well for companies unable to get venture capital financing, but which have strong appeal for "affinity" investors who like the company's product. This mechanism may be especially intriguing for Internet-oriented companies, which presumably have an appeal to the Internet-savvy investors who might be the most likely to purchase stocks in a cyber-offering.

Be aware though, that "going public" is not a typical funding strategy for startup businesses, and this is a *very* new area. While this method does avoid certain transaction costs, there are substantial, unavoidable costs in raising money by *any* method. If you are proceeding under a Regulation A exemption from registration, there is also a cap of $5 million on the amount of funds you can raise through this method in any twelve-month period. If liquidity is an issue—which it often is—you also need to carefully plan how you are going to provide for post-issuance trading of the stock. (To be fair, however, the $5 million or less cyber-offering option may function as a replacement for venture capital, private placements, or mezzanine financing, which often has almost no tradability.) The SEC has recently released a no-action letter allowing entrepreneurs to set up Web-based bulletin board–like listings for "bid" and "ask" offers to buy and sell securities, facilitating private investors' after-issuance trading of stock not listed on the NASDAQ or other exchanges. Andrew Klein has now founded a new online investment banking firm, Wit Capital Corporation, to act as an online underwriter to assist other companies in going public directly over the Internet. For more information, you can visit their Web site (**http://www.witcap.com**) or contact his colleague Gary Knight at 212-228-5787.

The Funding Process and Beyond

Be aware that it takes a *long* time and a huge amount of effort to obtain financing. Typically, private investors are capable of making a decision relatively quickly. But the process of approaching venture capitalists and strategic investors, meeting with them, allowing them to do due diligence on your company (to discover, among other things, whether you have as much going for you as you claim), and negotiating the final deal terms can take six months or longer, even if the process is successful. So don't wait until you are almost out of money to go looking for more. (Besides, investors are often far more cautious about putting money into a company that is almost completely out of cash, and in your desperation, you won't have much leverage to obtain the best terms with your financing source. Perspiration dripping off your nose onto the term sheet doesn't enhance your negotiating position on valuation.)

Also be aware that there are substantial legal issues whenever you are raising equity money (or any kind of money where the investor's return is tied to the financial success of your project). A variety of very specific securities laws apply to these transactions, and you should consult an attorney.

It takes substantial capital to make the most of interesting commercial opportunities on the Internet, and by looking beyond bootstrap financing, you may be able to take advantage of today's (and tomorrow's) unique opportunities.

CHAPTER 27

Avoid any legal liabilities in making content available on the Internet.

Untangling Legal Knots on the Web

By, Dean M. Gloster, Farella Braun & Martel LLP
(415) 954-4472 or glosterd@fbm.com

Thousands of companies and entrepreneurs are making use of the World Wide Web for advertising, public relations, and even commercial transactions. Unfortunately, along with business and technical hurdles, there are dangerous legal uncertainties about some activities on the Web. Several techniques, however, can minimize legal exposure for businesses positioning themselves for Internet opportunities, as well as for the Web developers assisting them. These include carrying out the online business in a separately incorporated subsidiary, exercising caution to avoid defamation or copyright infringement liability, and getting an indemnity from clients so that any legal difficulties are their problem, not yours.

The World Wide Web

Companies are now commonly using Web sites to:

- Further their public relations goals

- Distribute information internally or externally at reduced cost

- Generate advertising revenue as high-volume destinations

- Create transactional revenue by selling information, services, or merchandise

Although commerce on the Web is in its early stages, an August 1996 report by Montgomery Securities predicts that the Internet commerce and content market will exceed $50 billion in 2000. Another study released by Input in March 1996 predicted that Internet-based commerce would exceed $255 billion by the year 2000.

To take advantage of emerging opportunities, many developers are creating content-rich Web sites, and some of these even have interactive "soundoff" or comment features similar to newsgroup postings. The more interesting and interactive a Web site is, however, the greater the legal risks that those who set it up may face, given the current uncertain state of the law. The law is a slow-moving creature that follows far behind the pace of technological and business innovation. Typically, when courts are required to determine the applicability

---

Dean M. Gloster is a lawyer and a partner in the Internet and Multimedia Group of the San Francisco law firm of Farella Braun & Martel LLP, where he specializes in representing multimedia and online companies.

of legal principles to new areas, they resort to analogies to older (and hopefully related) areas of the law or businesses. Thus, courts sometimes resolve complicated issues involving communications satellites gone astray in space by citing old admiralty law cases involving wooden ships. (I'm not making this up.) With content made increasingly available over the Internet, however, we can predict that long-standing rules regarding copyright and trademark infringement, defamation, and other legal principles will be applied increasingly to content on the Web.

There have been very few Internet content-related lawsuits in the past, but with the advent of widespread commercial Web sites this may change. In the good old days (like three years ago), there may have been hundreds of GIF files floating around on alt.binaries [fill in the blank, naughty reader] that were infringing copies of photographs where some magazine owned the copyright—but who was *Playboy* going to sue? Some anonymous Internet user with no money? (And, frankly, the copyright owners may have figured that only a relative handful of people really knew how to decode binary files anyway.) Today, when those same copyright owners are busy setting up their own Web sites and trying to charge consumers for viewing the images, I'm sure that they take a much dimmer view of someone else's commercial Web site trying to generate revenue (or traffic) by distributing their copyright-infringing works.

Some of the copyright infringement, defamation, and other legal issues in content-based Web sites are illustrated in the following example.

Trouble on the Web

Imagine that you have been asked to design a wonderfully interactive Web site for Huge Media Company, a sprawling entertainment conglomerate. You develop a Web site that includes specialized news areas about recent developments behind the scenes at some of the television programs, films, and music groups distributed by Huge Media Company; "chat" areas where fans and consumers can type in their own comments, messages, and questions, organized in different topic areas; and separate areas that would allow consumers to buy merchandise and even download and sample short clips of music before ordering Huge Media Company music CDs at a discount.

After thousands of people view the site, you also take action to preserve the character of some of the areas, deleting crude propositions and messages with inflammatory claims about relationships between third parties and the star of a Huge Media Company television show.

What are the legal risks involved here for Huge Media Company or for you?

Defamation

Traditionally, the law drew a distinction between a "publisher" like a newspaper, liable when it publishes untrue and reputation-injuring comments about a noncelebrity, and "distributors" like bookstores or libraries, only liable for defamation if they have reason to know of the defamatory character of what they are distributing. Those of us familiar with the Internet generally believe (or at least hope) that Web site operators, online services, Internet service providers, and similar organizations should *not* be liable as publishers for information posted by users, because there is usually no opportunity for the organization to review the material before it is made available.

Unfortunately, the few legal decisions addressing this area have not always agreed. For example, in one case the online service Prodigy was held potentially liable as a publisher for defamatory statements that a third party had posted on its service. Because Prodigy had certain content guidelines, a software screening program to filter out offensive language, and had exercised some editorial control over messages posted on its bulletin boards, the court had no difficulty in finding it liable as a publisher in the case *Stratton Oakmont, Inc. v. Prodigy*, 1995 WL 323710 (N.Y.Sup.) (May 24, 1995).

A different court reached an opposite result in a case involving the online service CompuServe, because CompuServe exercised no editorial control, so it was more like an electronic library and thus a distributor like a news vendor or bookstore, rather than a publisher for defamation law. Accordingly, in *Cubby, Inc. v. CompuServe*, 776 F.Supp. 135 (S.D.N.Y. 1991), CompuServe was held not liable unless it knew or had reason to know of the defamatory nature of statements posted on its service.

Copyright Infringement

Providing any service that allows individual users to post or transmit material that is the copyrighted work of others (like a Dave Barry humor column) raises the risk that a company may be held liable for direct, contributory, or vicarious copyright infringement. Many Web sites also contain links that allow a user to reach other Web sites which may contain copyright-infringing materials. In a decision that has implications for the online area, the Ninth

Circuit Court of Appeals, a federal court governing appeals in the Western nine states of the United States, recently broadened potential liability for copyright infringement in a case involving a flea market that permitted someone's regular on-premises sale of pirated music tapes. The court held that because the flea market owners had the right to terminate access to the site and derived a financial benefit (the pirates rented space, and the pirated music was a "draw" for customers, creating an indirect benefit through admission, parking, and other fees), the site owner could be held for "vicarious" copyright infringement.

The court explained in *Fonovisa, Inc. v. Cherry Auction*, 76 F.3d 259, (9th Cir. 1996) that the site owner could also be held liable for "contributory" infringement because the site owner materially contributed to the infringement by providing space, advertising, and customers. Although the Fonovisa case did not involve online content, the court's reasoning suggests there may be potential liability if a Web site creator or maintainer gets advertising or other revenue from activities that indirectly pass on copyright-infringing materials or assist third parties in profiting from copyright infringement.

Avoiding Liability

In the Huge Media Company example, even the modest editorial actions at the Web site might allow someone to claim that Huge Media Company is a publisher, and thus is strictly liable for defamatory statements posted by users in its discussion areas. Even if Huge Media Company did nothing to police its site, that might not be enough to avoid any potential liability: First, even distributors under defamation law are liable when they have reason to know of the defamatory character of statements they are passing along. Finally, exercising no discretion over what appears in a chat area may be dangerous under some court decisions, which suggest that there is an affirmative duty to remove offending information once you have become aware of its character. One example of this is the copyright infringement ruling in *Religious Technology Center v. Netcom*, 907 F.Supp. 1361 (N.D. Cal. 1995), where a lawsuit was brought against Internet service provider Netcom for passing on postings of copyrighted Church of Scientology works and refusing to delete the postings after notice of their copyrighted nature.

Finally, in the Huge Media Company example, it would be surprising if all of the recording artists had contracts that clearly gave the company the right to distribute clips of their music over the Internet royalty-free, and these types of

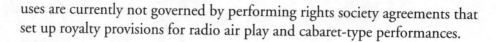

uses are currently not governed by performing rights society agreements that set up royalty provisions for radio air play and cabaret-type performances.

Safety Rules

Don't Panic

A creative or business person faced with this legal uncertainty might just give up on the idea of doing anything interesting online. But, for a business in a fast-moving area, sometimes the riskiest strategy is to do nothing while your competitors take advantage of the new media. Thus, proceeding with some common-sense guidelines may be the best course.

Have Clear Rights to the Online Content You Are Distributing

If you are distributing anything (pictures, sound, or text) online, make sure that you actually have the right to electronically distribute that content. Even if you do have some rights to specific content, many older agreements (like the recording artist's contract with Huge Media Company in the example) may not give you the right to distribute audio or pictures over the Internet royalty-free.

Come Up with Sensible Guidelines for Posting

If you are planning on a truly interactive Web site, there are even thornier issues. This is a difficult area, because the more guidelines and precautions you enforce, the more likely a court may find you liable to a higher standard for defamation. As a practical matter, though, a business may have to impose all kinds of limitations just to preserve the character of its Web site.

Incorporate Your Online Activities Separately

An online business division can be incorporated as a separate subsidiary, isolating the risk of large damage awards, if the company is careful to preserve the separate existence of the online corporation.

Get an Indemnity from Your Client

Other businesses, like advertising agencies, routinely get blanket indemnities from their clients so that if there is any lawsuit or dispute with a third party over copyrights, trademarks, defamation, commercial disparagement, or any other legal claim arising out of the work done for the client, the client will "indemnify, defend, and hold harmless" the outside consultant. These are fancy legal terms, meaning that the client will:

- Pay any expenses incurred (including a judgment in a lawsuit) by the contractor when some third party raises a claim

- Pay the contractor's legal fees in any dispute with a third party

- Not ever sue the contractor if the client has to shell out money to a third party in connection with some claim over the work

This is a useful clause to add to all of your appropriate contracts, although even the world's most carefully drafted indemnification provision won't do you any good if your client ends up insolvent and you yourself have enough money to be an attractive target in litigation.

There are almost limitless creative and substantial commercial possibilities on the World Wide Web. By having a general awareness of some of the legal issues involved in making content available over the Web, creative developers and new Internet-based businesses may be able to take advantage of these opportunities without running into legal problems.

APPENDIX A

Magazines for Web Developers

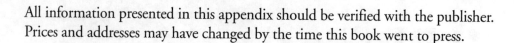

All information presented in this appendix should be verified with the publisher. Prices and addresses may have changed by the time this book went to press.

General Interest/General User

Internet World

Mecklermedia Corp.
20 Ketchum Street
Westport, CT 06880
Phone: 203-341-2872
Fax: 203-454-5840
WWW: http://www.iworld.com
Subscription: $29.00
Newsstand: $4.95
Frequency: Monthly
Pages: 130

Internet World is the premiere Internet publication of Mecklermedia, which produces the trade show of the same name. *Internet World* focuses on the computer professional who is developing, using, or dealing with anything that has to do with the Internet, particularly the World Wide Web. Feature articles and reviews cover Web development products, hardware, people who are doing amazing things on the Internet, and the usual smattering of news.

NetGuide

CMP Media
600 Community Drive
Manhasset, NY 11030
Phone: 516-562-5000
Fax: 516-562-7830
WWW: http://www.netguide.com
Subscription: $22.97
Newsstand: $3.95
Frequency: Monthly
Pages: 150

NetGuide is CMP Publications' premiere Web-site magazine, and is aimed at regular computer users who surf for work and pleasure, rather than surf junkies who may not be very computer savvy. *NetGuide* follows the biz of the Net, and has reviews of sites, development tools, and power-user applications. The magazine also features a column by Robert Seidman, whose insights on the Web, the Net, and online companies are among the most interesting around.

WEBster—The Cyberspace Surfer

Tabor Griffin Communications
8445 Camino Santa Fe, Suite 204
San Diego, CA 92121
Phone: 619-625-0070
Fax: 619-625-0088
WWW: http://www.tgc.com/webster.html
Subscription: $29.00
Newsstand: via the Web
Frequency: Biweekly
Pages: n/a

A Web-based publication, *WEBster* covers Web news and provides features and analysis on Web issues and development. It was named Runner-Up Best Online Publication at the 1994 Computer Press Association Awards.

Online Access

Red Flash Internet Inc.
WWW: http://www.oamag.com
Subscription: n/a
Newsstand: n/a
Frequency: Monthly
Pages: 100

Aimed at the experienced online user, this general-interest magazine covers the realm of online services, including the Internet, commerical online services, the Web, and Web-based online networks.

ONLINE USER

Online Inc.
462 Danbury Road
Wilton, CT 06897
Phone: 606-331-6345

Fax: 606-331-7261
WWW: http://www.onlineinc.com/oluser/
Subscription: $24.00/free to qualified subscribers
Newsstand: $3.99
Frequency: Monthly
Pages: 100

ONLINE USER is aimed at professionals who work extensively with online services and the Web. It covers new products, the online business, and more from a power-user's point of view.

Internet.com Magazine (Colombian)

Elqui Communications
Calle 90 # 13 -40. Piso 4
Santafé de Bogotá
Colombia
Phone: 571-6105418
Fax: 571-2362947
WWW: http://www.colomsat.net.co/internetcom/
Subscription: n/a
Newsstand: n/a
Frequency: Bimonthly
Pages: 80

My Spanish isn't too good, so it was hard to tell if foreign subscriptions are available, but this appears to be a very well-done Internet magazine that serves the computer and Internet communities of Colombia.

WWWiz Magazine

GRAFX Group, Inc.
17971 Sky Park Circle, Suite 33B
Irvine, CA 92714
Phone: 714-474-0554
Fax: 714-474-0668
WWW: http://wwwiz.com
Subscription: $24.95
Newsstand: $4.99
Frequency: Monthly
Pages: 120

A general-interest magazine aimed at average users of the World Wide Web.

Internet Australia

WWW: http://www.interaus.net/magazine/index.html
Subscription: $65.00
Newsstand: n/a
Frequency: Monthly
Pages: n/a

Aimed at the general-to-professional Web user, this is one of Australia's largest Internet and Web mags.

InternetUser

Ziff-Davis Publishing
One Park Avenue
New York, NY 10016
Phone: 212-503-3500
Fax: 212-503-4599
WWW: http://www.pcmag.com/iu/iuser.htm
Subscription: $24.95
Newsstand: $4.99
Frequency: Monthly
Pages: 120

InternetUser is a general-interest magazine for the Web from Ziff-Davis and the editorial staff of Ziff's leading magazine, *PC Magazine*. *InternetUser* has articles about surfing, building your own sites, and tools and hardware reviews, as well as feature articles.

Axcess

WWW: http://www.axcess.com
Subscription: $12.00
Newsstand: $3.00
Frequency: Bimonthly
Pages: 100

Axcess is what I'd expect *Wired* to be like if it was located in the East Village of New York. The magazine includes articles on music and various multimedia happenings and also includes a lot of content about the Internet and Web. It's aimed at the Generation X crowd—it's definitely not for Web development professionals, though some of the people and sites they cover are worthwhile for designers.

Wired

Wired Ventures
520 Third Street, 4th Floor
San Francisco, CA 94107
Phone: 415-222-6200
Fax: 415-222-6209
WWW: http://www.hotwired.com
Subscription: $39.95
Newsstand: $4.95
Frequency: Monthly
Pages: 220

You must have been living on another planet to not have heard of *Wired* magazine. *Wired* isn't exactly a Web magazine (believe it or not)—in fact, most of their articles don't have as much to do with Web stuff as they do with the culture and fads of cyberspace and the digital economy. Still, the trends that surface here and the personalities it covers are very much at play on the Web. Some may dislike *Wired* for its cutting-edge layout, others may dislike it for its editorial bent, but no one can deny the impact it has had (and still has) on the cyberspace community.

CyberMedia 2001

10410 San Fernando Avenue
Cupertino, CA 95014
Phone: 408-255-5007
Fax: 408-255-5730
WWW: http://www.cybrmda.com
Subscription: n/a
Newsstand: n/a
Frequency: Monthly
Pages: n/a

CyberMedia 2001 examines trends and issues about the Web and other digital convergence technologies.

Surfer-Oriented Guides

Yahoo! Internet Life

Ziff-Davis Publishing

One Park Avenue
New York, NY 10016
Phone: 212-503-3500
Fax: 212-503-4599
WWW: http://www.yil.com
Subscription: $24.95
Newsstand: $2.99
Frequency: Monthly
Pages: 115

Building on the brand recognition of its Yahoo! property, Softbank/Ziff-Davis
have repositioned *Internet Life* as *Yahoo! Internet Life*. The magazine is aimed
at surfers, and includes Yahoo! reviews of sites, Web news, and feature articles
on Net personalities.

The Net

Imagine Publishing Inc.
150 North Hill Drive
Brisbane, CA 94005
Phone: 415-468-4684
Fax: 415-468-4686
WWW: http://www.thenet-usa.com
Subscription: $45.95
Newsstand: $6.99
Frequency: Monthly
Pages: 100

The Net is a general-interest publication aimed at power-users and major
surfers. Articles include reviews, news about the Web, Web-site roundups, and
how-tos. A major part of the magazine is The Blue Pages, filled with mini-
reviews of various Web sites in different categories.

Iway

Connell Communications
86 Elm Street
Peterborough, NH 03458
Phone: 603-924-7271
Fax: 603-924-6972
WWW: http://www.cciweb.com/iway.html
Subscription: $29.97

Newsstand: $5.95
Frequency: 10/year
Pages: 90

Iway is aimed at Web surfers and is most well known for its *IWAY 500* issue, which lists its opinion of the top 25 Web sites in 20 categories.

Internet Underground

Ziff-Davis Publishing
One Park Avenue
New York, NY 10016
Phone: 212-503-3500
Fax: 212-503-4599
WWW: http://www.underground-online.com
Subscription: n/a
Newsstand: n/a
Frequency: Monthly
Pages: 80

This Web surfer's zine is aimed more at the younger set and tries to focus on what it calls "the cool side of the Internet."

Netsurfer Digest and Netsurfer Focus Magazine

Netsurfer Communications
333 Cobalt Way, Suite 107
Sunnyvale, CA 94086
Phone: 408-249-6346
Fax: 408-249-6346
WWW: http://www.netsurf.com/nsd/
Subscription: Free
Newsstand: via email
Frequency: Monthly
Pages: 10

Free email zines that gives you reviews and interesting information about different online sites.

Internet Voyaging

WWW: http://fan.nb.ca/cfn/info/ip_info/voyager/
Subscription: Free

Newsstand: n/a
Frequency: Biweekly
Pages: 1

This is the online archive for Richard Anderson's newspaper column about the Internet. He covers Web issues, Internet developments, and more, every second Thursday in the *Fredericton Daily Gleaner*. The focus is mostly toward average users, but some technical subjects are covered.

Online World (Australia)

IDG Communications Australia
P.O. Box 295
St Leonards, NSW 2065
Australia
Phone: 61-2-9439-5133
Fax: 61-2-9439-5512
WWW: http://idg.com.au/online.world
Subscription: n/a
Newsstand: n/a
Frequency: Monthly
Pages: 120

IDG's major online publication about Australia's online world.

WebMaster (Australia)

Australian
IDG Communications Australia
P.O. Box 295
St Leonards, NSW 2065
Australia
Phone: 61-2-9439-5133
Fax: 61-2-9439-5512
WWW: http://idg.com.au/webmaster/
Subscription: n/a
Newsstand: n/a
Frequency: Monthly
Pages: 120

Australia's leading Web professional magazine.

Internet (U.K.)

EMAP Readerlink
Audit House, Field End Road, Eastcote, Ruislip,
Middlesex, HA4 9LT
United Kingdom
Fax: 44-181-429-3117
WWW: http://www.emap.com/internet/
Subscription: £59.95
Newsstand: £2.99
Frequency: Monthly
Pages: 130

England's biggest-selling Internet magazine covers all sorts of Internet issues
and is aimed at general Web and Internet users, with some articles of interest
to the Web developer and power-user.

Websight Magazine

9520 Jefferson Boulevard
Culver City, CA 90232
Phone: 310-838-6200
Fax: 310-838-0359
WWW: http://websight.com
Subscription: $19.95
Newsstand: $3.95
Frequency: Monthly
Pages: 100

Another surfer-oriented magazine aimed at the Generation X-style crowd,
Websight offers reviews of sites, features on Web personalities, and future Web
trends.

theWEB (U.K.)

IDG Media
Ellesmere Port, Freepost
South Wirral, L65 3EB
United Kingdom
Phone: 44-151-357-1275
Fax: 44-151-357-2813
WWW: http://www.wcentral.co.uk

Subscription: n/a
Newsstand: n/a
Frequency: Monthly
Pages: 100

A leading Web publication in England from IDG Publications. Aimed at general users with site listings, news, and feature articles about the growing Web world.

Web-Developer Magazines

InterActivity

Miller Freeman
411 Borel Avenue, Suite 100
San Mateo, CA 94402
Phone: 415-358-9500
Fax: 415-358-9966
WWW: http://www.interactivity.com
Subscription: Free to qualified subscribers
Newsstand: $4.95
Frequency: Monthly
Pages: 80

InterActivity covers multimedia development issues with reviews, news, and feature cases about how certain multimedia products have been built. While not all of it is focused on the Web, there is a significant amount of information of concern to Web developers.

Web Informant

Informant Communications Group, Inc.
10519 E. Stockton Boulevard, Suite 142
Elk Grove, CA 95624-9704
Phone: 916-686-6610
Fax: 916-686-8497
WWW: http://www.informant.com/wi/
Subscription: $39.95
Newsstand: $5.99
Frequency: Monthly
Pages: 90

From the publishers of *Delphi Informant* and other leading computer technical magazines comes *Web Informant*, a monthly technical guide to developing Web and intranet sites. *Web Informant* includes how-to articles, product reviews, books, news, and development tips of interest to professional designers and programmers working in the Web field.

The Web Developer's Journal

Markland Communities, Inc.
Route 2, Box 80
Burbank, SD 57010
Phone: 605-624-7113
WWW: http://www.awa.com/nct/software/eleclea.html
Subscription: Free
Newsstand: via the Web
Frequency: Monthly
Pages: n/a

News and reviews about HTML, Web development tools, techniques, and tips. Entirely based on the Web.

Web Developer

Mecklermedia
20 Ketchum Street
Westport, CT 06880
Phone: 203-226-6967
Fax: 203-454-5840
WWW: http://www.iworld.com
Subscription: $24.95
Newsstand: $4.99
Frequency: Monthly
Pages: 120

Mecklermedia's main publication that contains information specifically geared toward Web development professionals.

WebMaster

CIO Communciations
492 Old Connecticut Path
Framingham, MA 01701
Phone: 508-935-4280

Fax: 508-872-0618
WWW: http://www.web-master.com
Subscription: Free to qualified subscribers
Newsstand: $4.99
Frequency: Monthly
Pages: 100

WebMaster, from the publisher of *CIO* magazine, is aimed not only at the networking and back-end experts of the Web, but anyone working in the Web and intranet fields.

WebServer Magazine

Computer Publishing Group, Inc.
320 Washington Street
Brookline, MA 02146
Phone: 617-739-7001
Fax: 617-739-7003
WWW: http://www.cpg.com/ws/
Subscription: Free to qualified subscribers
Newsstand: n/a
Frequency: Monthly
Pages: 80

WebServer magazine focuses on back-end and network technologies. Topics like TCP/IP, servers, and more are covered in this monthly magazine.

Web Techniques

Miller Freeman, Inc.
411 Borel Avenue
San Mateo, CA 94402
Phone: 415-358-9500
Fax: 415-358-9966
WWW: http://www.webtechniques.com
Subscription: $24.95
Newsstand: $4.95
Frequency: Monthly
Pages: 100

From the publisher of *InterActivity* and *Dr. Dobbs* comes *Web Techniques*, which covers all sorts of key Web and intranet development issues, including Java, HTML, Shockwave, and much more.

Internet & Java Advisor

Advisor Publications Inc.
5675 Ruffin Road
San Diego, CA 92123-5675
Phone: 619-278-5600
Fax: 619-278-0300
WWW: http://www.advisor.com/ia.htm
Subscription: $49.00/$139
Newsstand: $3.99
Frequency: Monthly
Pages: 100

Internet & Java Advisor covers Web development for Web, intranet, Java, and design professionals. Articles focus on tools, tips, and technical how-tos concerning programming, scripting, database design, and much more.

ZD Internet Magazine

Ziff-Davis Publishing
One Park Avenue
New York, NY 10016
Phone: 212-503-3500
Fax: 212-503-4599
WWW: http://www.zdnet.com
Subscription: $19.95
Newsstand: 3.95
Frequency: Monthly
Pages: 100

This is a new monthly from Ziff-Davis that's aimed at heavy professionals developing Web/intranet strategies and sites.

The WWW Journal

101 Morris Street
Sebastopol, CA 95472
Phone: 800-998-9938
Fax: 707-829-0104
WWW: http://www.w3.org/pub/WWW/Journal/
Subscription: $75.00
Newsstand: $3.95

Frequency: Monthly
Pages: 120

The World Wide Web Journal is jointly published by O'Reilly & Associates and the World Wide Web Consortium, which is the standards body headed by WWW inventor Dr. Tim Berners-Lee. It includes technical articles about standards development, new protocols, HTML and SGML advancements, legal issues, and much more.

Industry-Oriented Trades and Tabloids

Inter@ctive Magazine

CMP Media
600 Community Drive
Manhasset, NY 11030
Phone: 516-562-5000
Fax: 516-562-7830
WWW: http://techweb.cmp.com/ia/current/
Subscription: Free
Newsstand: via the Web
Frequency: Monthly
Pages: n/a

This publication used to be a paper publication, but due to the audience and the nature of the Web and other print competition, CMP turned this into a Web-only magazine accessible on their terrific TechWeb service.

Web Week

Mecklermedia
20 Ketchum Street
Westport, CT 06880
Phone: 203-226-6967
Fax: 203-454-5840
WWW: http://www.iworld.com
Subscription: Free to qualified subscribers
Newsstand: n/a
Frequency: Biweekly
Pages: 70

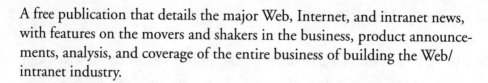

A free publication that details the major Web, Internet, and intranet news, with features on the movers and shakers in the business, product announcements, analysis, and coverage of the entire business of building the Web/intranet industry.

Inter@ctive Week

Ziff-Davis Publishing
One Park Avenue
New York, NY 10016
Phone: 212-503-3500
Fax: 212-503-4599
WWW: http://www.zdnet.com/intweek/
Subscription: Free to qualified subscribers
Newsstand: n/a
Frequency: Weekly
Pages: 80

Inter@ctive Week is a free Softbank/Ziff-Davis publication which covers various issues concerning the Web, the Net, and other interactive telecommunications mediums like interactive TV.

Media Central Digest

Cowles/Simba
P.O. Box 4234
11 Riverbend Drive South
Stamford, CT 06907
Phone: 203-358-4287
Fax: 203-358-5824
WWW: http://www.mediacentral.com
Subscription: Free
Newsstand: via email
Frequency: Weekly
Pages: 4

This free weekly from Cowles/Simba is a great resource. It covers news about the Web and its use by traditional media sources and marketing campaigns such as newspapers, movie studios, TV, or consumer brand launches. Each week you're given quick headlines and a synopsis of significant new Web sites, such as new movie sites, marketing campaigns, and the like.

Newsletters

The COOK Report on the Internet

COOK Network Consultants
431 Greenway Avenue
Ewing, NJ 08618
Phone: 609-882-2572
WWW: http://pobox.com/cook/
Subscription: $24.95
Newsstand: $4.99
Frequency: Monthly
Pages: 120

This is a newsletter for Internet-oriented professionals. *The COOK Report* is written for those who need to understand the details of the forces driving the evolution of Internet infrastructure, so they can prepare strategies for the future. It is intended both for the technical Internet professional and the non-technical manager who needs to understand the Internet for business reasons.

Inside the Internet

The Cobb Group Online
9420 Bunsen Parkway, Suite 300
Louisville, KY 40220
WWW: http://www.cobb.com/int/index.htm
Subscription: $39.00
Newsstand: n/a
Frequency: Monthly
Pages: 20

Inside the Internet, a monthly print newsletter from The Cobb Group, shows you how to make the most out of the Internet.

Internet Business Advantage

The Cobb Group Online
9420 Bunsen Parkway, Suite 300
Louisville, KY 40220
WWW: http://www.cobb.com/iba/index.htm
Subscription: $59.00
Newsstand: n/a

Frequency: Monthly
Pages: 20

The Cobb Group's new monthly journal of online strategies and solutions for Internet entrepreneurs.

Internet Business Report

Jupiter Communications
627 Broadway, 2nd Floor
New York, NY 10012
Phone: 212-780-6060
WWW: http://jup.com/newsletter/business/
Subscription: $24.95
Newsstand: $4.99
Frequency: Monthly
Pages: 40

Internet Business Report covers the issues and news that affect the commercialized development of the Internet and Web. It mainly features news stories, but also offers the occasional analysis or abstract from Jupiter Communication researchers and reports.

Internet Bulletin for CPAs

Kent Information Services, Inc.
227 East Main Street
Kent, OH 44240
Phone: 800-935-2329
Fax: 800-834-1996
WWW: http://www.kentis.com/ib.html
Subscription: $225.00
Newsstand: n/a
Frequency: Monthly
Pages: 20

Do CPAs need their own magazine concerning the Web? Well, why not? There's a ton of valuable information for CPAs on the Web, and many CPAs are independent business people who can benefit from doing business on the Web, not to mention advising others about tax issues resulting from online business. This unique publication, which is written by CPAs, discusses everything about the Web of value to CPAs.

INFORMATION highways

162 Joicey Boulevard
Toronto, Ontario
M5M 2V2
Phone: 416-488-7372
Fax: 416-488-7078
WWW: http://www.flexnet.com/~infohiwy/
Subscription: $105.00
Newsstand: n/a
Frequency: Bimonthly
Pages: 80

A magazine that is focused on business professionals using or working on the information superhighway. *INFORMATION highways* covers topics like how to access the Internet, how businesses are using the information highway, tools, and the latest developments that can help companies do business on the Internet.

InterAd Monthly

Jupiter Communications
627 Broadway, 2nd Floor
New York, NY 10012
Phone: 212-780-6060
WWW: http://www.webtrack.com/interad/interad.html
Subscription: $375.00
Newsstand: n/a
Frequency: Monthly
Pages: 30

This newsletter is a product of Jupiter's WebTrack service, which tracks the growth and distribution of Internet-based advertising. It includes articles about Web advertising, data and news about online marketing, and information for publishers on the Web.

Online MarketPlace

Jupiter Communications
627 Broadway, 2nd Floor
New York, NY 10012
Phone: 212-780-6060
WWW: http://jup.com/newsletter/marketplace/
Subscription: $545.00

Newsstand: n/a
Frequency: Monthly
Pages: 35

Online MarketPlace from Jupiter covers the transaction scene on the Web and Internet. This newsletter tracks the growth of the Internet consumer population and the trends in electronic commerce, and serves up analysis and news of concern to anyone doing commerce directly over the Web.

Online Tactics

Cowles/Simba
P.O. Box 4234
11 Riverbend Drive South
Stamford, CT 06907
Phone: 203-358-4287
Fax: 203-358-5824
WWW: http://www2.simbanet.com/simba/sources/art1.html#AJ
Subscription: $345.00
Newsstand: n/a
Frequency: Monthly
Pages: 10

Cowles/Simba is one of the biggest newsletter and research firms that publishes information about media. Now they've moved on to the emerging media of the Web. *Online Tactics* is a newsletter that serves those companies trying to build online businesses. The newsletter covers successful strategies, content development, marketing, sales, and more of interest to budding online entrepreneurs.

Internet Business Journal

Strangelove Internet Enterprises
45 Rideau Street, Suite 502
Ottawa, ON K1N 5W8
Canada
Phone: 613-241-0982
Fax: 613-241-4433
WWW: http://www.strangelove.com/ibj/
Subscription: $149.00
Newsstand: n/a
Frequency: Monthly
Pages: 20

This is a business-oriented newsletter that focuses on the development of the commercial Web world. Articles focus on business ideas, marketing and industry news and trends, and more.

Internet Research

MCB University Press
60/62 Toller Lane
Bradford, West Yorkshire BD8 9BY
England
Phone: 44-1274-777-700
Fax: 44-1274-785-200
WWW: http://www.mcb.co.uk/liblink/intr/jourhome.htm
Subscription: $24.95
Newsstand: $4.99
Frequency: Monthly
Pages: 120

This is an academic-based publication that focuses on many Internet issues including, policy, research, resources, and new technologies.

Interactive Publishing Alert

NetCreations
47 Joralemon Street
Brooklyn, NY 11201
Phone: 718-237-1624
Fax: 718-237-2347
WWW: http://www.netcreations.com/ipa/
Subscription: $395.00
Newsstand: via email only
Frequency: 24/year
Pages: 20

This newsletter is published by Rosalind Resnick, a recognized expert in online/Internet issues and president of NetCreations, a major Internet software developer. *IPA* is published on the Web, and you can subscribe to an email list informing you of new issues, recent events, and more. *IPA* also publishes a number of significant studies and reports about online publishing, women on the Net, and much more.

Internet Week

Phillips Business Information, Inc.
1201 Seven Locks Road
Potomac, MD 20854
Phone: 301-424-3338
Fax: 301-309-3847
WWW: http://www.phillips.com/iw/index.html
Subscription: $596
Newsstand: n/a/
Frequency: Weekly
Pages: 8

A weekly informative newsletter which recaps the week in Internet news and analysis.

The Intranet Journal

WWW: http://www.brill.com/intranet/
Subscription: Free
Newsstand: n/a
Frequency: Monthly
Pages: n/a

The Intranet Journal is a Web-based publication that publishes articles, news, and information of concern to people building corporate intranets. The site includes links to tools, full length articles, and how-tos.

Web Marketing Today

Wilson Internet Services
P.O. Box 308
Rocklin, CA 95677
Phone: 916-652-4659
WWW: http://www.wilsonweb.com/wmt/
Subscription: Free
Newsstand: via email
Frequency: Biweekly
Pages: n/a

Web Marketing Today is a free email publication and supporting Web site that helps people learn to do effective online marketing of their products, sites, and services. Articles cover tips from savvy Web marketers, news about online marketing, and marketing strategies.

CyberWire Dispatch

WWW: http://cyberwerks.com:70/1/cyberwire
Subscription: Free
Newsstand: via Web
Frequency: n/a
Pages: 1

CyberWire Dispatch is written by Brock N. Meeks and is a free publication.
Meeks, a top new media/Web reporter, does investigative reporting and
analysis on Web/Internet issues and is known for his focus on legislative issues
as he reports from Washington, D.C. He is currently Chief Washington
Correspondent for *Wired/HotWired* and was previously the Washington
Bureau Chief for *Inter@ctive Week*.

Seidman's Online Insider

CMP Media
600 Community Drive
Manhasset, NY 11030
Phone: 516-562-5000
Fax: 516-562-7830
WWW: http://www.netguide.com
Subscription: Free
Newsstand: via email
Frequency: Weekly
Pages: 8

A free weekly email-based newsletter from former IBM staffer and current
NetGuide columnist Robert Seidman, this is an excellent recap of issues
concerning the big picture reports, studies, and strategic moves by the players
on the Web and online universe.

InterActive Consumers

FIND/SVP, Inc.
625 Avenue of Americas
New York, NY 10011
Phone: 212-645-4500
WWW: http://etrg.findsvp.com/iac_mprr/iacindex.html
Subscription: $395.00
Newsstand: n/a

Frequency: Monthly
Pages: 20

This newsletter focuses on consumers' views concerning buying items over the Web and how people's purchasing decisions are changing as a result of the digital age.

Interactive Content

Jupiter Communications
627 Broadway, 2nd Floor
New York, NY 10012
Phone: 212-780-6060
WWW: http://jup.com/newsletter/content/
Subscription: $555.00
Newsstand: n/a
Frequency: Monthly
Pages: 30

Jupiter's *Interactive Content* is a newsletter that focuses on consumer-oriented online and Web-based services. It gives analysis of subscribers to these services, strategic moves and partnerships, and a look at the content they are developing.

The Internet InfoScavenger

InfoScavenger Communications, Inc.
1153 Bergen Parkway, Suite M473
Evergreen, CO 80439
Phone: 303-674-2794
Fax: 303-674-4184
WWW: http://www.infoscavenger.com
Subscription: $149.00
Newsstand: n/a
Frequency: Monthly
Pages: 5

The *Internet InfoScavenger* is a newsletter for marketing and business professionals that reports on new sites, tools, and resources to help get the most out of the Web.

The Digital Kids Report

Jupiter Communications
627 Broadway, 2nd Floor
New York, NY 10012
Phone: 212-780-6060
WWW: http://jup.com/newsletter/kids/
Subscription: $425.00
Newsstand: n/a
Frequency: Monthly
Pages: 30

Kids are a major part of the Web, and many developers are targeting them. Jupiter's *Digital Kids* newsletter focuses on the special content issues, legal and ethical issues, and data of direct concern to developers and marketers targeting CD, online, and Web products to the under-18 age group.

Interactive Marketing Communications Magazine

Interactive Marketing Communications
34700 Coast Highway #200
Capistrano Beach, CA 92624
Phone: 714-489-8649
Fax: 714-489-8752
WWW: http://www.imcweb.com
Subscription: n/a
Newsstand: n/a
Frequency: Monthly
Pages: n/a

Interactive Marketing Communications Magazine is a new publication that was launched in October 1996. The magazine covers the entire realm of interactive marketing, with articles on case studies, industry trends, news, and advice from Internet and interactive marketing gurus.

NetWatchers Cyberzine

WWW: http://ion1.ionet.net/~mdyer/text.shtml
Subscription: Free
Newsstand: via the Web
Frequency: Monthly
Pages: n/a

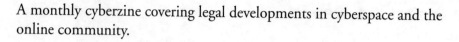

A monthly cyberzine covering legal developments in cyberspace and the online community.

The Online TrailBlazer

WWW: http://www.intercom.net/biz/lma/trailblazer/
Subscription: Free
Newsstand: via email
Frequency: Monthly
Pages: 5

A general recap of monthly news for Web and Internet professionals delivered via email.

Ad Age: Interactive Media & Marketing

Crain Communications
740 N. Rush Street
Chicago, IL 60611
Phone: 312-649-5200
Fax: 312-280-3179
WWW: http://www.adage.com/IMM/
Subscription: Free
Newsstand: via the Web
Frequency: Weekly
Pages: 5

This section of the *Ad Age* Web site is devoted to magazine coverage of Web-based advertising and marketing.

Corporate Internet Strategies

Cutter Information Corp.
37 Broadway, Suite 1
Arlington, MA 02174-5552
Phone: 617-648-8702
WWW: http://world.std.com/~cic/cis/cis.htm
Subscription: $517.00
Newsstand: n/a
Frequency: Monthly
Pages: 20

Corporate Internet Strategies, edited by Internet consultant Ed Yourdon, is billed as a personal guide and consultant on helping corporations build strategies for conducting business on the Web.

dot.COM

Business Communications, Inc.
25 Van Zant Street
Norwalk, CT 06855
Phone: 203-853-4266
Fax: 203-853-0348
WWW: http://www.buscom.com/internet.html
Subscription: $375.00
Newsstand: n/a
Frequency: Monthly
Pages: 20

dot.COM is yet another Internet publication for businesses looking to follow the online and Web scene. dot.COM tracks software and hardware developments, encryption, transacations, advertising, and much more. Each issue focuses on news, trends, and lots of analysis.

APPENDIX B

Conferences and Organizations

General Interest/Trade Shows

Consumer Electronics CES

Electronic Industries Association
2500 Wilson Boulevard
Arlington, VA 22201
Phone: 703-907-7600
Fax: 703-907-7690
WWW: http://www.eia.org/CEMA/cesnews/ontext11.htm

The Consumer Electronics Show isn't exactly the hotspot of Web conferences, but if you're a developer looking to see what this industry is doing in relation to the Web, then this is the place to go. As I showed you in Chapter 17, many of the major consumer electronics companies are creating Web-capable devices like TVs. CES will be a major showcase for these types of Web-related electronics.

Comdex/Windows World

Softbank Expos
303 Vintage Park Drive
Foster City, CA 94404
Phone: 415-578-6900
WWW: http://www.sbexpos.com and http://www.comdex.com

Comdex, along with its sister show Windows World, is the largest computer-oriented general trade show in the world. Even though it focuses on the entire realm of the computer business, this will become a much more interesting show for Web developers as the Web becomes a more integral part of the computer business.

MACWORLD Expo

MHA Event Management
Phone: 617-551-9800
WWW: http://www.mha.com/macworld/

MACWORLD Expo, which is produced by MHA in conjunction with IDG and *MacWorld* magazine, is held in Boston and San Francisco. MACWORLD Expo is the leading conference for examining the state of the Macintosh and Mac Web products.

ABA Tradeshow

American Booksellers Association
828 South Broadway
Tarrytown, NY 10591
Phone: 800-840-5614 or 800-591-2665
WWW: http://www.bookweb.org/aba/

The ABA Tradeshow is the largest gathering of publishers in the world. While Web developers will have more important shows to go to than this one, as publishers become a key area of investment and content development for the Web, the ABA show is certain to be an interesting place to be.

Web/Intranet Development

Internet World

Mecklermedia Corp.
20 Ketchum Street
Westport, CT 06880
Phone: 203-341-2872
Fax: 203-454-5840
WWW: http://www.iworld.com

Mecklermedia's Internet World is one of the largest of the Internet/Web-specific shows. Mecklermedia is now hosting Internet World shows all over the world and twice yearly in the U.S.

Web Design & Development

Miller Freeman
411 Borel Avenue, Suite 100
San Mateo, CA 94402
Phone: 415-358-9500
Fax: 415-655-4360
WWW: http://www.mfi.com

Miller Freeman's Web Design & Development show runs alongside its long-running Software Development conference, which is held twice yearly in San Francisco and Washington, D.C. Living up to its name, it is very much a technically oriented conference aimed at people building Web and intranet sites.

Netscape Internet Developers' Conference

Softbank Expos
303 Vintage Park Drive
Foster City, CA 94404
Phone: 415-578-6900
Fax: 415-525-0199
WWW: http://developer.netscape.com/devcon/

Run by Softbank for Netscape, this is the official conference for covering the development of Internet and intranet sites using Netscape-based technology.

Microsoft Sitebuilder Conference

Softbank Expos
303 Vintage Park Drive
Foster City, CA 94404
Phone: 415-578-6900
WWW: http://206.13.56.30

Run by Softbank in conjunction with Microsoft, this is Microsoft's premiere conference for developers of Internet and intranet products using Windows and Microsoft Web development tools and technologies.

Web Developer

Mecklermedia Corporation
20 Ketchum Street
Westport, CT 06880
Phone: 203-341-2872
Fax: 203-454-5840
WWW: http://www.iworld.com

While Mecklermedia's Internet World tries to be a conference for everybody from a general user to a corporate user to a developer, this other Mecklermedia-produced conference focuses only on developers and designers.

Webgrrls Expo

Webgrrls c/o Cybergrrl
50 Broad Street #1614
New York, NY 10004
WWW: http://www.webgrrls.com/expo.html

Webgrrls has a growing network of chapters around the country promoting the inclusion, development, impact, and roles of women in new media—specifically the Web. The movement, which began in New York, has brought forth the first Webgrrls Expo in New York in the early fall of 1996.

Web Innovator

Softbank Expos
303 Vintage Park Drive
Foster City, CA 94404
Phone: 415-578-6900
WWW: http://www.sbexpos.com

Another large conference focusing on Internet developers, Web developers, content developers, and Webmasters.

Seybold

Softbank Expos
303 Vintage Park Drive
Foster City, CA 94404
Phone: 415-578-6900
WWW: http://www.seyboldseminars.com

Each year Seybold and Softbank produce the Seybold conference, which focuses on the entire realm of electronic publishing—from desktop, to CD-ROM, and now the Web. This is a top show for many Web- and desktop publishing-oriented companies like Adobe, Apple, Kodak, Netscape, and others.

Web Nation

Softbank Expos
303 Vintage Park Drive
Foster City, CA 94404
Phone: 415-578-6900
WWW: http://www.webinn.com/index.html

Web Nation, which is produced by Seybold, Softbank Expos, and a variety of vendors, is a series of conferences that cover several important areas of Web development. The three conferences are Web Innovator, World Movers, and The Searcher. Web Innovator focuses on hard-core Web development issues like programming, designing, and engineering Web sites. World Movers is a

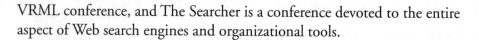

VRML conference, and The Searcher is a conference devoted to the entire aspect of Web search engines and organizational tools.

Plug.In

Jupiter Communications
627 Broadway, 2nd Floor
New York, NY 10012
Phone: 212-780-6060
WWW: http://www.jup.com

Held at the same time as the infamous New York Music Festival, Plug.In is a show dedicated to the merger of new media and music, especially the Web. Conference topics and exhibitors focus on digital distribution, online music, advertising and PR, and Webcasting concerts.

RSA Data Security Conference

Produced by LKE Productions
1620 Montgomery Street, Suite 120
San Francisco, CA 94111
Phone: 415-544-9300
Fax: 415-544-9306
WWW: http://www.rsa.com

RSA is the dominant technology in the cryptography field. Cryptography is a key element in creating a host of Web technologies, including secure commerce and password protection. This conference, which attracts over 2,000 attendees, focuses on cryptography, RSA technology, and the technologies that RSA plays a key role in.

VRML

World Movers

P.O. Box 45295
San Francisco, CA 94145
Phone: 415-578-6900
Fax: 415-525-0199
WWW: http://www.webinn.com

Held during the Web Nations conference week, this Softbank-, Seybold-, and SGI-backed conference is going to be the leading conference on VRML 2.0 technology. VRML 2.0 is based on SGI's "Moving Worlds" specification.

Java

JavaOne

Sun Microsystems
2550 Garcia Avenue
Mountain View, CA 94043
Phone: 415-960-1300
Fax: 415-969-9131
WWW: http://www.sun.com

Produced by Sun, JavaOne is the premiere conference for Java developers world-wide. With technical seminars, exhibitors, and tons of cool Java, this is a show for the hooked-on-Java crowd—no decaf here.

Web/Online Marketing and Business Oriented

Online Advertising '97

Jupiter Communications
627 Broadway, 2nd Floor
New York, NY 10012
Phone: 212-780-6060
WWW: http://www.jup.com

Jupiter Communications is a major producer of information and research about the rising business of Web-based advertising. This Jupiter-sponsored conference focuses on this major area of advertising growth.

Consumer Online Services IV

Jupiter Communications
627 Broadway, 2nd Floor
New York, NY 10012
Phone: 212-780-6060
WWW: http://www.jup.com

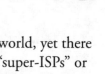

Many people say that the Web will take over the entire online world, yet there are also those who feel that commercial online services, either "super-ISPs" or traditional- and Web-based services, will survive and prosper. This conference is aimed at bringing together the key players and developers who are working to build consumer-oriented online services, either on the Web or as proprietary properties.

Web Advertising

Thunder Lizard Productions
1619 Eighth Avenue North
Seattle, WA 98109
Phone: 206-285-0305
Fax   206-285-0308
WWW: http://www.thunderlizard.com/WebAdv.html

An industry and general interest conference focusing on Web advertising. Sessions at the conference include finding good sites for ads, analyzing response, banner creation, traffic generation, and more.

Interactive Media

IMA Expo

Interactive Multimedia Association
48 Maryland Avenue, Suite 202
Annapolis, MD 21401-8011
Phone: 410-626-1380
Fax: 410-263-0590
WWW: http://www.ima.org

The Interactive Multimedia Association is one of the biggest developer organizations in the country, and the IMA Expo covers everything in the realm of interactive multimedia, including CD-ROMs, the Web, digital video, and much more.

Interactive

Softbank Expos
303 Vintage Park Drive
Foster City, CA 94404
Phone: 415-578-6900
WWW: http://www.sbexpos.com/interactive/

This Softbank-produced show centers on the growing interactive development industry. Specific topics at past shows have included Web technology, distance learning, online information services, design, and the interactive classroom.

Digital Kids '96

Jupiter Communications
627 Broadway, 2nd Floor
New York, NY 10012
Phone: 212-780-6060
WWW: http://www.jup.com

Named after the Jupiter publication of the same name, Jupiter's Digital Kids conference focuses on the development and marketing of digital content for the under-18 crowd. Digital Kids looks at topics like educational content, design, game development, the Web, advertising to kids online, CD-ROMs, and much more.

Programming

Software Development

Miller Freeman
411 Borel Avenue, Suite 100
San Mateo, CA 94402
Phone: 415-358-9500
Fax: 415-655-4360
WWW: http://www.mfi.com

Software Development is probably the number one conference for professional programmers of all kinds. Web developers who aren't bitten by the programming bug may opt to attend the show anyway, because Miller Freeman launched Web Development to run right along side it—both shows, which run in San Francisco and Washington, D.C., are held twice yearly.

Traveling Training Camps

Wave Technologies

Wave Technologies International, Inc.
10845 Olive Boulevard, Suite 250
St. Louis, MO 63141

Phone: 314-995-5767
Fax: 314-995-3894
WWW: http://www.wavetech.com

Wave Technologies is a large producer of training and miniregional conferences on topics of use for Web developers. Contact them about conferences in
your area of the country (or even the world) on such topics as Java, Microsoft
Internet Server, HTML, and more.

Other

Online Developers

Jupiter Communications
627 Broadway, 2nd Floor
New York, NY 10012
Phone: 212-780-6060
WWW: http://www.jup.com

Online Developers is emerging as the premiere conference covering the
development of Web- and online-based games. It's held once a year in San
Francisco.

Computer Game Developer's Conference

Miller Freeman
411 Borel Avenue, Suite 100
San Mateo, CA 94402
Phone: 415-358-9500
Fax: 415-655-4360
WWW: http://www.mfi.com

Are you developing Web games, TCP/IP-based game engines, online service
games, or email games? Well, no matter what kind of game you're creating, the
amount of cool discussions, tools, techniques, and expert help you can find at
the Computer Game Developer's Conference is unparalleled.

Adobe Internet Conference

Thunder Lizard Productions
1619 Eighth Avenue North
Seattle, WA 98109

Phone: 206-285-0305
Fax: 206-285-0308
WWW: http://www.thunderlizard.com

As one of the biggest and most important software companies providing key tools (Photoshop, PageMill) and technologies (PostScript, Acrobat), Adobe has developed the Adobe Internet Conference to bring together Web designers and developers for in-depth sessions about Adobe products and the Web. If you're a key user of Adobe products, or just looking into what Adobe is doing as a major Web technology player, this is a good conference for you.

Visual Basic VBITS

Fawcette Technical Publications
209 Hamilton Avenue
Palo Alto, CA 94301
Phone: 415-833-7100
Fax: 415-853-0230
WWW: http://www.windx.com

Produced by the publisher of *Visual Basic Programmers Journal*, VBITS is the best conference and tradeshow for programmers using Visual Basic and other key VB technologies from Microsoft, such as VBScript, Visual Basic for Applications, ActiveX, and more. VB is a major language and programming environment for Web developers, and this conference will be a major place to learn about VB and its relevance for Web developers. Also look for VBITS Interactive, a special version of the conference aimed directly at intranet and Internet solutions.

SIGGRAPH

SIGGRAPH 97 Conference Management
Smith, Bucklin & Associates, Inc.
401 North Michigan Avenue
Chicago, IL 60611
Phone: 312-321-6830
Fax: 312-321-6876
WWW: http://www.siggraph.org

The premiere conference for computer graphic programmers, artists, developers, tool companies, and researchers, SIGGRAPH is increasingly important to Web developers as the Web incorporates more and more 3D graphics, either

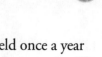

through VRML or other technologies. SIGGRAPH, which is held once a year in various locations, will take you on a trip through the future of computers. If you're looking to see the latest products and technologies like VRML, VR, 3D interfaces, realtime 3D graphics, 3D tools, and more, head to SIGGRAPH.

Online Expo

International Marketing Associates
2118 Wilshire Boulevard, Suite #594
Santa Monica, CA 90403
Phone: 800-453-4363
Fax: 310-315-7394
WWW: http://www.onlineexpo.com/index.html

Online Expo, which is held in New York and L.A. in the fall, is smaller in size than Internet World, but is similar in its purpose. It's a general trade show and conference on the entire range of online and Internet opportunities and markets available to developers, consumers, and businesses.

Macromedia User Conference

Macromedia, Inc.
600 Townsend Street
San Francisco, CA 94103-4945
Phone: 415-252-2000
Fax: 415-626-0554
WWW: http://www.macromedia.com

The top conference for those using Macromedia products, especially Director, Authorware, and Shockwave. The Macromedia User Conference is held every year in the fall in San Francisco.

Organizations

World Wide Web Consortium (W3C)

Massachusetts Institute of Technology
Laboratory for Computer Science
545 Technology Square
Cambridge, MA 02139
Phone: 617-253-2613

Fax: 617-258-5999
WWW: http://www.w3.org

The W3C is arguably the most influential Web organization around. It was founded by MIT, the major Web industry players, and Dr. Tim Berners-Lee, the inventor of the WWW, as the consortium to develop, review, organize, and promote standards for the Web and Web products.

Individuals can't join, but companies and other interested parties can get information about joining at **http://www.w3.org/pub/WWW/Consortium/ Prospectus/FAQ.html**.

The W3C encourages individuals to participate by subscribing to their publication, the *WorldWideWeb Journal,* published four times a year by O'Reilly and Associates. Information about the journal is located at **http:// www.w3.org/pub/WWW/Journal/**.

Internet Engineering Task Force
http://www.ietf.cnri.reston.va.us/home.html

The IETF is, along with the W3C, the most important Internet organization for setting the standards and technologies that drive the Internet and the Web forward. The IETF describes itself as "the protocol engineering and development arm of the Internet." Its members work on many of the low-level standards (like TCP/IP) that result in the defining of the Internet's most fundamental architectures.

You can find out much more on their Web site and browse many of the working drafts the IETF is building about next-generation Internet technologies and systems.

The Interactive Multimedia Association
Interactive Multimedia Association
48 Maryland Avenue, Suite 202
Annapolis, MD 21401-8011
Phone: 410-626-1380
Fax: 410-263-0590
WWW: http://www.ima.org

Founded in 1988, the IMA is a very large organization of multimedia developers. The IMA offers its members a journal, conferences, discounts on products, and access to the IMA job bank. The organization promotes various multimedia causes, such as intellectual property and copyright protection.

Computer Game Developers' Association

CGDA Main Office
960 North San Antonio Road #125
Los Altos, CA 94022
Phone: 415-948-2432
Fax: 415-948-2744
WWW: http://www.cgda.org

The CGDA is the premiere organization for game developers of all kinds, from small companies to individuals, and from those doing packaged products, to shareware authors, and now online game developers. Each year they gather in Santa Clara for the Computer Game Developers' Conference. During the year, members receive the newsletter and discounts on products, and the organization works to boost industry and developer issues.

Webgrrls

Webgrrls c/o Cybergrrl
50 Broad Street #1614
New York, NY 10004
WWW: http://www.webgrrls.com

Webgrrls is a network of group chapters that work to promote women's efforts on the Web, as developers, designers, consultants, and Webmasters. Women are flocking to the Web, and Webgrrrl chapters are forming in cities all around the world to provide a forum for women to exchange information, give job and business leads, learn about new technologies, mentor, intern, train, and more. Look in the Web/Intranet Development section for more info about their Expo.

The Electronic Frontier Foundation

1550 Bryant Street, Suite 725
San Francisco, CA 94103
Phone: 415-436-9333
Fax: 415-436-9993
WWW: http://www.eff.org

Founded by former Lotus founder Mitch Kapor, the Electronic Frontier Foundation is best described as the ACLU of cyberspace. It works overtime to protect the civil liberties of people using the information superhighway. It works to promote free speech online, lobby government, provide public information about new media, and generally support the proper, free, and fair use of information, new media, and the online universe.

Recreational Software Advisory Council

1050 Waltham Street, Suite 420
Lexington, MA 02173
Phone: 617-860-9888
Fax: 617-860-9604
WWW: http://www.rsac.org

Originally formed to promote a fair and easy-to-use labeling system for game and multimedia content as the problem of Web ratings took off late in 1994, the RSAC also helped devise a ratings standard for Web sites, and is now a major force in that area of the Web. The RSAC is a coalition of game developers, new media companies, and Web developers that works with industry, parents, educators, and others to work out criteria for publishers to use to rate their site or game in terms of various content categories. Many sites are voluntarily rating themselves using the RSAC system, which parents and educators use to control the type of content their children get access to.

Information Systems Security Association

1926 Waukegan Road, Suite 1
Glenview, IL 60025-1770
Phone: 847-657-6746
Fax: 847-657-6819
WWW: http://www.uhsa.uh.edu/issa/

The ISSA is an international organization of Web and Internet professionals that specialize in security practices, software, hardware, and other issues.

Internet Society

Internet Society International Secretariat
12020 Sunrise Valley Drive, Suite 210
Reston, VA 20191
Phone: 703-648-9888

Fax: 703-648-9887
WWW: http://www.isoc.org

The Internet Society is a major international organization that promotes coordination and growth of the Internet on a worldwide basis. Its members include companies, government agencies, academics, and other organizations working with the Internet.

New York Media Association

Phone: 212-826-2399
Fax: 212-207-8850
WWW: http://www.nynma.org

If you're in New York and doing multimedia/Web development, the New York Media Association is a good group to check out. New York is arguably the content capital of the world, and is becoming a rapidly growing force in the Web and new media industries. This group was founded to organize the growing group of developers in the area building Web sites, CD-ROMs, and other new media-oriented products. The group holds monthly meetings and conferences for its members.

Internet Advertising Bureau

Phone: 212-704-4446

The IAB was created by a cross-section of advertisers and Web development companies to represent companies that actively sell advertising on the Internet and online services. The IAB, which held its first meeting in 1996, has broken into 11 working groups to deal with various issues. Those committees include standards and practices, audience measurement, membership, marketing and conferences, advertising to children, technology, industry liaison, and international. You can attain membership (non-voting) by paying a $1,000 fee. Money will go toward running the association, conferences, and a research program being done by Coopers & Lybrand.

Spiderwomen

http://www.amazoncity.com/spiderwoman/swomen.html

Existing mainly as a mailing list, the Spiderwomen are a community of women and men dedicated to supporting women Web designers.

HTML Writers Guild
http://www.hwg.org

The HTML Writers Guild is the premiere international organization of World Wide Web authors and Internet publishing professionals. Guild members have access to resources, including HTML and Web business mailing lists, information repositories, and interaction with their peers.

Internet Professional Publishers Association
http://www.ippa.org

A professional association of commercial Web design agencies working to build a new marketing medium for businesses through the Internet.

Webmasters' Guild
http://www.webmaster.org

This not-for-profit organization is for Webmasters and works to promote the Webmaster position and career path. The Webmasters' Guild is working to become the forum for sharing information about and with Webmasters and developers around the world.

Voice on the Net Coalition (VON)
Phone: 802-879-3751
WWW: http://www.von.org

The Voice on the Net Coalition is a group of software and hardware companies that have banded together to develop standards and promote the use of Internet phone products. It works to fend off the growing criticisms of various phone company coalitions, who are afraid that the Internet phone movement could significantly cut into their business.

APPENDIX C

The Wrap-Up Appendix

Some days I wake up despising two of the words contained in the title of this book: The first is the word *Ultimate* and the second is *Web*. In using the word ultimate, this book sets a standard that is more of a goal than a guarantee; and by writing a book about the Web, I've probably set myself up for *Mission Impossible.*

Problem number one is that the product development cycle on the Web is so quick, and the competition is so intense, that in the course of writing this book over a four-month period I have watched some of the work already written be augmented by new product introductions or updates. In other cases, the Web is so big that by the time I've found out about something, the chapter had been closed and sent to production. Finally, this book is trying to be the *Ultimate Web Developer's Sourcebook,* so opting not to mention or fix those shortcomings wasn't acceptable to me. So I persuaded my publisher that at the end of the book we'd include a catch-all section that tries to shore up some of these problems.

As I write this appendix, what I realize most is that this chapter is a testament to both the amazing upheaval the Web has brought to computer and software development and the dedication of thousands of programmers who probably aren't getting enough sleep.

Graphic Technologies

During production of this book, Adobe released the Photoshop 4.0 package, and shareware developer JASC released a new version of its Paint Shop Pro package. Be sure to check out both products; especially Photoshop 4.0's Web-centered features, such as digital watermarking (to safeguard online original art) and new support for various Web file formats. One art package I failed to mention was Macromedia's xRes 2.0—check it out at **http://www. macromedia.com/software/xres/index.html**. Finally, Microsoft, Netscape, Kodak, and other leading vendors announced they would support the new Flashpix graphic format on the Web. You can read more about it at the unofficial FlashPix Web site, located at **http://www.flashPix.com** and on Kodak's site at **http://www.kodak.com/daiHome/flashPix/flashPix.shtml**. Also check out the exciting software for digital photography being produced by Live Picture (which is headed by John Sculley, Apple's former CEO) at **http://www.livepicture.com**, including its LivePix product, which is aimed at consumers (**http://www.livepix.com**).

Artbeats

Artbeats Software Inc.
P.O. Box 709
Myrtle Creek, OR 97457
Phone: 541-863-4429
Fax: 541-863-4547
WWW: http://www.artbeats.com

I left out this great company when discussing some of the better graphic background and texture resources. Artbeats has been around since the dawn of desktop publishing and produces some of the best backgrounds and useful clip art around. They have recently begun developing several products dedicated specifically to Web development.

Atomic3D

Nucleus Interactive
WWW: http://www.atomic3d.com

Atomic3D is a 3D animation and Web broadcast technology that presents 3D animations over the Internet in realtime. The animation, using a plug-in and, depending on the number of users, a special server program, streams across in realtime. You can find out about the plug-in, authoring, and server products on their home page.

Pantone Color Matching System

Pantone, Inc.
590 Commerce Boulevard
Carlstadt, NJ 07072
Phone: 201-935-5500
Fax: 201-896-0242
WWW: http://www.pantone.com

The company that revolutionized color matching and color printing has brought its technology to the Web. Pantone announced in September of 1996 that it was producing a product called Pantone ColorWeb. This set of tools allows designers and Web publishers to manage color reproduction of Web sites. This may not seem important, but a number of Web designers have been very vocal about the need to calibrate the color system of the Web. This is especially important to clothing manufacturers (like L.L. Bean) and other retailers that want to give the highest level of accuracy to customers.

The Pantone ColorWeb system uses Pantone's Internet Color System (PICS) as "a cross-platform, dither-free palette of numbered and chromatically organized colors, to provide Web designers with a method for using colors that can be viewed accurately, with the best possible results, regardless of monitor or platform."

Users will have to use a special Netscape plug-in with their browser, but the result is the truest color representation you'll ever see on the Web.

PhotoGIF, ProJPEG, and GIFmation

BoxTop Software, Inc.
One Research Boulevard, Suite 201
Starkville, MS 39760
Phone: 601-323-6436
WWW: http://www.aris.com/boxtop/

Mac-oriented Web developers will want to check out BoxTop software's tools. The software company makes two major plug-ins for Photoshop. PhotoGIF helps create perfect GIF files for the Web (enhance and optimize the pallete, lower the file size, and so on). ProJPEG does the same for JPEG images, and GIFmation is a standalone product for creating GIF89a-compatible animation files.

Multimedia Technologies

Perhaps the fastest-moving section of the Web development scene is the multimedia technologies, particularly the streaming technologies. A lot has happened and been announced since even this book was started!

The audio section of the Internet continues to be a hotbed of updates and new products. Over the course of this book's development, RealAudio 2.0 was joined in the streaming technology market by Xing Technologies' Streamworks 2.0, and then Macromedia jumped in with Shockwave Streaming Audio—which for two weeks was the best streaming audio I had heard on my 28.8 Kbps modem. Then Progressive Networks shot back with RealAudio 3.0, which matched the quality and added more new features. RealAudio 3.0 now supports FM-stereo-quality at 28.8 modem speeds, and is completely scalable all the way up to T1 speeds for CD-quality sound.

The overall streaming video and audio scene got a big wake-up call when several heavyweights announced cool new products in this area. Microsoft announced it was debuting a product called NetShow to offer streaming sound and video, and Netscape said it would market its own audio server (which right now is code-named Salmon) with a browser plug-in currently code-named Trout. AT&T's Lucent Technologies also announced it was going to debut its own suite of streaming technologies, and was starting a new division called Elemedia to head up the work.

KoanMusic Plug-In

SSEYO Ltd
Pyramid House
Easthampstead Road
Bracknell, RG12 1YW UK
Phone: 44-1344-712017
Fax: 44-1344-712005
WWW: http://www.sseyo.com

This special plug-in music format allows you to create special "MIDI-like" songs which play back over the Web using the Koan plug-in. KoanMusic is different from standard composed songs because it is actually played back by the computer, which determines the music based on a composed outline. Koan essentially takes the framework of a composition from a musician and creates the note-by-note song with it. The results, while in a certain range and style, can be different every time. Koan is great for theme music and can go for a long time without repetition. This reduces file size and monotony as well. KoanMusic is created with the Koan Pro composer package, which is available from SSEYO.

VXtreme

VXtreme, Inc.
701 Welch Road, Building C
Palo Alto, CA 94304
Phone: 415-614-0700
Fax: 415-614-0710

What would a few passing months be on the Web without yet another interesting entrant into the streaming audio or video field. While I was writing this book, VXtreme debuted its streaming video package called Web Theater. The entire suite of products includes Web Theater Server, Web Theater Client, and Web Theater Producer—which makes the system similar to VDOLive in its

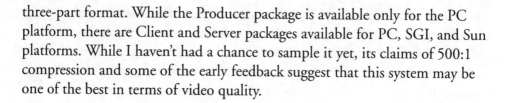

three-part format. While the Producer package is available only for the PC platform, there are Client and Server packages available for PC, SGI, and Sun platforms. While I haven't had a chance to sample it yet, its claims of 500:1 compression and some of the early feedback suggest that this system may be one of the best in terms of video quality.

More Development Tools

The development tool scene is also rapidly evolving, and part of the acceleration is due to the war between Microsoft and Netscape to dominate the Web development, server, and browser markets. Both companies debuted large development programs that featured new tools and boosted some cutting-edge third-party products. Netscape started AppFoundry (**http://home.netscape.com/one_stop/intranet_apps/index.html**) and Microsoft started Site Builder (**http://www.microsoft.com/workshop/**). Both feature free downloads of cutting-edge tools, code, and examples, and will become the focus points of their development programs on the Web. Sun's JavaSoft subsidiary also launched its developer program, the Java Developer Connection. You can register and pay online (**http://java.sun.com**) or call 1-800-JAVASOFT.

After visiting these sites I decided I needed to add a few more "heads ups" on some key development tools and resources. Forgive me for omitting them—or forgive some of them for not being out when I originally was looking for them.

The ForeFront Group

1330 Post Oak Boulevard, Suite 1300
Houston, TX 77056
Phone: 713-961-1101
Fax: 713-961-1149
WWW: http://www.ffg.com/internet.html

The ForeFront Group has developed a number of cool Web products; two that you may find particularly interesting are:

- WebPrinter—This product improves the printing abilities of Web browsers. Printing out Web pages has never been handled very well, and WebPrinter is designed to help improve that. You can even print pages in booklet form.

- Surf 'n' Print—Using their book-printing software technology, Surf 'n' Print helps take data off the Internet and turn it into a booklet right from your printer.

Check out these and several other cool utilities on their Web site.

NetImpact Studio

Powersoft
561 Virginia Road
Concord, MA 01742
Phone: 508-287-1500
Fax: 508-287-1600
WWW: http://www.powersoft.com

Powersoft is one of the premiere database development software companies in the world, and NetImpact Studio is Powersoft's answer to Web development. NetImpact is built to not only do Web page/HTML editing, but more importantly to ease the development of database backed Web sites. The package includes lots of help for developing, managing, and testing Web sites and HTML pages developed specifically to deliver information to and from databases.

NetDynamics

NetDynamics, Inc.
185 Constitution Drive
Menlo Park, CA 94025
Phone: 415-462-7600
Fax: 415-617-5920
WWW: http://www.netdynamics.com

NetDynamics combines two potent Web forces—Java and databases—and brings them together within a custom visual Web development environment. With NetDynamics, developers can create new Web applications using databases and Java. The program generates Java code automatically and hides the work needed to create database-backed Java applets.

Now Up-to-Date's Web Publisher 1.0

Now Software, Inc.
921 SW Washington Street, Suite 500
Portland, OR 97205-2823
Phone: 503-274-2800
Fax: 503-274-0670
WWW: http://www.nowsoft.com

Now Up-to-Date is one of the leading schedule and calendar packages around. Its new Web Publisher version helps you design and distribute calendar information via the Web. The product automatically creates calendars and address books without needing to do the HTML for them. Users can download three specific plug-ins to enhance working with the published data via their browser:

- AboutTime—Used to view calendars in Netscape.

- AboutPeople—Used to view the searchable address books.

- Now Passports—Used to access time and people information; capture calendar and book information for your personal use.

Now has even published the complete NFL 1996 schedule on their site to demonstrate the power of this product to help with that office football pool. <grin>

Site@rchitect

MediaShare
5927 Priestly Drive, Suite 101
Carlsbad, CA 92008
Phone: 619-931-7171
Fax: 619-431-5752
WWW: http://www.mediashare.com

In the vein of NetObjects Fusion's site, Site@rchitect is a fourth-generation Web site development tool. While NetObjects is the new wave of page design, Site@rchitect is a major leap forward in the entire content-management side of Web production.

WebObjects

NeXT Software, Inc.
900 Chesapeake Drive
Redwood City, CA 94063
Phone: 415-366-0900
FAX: 415-780-3929
WWW: http://www.next.com

WebObjects is hard to describe because it really is an amazingly powerful product. Essentially, WebObjects attempts to simplify the process of integrating large databases onto the Web by providing you with a software layer that makes it easy to extract information from databases and then display it dynamically over the Web in HTML. WebObjects comes in three flavors: WebObjects, WebObjects Pro, and WebObjects Enterprise. WebObjects Pro adds the ability to compile WebObjects programs into C/C++ applications. The Enterprise edition adds extensive features for the high-end databases found in large corporations.

Even More Media Sources

The Web Magazine

IDG Publishing
501 Second Street, Suite 110
San Francisco, CA 94106
Phone: 415-267-4558
Fax: 415-267-4586
WWW: http://www.webmagazine.com

The Web, which just premiered, is IDG's general-interest magazine for Web enthusiasts and surfers. It focuses mostly on reviews of sites, information about Web personalities, and feature articles on major Web news and trends of interest to surfers.

David Strom's Web Informant Mail-Zine

http://www.strom.com

David Strom is a leading freelance writer and networking/communications consultant. His weekly Web Informant newsletter is available for free via email. It's a good round-up of interesting information and for Web developers and professionals.

TV Shows

One area I forgot to address in the magazine section were the many TV shows that have debuted that focus on the Web. I've taken these from an article I put together on TV technology media outlets.

The Site

Ziff-Davis Publishing (ZDTV)
One Park Avenue
New York, NY 10016-5801
Phone: 212-503-3500

Phone: 212-503-3500
Fax: 212-503-4599
WWW: http://www.thesite.com

The Site covers Web sites in a TV news magazine style. Each episode goes through several segments including The Day in Review, Site of the Nite, Showtime, and Altered Egos.

Schedule Information:
Show airs on MSNBC Mondays-Thursdays, 10-11PM.

The Web

CNET, Inc.
150 Chestnut Street
San Francisco, CA 94111
Phone: 415-395-7800
Fax: 415-395-9205
WWW: http://www.cnet.com/Content/Tv/Web/index.html

The Web is, as its title implies, focused solely on the Web. There are interviews with designers, reviews of sites, and discussion about the Web and where it's going.

Schedule Information:
The Web broadcasts directly after C|NET Central on The Sci-Fi network. It's also broadcast in the San Francisco Bay Area on KPIX Channel 5, and is shown in Tokyo, Japan.

TV.COM

CNET, Inc.
150 Chestnut Street
San Francisco, CA 94111
Phone: 415-395-7800
Fax: 415-395-9205
WWW: http://www.tv.com

TV.COM is a syndicated show produced by in partnership by C|NET and top syndicator Golden Gate Productions (GGP). TV.COM focuses on the Internet and Online world with an Entertainment Tonight–like feel.

Schedule Information:
TV.COM is broadcast at various times in over 30 local TV markets across the country. Check the Web site for exact locations and scheduling information.

Netizen

Wired Ventures
520 Third Street, 4th Floor
San Francisco, CA 94107-1815
Phone: 415-222-6200
Fax: 415-222-6209
WWW: http://www.hotwired.com

Netizen is Wired Ventures' show about the people, politics, and issues of the Internet. Based on the monthly magazine section found in *Wired* magazine, the show has yet to air.

Schedule Information:
Show will begin airing this fall on MSNBC.

Cyberlife

Discovery Communications
7700 Wisconsin Avenue
Bethesda, MD 20814
Phone: 301-986-1999
Fax: 301-986-1889
WWW: http://www.discovery.com

Cyberlife is Discovery's main show about the Internet. Regular segments are aired each night and a full slate of segments is aired later in the week.

Schedule Information:
Cyberlife features new programs each weeknight at 7:25 and 11:25 p.m. ET and again on Saturdays at 2:30 p.m. ET or Sundays at 11:30 a.m. ET.

Even More Web Sites

Either I had no chapter that these sites fit into naturally, or I just found them as the book was finishing up, either way they're all worth a visit.

Amazon.com's Build Your Own Bookstore Program

`http://www.amazon.com`

Amazon.com, the big-time bookseller on the Internet, has a unique developer program you might want to check out. Refer your Web site's customers to books you like, and if they jump to that book from a link on your site and purchase it, you earn a commission. For example, if you were doing a huge

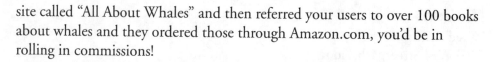

site called "All About Whales" and then referred your users to over 100 books about whales and they ordered those through Amazon.com, you'd be in rolling in commissions!

Project Cool Developer Zone
http://www.projectcool.com/developer/

This new site provides a lot of good information about Web design, HTML tutorials and tips, low-bandwidth ideas, and more.

Sun's Java Enterprise White Paper
http://www.sun.com/javacomputing/

This white paper on Java, from Java's creator Sun Microsystems, explains the reach Java will have as Sun builds all the additional framework I described in the Java chapter.

The Web Developer's Virtual Library
http://www.stars.com

I should have no excuse for forgetting to include this site somewhere in this book, but it's so comprehensive and covers so many things, there was no major chapter to put it in so I left it for this section. This is a page every Web developer should bookmark. It's simply massive in scope and has links to hundreds of useful sites for Web developers.

The Web Designers' Mailing List
http://www.lynda.com/webdesign-faq.html

This is a mailing list you should consider subscribing to. Run by Lynda Weinman, a leading author on Web design, this mailing list of over 2,000 Web development professionals fosters excellent discussion on the latest HTML tricks, new products, technologies, and more. Check out the FAQ for subscription information and list rules.

Microsoft IE 4.0 Preview
http://www.microsoft.com/win32dev/ui/ie40.htm

Get the lowdown on Microsoft's Internet Explorer 4.0 browser, the first version of Microsoft's vision to embed the browser application directly into the Windows operating system.

Index

C

X

Y

You Already Smelled The Coffee.
Now Move On To The Hard Stuff...

Web Informant will get you there

Developing successful applications for the Web is what you really like to do. You like your information straight. You want it bold and to the point.

Web Informant Magazine is the only source you need, offering nuts and bolts programming solutions, specific coding techniques, actual code and downloadable files—no gimmicks, trends or fluff.

It's a powerful source of information, and it's the only source of information challenging enough to keep you on the edge. It's tough. It's Java®, Perl, JavaScript, HTML, and VRML. It's unexplored territory, and you like it that way.

Web Informant will get you there.